Protestant Nationalists in Ireland, 1900–1923

D1584835

From the turn of the twentieth century until the end of the Irish Civil War, Protestant nationalists forged a distinct counterculture within an increasingly Catholic nationalist movement. Drawing on a wide range of primary and secondary sources, Conor Morrissey charts the development of nationalism within Protestantism, and describes the ultimate failure of this tradition. The book traces the re-emergence of Protestant nationalist activism in the literary and language movements of the 1880s and 1890s, before reconstructing their distinctive forms of organization in the following decades. Morrissey shows how Protestants, mindful of their minority status, formed interlinked networks of activists and developed a vibrant associational culture. He describes how the increasingly Catholic nature of nationalism – particularly following the Easter Rising – prompted Protestants to adopt a variety of strategies in an attempt to ensure their voices were still heard. Ultimately, this ambitious and wide-ranging book explores the relationship between religious denomination and political allegiance, casting fresh light on an often-misunderstood period.

CONOR MORRISSEY is Lecturer in Irish/British History at King's College London. He previously held appointments at the National Museum of Ireland, Trinity College Dublin, and Hertford College, University of Oxford.

Protestant Nationalists in Ireland, 1900–1923

Conor Morrissey

King's College London

CAMBRIDGE
UNIVERSITY PRESS

CAMBRIDGE
UNIVERSITY PRESS

University Printing House, Cambridge CB2 8BS, United Kingdom

One Liberty Plaza, 20th Floor, New York, NY 10006, USA

477 Williamstown Road, Port Melbourne, VIC 3207, Australia

314-321, 3rd Floor, Plot 3, Splendor Forum, Jasola District Centre, New Delhi - 110025, India

103 Penang Road, #05-06/07, Visioncrest Commercial, Singapore 238467

Cambridge University Press is part of the University of Cambridge.

It furthers the University's mission by disseminating knowledge in the pursuit of
education, learning and research at the highest international levels of excellence.

www.cambridge.org
Information on this title: www.cambridge.org/9781108462877
DOI: 10.1017/9781108596251

© Conor Morrissey 2019

First published 2019
First paperback edition 2021

A catalogue record for this publication is available from the British Library

Library of Congress Cataloging in Publication data
Names: Morrissey, Conor, 1985- author.
Title: Protestant nationalists in Ireland, 1900-1923 / Conor Morrissey.
Description: Cambridge, United Kingdom ; New York, NY : Cambridge
   University Press, 2019. | Includes bibliographical references and index.
Identifiers: LCCN 2019008056 (print) | LCCN 2019013347 (ebook) |
   ISBN 9781108473866 (Hardback) | ISBN 9781108462877 (Paperback) |
   ISBN 9781108473866
Subjects: LCSH: Nationalism–Ireland–History–20th century. |
   Nationalists–Ireland–History–20th century. | Protestants–Ireland–History–
   20th century. | Religion and politics–Ireland–History–20th century. |
   Ireland–Politics and government–20th century. | Ireland–History–20th
   century.
Classification: LCC DA960 (ebook) | LCC DA960 .M675 2019 (print) |
   DDC 320.54094150888409041–dc23
LC record available at https://lccn.loc.gov/2019008056

ISBN 978-1-108-47386-6 Hardback
ISBN 978-1-108-46287-7 Paperback

To my parents

Contents

Tables

Acknowledgements

My first debt is to Professor David Fitzpatrick, for his many years of unfailing kindness, patience, and generosity. David's early death in February 2019 has robbed Irish history of one of its most brilliant practitioners. He will be sorely missed.

I must next express my gratitude to four brilliant historians: Roy Foster, Anne Dolan, Ian McBride, and Eunan O'Halpin, who have each proved a source of encouragement and strength. In Oxford, Senia Paseta, Marc Mulholland, and David Dwan have proved remarkably kind colleagues.

This book could not have been completed without the support of the Irish Research Council, which awarded me a doctoral fellowship and a postdoctoral fellowship, and the Board of Trinity College Dublin, who awarded me a postgraduate research studentship. I would like to express my sincere thanks to the librarians and archivists in Ireland and Britain who assisted me in my research. In particular, I must acknowledge the staff of the National Library of Ireland, the Military Archives, Dublin, the library of Trinity College Dublin, and the National Archives, Kew.

This book took a long time to write. I must record my gratitude to Jakub Beneš, John Borgonovo, John Cunningham, Peter Crooks, David Dickson, Jennifer FitzGerald, Sorcha Geoghegan, Tomás Irish, Martin Maguire, Edward Molloy, Eve Morrison, William Murphy, Cormac Ó Comhraí, Pádraig Óg Ó Ruairc, Eda Sagarra, Thomas Tormey, Ciarán Wallace, Fionnuala Walsh, and Tim Wilson. At Cambridge University Press, Liz Friend-Smith and Michael Watson have shown great faith in this project. I must thank my uncle and aunt, Patrick F. O'Donovan and Olive O'Donovan, who have always been an enormous source of encouragement. My grandmother, Ann O'Leary, has always believed in me.

Finally, my family. My siblings, Cian, Eva, and Elise, provide not just encouragement, but a never-ending supply of fun as well. But the final word belongs to my parents. Liz and John Morrissey have been an inspiration. Although no words can express the debt I owe, I hope this dedication is some small recompense.

Irish-Language Terms Used

Ard fheis	Annual party conference
Céilí/Céilithe	Irish dancing session/sessions
Clan na Gael	'Family of the Gaels': separatist organisation sister of the IRB
Coisde Gnótha	Gaelic League executive
Comhluadar Gaodhalach na Fiadhnuise	Irish Guild of Witness
Craobh na gCúig gCúigí	Branch of the Five Provinces
Cumann	Branch of society
Cumann Gaedhealach an Cólaiste	College Gaelic Society (QUB)
Cumann Gaelach na hEaglaise	Irish Guild of the Church
Cumann na nGaedheal	'Society of the Gaels': Republican front in the 1900s; later Irish Free State political party
Cumann na Saoirse	'Society of Freedom': Pro-Anglo-Irish Treaty women's group
Dáil Éireann	Irish parliament
Feis/Feiseanna	Festival/festivals
Fianna Fáil	'Soldiers of destiny': political party, 1926–
Na Fianna Éireann	'Soldiers of Ireland': republican youth group
Sinn Féin	'We ourselves': political party, 1905–
Taoiseach	'Chief': prime minister of Ireland
Teachta Dála	'Deputy to the Dáil': Member of Parliament

Abbreviations

AOH	Ancient Order of Hibernians
BL	British Library
BMH, WS	Bureau of Military History, Witness Statements
CBS	Crime Branch Special Records
CCCA	Cork City and County Archives
CD	Contemporary documents
CIG	*Church of Ireland Gazette*
DIB	*Dictionary of Irish Biography*
DL	Deputy Lieutenant
DSO	Distinguished Service Order
FJ	*Freeman's Journal*
GAA	Gaelic Athletic Association
GOLI	Grand Orange Lodge of Ireland, Belfast
GPO	General Post Office, Dublin
ICA	Irish Citizen Army
II	*Irish Independent*
ILPI	Independent Labour Party of Ireland
IPHRA	Irish Protestant Home Rule Association
IRA	Irish Republican Army
IRB	Irish Republican Brotherhood
IT	*Irish Times*
IWA	Irish Women's Association
MAD	Military Archives, Dublin
McC	Denis McCullough papers
MRIA	Member, Royal Irish Academy
MSPC	Military Service Pensions Collection
NAI	National Archives of Ireland
NLI	National Library of Ireland
PFOI	Protestant Friends of Ireland
PNS	Protestant National Society
PRONI	Public Record Office of Northern Ireland, Belfast
QC	Queen's Counsel

RCBL	Representative Church Body Library, Dublin
RCPI	Royal College of Physicians of Ireland
RIC	Royal Irish Constabulary
TCD	Trinity College Dublin
TD	*Teachta Dála*
TNA	The National Archives, Kew
UCD	University College Dublin
UG	*Ulster Guardian*
UIL	United Irish League
ULT	Ulster Literary Theatre
UVF	Ulster Volunteer Force
VC	Victoria Cross

Introduction

It is June 1918, and Ireland is once again close to rebellion. The British government's efforts to extend conscription to Ireland has caused outrage, and all nationalist groups, as well as the Catholic hierarchy, have combined to resist the measure. Beginning in April 1918, there was large-scale public agitation against conscription, which led some British officials to fear that just two years after the Easter Rising, there would be another outbreak of violence. The 9th of June was designated 'Women's Day', and tens of thousands of women converged on Dublin to sign an anti-conscription pledge. Nelly O'Brien, a nationalist activist, organised a separate Protestant women's protest. On the morning of the 9th, the women sought to meet at Christ Church Cathedral for prayer prior to attending the main rally. Receiving no reply from the Dean as to their request for the cathedral to be opened early, they assembled at the appointed time, but found the doors shut. They were forced to hold their prayer service outside, kneeling down in the rain. Before the group departed, the doors were opened and the women were met by an official. He snatched a copy of the women's pledge from them, tore it into pieces, and stated that he would not allow 'rubbish' like that in the cathedral.[1]

This incident is illuminating for several reasons. First, the women felt the need to form their own, explicitly Protestant, organisation. Second, the women, who came from respectable families, were treated discourteously by a Church of Ireland official. Third, when the group made their way to the main rally, they were warmly received by their fellow (Catholic) nationalists and their presence was highlighted in several accounts. And finally, for D. P. Moran, a Catholic-chauvinist newspaper editor, the incident substantiated his long-held view that the vast majority of Irish Protestants were entirely opposed to Irish nationalism, and that Protestant nationalists were a tiny, unrepresentative minority.[2] This book will explore these themes.

---

[1] *Irish Independent (II)*, 10 June 1918. See also *Nenagh Guardian*, 15 June 1918.
[2] *The Leader*, 15 June 1918.

This is the story of a counterculture. From about 1900, and continuing until the end of the Irish Civil War in 1923, a substantial group of Irish Protestants eschewed the unionist views typically held by their co-religionists, and instead played an active role in the advanced nationalist movement. There are three overarching themes of this book. The first is motivation. Although Protestant nationalism was a widespread phenomenon, its support within the broader community was always low. This book assesses the formative influences that caused a minority to reject unionism for a nationalist perspective that would cause them to be isolated from their own communities. It will chart the striking tendency for Protestant nationalists to form self-perpetuating networks of activists, where individuals, bound by ties of family and intense friendship, forged alliances that allowed them to repudiate the views of Protestant unionists. It will also discuss the tendency for some to have a tradition of nationalism in their family, and for others to explicitly reject a unionist inheritance.

Second, this book will detail the extent of Protestant involvement in, and influence on, Irish nationalism. Although the nationalist movement during the period 1900–1923 included many Protestants in leadership positions, the extent of 'grassroots' Protestant nationalist activism has been under-researched. Where nominal data can be traced, a prosopographical methodology will be adopted to assess the denominational and socioeconomic composition of nationalist organisations. Furthermore, Protestant nationalist influence on wider nationalism (for example, in reviving the Irish Republican Brotherhood (IRB) or planning the Howth gun-running) will be discussed.

Third, it will examine the fraught relationship between religious identity and Irish nationalism. How did Protestant nationalists fit into the nationalist movement? How did Catholics view them? One key theme is the changing nature of nationalism. After 1916, the nationalist movement grew steadily more Catholic in nature. How did Protestant nationalists react to this? This book will discuss evidence that Protestants suffered discrimination from Catholic nationalists, and will highlight the hostility that Protestants faced from their unionist co-religionists, especially in Ulster. Some Protestant nationalists converted to Catholicism. How common was this? And for those who remained Protestant, how did they view Catholics, and Catholicism? Did traditionally hostile attitudes endure?

Irish nationalism in the early 1900s was divided into two wings: moderate nationalists, whose objective was home rule, and advanced nationalists, who sought a significantly larger degree of independence, usually a republic, and who incorporated a substantial physical-force

element. Although some scholars have drawn attention to the commonalities between moderate and advanced nationalists,[3] a study of Protestant nationalists must choose which tradition to focus on. Protestant
advanced nationalists and Protestant home rulers had little in common:
the former sought an independent state, whereas the latter could be
notably tepid in their convictions, tending to view home rule primarily
as another liberal reform, which would ultimately strengthen the
Empire. Protestants within the advanced nationalist movement are the
focus of this book.[4] Advanced nationalists were a disparate group,
bringing together political, literary, theatrical, journalistic, cultural,
sporting, trade union, and militant elements, largely uncoordinated
until 1917, and by and large represented by Sinn Féin after that. The
contrast with the home rulers' Irish Parliamentary Party and grassroots
United Irish League is stark, but individual advanced nationalists
understood that even though their movement was comprised of small,
heterogeneous groups, they saw themselves as working towards a
common goal. A classic expression of this perspective comes from
Sydney Czira, née Gifford (1889–1974), a Rathmines Anglican and a
prolific nationalist journalist under the pen name 'John Brennan'. She
stated that:

a new political force was coming into existence, and which, with a touch of
prophetic vision, we called 'The Movement' ... It was not organised into one
body, and it had no recognised leaders. But the Movement did move, slowly at
first, and then with tremendous momentum from 1910 to 1916. Many of the men
and women of the Movement were very obscure individuals ... They had little or
no political influence. They belonged to a number of small societies and groups.
Some were in Sinn Féin; others in the Irish Republican Brotherhood; others in
the Inghinidhe na hÉireann. Still more were in the ranks of the Gaelic League or
GAA. Within a few years these scattered groups had coalesced, and an Irish
revolutionary force came into being. The obscure men and women of
1908 became the acknowledged leaders of Ireland in 1916 and the years that
followed.[5]

---

[3] For example, Patrick Maume, *The long gestation: Irish nationalist life 1891–1918* (Dublin, 1999); D. George Boyce, *Nationalism in Ireland* (London, 1995).

[4] We lack a full study of Protestant home rulers, but see four useful recent biographies: Colin Reid, *The lost Ireland of Stephen Gwynn: Irish constitutional nationalism and cultural politics, 1864–1950* (Manchester, 2011); Jennifer Regan-Lefebvre, *Cosmopolitan nationalism in the Victorian Empire: Ireland, India and the politics of Alfred Webb* (Basingstoke, 2009); Otto Rauchbauer, *Shane Leslie: sublime failure* (Dublin, 2009); Jasper Ungoed-Thomas, *Jasper Wolfe of Skibbereen* (Cork, 2008).

[5] Sidney Gifford Czira, *The years flew by* (John Hayes, ed.) (Galway, 2000 [1974]), 39. Both 'Sydney' and 'Sidney' spellings appear of Czira's first name.

It is the Protestants of Czira's 'Movement', the advanced nationalist movement, which this book will trace.

Why is religion relevant to the study of nationalism? Although often taken for granted in Ireland, the extent to which nationalism has a religious origination has been the subject of dispute. First published in 1960, Elie Kedourie's work *Nationalism* advanced the theory that nationalism was a concept that was invented in Europe in the early nineteenth century.[6] This text has proved influential, and has given rise to the modernist perspective, whose adherents claim a comparatively recent history for nationalism. Most modernists hold that nations and nationalism are recent constructions that have been created by social elites to achieve political and economic ends, and were little influenced by religion or pre-industrial experience. The most influential modernist thinkers include Ernest Gellner, Benedict Anderson, and Eric Hobsbawm.[7] The modernist approach is disputed by advocates of the perennialist perspective. Perennialists contend that nations and nationalism are continuous or recurrent throughout history, with their roots in vernacular culture and religion. Adrian Hastings's *The construction of nationhood* has become the seminal work.[8] Hastings adopted an empirical approach to demonstrate that nations frequently have origins deep in medieval history and argues that religion is central to the creation of nations and nationalism.[9] Anthony D. Smith's *Nationalism and modernism* criticises the modernists for what he contends is a lack of historical depth to their analyses, and argues that religion plays a strong role in forging nationalism.[10] Steven Grosby's recent critique offers a perennialist interpretation, which uses examples from ancient Israel, Buddhist Japan, and Catholic Poland to demonstrate both the antiquity of nationalism and its primarily religious origination.[11] But can these theories be applied to Ireland? Or to the Protestant nationalist tradition?

The Tudor conquest of Ireland, generally seen as lasting from 1534 to 1603, saw English sovereignty extended beyond the Pale, to encompass the entire island. The trauma of conquest was exacerbated by attempts

---

[6] Elie Kedourie, *Nationalism* (London, 1960).

[7] See, for example, Ernest Gellner, *Thought and change* (London, 1964); Ernest Gellner, *Nations and Nationalism* (Oxford, 1983); Benedict Anderson, *Imagined communities: reflections on the origin and spread of nationalism* (London, 1983); Eric Hobsbawm, *Nations and nationalism since 1780: programme, myth, reality* (Cambridge, 1990).

[8] Adrian Hastings, *The construction of nationhood: ethnicity, religion and nationalism* (Cambridge, 1997).

[9] Hastings, *The construction of nationhood*, 2.

[10] Anthony D. Smith, *Nationalism and modernism: a critical survey of recent theories of nations and nationalism* (London, 1998), 112–116, 219, 227.

[11] Steven Grosby, *Nationalism: a very short introduction* (New York, 2005).

by the English authorities to enforce the Reformation. However, weak state power meant that the Gaels and Old English generally resisted conforming, which gave Irish Protestantism the appearance of an English imposition, an image it has never quite lost. D. George Boyce has argued that the Gaels (the native, Irish-speaking inhabitants) developed some sense of national identity during the Tudor plantations.[12] The Ulster plantation, an attempt to subdue this most recalcitrant province, saw the native Irish removed from their lands and replaced by Protestant Scottish and English planters. The natives, who never accepted their expropriation, sought in 1641 to overturn the plantation. The 1641 rebellion was enormously significant, acting as an 'occult force' on Irish Protestants, and providing later generations with evidence of the natives' capacity for murderous retribution for past dispossession.[13] Equally significant was the decision of the Old English gentry of the Pale to cast aside ethnic difference and support their co-religionists in rebellion, culminating in the Confederate war. This religious front had been prefigured by the writings of the Gaelicised Old English priest Geoffrey Keating (c. 1580–1644), who in 'Foras feasa ar Éirinn' (c. 1634) defined the 'Éireannaigh', or Irish people, as the Gaels and the Catholic Old English, excluding the New English settlers and Protestants from his definition. Perennialist scholars sometimes trace the origin of Irish nationalism to Keating's work.[14] The dual disasters of the Cromwellian land settlement and the expropriation that followed the defeat of the Catholic King James II offered a final crystallising moment. 'Old English and native Irish were once more involved in a common ruin; and the long period of oppression that followed all but eradicated the memory of any division between them.'[15] Marianne Elliott adopts a perennialist approach in tracing the origin of Irish nationalism to this fusion of the Gaels and Old English in the seventeenth century.[16]

The eighteenth-century penal laws, although imperfectly implemented, discriminated against Catholics in favour of members of the established church, the Church of Ireland, resulting in a Protestant parliament, constitution, and land ownership, which actively excluded

---

[12] Boyce, *Nationalism in Ireland.*
[13] A. T. Q. Stewart, *The narrow ground: aspects of Ulster 1609–1969* (Belfast, 1997 [1977]), 49.
[14] See, for example, Tom Garvin, 'National identity in Ireland', *Studies: An Irish Quarterly Review*, Vol. 95, No. 379 (Autumn, 2006), 243.
[15] J. C. Beckett, *The Anglo-Irish tradition* (London, 1976), 42.
[16] Marianne Elliott, *When God took sides: religion and identity in Ireland – unfinished identity* (Oxford, 2009).

the Catholic majority from influence.[17] Although grievously wounded by the loss of its gentry to emigration and religious conversion, Catholic identity was in fact strengthened during the penal era. Gaelic poets, in declaiming the ruin of their people, provided later generations of Catholic patriots with a rich literature of past injustice to mine. One paradox of the penal era is that Protestants themselves became assertively Irish. Although remaining culturally English, they discarded the terms 'New English' or 'English in Ireland' and began to refer to themselves as the 'Irish nation'.[18] Partially born of grievance with the British government's treatment of the subordinate legislature in Dublin, the Protestant 'Patriot' movement developed. This movement, which sought legislative independence from Britain, originally excluded Catholics from their conception of the Irish nation.[19] Although the late eighteenth-century genesis of the 'Protestant nation' suggests it corresponds to the modernist model, it must be noted that Protestant nationalism was propelled by religious identity. Eventually, prominent Patriots, inspired by Enlightenment principles, came to support Catholic relief. Protestant patriotism spawned the Volunteer movement, whose Convention at Dungannon in 1782 prompted the eventual concession of legislative independence from Britain.[20] One of the themes of this study will be the extent to which nostalgia for the Patriots, Volunteers, and Dungannon informed later Protestant and Catholic nationalism.

The Society of United Irishmen was founded in 1791. Its ideology was a synthesis of influences: Protestant patriotism, Presbyterian democracy, Catholic unrest, and the spirit of the American and French revolutions. Theobald Wolfe Tone (1763–1798), an Anglican barrister, was the group's most powerful personality and is generally regarded as the father of Irish nationalism.[21] Its commitment to the union of 'Catholic, Protestant and Dissenter' was historically significant, and has provided both an aspiration and a source of rhetorical ammunition for generations of Irish nationalists. The 1798 rebellion, in which the United Irishmen sought to create a republic on French lines, ended in failure, and was

---

[17] S. J. Connolly, *Religion, law and power: the making of Protestant Ireland, 1660–1760* (Oxford, 1992); T. P. Power and Kevin Whelan (eds.), *Endurance and emergence: Catholics in Ireland in the eighteenth century* (Dublin, 1990).

[18] Elliott, *When God took sides*, 34; David Hayton, 'Anglo-Irish attitudes: changing perceptions of national identity among the Protestant ascendancy in Ireland, ca. 1690–1740', *Studies in Eighteenth-century culture*, Vol. 17 (1987), 151–152.

[19] See Jacqueline Hill, *From Patriots to unionists: Dublin civic politics and Irish Protestant Patriotism, 1660–1840* (Oxford, 1997).

[20] Thomas Bartlett, *The fall and rise of the Irish nation: the Catholic question, 1690–1830* (Dublin, 1992), 34–38.

[21] Marianne Elliott, *Wolfe Tone: prophet of Irish independence* (New Haven, 1989).

followed by the Act of Union in 1800, which dissolved the Irish parliament and created the United Kingdom of Great Britain and Ireland.

Marianne Elliott has argued that Protestant – in particular, Presbyterian – support for the United Irishmen should be understood in the context of a widespread belief that Catholicism had lost its menace.[22] When it became clear throughout the nineteenth century that Catholicism was in fact resurgent, Presbyterians began to identify with wider British culture and support the Union.[23] This did not prevent later generations of Catholic nationalists from citing the example of 1798 in exhorting Presbyterians to rediscover their radicalism, nor for a small but active tradition of Presbyterian radicalism to remain active, especially in Ulster. Protestant nationalists frequently looked back to the late eighteenth century. One such figure was the novelist and Church of Ireland clergyman George A. Birmingham. Speaking of his co-religionists, he wrote:

> They have quite forgotten that their grandfathers stood for Irish nationality. They have chosen to call themselves English … They conceived of themselves as an English garrison, and held loyalty to England as their prime duty.[24]

The few scholars of Irish nationalism to endorse the modernist view trace the formation of Irish nationalism to the eighteenth century. John Hutchinson traces the origin of cultural nationalism to the mid-eighteenth century.[25] Richard English, in his wide-ranging empirical and theoretical survey, offers a useful compromise between the perennialists and modernists: he dates the origins of Irish nationalism to the United Irishmen, although he stresses its more ancient roots.[26]

This study argues that the United Irishmen, alongside the Patriots and Volunteers, formed an alternative moment of crystallisation, when a Protestant nationalist tradition was created in Ireland. This tradition, while always having the adherence of only a minority of Protestants, co-existed alongside the Catholic nationalist tradition. The existence of a separate Protestant nationalist tradition helps explain, for example, the prejudice against the institution of the Church of Rome held not only by United Irishmen such as Tone and William Drennan, but also by later generations of Protestant nationalists, a fact that occasionally perplexes

---

[22] Elliott, *When God took sides*, 128.

[23] Peter Brooke, *Ulster Presbyterianism: the historical perspective 1610–1970* (Dublin, 1987), 194, 208.

[24] George A. Birmingham, *The seething pot* (London, 1905), 134–135, originally quoted in Elliott, *When God took sides*, 98. For Birmingham, see below, Chapter 1.

[25] John Hutchinson, *The dynamics of cultural nationalism: the Gaelic Revival and the creation of the Irish nation state* (London, 1987). See also R. V. Comerford's guarded endorsement: *Ireland* (London, 2003).

[26] Richard English, *Irish freedom: the history of nationalism in Ireland* (London, 2006), 492ff.

modern scholars.[27] It is possible that there are two Irish nationalisms: one, a Catholic strain, with its perennialist roots in the seventeenth century or earlier, and the other, a more modern, Protestant strain. Protestant nationalism, like Catholic nationalism, had its origin in religious identity, and, in its evolved, United Irishman form, gave ideological sustenance to later generations of Irish nationalists, from all religious backgrounds.

What European parallels with Protestant nationalists can we discern? Central European history is replete with borderland peoples who, forced to declare a national allegiance, chose an identification seemingly at odds with language or religion. One parallel is that of the Protestant Masurian Poles of East Prussia, who, following a plebiscite in 1920, essentially became German by rejecting the politics of their Catholic co-nationals and voting almost unanimously to remain in Germany.[28] There is a burgeoning historiography on 'side-switching' in Central Europe. James Bjork has examined, again in the post–Great War period, the Upper Silesians, some of whom adhered to Germany, some to Poland, and others wavering in between.[29] Chad Bryant has charted the fair degree of opportunism that led some Czechs, living under Nazi occupation, to declare themselves German.[30] Tara Zahra, in an important article, has claimed that national 'indifference' constituted a distinct form of political agency in Central Europe.[31] It is difficult, however, to meaningfully place Protestant nationalists within these frameworks. The wartime Czech experience aside, most Central European side-switching involved substantial population groups, who may have appeared one thing, but became another. Only the relatively small number of Protestant nationalist converts to Catholicism really fit into this category.[32] Likewise, national indifference can scarcely be detected among the subjects of this book, although Protestant National Army servicemen may come close.[33]

---

[27] See, for example, discussion of Independent Orange Order, below, Chapter 2.

[28] Richard Blanke, '"Polish-speaking Germans?": language and national identity among the Masurians', *Nationalities Papers*, Vol. 27, No. 3 (1999), 429–453.

[29] James E. Bjork, *Neither German nor Pole: Catholicism and national indifference in a Central European borderland* (Michigan, 2008). See also an important comparative study, T. K. Wilson, *Frontiers of violence: conflict and identity in Ulster and Upper Silesia 1918–1922* (Oxford, 2010).

[30] Chad Bryant, *Prague in black: Nazi rule and Czech nationalism* (Cambridge, MA, 2007), 51–55, 71–76ff.

[31] Tara Zahra, 'Imagined noncommunities: national indifference as a category of analysis', in *Slavic Review*, Vol. 69, No. 1 (Spring, 2010), 93–119. Cf. Jakub S. Beneš, *Workers and nationalism: Czech and German social democracy in Habsburg Austria, 1890–1918* (Oxford, 2016), 11–12.

[32] See Chapter 3.   [33] See Chapter 8.

More promising may be the pan-European phenomenon of aristocratic rebellion, where upper-class figures transgress class lines and support socialist, communist, or anarchist causes. Examples are legion: Katharine Stewart-Murray, the 'Red Duchess' of Atholl, who supported the Republicans in the Spanish Civil War; Mihály Károlyi, the 'Red Count', who served as president of the short-lived First Hungarian People's Republic; Gavin Henderson, 2nd Baron Faringdon, a socialist, pacifist, and Fabian; and Leo Tolstoy. Indeed, the 'repentant gentry' is a recurring theme in Russian literature.[34] Certain Protestant nationalists bear this comparison well: Roger Casement, Albinia Brodrick, and, above all, Constance Markievicz. But we should be careful. As we will see throughout this book, Irish aristocratic revolutionaries usually allied and formed networks with decidedly bourgeois co-religionists. It is difficult to escape the conclusion that Protestant nationalism is better understood as a minority response to the history of Irish Protestantism and the growth of Catholic democracy, rather than an Irish expression of a pan-European phenomenon.

Any study of Protestant nationalists is indebted to, and builds upon, the work of earlier scholars. Protestant nationalists have fascinated historians of Ireland, who have frequently sought to decode and analyse the ambiguities and ambivalences that underlay their experiences. The existence of a substantial political dissident tradition within Irish Protestantism, whose members frequently exhibited liberal or cosmopolitan views that diverged from the ethos that would dominate Northern Ireland, the Irish Free State, or the Republic of Ireland, has excited the curiosity of generations of scholars. Historians, as well as literary critics and political scientists, have employed a diverse range of methods to reconstruct the political trajectories, ideology, and social milieu of these figures.

The importance of religious and social background in determining political development has proved controversial. F. S. L. Lyons's study *Charles Stewart Parnell* portrayed the Irish Party leader as a skilled practitioner of political power, though one whose views did not follow any fixed programme.[35] A younger scholar, Paul Bew (b. 1950), in his short, sharp *C. S. Parnell*, disagreed, arguing that Parnell followed an essentially conservative programme, aimed at securing the leadership of the Protestant gentry in a home rule parliament. Bew claimed that Parnell's views were informed by ancestral memory of the eighteenth-century Patriot tradition, the nationalist leanings of members of his immediate family, as

---

[34] See, for example, Caryl Emerson, *The Cambridge introduction to Russian literature* (Cambridge, 2008), 12.
[35] F. S. L. Lyons, *Charles Stewart Parnell* (London, 1977).

well as class consciousness.[36] This book will demonstrate that these themes projected into the twentieth century: we will see how the importance of residual memories of the eighteenth century, the influence of relations who exhibited nationalist sympathies, and even the desire for the perpetuation of Protestant influence informed the actions of those who lived a generation and more after Parnell.

Among individuals active during 1900–1923, the field of biography is particularly well served. The romantic, often tragic experiences of prominent Protestant rebels have been subjected to repeated analysis: there have been at least twelve full biographies of Roger Casement, seven of Erskine Childers, and nine of Constance Markievicz.[37] Since 2000, biographies have been produced of Bulmer Hobson, Rosamond Jacob, Captain Jack White, Alice Milligan, Albinia Brodrick, Kathleen Lynn (twice), Ella Young, Maud Gonne, Grace Gifford, Louie Bennett, Eva Gore-Booth, Anna Parnell, Francis Stuart, and Sam Maguire, as well as a collective biography of the Gifford sisters. Marnie Hay's *Bulmer Hobson* is a fine biography of an occasionally neglected figure, and has proved an invaluable source for this study. Margaret Ó hÓgartaigh's *Kathleen Lynn* reconstructs Lynn's career as a pioneering female physician and socialist republican, while probing her troubled relationship with her unionist family. Colin Reid's *The lost Ireland of Stephen Gwynn* offers, inter alia, a fine discussion of the 'O'Brien inheritance': the amalgam of maternal-line influences that inspired his subject's (moderate) nationalism. Catherine Morris's evocative *Alice Milligan and the Irish cultural revival* highlights Milligan's influence on the development of cultural nationalism.[38]

---

[36] Paul Bew, *C. S. Parnell* (Dublin, 1980). See also a later, expanded life by the same author: *Enigma: a new life of Charles Stewart Parnell* (Dublin, 2011).

[37] The fullest account of Casement's life is Séamas Ó Síocháin, *Roger Casement: imperialist, rebel, revolutionary* (Dublin, 2008). For a fine portrait that stresses the extent to which his self-image as an Irish Protestant informed his nationalist activism, see Brian Inglis, *Roger Casement* (London, 1973). For Childers, the fullest treatment is Andrew Boyle, *The riddle of Erskine Childers* (London, 1977). Important studies of Markievicz include Diana Norman, *Terrible beauty: a life of Constance Markievicz* (Dublin, 1988), and Lauren Arrington, *Revolutionary lives: Constance and Casimir Markievicz* (Princeton, 2016). An earlier work by Seán O'Faoláin, *Constance Markievicz: or, the average revolutionary; a biography* (London, 1934), is implicitly hostile.

[38] Marnie Hay, *Bulmer Hobson and the nationalist movement in twentieth-century Ireland* (Manchester, 2009); Margaret Ó hÓgartaigh, *Kathleen Lynn: Irishwoman, patriot, doctor* (Dublin, 2006); Catherine Morris, *Alice Milligan and the Irish cultural revival* (Dublin, 2012).

The late Valerie Jones's *Rebel Prods* adopts a wide lens to examine radical Protestant nationalists, with a focus on the 1916 Rising.[39]

It is possible that one impact of this biographical focus has been to skew scholarly understanding of the nature of Protestant nationalism. Frequently the conversion from youthful unionism to nationalism – a typical trajectory for the subjects of these studies – is viewed as a sort of complex biographical puzzle to be solved. The Gifford sisters are 'unlikely rebels', Anna Parnell mounted a 'petticoat rebellion', and such is the 'riddle of Erskine Childers' that this is the title of two books about the man.[40] The way forward for historiography is to follow up the implications of the circles that have been reconstructed, to define what networks they formed, and what political organisations attracted them. This would, additionally, provide a context in which new biographies might be placed. A study of this sort allows the abnormality or otherwise of individual Protestant nationalists to be assessed, as well as highlighting the degree to which these individuals, although politically marginalised in their own religious community, formed recognisable networks and developed a distinctive associational culture, explicitly at odds with mainstream Protestant society. That is the primary object of this book.

Methods, Sources, and Definitions

> 99% of Catholics and 98% of Protestants approximately could be relied on to vote for their natural hereditary side. I think I am right in saying that the percentage of 'rotten Protestants' (it was the term always employed) was appreciably greater than that of backsliding Catholics … The faculty of independent judgement is more cultivated among Protestants.[41]

During the period between the turn of the twentieth century and the cessation of hostilities in the Irish Civil War in 1923, Protestants played an influential role in the advanced nationalist movement. Protestant nationalists, as a religious minority among nationalists, and a political minority among their co-religionists, formed a vibrant counterculture within Irish life. Analysis of this group enhances our understanding of religious and political identity during this era. Counterculture has been

---

[39] Valerie Jones, *Rebel Prods: the forgotten story of Protestant radical nationalists and the 1916 Rising* (Dublin, 2016).

[40] Anne Clare, *Unlikely rebels: the Gifford girls and the fight for Irish freedom* (Cork, 2011); Patricia Groves, *Petticoat rebellion: the Anna Parnell story* (Cork, 2009). The second biography of Childers to bear this name is Michael McInerney, *The riddle of Erskine Childers* (Dublin, 1971).

[41] Stephen Gwynn, *Experiences of a literary man* (London, 1926), 277.

defined as 'a social group or movement whose values and way of life are opposed to the mainstream of society to some degree'.[42] Although frequently applied to the student and hippy cultures identified with youth conflicts around 1968, the term has a wider usage, and has been applied to the Romantic movement in the first half of the nineteenth century, the bohemians from the latter part of the century, and other groups that challenge the political, social, or behavioural norms prevalent in mainstream society. Protestant nationalists, in, for example, rejecting the political views of the vast majority of their co-religionists (especially that of the older generation), frequently changing their given names, and departing from typical modes of language, pastimes, and dress represent an important Irish counterculture during this era.[43]

A variety of methods have been used to trace this counterculture. Where nominal data has survived, a prosopographical approach has been employed. Prosopography, defined as 'the investigation of the common background characteristics of a group of actors in history by means of a collective study of their lives', provides a useful analytical framework for collective biography.[44] By submitting a historical group, whose individual biographies may be untraceable, to analysis under such headings as dates, religious denomination, profession, father's profession, and membership of political organisations, one can trace the patterns of relationships and political activity of the chosen set, and determine how this group evolved over the chosen time frame. One of the principal benefits of prosopography is that it mitigates against 'drawing conclusions from a handful of individual cases and of generalising from a handful of eloquent examples'.[45] To this end, membership lists have been reconstructed for the Dungannon Clubs, Irish Citizen Army, Irish Guild of the Church, Irish Guild of Witness, and the Branch of the Five Provinces. Protestant advanced nationalist women, a major topic of this book, are examined as an individual group. Lists have been assembled of all known Protestant 1916 rebels, as well as Protestant members of the Irish Republican Army and anti-Treaty forces. Chapter 8 includes a

---

[42] Noel Castree, Rob Kitchin, and Alisdair Rogers, *A dictionary of human geography* (Oxford, 2013).
[43] See, for example, Dick Hebdige, *Subculture* (London, 1979), 127ff.
[44] Lawrence Stone, 'Prosopography', *Daedalus*, Vol. 100, No. 1 (Winter, 1971), 46.
[45] K. S. B. Keats-Rohan (ed.), *Prosopography approaches and applications: a handbook* (Oxford, 2007), 36. For two fine examples of prosopography in an Irish context, see Fergus Campbell, *The Irish establishment: 1879–1914* (Oxford, 2009); James Richard Redmond McConnel, 'The view from the backbench: Irish nationalist MPs and their work, 1910–1914', PhD thesis, University of Durham, 2002. See also the much recast, and highly valuable, published version of the latter work: James McConnel, *The Irish Parliamentary Party and the third home rule crisis* (Dublin, 2013).

substantial prosopographical analysis of Protestants in the Free State, or National Army. In all, data has been assembled on about 500 Protestant nationalist activists and 220 Protestant National Army servicemen. As we have noted, much of the literature on Protestant nationalists is largely biographical; this study, in reconstructing Protestant nationalist associational culture, will contribute to a better understanding, of not merely well-known figures, but the denominational, socioeconomic, and geographic context in which they operated. Scholarship of Irish nationalism – particularly in its revolutionary strain – has seen enormous growth in recent years. However, there have been few efforts to quantitatively examine the backgrounds of substantial numbers of advanced nationalists.[46] This book, in exploring the backgrounds, careers, and connections of a substantial group of activists, will also make a significant contribution to the study of Irish nationalism more generally. Where sources preclude prosopography, or such analysis would render little, this study has recourse to a qualitative investigation of a variety of other nationalist organisations, including the Protestant National Society, the Ulster Literary Theatre, Sinn Féin, the Protestant Friends of Ireland, and the Gaelic League. And so, in combining quantitative and qualitative methods, a full picture of Protestant advanced nationalist activity will emerge.

Irish history during this period is famously – or notoriously – well documented, and in preparing this book reference has been made to a wide variety of source material. Nominal data for organisations such as the Dungannon Clubs and the Irish Guild of the Church has been derived from surviving minute books, and in the case of the National Army, an underused census. Biographical data (i.e., the denomination, place of birth, profession, and father's profession of activists) has been gleaned from a wide variety of sources, notably the 1901 and 1911 census returns, the *Dictionary of Irish Biography*, press obituaries, and secondary accounts. The Military Service Pensions Collection (MSPC) is a revelatory source, which includes the most reliable membership lists for the Irish Citizen Army (ICA), Irish Republican Army (IRA), and Cumann na mBan. Likewise, the Bureau of Military History Witness Statements include a large amount of material related to Protestant nationalists.

In general, Protestant nationalists were curiously unreflective: memoirs rarely record their responses to being a *Protestant* nationalist,

---

[46] But see David Fitzpatrick, *Politics and Irish life, 1913–1921: provincial experience of war and revolution*, rev. ed. (Cork, 1998 [1977]); Peter Hart, 'The social structure of the Irish Republican Army, 1916–1923', *The Historical Journal*, Vol. 42, No. 1 (March 1999), 207–231.

possibly owing to a desire to cast their political choices in a conventional light. However, the Protestant nationalist mentality can be discerned from analysis of the rich periodical literature of the period, including the *Gaelic Churchman, Red Hand Magazine,* the *Gaelic American,* and the *Church of Ireland Gazette,* as well as national, mass-circulation newspapers. A large number of manuscript sources have also been examined. Roger Casement's correspondence with Alice Stopford Green is a valuable source. The manuscript diaries of Nancy Campbell and Rosamond Jacob provide insight into the formative influences of advanced nationalist women. Thomas Johnson's and Lindsay Crawford's papers detail Protestant nationalist reactions to changing times. Memoirs, intelligence files, pamphlets, and annual reports complete the picture. These sources have been combined to produce a collective biography that highlights the experiences of both well-known and unfamiliar figures.

What is a Protestant? Until the disestablishment of the Church of Ireland was enacted in 1869, the term 'Protestant' was often applied solely to Anglicans, excluding Presbyterians and other dissenters. However, after disestablishment the word came to be applied to all members of the reformed churches, and this definition is used here.[47] There was some (as we will see, occasionally exaggerated) tendency for Protestant nationalists to convert to Catholicism. This book will seek to establish how many are known to have converted to Rome, and will gauge how typical this decision was. Therefore, this study includes all those who were *baptised* or *raised* in the Protestant churches, and has used obituaries, memoirs, and secondary books to identify converts.

Many scholars have chosen to avoid the term 'Protestant' and instead – particularly when talking of upper-class or Church of Ireland figures – to refer to the 'Anglo-Irish'.[48] Although used for centuries, the term became more frequently used at the turn of the late nineteenth century but gained special currency in the decades after independence. Irish Protestants rarely described themselves as Anglo-Irish: the few who did, such as Trinity College Dublin (TCD) provost John Pentland Mahaffy, were determined iconoclasts.[49] The term 'Anglo-Irish' has now been applied quite indiscriminately, with even an individual such

---

[47] Donald Harman Akenson, *Small differences: Irish Catholics and Irish Protestants 1815–1922: an international perspective* (Kingston, 1988), 229 n.

[48] See, for example, Beckett, *The Anglo-Irish tradition,* 98.

[49] W. B. Stanford and R. B. McDowell, *Mahaffy: a biography of an Anglo-Irishman* (London, 1971).

as the Catholic surgeon's son Douglas ffrench-Mullen being described as such.[50] Another problematic term is 'Ascendancy'. This eighteenth-century coinage, which originally referred to the Church of Ireland upper class in the 1700s, is sometimes applied to the late nineteenth and early twentieth-century gentry, frequently by those who regret the passing of this social order.[51] It may be more useful to describe these figures as Irish Protestants, which was the expression they themselves used, and to pay close attention to the denominational and class divisions in their society.

From what sort of community did the Protestant nationalist counter-culture emerge? By 1900, the lines of demarcation between religious confession and political affiliation were closely drawn, the result of a century-long process of stratification. During the nineteenth century, Protestants, initially ambivalent about the loss of their parliament, accepted the security of rule from Westminster as a trade-off for independence. The link between unionism and Protestantism strengthened, aided by the influence of Daniel O'Connell, whose campaigns for Catholic emancipation and repeal of the union drew an explicit link between Catholicism and Irishness. The advance of the Catholic middle class, particularly after emancipation was secured in 1829, further convinced Protestants that the Union was the sole guarantor of their liberties. However, a short-lived Protestant nationalist movement re-emerged in the 1840s. Young Ireland, the name given to a group of middle-class Catholics and Protestants associated with TCD and the *Nation* newspaper, promoted cultural revival, a non-sectarian vision of Irishness, and national independence. The group supported O'Connell's repeal campaign but eventually clashed with the nationalist leader, with some members viewing his conflation of Catholicism and the Irish nation with distaste. The disestablishment of the Church of Ireland enacted in 1869 was traumatic, with clergy and laity spending the following decades accustoming themselves to their church's loss of prestige. However, there is evidence that even in the 1870s the Patriot tradition continued to exert a powerful influence on some Irish Anglicans. The first three leaders of the home rule movement, Isaac Butt, William Shaw, and Charles Stewart Parnell, in seeking to restore Irish Anglicans to a leadership role in Irish life, were influenced by this tradition. This remained a minority

---

[50] For criticism of the use of this term, see, for example, Elliott, *When God took sides*, 33; Nicholas Canny, *Making Ireland British, 1580–1650* (Oxford, 2001), vii–viii; Jack White, *Minority report: the Protestant community in the Irish Republic* (Dublin, 1975), 17, 31, 67.

[51] For a notably rose-tinted treatment, see Mark Bence-Jones, *Twilight of the Ascendancy* (London, 1987). For criticism of the use of this term, see David Fitzpatrick, *Descendancy: Irish Protestant histories since 1795* (Cambridge, 2014), 3.

perspective, however, and by the end of the nineteenth century, the link between Protestantism and unionism, and Catholicism and nationalism, was firmly established, despite growing efforts by Protestant nationalists to disturb it.

According to the 1901 census there were 1,150,114 Protestants in Ireland, amounting to 25.79 per cent of total.[52] In 1911 the Church of Ireland was the largest Protestant denomination, with its 576,611 members representing 13.1 per cent of the total population and 50.2 per cent of Protestants. Geographically, members were most prevalent in Ulster, where they amounted to 23.2 per cent of total. There were more than 140,000 Episcopalians in Leinster, totalling over 12 per cent. However, in Munster and Connaught their numbers were few, only 4.89 per cent and 3.11 per cent, respectively. Despite a reputation for being synonymous with the landed and professional interest, the church always included a substantial working class, especially in Ulster and Dublin.[53] However, Episcopalians remained over-represented in the gentry and professional classes. The Wyndham land act of 1903 eroded Episcopalian landed dominance, but they retained disproportionate economic influence, as well as a close connection with TCD, where the church had its divinity school. Presbyterians were the second-largest Protestant denomination. There were 443,276 Presbyterians in Ireland in 1901, amounting to 9.94 per cent of the total population.[54] Presbyterianism in Ireland traces its origins to planters from Scotland who settled in Ulster during the plantation. As such, Irish Presbyterianism has always had a strongly northern aspect. In 1901, 95.9 per cent of Presbyterians resided in Ulster.[55] Presbyterians made up 50.8 per cent of County Antrim, 34.4 per cent of residents of Belfast, and 38.9 per cent of County Down. The striking concentration of Presbyterians in the north-east gave rise to a sense of Ulster exceptionalism from the 1890s, which made it particularly easy for members of this church to contemplate partition. Irish Protestants, then, were most numerous in Dublin and the north-east. These communities were highly developed, with a tradition of internal dissent, and, by comparison with the rest of the country, a sense of confidence about the future. As we will see, it was here,

---

[52] W. E. Vaughan and A. J. Fitzpatrick, *Irish historical statistics: population, 1821–1971* (Dublin, 1978), 49. Vaughan and Fitzpatrick's figure includes tiny numbers of atheists, Jews (numbering 3,771), and those who refused to answer the religious question on the census return.

[53] See, for example, Martin Maguire, 'A socio-economic analysis of the Dublin Protestant working class, 1870–1926', *Irish economic and social history*, 20 (1993), 35–61.

[54] Vaughan and Fitzpatrick, *Irish historical statistics: population, 1821–1971*, 49.

[55] Vaughan and Fitzpatrick, *Irish historical statistics: population, 1821–1971*, 63–65.

in Dublin and the north-east, where Protestants were most numerous, that a Protestant nationalist counterculture would emerge.

This book takes a broadly chronological approach, interspersed with thematic sections at relevant points. Chapter 1, 'Radicals, c. 1900–1910', focuses on the nexus that was forged between republicanism and the literary movement, initially due to the efforts of Protestant figures such as W. B. Yeats and Maud Gonne, aided by supportive Catholics such as John O'Leary and Arthur Griffith. The Boer War, which led some Protestants to question their allegiance to unionism, and gravitate towards nationalist politics, is assessed. Opposition to this conflict was a leading factor in the revival of the advanced nationalist movement from around 1900. This chapter also discusses two of the most prominent newspaper editors of the period, Arthur Griffith and D. P. Moran, whose differing conceptions of the role Protestants should play in Irish life had implications for the nature of Protestant engagement with nationalism. The final section assesses the Gaelic League, and charts how the increasingly Catholic nature of the organisation both alienated Protestants and precipitated the creation of two new bodies, with a largely Protestant membership, one of which would later become a substantial forum for republican members of the Church of Ireland.

If Chapter 1 largely focuses on activism in Dublin and the south of the country, in Chapter 2, 'Dissidents, 1900–1910', the emphasis shifts to the separate development of Protestant nationalist politics in Belfast and Ulster. It discusses efforts by Ulster Protestant nationalists to encourage their co-religionists to convert to nationalism, by means of enterprises such as the Ulster Literary Theatre. It also analyses the efforts of republicans, principally Bulmer Hobson, to create organisations that would appeal to Protestants, such as the Protestant National Society and the Dungannon Clubs. The chapter also discusses the efforts of Robert Lindsay Crawford to radically reorient Orangeism towards republicanism. Belfast in this period became home to a vibrant Protestant nationalist counterculture, centred on figures such as Francis Joseph Bigger. The eventual dispersal of this group, which owed much to unionist hostility, will be examined.

Chapter 3, 'Converts, c. 1910–1916', largely focuses on the behaviour of Protestants from unionist backgrounds who adopted nationalist politics. The first section assesses the ideology of pre-1916 Sinn Féin, whose efforts to encourage Protestant participation led certain intellectuals to believe it posed a threat to unionist hegemony, but whose failure to develop a secularist programme ultimately impeded its efforts. The next section discusses 'synthetic Gaels': those Protestant converts to nationalism whose extravagant attempts to fit in could raise smiles or prompt hostility. In the next section, Protestant advanced nationalist women are assessed as a group, by means of a denominational, socioeconomic, and geographical examination. Their writings are used to assess their motivation for converting to an advanced nationalist position. The final section deals with conversion to Catholicism, and argues that religious conversion was rare, being most common among advanced nationalist women.

Chapter 4, 'Militants, 1912–1916', focuses on the efforts of Protestant advanced nationalists to bring about political change using extra-parliamentary methods. The first section describes the creation of the Irish Volunteers as a nationalist counterpoint to the Ulster Volunteers, and how this body came to be armed by a committee primarily composed of Protestants. The second section discusses labour and the Irish Citizen Army, whose leadership, at least initially, included several Protestants. The extent to which socialist leaders sought to fashion a nationalism that would appeal to working-class Protestants is also examined. Chapter 5 discusses the Easter Rising of 1916 and its aftermath. The rebellion had a largely Catholic cast, which has produced a belief that Catholicism and republicanism are connected. This chapter traces the experiences of those Protestants who did rebel in 1916. Many Protestant rebels first realised the increasingly Catholic nature of their movement in internment camps in Britain. The final section assesses the occasionally negative reactions of Protestant republicans to this change.

Chapter 6, 'Outsiders?, 1918–1921', assesses the political behaviour of Protestant republicans during the revolutionary period, as well as the attitude of the wider Irish advanced nationalist movement to Protestants. It describes the various means by which some Irish Protestants sought to demonstrate loyalty to the idea of an Irish republic. It discusses the conscription crisis, which prompted the creation of a specifically Protestant anti-conscription movement. It analyses the Irish Guild of the Church, the bulk of whose membership had by 1918 come to sympathise with the rebels, and the Irish Guild of Witness, a splinter group, whose members remained loyal to the Crown. The next section deals with the Ulster problem, which forced Protestant republicans to reorient their message in an effort to detach the Protestant working class from unionism. Finally, it discusses the Protestant Friends of Ireland, an American-based nationalist body, and examines the rhetoric Éamon de Valera used about Irish Protestants during his American tour, in 1919–1920.

Chapter 7, 'Revolutionaries, 1919–1923', describes Protestant active rebels in the War of Independence and on the republican side in the Irish Civil War. It discusses the formative influences of Protestant IRA men, their activities during the conflict, and their tendency to support the anti-Treaty side during the succeeding Civil War. The extent to which Irish Protestants were victims of a campaign of sectarian-based harassment and intimidation during this era has been controversial. The final section contributes to this discussion, by tracing the reaction of some Protestant nationalists to events such as those of Dunmanway in late April 1922, when thirteen Protestant men were killed. Finally, Chapter 8, 'Free Staters, 1922–1923', focuses on Protestants who supported the Anglo-Irish Treaty. It includes an analysis of Protestants who served in the National Army during the Civil War, and argues that this prefigures later Protestant engagement with the Irish Free State. Finally, the Conclusion follows the experiences of a number of carefully chosen individuals in the Free State, and assesses their responses to life in independent Ireland.

Protestant nationalism was a complex, vibrant counterculture in Ireland during the period 1900–1923. This book will provoke new questions as to the nature of Irish Protestantism and Irish nationalism, and about the intersection of religious identity with nationalism.

1   Radicals, c. 1900–1910

Origins: The Cultural Revival

Early on the morning of 19 January 1885, an elderly-looking gentleman disembarked at North Wall, Dublin. Tall, slightly built, with distinguished angular features, the figure was met, probably at his own insistence, by only a small party of supporters. Nineteen years and one month after his conviction for treason-felony, and after many years abroad, John O'Leary, veteran Fenian and Young Ireland relic, had returned from exile.[1]

Why begin a study of Protestant nationalists with John O'Leary? Among the leading Irish separatists of his era, O'Leary was baptised Catholic, although he was religiously unobservant, and, in common with many Fenians, he was a staunch anti-clericalist.[2] His importance becomes clear in an address he delivered that same night, before a packed audience in the Rotunda Room, to the members of the Young Ireland Society, a quasi-Fenian group which sought to revive the spirit of the Mitchel and Davis. The Protestant nationalist tradition that will be discussed in this book depended as much on cultural influences as it did on political. In his speech, 'Young Ireland – the old and the new', O'Leary outlined a new path for Irish nationalism. The Fenian movement, of which he was a senior member, had neglected the cultural sphere. O'Leary suggested that nationalism could be reinvigorated through greater engagement with Irish culture, especially history and literature.[3] In fact, the Young Ireland Society had, since their foundation in 1881, been doing exactly that: organising lectures, holding commemorations, and raising monuments to the nationalist dead.[4] However, O'Leary, elected president of the

---

[1] Marcus Bourke, *John O'Leary: a study in Irish separatism* (Tralee, 1967), 172–173.
[2] John O'Leary, *Recollections of fenians and fenianism*, Vol. II (London, 1896), 12–16, 32–42, 48–54.
[3] John O'Leary, *Young Ireland: the old and the new* (Dublin, 1885).
[4] For the Young Ireland Society, see M. J. Kelly, *The fenian ideal and Irish nationalism, 1882–1916* (Woodbridge, 2006), ch. 1.

20

organisation that night, would take this tendency further. The intimate, largely elitist synthesis of cultural and political nationalism he helped fashion would prove so seductive that by the early 1900s there was a more significant Protestant nationalist milieu in Ireland than at any time since 1798. John Hutchinson, in his seminal *The dynamics of cultural nationalism*, makes the contestable claim that 'Cultural nationalism ... has a politics, but it is very different from that of the political nationalist in its goals and modes of organisation.'[5] In fact, what we see in Ireland from this era is the drawing together of cultural and political nationalists, on a combined programme of national revival.

O'Leary's conception of Irish nationalism was aristocratic – he opposed the working man's franchise and priests in politics, and was hostile to the Land League (he held town property in Tipperary, and was considered a harsh landlord). This vision proved seductive for a group of Protestant intellectuals who expected self-government and yearned to play a prominent part in it. Furthermore, O'Leary himself understood their value; he would devote much of the rest of his life to winning well-to-do Protestants to nationalism.[6] According to Maud Gonne, his 'chief interest in life was getting new recruits for Ireland, especially from the Unionist element from which he wanted to form an intellectual backing for the Separatist movement'.[7] O'Leary expected that the Protestant 'quality' would populate a future Irish parliament, where they would ensure a gratifyingly conservative ethos. W. B. Yeats, most famously, came under O'Leary's spell. The poet, aged twenty in 1885, was the sort of marginalised Protestant – his father was a barrister turned impecunious painter – who was attracted by the Young Ireland vision of a pluralistic independent Ireland, in which Protestants and the gentry would still play a role. For Yeats, O'Leary, far from being the Fenian bogey of Protestant imagination, seemed to exemplify antique and noble virtue; the older man would help inspire the poet's patriotism. Yeats, encouraged by Maud Gonne, a Surrey-born army officer's daughter and convert to nationalism, flirted with Fenianism himself during this period.[8]

In 1880 Charles Stewart Parnell, a County Wicklow landlord and member of the Church of Ireland, was elected chairman of the Irish Parliamentary Party. It was never Parnell's intention to be prime minister in a restored Irish parliament primarily comprised of Catholic land

---

[5] Hutchinson, *The dynamics of cultural nationalism*, 15.
[6] Bourke, *John O'Leary*, 16, 196.
[7] Maud Gonne MacBride, *A servant of the Queen: reminiscences* (London, 1938), 89–90.
[8] R. F. Foster, *W. B. Yeats: a life, Vol. I: the apprentice mage* (Oxford, 1997), 44.

agitators, ex-Fenians and middling businessmen. Parnell saw land ownership as the issue that prevented the gentry taking what he saw as their
natural role as leaders of the home rule movement, and embarked
on a strategy of increasing the Protestant representation in his party.[9]
However, despite his attempts to lure suitable Protestants onto the Irish
benches, Parnell's leadership style alienated two important centres of
Protestant nationalist opinion, which instead gravitated towards the Irish
Protestant Home Rule Association (IPHRA).[10] The IPHRA was
founded in May/June 1886, with the purpose of undermining unionist
claims that Irish Protestants were unanimously opposed to home rule.
The organisation, which was chiefly active from 1886 to 1887 and again
briefly in 1893, held public meetings and published pamphlets in its
attempt to inculcate nationalist sentiment in Protestants, as well as
providing a pool of speakers for Irish Party rallies.

The IPHRA, although small, formed two distinct and sometimes
antagonistic wings, both of which were comprised of sections of Protestant nationalist opinion that were neglected or ignored by Parnell.[11] The
Belfast executive was dominated by mainly-Nonconformist representatives of Ulster tenant farmers, such as Thomas Shillington (d. 1925), a
Portadown-based Methodist and linen manufacturer who was president
of the organisation; T. A. Dickson, a Presbyterian who became Liberal
member for St Stephen's Green; and John Pinkerton, a Unitarian who
became Irish Party member for Galway. The Ulster IPHRA was characterised not by romantic attachment to a restored Irish parliament, but
rather by adoration of Gladstone and obsession with the land issue. For
the bulk of these men, home rule was merely another liberal reform,
designed to improve the government of Ireland.[12] The Dublin executive
was dominated by a talented circle of young, mostly Church of Ireland
activists from landed, clerical and professional backgrounds. Its most
important figures were the economist C. H. Oldham and the poet and
journalist T. W. Rolleston. Oldham, a close friend of John O'Leary, was
the co-founder of the *Dublin University Review*, which sought to emulate
the ethos of the *Dublin University Magazine* of fifty years before. Rolleston

[9] Bew, *C. S. Parnell*, 13–14, 28–29, 33, 40; Gwynn, *Experiences*, 56.
[10] See Oliver McCann, 'The Protestant home rule movement, 1886–1895', MA thesis, University College Dublin, 1972; James Loughlin, 'The Irish Protestant Home Rule Association and nationalist politics, 1886–93', *Irish Historical Studies*, Vol. 24, no. 95 (May 1985), 341–360.
[11] For evidence of north/south animus, chiefly due to the Ulstermen's desire to control the movement, see National Library of Ireland (NLI), MS 3657, minute book of Dublin branch of the Irish Protestant Home Rule Association (IPHRA), 3, 5, 7, 9, 11, 14 June 1886.
[12] Loughlin, 'The Irish Protestant Home Rule Association', 343–344.

was his partner in this venture. Another disciple of O'Leary, Rolleston was among the leading young literary figures of the decade. He, like Oldham, worshipped Thomas Davis (1814–1845), the writer and leading figure in Young Ireland.[13] The group's broad circle included Yeats, Maud Gonne, and the *litterateur* Stephen Gwynn (1864–1950), who was elected Irish Party member for Galway in 1906. They idolised John O'Leary, and adopted an advanced, sometimes republican rhetoric.[14] The pseudo-aristocratic nature of the group was underlined by members' lack of interest in the land question, and staunch defence of the role of landlords in Irish life.[15] The refusal of Oldham and Rolleston to take the Party pledge, which they saw as illiberal, precluded their standing for parliament. Parnell was recruiting Protestants, but his leadership style prevented some of his most promising co-religionists from joining his movement.[16] IPHRA members were prominent in the Contemporary Club, a Saturday-night discussion forum on literary and political topics that sought to encourage Protestant interest in nationalism. The Contemporary Club can be seen as part of wider culture of Young Ireland and literary societies that harked back to the 1840s in the hope of encouraging a national literature.[17] Technically non-political, the Contemporary included, besides the usual suspects of O'Leary, Oldham, Rolleston, and Yeats, several unionists, including Edward Dowden, professor of English literature in TCD.[18] Originally men-only, Maud Gonne was admitted; she would find that her charisma and social status allowed her access to places barred to others of her sex.[19]

Yeats would claim that the Irish literary revival, and indeed 'all that stir of thought which prepared for the Anglo-Irish War', began when Parnell fell from power in 1891, following the revelation of a long, adulterous love affair.[20] However, Roy Foster has shown that it was not in the 1890s,

---

[13] T. W. Rolleston (ed.), *Prose writings of Thomas Davis* (London, 1890).

[14] Foster, *W. B. Yeats: a life*, Vol. I, 39–41. John O'Leary even attended a meeting of the IPHRA Dublin executive, perhaps the sole Catholic to do so: NLI, MS 3657, minute book of Dublin branch of the IPHRA, 30 June 1886.

[15] *North and South*, 5, 26 March, 25 June 1887.   [16] Gwynn, *Experiences*, 57.

[17] See R. F. Foster, *Words alone: yeats and his inheritances* (Oxford, 2011), 129–131ff. For a fine study of the Yeats/Young Ireland relationship, see David Dwan, *The great community: culture and nationalism in Ireland* (Dublin, 2008), esp. 79–137.

[18] See Harry Nicholls, 'Memories of the Contemporary Club', parts I and II, *Irish Times* (*IT*), 20, 21 December 1965.

[19] Gonne MacBride, *A servant of the Queen*, 89.

[20] W. B. Yeats, 'The Irish dramatic movement: a lecture delivered to the Royal Academy of Sweden', in William H. O'Donnell and Douglas N. Archibald (eds.), *The collected works of W. B. Yeats, Vol. III: autobiographies* (New York, 1999), 410.

but in the heady atmosphere of the mid-1880s that the revival truly began,[21] when self-government seemed imminent, and young Protestant intellectuals sought to elbow themselves from the margins into the intellectual vanguard of the coming state. For F. S. L. Lyons, this group's attraction to cultural nationalism was 'a means of attaching themselves to their native country and at the same time holding at arm's length the English connection which the more perceptive of them already sensed to be both dangerous and unreliable'.[22] Progress was swift from this period, much of it led by Yeats. Still looking back to the 1840s, an important anthology, *Poems and ballads of Young Ireland*, was published in 1888, which included contributions by the young writers in O'Leary's circle, including Yeats, Rolleston, Katharine Tynan, George Sigerson, and Douglas Hyde.[23] For Yeats, much of this activity was designed to secure Protestant leadership of a revived national life. Ben Levitas argues that the poet believed 'Catholic demotic formlessness required the discipline of educated Protestant elites.'[24] In 1892 Yeats founded the Irish Literary Society in London along with Rolleston and Charles Gavin Duffy, and that same year he helped set up the National Literary Society in Dublin, with Douglas Hyde as president. The following year, as will be discussed further in this chapter, Hyde would co-found the Gaelic League, dedicated to the revival of the Irish language. Taken together, the literary revival, sparked by Yeats and his set, and the Gaelic revival, led by Hyde, would give catalyst to a new advanced nationalism, through which a substantial Protestant nationalist counterculture would emerge.

Around this time another important figure, George Russell (1867–1935), was coming to prominence. Russell, a journalist, writer, artist, cooperative administrator and political thinker, first met Yeats at the Metropolitan School of Art, and they forged a close, if occasionally strained, friendship. From an Ulster Methodist background, Russell left behind Lurgan, County Armagh, to throw himself into Dublin's artistic and literary avant-garde. Russell, who was generally known by the pseudonym 'Æ', published his first collection of poetry, *Homeward: songs by the way*, in 1894. *Homeward* displayed Æ's long-time absorption in the occult, an interest he shared with Yeats; Æ, as we will see, would do much to stimulate such ideas among his fellow Protestant nationalists.[25]

---

[21] Foster, *Words alone*, 143ff.

[22] F. S. L. Lyons, *Culture and anarchy in Ireland, 1890–1939* (Oxford, 1979), 28.

[23] [Various authors], *Poems and ballads of Young Ireland* (Dublin, 1888).

[24] Ben Levitas, 'A temper of misgiving: W. B. Yeats and the Ireland of Synge's time', in Senia Paseta (ed.), *Uncertain futures: essays about the Irish past for Roy Foster* (Oxford, 2016), 115.

[25] See Chapter 3.

That same year Yeats met Augusta, Lady Gregory (1852–1932), the owner of Coole Park, County Galway, who was destined to become his literary partner and greatest supporter. Recently widowed, and free to live her life largely as she chose, Gregory, a member of the Church of Ireland, was slowly developing nationalist views, and becoming fascinated by Gaelic culture. Seeking to put on plays with Irish themes, Gregory, Yeats and Edward Martyn, a Catholic landlord and patron of the arts, founded the Irish Literary Theatre in 1899. Three years later this was succeeded by the Irish National Theatre Society, which led to the foundation of the Abbey Theatre in 1904. In 1902 Yeats and Gregory's startlingly unsubtle *Cathleen ni Houlihan* was performed. Maud Gonne played the title role, as an elderly woman/allegory of Ireland, who convinces a young man to fight to restore her 'four green fields'. When he is convinced to do so, the old women is transformed into a young girl with 'the walk of a queen'.[26] The play, with its call for blood sacrifice, 'They shall be remembered for ever, / They shall be alive for ever, / They shall be speaking for ever, / The people shall hear them for ever', was in fact co-written by a man whose days of fiercest nationalism were behind him. During the first decade of the new century, Yeats's advanced nationalist sympathies (which had owed much to a desire to impress Maud Gonne) gave way to disenchantment with what he viewed as a new, narrow-minded, Catholic-dominated tendency.[27] But the nexus between those of Fenian sympathies and literary-minded men that Yeats helped forge after 1885 played a key role in creating a broad, multifaceted advanced nationalism, that would before long challenge the authority of home rulers to speak for Ireland. This movement, self-consciously harking back to the spirit of 1798 and 1848, and owing as much to literary culture as it did Fenianism, would prove seductive to numerous young Protestants.

The New Nationalism

The advanced nationalist threat to constitutional nationalism became evident in the run-up to the centenary of 1798. John O'Leary, hoping that the commemorations would bolster the separatist movement, took the initiative, chairing the Provisional Centenary Committee, which included Yeats, Maud Gonne, and a strong Fenian element. However, the home rule leadership, who often appropriated republican

---

[26] David R. Clark and Rosalind E. Clark (eds.), *Cathleen ni Houlihan,* in *The collected works of W. B. Yeats, Vol. II: the plays* (New York, 2001), 83–94.
[27] Foster, *W. B. Yeats: a life,* Vol. I, 179, 196, 265, 300, 367, 405ff.

anniversaries in an attempt to gain an air of radicalism otherwise lacking, outmanoeuvred O'Leary, and ended up dominating proceedings.[28] The secretary of the Centenary Committee was Frederick Allan (1861–1937), a Dublin-born Methodist, the business manager of the *Irish Daily Independent*, and, since 1894, the secretary of the supreme council of the IRB.[29] Allan's religion made him an unlikely leading figure in the IRB during this period. During the organisation's 1860s heyday, only one senior member, Thomas Clarke Luby, came from a Protestant background. However, although it never had anything resembling the religious composition of the United Irishmen or Young Ireland, the IRB always included a small number of Anglicans and Presbyterians in its ranks. The Fenian vision of a secular Irish republic, and its lack of concern with the agrarian issue, made it attractive to some liberal Protestants.[30] When Dublin Castle suppressed the Fenian *Irish People* in 1865, numerous Protestants, some from landed backgrounds, were found on its subscription list.[31] The strong anti-clerical element of the organisation (which had been denounced by the Vatican in 1870) was a factor that ensured that when the IRB began to revive in the early 1900s, a group of young Protestants would come to prominence, and do much to change the complexion of the group.[32] Allan's attempts to resuscitate Fenianism in the 1890s met with little success. Fenianism, and advanced nationalism in general, would require more stimulus than the 1798 centenary. This would come courtesy of the Boer War.

The Second Boer War was fought from 1899 to 1902, between the British Empire and the two independent Boer republics of the Transvaal and the Orange Free State. If the war, which led to the creation of the Union of South Africa, proved controversial in British society, it was doubly so in Ireland. Most Irish unionists supported the war, whereas the conflict proved deeply unpopular among Irish nationalists, the vast majority of whom sympathised with the Boers.[33] The Irish Parliamentary Party opposed the conflict in the Commons. Among advanced nationalists the war provoked outrage, with figures such as James Connolly and Arthur Griffith taking an explicitly pro-Boer position. John MacBride,

---

[28] See Senia Paseta, '1798 in 1898: the politics of commemoration', *The Irish Review*, No. 22 (Summer, 1998), 46–53.

[29] See Owen McGee, 'Fred Allan (1861–1937): Republican, Methodist and Dubliner', in *Dublin Historical Record*, Vol. 56, No. 2 (Autumn, 2003), 205–216.

[30] Tom Garvin, *The evolution of Irish nationalist politics* (Dublin, 1981), 60.

[31] *Gaelic American*, 28 July 1917. John Devoy, the *Gaelic American* editor, served as a Fenian in Ireland in the 1860s.

[32] See Chapter 2.

[33] See Donal P. McCracken, *The Irish Pro-Boers* (Johannesburg, 1989).

later to marry Maud Gonne, went even further: he raised an Irish brigade to fight on the Boer side in South Africa.

Conflict between the British Empire and the Boers gave impetus to the nationalist movement. Progress in women's education and a changing attitude to female involvement in public life ensured that for first time since the Ladies' Land League, small numbers of women became involved in nationalist public agitation. Maud Gonne became heavily involved in anti–Boer War protests.[34] In October 1899, Gonne, along with James Connolly, Arthur Griffith, W. B. Yeats, and John O'Leary, founded the Irish Transvaal Committee. The organisation, which received financial support from Gonne, encouraged Irish recruitment to MacBride's brigade.[35] In 1900 Gonne founded Inghinidhe na hÉireann, an explicitly separatist women's organisation, and an important precursor to greater female involvement in advanced nationalism. Gonne's pro-Boer activities were criticised by unionists who – not unreasonably – highlighted her tenuous links with Ireland, and her father's military service.[36] Nationalists could distrust her as well: Michael Davitt, for example, suspected she was a spy.[37] Gonne's anti-war activities led to the Castle keeping track of her movements.[38]

If the war offered Maud Gonne an opportunity for activism, for another significant figure, it prompted a move towards nationalism. At the outset, the Hon. Albinia Brodrick's sympathies were with Britain. Brodrick (1861–1955) was the English-born daughter of William Brodrick, 8th Viscount Midleton, the owner of an estate in County Cork. At the beginning of the war she worked at the War Office, where her brother, St John Brodrick, was from 1900 the secretary of state. Despite this initial support she came to have serious doubts about the morality of Britain's position, particularly following the deaths of friends of her family in the conflict. Leaving the War Office with a hatred for British imperialism, she would describe the years 1900–1903 as a 'period of mental and spiritual solitude'.[39] The fact that her brother was secretary

---

[34] See, for example, *United Irishman*, 7 October 1899.

[35] McCracken, *The Irish Pro-Boers*, 49; James McGuire and James Quinn (eds.), *Dictionary of Irish biography* (Cambridge, 2009) (print and online) (hereafter *DIB*), article on Maud Gonne MacBride.

[36] *Freeman's Journal* (*FJ*), 21 October 1899; Ramsay Colles, *In castle and court house: being reminiscences of thirty years in Ireland* (London, 1911), 51–56.

[37] Maud Gonne to W. B. Yeats, early March 1897, in Anna MacBride White and A. Norman Jeffares (eds.), *The Gonne–Yeats letters, 1893–1938: always your friend* (London, 1992), 65–66.

[38] NAI, Crime Branch Special Records, 20957/s. See also Gonne MacBride, *A servant of the Queen*, 99–103.

[39] Albinia Brodrick, *Verses of adversity* (London, 1904), preface.

of state for war appears to have made Brodrick associate her own family with British aggression – from 1903 she was to be entirely estranged from her family.[40] After this date Brodrick, formerly an English Conservative and unionist, became associated with radical social causes and radical politics, and looked to Ireland as her nation. In 1903 she trained as a nurse, becoming a prominent nursing leader, and in 1908 she purchased some land in Sneem, County Kerry, where she built a hospital which she named Ballincoona, founded a cooperative, adopted the name Gobnaít Ní Bhruadair, and developed steadily more radical nationalist views.[41] Brodrick may have changed her name and her politics, but she retained an extremely high-handed manner: her dismissal of staff who failed to attend Mass did not endear her to all the locals.

Those nationalist activists who were children at the time of the war inherited their views from their parents. Rosamond Jacob, aged eleven when the conflict began, and from a Quaker, pro–home rule background, condemned the 'degenerate Irishmen' who joined the British army.[42] She recorded her satisfaction with Boer successes, stating: 'The Boers are still continuing the war, and are not much worse off than they were a year ago, thank heaven. In Nov. Col. Lynch ... was elected MP for Galway, and the Jingoes are very much flabbergasted.'[43] By contrast, for Edie and Dorothy Stopford, being daughters of Irish unionists, British success in the Boer campaign was a cause of celebration:

We celebrated the relief of ... Mafeking by dancing and cheering round an evening bonfire ... scarcely noticing the booing of the local population which, pro-Boer to a man, had lined the low park wall some hundreds of yards away.[44]

Edie and Dorothy Stopford, the nieces of the nationalist historian Alice Stopford Green, would later develop entirely different political views.

Not everyone found their nationalism strengthened by the war. For T. W. Rolleston, it marked his departure from political nationalism and his endorsement of the Empire. Rolleston, as we have seen, was a leading figure in the literary and republican avant-garde in the 1880s and 1890s.

---

[40] *The Kerryman*, 26 December 1964, 2 January 1965.

[41] *British Journal of Nursing*, 23 January, 10 April 1909, 26 November 1910, 19 October 1912, 5 September 1914; *Sneem Parish News* (1998), 12–13; *Sneem Parish News* (2000), 24. See also Conor Morrissey, 'Albinia Brodrick: Munster's Anglo-Irish Republican', *Journal of the Cork Archaeological and Historical Society*, Vol. 116 (2011), 94–108.

[42] NLI, Rosamond Jacob papers, Rosamond Jacob diaries, MS 32,582, 25 March 1900.

[43] NLI, Rosamond Jacob diaries, MS 32,582, 31 December 1901. Arthur Lynch, who in 1900 raised an Irish brigade to fight alongside the Boers, was elected MP for Galway North in 1901, defeating unionist candidate Horace Plunkett, to the delight of Irish nationalists.

[44] NLI, MS 11,426, Typescript recollections of Miss [Edie] Stopford, undated.

He may have resembled Thomas Davis then, but by the late 1890s his support for separatism waned. Furthermore, although he would join, and became prominent in, the Gaelic League, he would grievously offend its members in 1896 when he cast doubt on possibility of restoring Irish. In 1900 Rolleston denounced the anti-war rhetoric of nationalists, and suggested that Irish people should support the conflict. Ireland, he believed, should take its place at the head of what he termed the 'Anglo-Celtic Empire'. This provoked a fierce response from the newspaper editor Arthur Griffith, who solemnly read him out of the nationalist movement. Griffith claimed that Rolleston was an opportunist, and never a nationalist by conviction, who supported home rule in the 1880s when it looked imminent, and the Empire now, when it was in the ascendant.[45] From then on he often referred to Rolleston as 'Mr Rollingstone'.[46] Griffith would write that if Rolleston 'had never called himself a Nationalist no one would have paid the least notice to his nonsense, but the converted rebel is ever dear to Englishmen, and their Irish counterparts'.[47] This belief would inform Griffith's later invective against other Protestant former-nationalist renegades.

Among the most influential Irish intellectuals of his age, Arthur Griffith (1871–1922) was an editor, journalist and political thinker. A Dublin-born Catholic, he edited several radical newspapers, including the *United Irishman* and *Sinn Féin*, and was the leading force behind the Sinn Féin party. As with John O'Leary, Griffith was fixated on converting Protestants to nationalism. More than any other Catholic separatist of his generation, Griffith strove – with little success – to fashion a nationalism that would appeal to Irish Protestants, especially those of Ulster. He hero-worshipped Protestant patriots Parnell, Mitchel and Davis, idolised the eighteenth-century parliament, and occasionally expressed a preference for Irish Protestant rule over that of England.[48] Family background seems to have had a role in formulating his views: Griffith came from Ulster Protestant stock: his grandfather appears to have converted to Catholicism. Desire to ensure Protestant support for independence was the primary motivation behind Griffith's dual-monarchy concept. Adopting an awkward parallel with recent central European history, he praised the Hungarians, whose representatives in 1867 withdrew from the imperial parliament and forced the Austrians to concede equal status

---

[45] T. W. Rolleston, *Ireland, the Empire, and the War* (Dublin, 1900), 7; *United Irishman*, 24 March, 12 May 1900.

[46] Brian Maye, *Arthur Griffith* (Dublin, 1997), 294.   [47] *United Irishman*, 9 June 1900.

[48] Richard Davis, 'Ulster Protestants and the Sinn Féin press, 1914–22', *Éire-Ireland*, Winter 1980, 61.

in the Austro-Hungarian dual monarchy. Although Griffith claimed to be a separatist, he proposed a compromise whereby Irish MPs would withdraw from Westminster, create a parliament in Dublin, and force Britain to grant Ireland similar status to Hungary. Ireland's demand should be the restoration of the 1782 constitution: an Irish 'King, Lords and Commons', independent of Britain, but connected through the Crown.[49] Far from retention of the monarchy proving seductive to Protestants and unionists, they generally ignored Griffith's scheme. Home rulers ridiculed the idea, and advanced nationalists saw it as no replacement for a republic. However, in formulating this concept in the hope of accommodating Protestants, Griffith showed an unusual imagination and ideological flexibility, as well as prescience about the danger unionism posed to the nationalist project.[50] The Sinn Féin organisation he founded in 1905 technically endorsed dual monarchy; however, few besides Griffith took this very seriously, and the group gained the adherence of numerous advanced nationalists, including sworn IRB men.

As with John O'Leary in the 1880s and 1890s, Griffith drew Protestant literary figures to his circle, such as the writers James Stephens and Herbert Moore Pim, as well as George Redding, a Guinness employee who wrote satirical verse.[51] A more important figure was the Rev. James Owen Hannay (1865–1950), the Belfast-born rector of Westport and author of numerous comic novels under the pseudonym George A. Birmingham. Neither a republican nor a physical-force man, he was the most prominent Protestant cleric to join the Gaelic League and associate with Sinn Féin.

On 26 January 1907 the Abbey Theatre first performed John Millington Synge's *The playboy of the western world*, an earthy and evocative tale of young man who claims to have killed his father. Throughout the next week, each performance was marked by rioting by young nationalists, outraged at what they viewed as a smear against peasants in the west, and an insult to Ireland itself. Significantly, many of the protesters called themselves Sinn Féiners, and Arthur Griffith, writing in *Sinn Féin*, led the charge against the play. It is difficult to avoid the sectarian connotations of the affair: a protest by young Catholic nationalists against the Abbey's Protestant directorate, and Synge, an Anglican

---

[49] See Arthur Griffith, *The resurrection of Hungary: a parallel for Ireland* (Dublin, 2003 [1904]). Griffith told P. S. O'Hegarty that although he was an ideological separatist he proposed a dual monarchy so as to ensure the greatest possible support for independence: P. S. O'Hegarty, *A history of Ireland under the union* (London, 1952), 652.

[50] See Richard Davis, *Arthur Griffith and non-violent Sinn Fein* (Dublin, 1974), ch. 8.

[51] Ulick O'Connor, *Oliver St. John Gogarty* (London, 1981 [1963]), 139.

landlord's son, its most promising playwright.[52] The *Playboy* riots were a significant cultural moment: Griffith may have been seeking Protestants for nationalist purposes, but only on his own terms, and he could be easily provoked by any perceived condescension by the landed class. And below Griffith was a new class of nationalist activists who could scarcely care if Protestants wished to join their movement.

Another editor who damned Yeats, Synge, the Abbey, and the *Playboy* was D. P. Moran (1869–1936). Moran's paper, *The Leader*, was an unashamedly Catholic-chauvinist counterpoint to Griffith's journals. Moran was a leading advocate of the growing Irish-Ireland movement, which sought the extirpation of English cultural influence and the restoration of a 'purer' Gaelic identity.[53] A gifted journalist with a talent for ridicule – a talent he shared with Griffith – Moran openly expressed distrust of Irish Protestants. He broke a nationalist taboo by openly drawing a connection between Catholicism and nationalism and Protestantism and unionism. Moran had contempt for Catholics who praised Protestant nationalists 'because they had the common decency to be nationalists', dismissing these 'tame Catholics' as 'tolerance provers'.[54] This sort of language horrified Griffith: he claimed the *Leader* appealed to 'the lowest, basest and meanest passion in man – religious bigotry'.[55]

If some wished to restore an ancient Gaelic nation, others seemed content merely to borrow from it. Demonstrating that everything Irish was becoming fashionable, even in the unlikeliest places, Dublin Castle on St Patrick's Day, 1907, featured a novel entertainment. One correspondent reported:

In former years Irish dances have been conspicuous by their absence. It was as if nothing Irish could flourish in the atmosphere of the grim old Castle. But [this year] the Castle on the Liffey saw a characteristic Irish event of the most picturesque kind. In the centre of St Patrick's Hall, Lady MacDonnell's set of eight formed a brilliant centrepiece, the ladies being dressed in green and gold, the Irish colours. Four other sets, organised by Countess Plunkett, Mrs Fournier, Countess Markievicz, and Mrs Moran, occupied the four corners of the square, and after filing past the throne they danced the Munster Figure Reel to Irish music. It was, without doubt, the most brilliant Irish dance ever performed.[56]

[52] See, for example, Robert Welch, *The Abbey Theatre, 1899–1999* (Oxford, 1999), 41.
[53] See for example, D. P. Moran, *The philosophy of Irish Ireland* (Dublin, 1905).
[54] Patrick Maume, *D. P. Moran* (Dundalk, 1995), 19.
[55] *United Irishman*, 12 January 1901.
[56] *Celtia: a Pan-Celtic monthly magazine*, March 1907.

Only nine years later Markievicz, one of the organisers of this event, would be fighting with the rebels on St Stephen's Green.

The Irish Language

In the modern period, Protestant interest in the Irish language dates to the founding of the Royal Irish Academy in 1785. The academy, among other things, undertook to preserve early Irish manuscripts, making possible the work of future scholars. A sense that preaching in Irish could help woo the western masses informed several initiatives. In 1818 the Irish Society was founded in Dublin, devoted to the expansion of popular education through schools and publishing ventures. It was generally viewed as a Protestant missionary undertaking.[57] In 1838 a professorship of Irish was founded within the divinity school in Trinity College; its main function was to prepare Anglican ministers to convert Irish-speakers. Throughout the nineteenth century, a significant number of Protestants, often teachers or clergymen, helped to sustain interest in the language. Their motives varied, from antiquarianism, to proselytism, to, in the case of figures such as James McKnight, a County Down–born agrarian reformer, a hope that a shared culture could reconcile Irish factions.[58] Another learned body, the Ossianic Society, founded in 1853, again had a largely Protestant membership. However, later in the century a new group of Protestants, such as the Rev. Maxwell Close, the Rev. Euseby Cleaver, and Thomas O'Neill Russell, repudiated pros-elytism and became interested in the restoration of Irish as a living language.[59]

In 1892, Douglas Hyde, in his inaugural address as president of the National Literary Society, gave an address entitled 'The necessity for de-anglicising Ireland'.[60] He called for the restoration of Irish as a spoken language and a concomitant decline in English, and English cultural influence. This lecture would inspire the formation of the Gaelic League

---

[57] Its full name was the Irish Society for Promoting the Education of the Native Irish through the Medium of Their Own Language.

[58] See Roger Blaney, *Presbyterians and the Irish language* (Belfast, 1996); Pádraig Ó Snodaigh, *Hidden Ulster: Protestants and the Irish language* (Belfast, 1995).

[59] See Seán Ó Tuama (ed.), *The Gaelic League idea* (Cork, 1972), 9–19. See also Breandáin Ó Conaire, 'Na Protastúnaigh, an Ghaeilge agus Dubhghlas de híde', *Seanchas Ardmhaca: Journal of the Armagh Diocesan Historical Society*, Vol. 15, No. 2 (1993), 130–150.

[60] 'Douglas Hyde on the necessity for de-anglicising Ireland', reprinted in Edmund Curtis and R. B. McDowell (eds.), *Irish historical documents, 1172–1922* (New York, 1968), 310–313.

the following year; Hyde, an Anglican clergyman's son from a landed background, became its first president. Among the leading figures in the new organisation was Eoin MacNeill, a Catholic and Gaelic scholar. The Gaelic League would have little in common with earlier antiquarian or proselytising groups; a mass movement based on endless classes, lectures, feiseanna and céilithe, it attracted the newly educated Catholic lower middle and middle classes eager for intellectual, social, and patriotic stimulation. From its inception, Hyde insisted that, so as to avoid the controversies that had bedevilled earlier initiatives, the organisation must be non-political and non-sectarian.[61] Believing restoration of the language to be pre-eminent he sought to build as wide a movement as possible, attracting unionists and Protestants while avoiding giving offence to the Catholic hierarchy. The desire to avoid entangling the Gaelic League in controversy became something of an obsession of Hyde's and eventually led to his resignation from the organisation's presidency. However, it is incorrect to state that Hyde was a mild unionist, as later detractors would allege.[62] As a young man he was a fiery pro-Fenian, and mixed in strongly advanced nationalist circles. These instincts remained with him, but they have been obscured by his desire to subordinate politics to the language issue.[63]

The long-existing tradition of Protestant interest in the language, alongside general curiosity, ensured strong Protestant involvement in the Gaelic League in its early years.[64] Oliver MacDonagh has also stressed what he terms 'Protestant identity crisis', which led them to dominate the League until the 1900s, when the largely Catholic nature of the movement became apparent.[65] For example, the predominantly Protestant Belfast Naturalists' Field Club had offered Irish, or 'Celtic' lessons a year before the Gaelic League was founded, and in 1895 this group voted to become the Belfast branch of the League.[66] The president

---

[61] 'No matter of religious or political difference of opinion shall be permitted into the proceedings of this Society'; 'Rules of the Gaelic League', in *Report of the Gaelic League for the year ended 30th September 1894* (Dublin, 1895), 9.

[62] Ó Tuama, *The Gaelic League idea*, 31–32.

[63] D. P. Daly, *The young Douglas Hyde: the dawn of the Irish revolution and renaissance* (Dublin, 1974), xi, xii, xvii, xviii, 21, 46, 53, 202 n.; Diarmid Coffey, *Douglas Hyde: President of Ireland* (Dublin, 1938), 48–49.

[64] Arthur E. Clery, 'The Gaelic League, 1893–1919', *Studies*, Vol. 8, No. 31 (September 1919), 401.

[65] Oliver MacDonagh, *States of mind: a study of Anglo-Irish conflict, 1780–1980* (London, 1985), 104–125.

[66] *Annual Report and Proceedings of the Belfast Naturalists' Field Club for the year ending 31 March 1895*, Series II, Part II, Volume IV, 1894–1895; *Annual Report and Proceedings of the Belfast Naturalists' Field Club for the year ending 31 March 1896*, Series II, Part III, Volume IV, 1895–1896; *Ulster Guardian (UG)*, 31 August 1907.

of the branch was the unionist and Presbyterian John St Clair Boyd, a popular figure who was a prominent surgeon and philanthropist in the city.[67]

The Boer War provided both impetus and strain, as members reacted to a more politicised atmosphere. Hyde later remembered that the conflict brought a large number of unionists and Protestants into the movement: 'a great many unionists, mostly ladies, were attracted into the [language] movement ... A year or two of this study usually ate away their unionist tendencies like an acid, and left them convinced Nationalists'.[68] Throughout the nineteenth century Magyar, Czech, Serb and Croat cultural revivalist movements had the effect of converting the linguistically curious into the politically committed. Ireland was no exception to this pattern.[69] The changing political complexion of the League caused an exodus of politically unconverted or unconvertible Protestants.[70]

Central to the Gaelic League's mission was a belief that the English language was an imposition, whose influence could be eradicated through education and activism. This view was publicly undermined by one of its leading figures, T. W. Rolleston. At a speech in 1896 Rolleston apportioned much of the blame for the decline of Irish not on British rule, but on the decision of native speakers to stop speaking the language. He compounded the heresy by casting doubt on the possibility of restoring Irish as the country's lingua franca.[71] This was characteristic: an iconoclastic figure, Rolleston, although a believer in the League, was unafraid to criticise its strongest-held beliefs. His speech was denounced by Gaelic Leaguers, including Alice Milligan and Gaelic Athletic Association (GAA) founder Michael Cusack.[72]

After a slow start, Gaelic League growth was steady: it had forty-three branches by 1897, and by 1904 (after the Boer War) it had almost six hundred branches and 50,000 members. As the League expanded, the proportion of Protestants dropped significantly: one contemporary observer estimated in 1907 that 5 per cent of members were Protestant.[73] The Gaelic League leadership's strategy for checking this decline seems to have been borrowed from that of the Irish Parliamentary Party, which

---

[67] *Belfast News-Letter*, 11 July 1918.   [68] *Gaelic Churchman*, February 1925.

[69] Nicholas Mansergh, *The Irish question, 1840–1921* (London, 1965), 246.

[70] Clery, 'The Gaelic League, 1893–1919', 401.

[71] *Irish Daily Independent*, 21 January 1896.

[72] *Irish Daily Independent*, 25, 27, 30 January 1896.

[73] Patrick Dinneen, 'The Gaelic League and non-sectarianism', *Irish Rosary*, Vol. 11, No. 1 (January 1907), 9. Less credibly, Anglican Gaelic Leaguer Margaret E. Dobbs put the figure at 10 per cent: *Church of Ireland Gazette* (*CIG*), 29 November 1907.

had a tendency to select Protestants to fill by-election vacancies: they placed prominent Protestants into high-profile positions, thus avoiding the appearance of religious homogeneity.[74] Attempts by Catholics to reach out in organised fashion to Protestants in rural Ireland met with little success. One activist claimed that on approaching a well-known Protestant 'gentleman' for a Gaelic League subscription, he was told he 'had considered that matter, long ago, all rot; better teach them [Catholics] knitting and sewing, and how to clean their dirty houses'.[75]

Despite claims of political neutrality, the tendency for Gaelic League membership to transform Protestant unionists into Protestant national-ists made it anathema to the pro-Union press. Elements of the Gaelic League programme were detested by unionists, particularly attempts to make Irish a compulsory subject in education, and make knowledge of the language a prerequisite for public appointments.[76] The *Church of Ireland Gazette* was a particularly stern critic. 'It is idle to say that the League offers a common platform to all Irishmen, so long as its practice includes so much which the great body of Irish Unionists are unable to accept as either useful or reasonable.'[77] The League's attempts to encourage temperance and native industry were scarcely expiating factors: 'The very fact that most of us think that the Gaelic League is doing a good deal of mischief should make us glad to admit that other energies which it has called into being are doing something to counteract this mischief.'[78] One prominent – and damaging – critic of the League was the Rev. J. E. H. Murphy, professor of Irish at TCD. Throughout late 1907 and early 1908, in a bad-tempered public correspondence, Murphy accused Douglas Hyde of leading a disloyal organisation, while Hyde struck back, claiming the former had failed to encourage the language.[79] Hyde stated that:

we [the Gaelic League] have treated Mr Murphy with the greatest courtesy … we invited him to our gatherings, asked him to take part in our examinations, and made him free of our platforms … but in turn he has only called us names, relying on his title in Trinity College to make them go down with the public.[80]

According to Hyde, Murphy's criticisms would mean more had they not 'come from … the occupant of a chair which, though in existence for over

---

[74] *Gaelic Churchman*, February 1921.   [75] *Peasant*, 25 May 1907.
[76] For education, see P. J. Mathews, *Revival: The Abbey Theatre, Sinn Féin, the Gaelic League and the Co-operative movement* (Cork, 2003), 25–27; for public appointments, see *CIG*, 19 January 1906.
[77] *CIG*, 10 August 1906.   [78] *CIG*, 20 April 1906.
[79] See *CIG*, 18 October, 1, 15, 29 November, 6 December 1907, 3 April 1908.
[80] *CIG*, 3 April 1908.

seventy years, has never produced, published, or edited, one single line of Irish literature'.[81]

Such controversies unsettled Protestant Gaelic Leaguers. Rolleston wrote an article in the *Gazette* encouraging Anglicans to join and criticising the attitude of the Church of Ireland to Irish reform movements generally:

> its general attitude towards things distinctly Irish has, for some three centuries, been one of aversion and distain, mingled perhaps in more recent times with something of alarm as well ... It has remained the Church of an alien minority; it has cut itself off from all development and all national influence, it lives, one might say, on an island within an island.[82]

Rolleston's article provoked controversy in the *Gazette*. One Anglican layman wrote:

> Should Protestants join the Gaelic League? Should house-holders join an association of hard-working burglars? ... We do not think loyal Irishmen should join such a league, most of the members of which are disloyal. Men do not comfort and sustain their avowed enemies.[83]

Frequently, the most trenchant critics of the League were those who had personal experience of it. For example, one Orangeman and unionist recalled having attended Irish classes, but realising the political tenor of the group, 'returned from it a sadder and wiser man'.[84] Besides a belief that the Gaelic League was subversive, another reason for Protestant reluctance to join has been overlooked. A large number of League activities, including feiseanna, committee meetings, and its annual Language Procession in Dublin, were held on Sundays. Violation of the fourth commandment contravened Protestant doctrine and was frequently cited against the League.[85] Refusal to break the Sabbath was also a factor that prevented many Protestants from joining the GAA.

The increasingly Catholic nature of the body also prevented some Protestants from participating in the League. Some Catholic clergy were initially hostile, but within a few years they had overcome their suspicions and became instrumental in creating a network of branches throughout the country.[86] Several Gaelic League priests were tactless – or perhaps openly exclusionary – in public. Fr Patrick Dinneen, the

---

[81] *CIG*, 15 November 1907.   [82] *CIG*, 17 November 1905.
[83] *CIG*, 8 December 1905. For critical replies, see *CIG*, 15, 22 December 1905.
[84] *The Republic*, 24 January 1907.
[85] See, for example, *CIG*, 5 January 1906, 29 November, 6 December 1907, 10 January 1908; Coffey, *Douglas Hyde*, 52–53.
[86] Timothy G. McMahon, '"All creeds and all classes"? Just who made up the Gaelic League?', *Éire-Ireland*, Vol. 37, Nos. 3–4 (Fall/Winter 2002), 125; Mathews, *Revival*, 24.

lexicographer, expressed scepticism of the desirability of Catholic/ Protestant co-operation in the movement.[87] Earlier in the decade a pamphlet by Fr Patrick Forde claimed that Catholicism was synonymous with the Irish language and Protestantism with the English.[88] This pamphlet outraged Rolleston.[89] He wrote to Hyde stating that unless action was taken against the 'sectarian and intolerant' party, he would lead a group of Protestant and liberal Catholics out of the League. Rolleston threatened to form a new body under the leadership of Lord Castletown of Upper Ossory, in alliance with his Celtic Association, a Pan-Celtic movement. There was already tension in the League between those who wished to build links with Pan-Celticists in Britain and those who wished to remain an Ireland-only association. Any Pan-Celtic–associated Gaelic association would have a mainland British and therefore pro-Union bias.[90] Rolleston wrote:

I am going to thrash the matter out with Lord C. and others, but at the same time I think it is a great pity that it should be so. There are only a million Protestants in Ireland, they cannot be driven out nor can they, like Catholics in England, be regarded as a more or less negligible quantity.[91]

Although Rolleston's plan did not transpire, in late 1904 a group of Dublin-based Protestant Gaelic Leaguers set up a Protestant-friendly branch, called Craobh na gCúig gCúigí (the Branch of the Five Provinces).[92] The driving force behind it was the artist Nelly O'Brien (1864–1925). O'Brien and the Rev. James Owen Hannay were vice-presidents of the branch, and Rolleston served as president. Wags labelled the group 'the branch of the five Protestants' because of its religious composition and supposedly puny membership.[93] A claim of a dearth of members seems unfair: within a few months it reported 128 members, and appears to have enjoyed growth afterwards.[94] A total of 64 members have been traced, of whom 39 were women.[95] Protestants

---

[87] Dinneen, 'The Gaelic League and non-sectarianism', 11.
[88] Patrick Forde, *The Irish language movement: its philosophy*, Gaelic League pamphlet No. 21 (London, n.d. [1901]), 27–28.
[89] See *All Ireland Review*, Vol. 2, No. 27 (20 July 1901), 206.
[90] Peter Berresford Ellis, *The Celtic dawn: a history of Pan Celticism* (London, 1993), 73–77.
[91] T. W. Rolleston to Douglas Hyde, quoted in Maria O'Brien, 'Thomas William Rolleston: the forgotten man', in Betsey Taylor FitzSimon and James H. Murphy (eds.), *The Irish Revival reappraised* (Dublin, 2003), 161.
[92] *IT*, 17 December 1904.
[93] See, for example, Earnán de Blaghd [Ernest Blythe], *Trasna na Bóinne* (Dublin, 1957), 128.
[94] *FJ*, 23 June 1905.
[95] Nominal data is derived from: *FJ*, 7 December 1904, 23 June, 7 November 1905, 3 January, 27 February 1906, 28 May 1907, 10 October, 22 November 1910; *II*,

dominated the branch: of the 45 members whose denomination has been traced, 34 belonged to a reformed church, and nine were Catholic. There were 29 Episcopalians, two Quakers, one Methodist, and two Protestants whose affiliation cannot be traced. There was also one Jew.[96]

O'Brien remembered that 'the primary object of [the branch] was to get Protestants and professed Unionists to join in the national move-ment'.[97] Although it had a Protestant majority, several Catholics, such as Colm O Murchadha, who gave classes there, and later served as clerk of the Dáil, and Kenneth Reddin, later a writer and district justice, were prominent. But it was, in the main, a Protestant society: Reddin later recalled of himself and O Murchadha that, 'we, being Catholics, were kind of interlopers'.[98] O'Brien was able to tap an embryonic network of upper-middle-class Protestants curious about the Revival but requiring the enticement of a Protestant-majority environment to engage with it. The branch counted among its members Dora French, Lily Duncan, Nora Cunningham, George Ruth, James Stephens, George Nicholls, George Irvine, Ernest Joynt, Ernest Blythe, Nelly O'Brien's cousin Conor O'Brien, W. B. Yeats's sister Elizabeth Yeats, Jack Morrow, Ada McNeill, and Lily Williams. This was an artistic set: there were so many artists in the branch (at least twelve of whom were professional) that for several years an annual exhibition of members' art was held.[99] The radicalising impact that learning Irish and engaging with cultural nationalism could have on Protestants is borne out by analysis of the Branch's members. Of those Protestant members who have not been identified as engaging in political nationalist activism before c. 1905, a total of twenty did so afterwards.

In early 1906 the Rev. James Hannay used a speech to the Branch to make a spirited defence of the League as non-political and non-sectarian.[100] Any positive effect of this was marred when he became

---

8 December 1905, 11 June 1906, 28 October 1908, 14 October 1912; *IT*, 14 May 1906, 5, 11 October 1913, 29 January 1940; *Irish Press*, 28 January 1941; Michael Hurley (ed.), *Irish Anglicanism, 1869–1969: essays on the role of Anglicanism in Irish life, presented to the Church of Ireland on the occasion of the centenary of its disestablishment, by a group of Methodist, Presbyterian, Quaker, and Roman Catholic scholars* (Dublin, 1970), 117; Leon Ó Broin, *Protestant nationalists in revolutionary Ireland: the Stopford connection* (Dublin, 1985), 38.

[96] The artist Estella Frances Solomons (1882–1968), who joined Cumann na mBan c. 1918.

[97] *Gaelic Churchman*, February 1921.   [98] *IT*, 29 January 1940.

[99] *IT*, 11 October 1913, 5, 17 October 1914. See also Hilary Pyle (ed.), *Cesca's diary, 1913–1916: where art and nationalism meet* (Dublin, 2005), 154–155.

[100] James Owen Hannay, *Is the Gaelic League political?: lecture delivered under the auspices of the Branch of the Five Provinces on January 23rd, 1906* (n.p., n.d.), esp. 6–10, 12, 19–20, 24.

embroiled in a holy row in Connaught. Hannay's hugely popular comic novels contained many uncomplimentary depictions of Catholic clergy. When Hannay was revealed as the author of these works, the parish priest of Westport, believing an unscrupulous character in *The seething pot* to be based on himself, organised a boycott of his Protestant opposite number. Despite Hannay's position in the League (he was a member of the Coisde Gnótha, the Gaelic League executive) he was excluded from the Connaught Feis. Although he found much support within the League, including from some Catholic clergy, Hannay resigned from the executive.[101] Hannay claimed to remain a supporter of the League, but in reality he was deeply hurt by the episode. While he did not name Hyde explicitly, Hannay had him in mind when wrote that he was perturbed to find the League's leaders 'becoming cowardly and trucking to priests and politicians'.[102] A gleeful *Gazette* found in the controversy vindication of its warnings. It stated it had no wish 'to make "capital" out of the Rev. J. O. Hannay's experience' before doing precisely that. 'The majority of Irish Churchmen will find in the incident strong confirmation of their fears concerning the Gaelic League.'[103]

A tendency for language activism to lead to republican militancy emerges during this period. In 1905 George Irvine (1877–1954) joined the Gaelic League. Irvine, a Fermanagh-born schoolteacher and Anglican, was destined to become one of the leading Protestant nationalists of his generation. Irvine may have followed the example of his older brother William John Irvine, a schoolteacher and Trinity College graduate, who was a member of the Drumcondra branch of the Gaelic League from at least 1902.[104] George Irvine also became an active member of the Drumcondra branch and formed an important friendship with his fellow Anglican, James Deakin (1874–1952), a chemist by trade. Another significant friendship was with Ernest Blythe. On coming to Dublin as a teenage civil service clerk in 1905, Blythe, a County Antrim–born member of the Church of Ireland, wanted to learn Irish but 'was afraid to join the Gaelic League because I believed that if it were discovered that I were a Protestant I should be put out'.[105] When he finally found the courage to join the Central Branch of the Gaelic League, Blythe was pleased to find Irvine, a fellow Protestant, in his class. Irvine converted

[101] See R. B. D. Trench, 'J. O. Hannay and the Gaelic League', *Hermathena* 102 (Spring, 1966), 26–52; Brian Taylor, *The life and writings of James Owen Hannay (George A. Birmingham), 1865–1950* (New York, 1995), 59–67.
[102] Hurley, *Irish Anglicanism, 1869–1969*, 115.   [103] *CIG*, 5 October 1906.
[104] *An Claidheamh Soluis*, 11 January 1902.
[105] National Archives of Ireland, Dublin (NAI), Bureau of Military History Witness Statements (BMH WS) 939, Ernest Blythe (accessible online).

Blythe to Sinn Féin after suggesting he read Griffith's *United Irishman* and *The resurrection of Hungary*.[106] Irvine would become a senior member of Sinn Féin, joining the party's executive in 1910.[107] Another figure Blythe met in the Gaelic League was Sean O'Casey, the future dramatist, who persuaded him to join the IRB. Irvine followed the common line of progression from the Gaelic League classroom to the IRB. Having initially rebuffed a Catholic associate's suggestion to join, in about 1907 he was successfully recruited by Deakin. Irvine first joined the Teeling Circle of the IRB, and in 1911 he was elected Centre of the Mangan Circle. In 1912 he was elected secretary of Dublin Centres' Board, the coordinating body for the IRB in Dublin.[108]

In 1907 an explicitly Protestant Gaelic League organisation was formed. This was the initiative of these four Dublin-based IRB men, Sean O'Casey, Ernest Blythe, Seamus Deakin, and George Irvine. These men provide a good example of a Protestant nationalist network: all four initially joined the Gaelic League; Irvine recruited Blythe to Sinn Féin; O'Casey recruited Blythe and (most likely) Deakin to the IRB; and Deakin convinced Irvine to join that organisation as well. O'Casey had been concerned for quite a while to bring more of his co-religionists into the League. The purpose of this initiative was simple: they would entice their co-religionists into the Gaelic League, and thereafter seek to convert them to republicanism. Using cultural revivalism to effect political conversion within a socially cordial environment parallels Bulmer Hobson's efforts in the same period.[109]

In early May 1907 a meeting of Protestant Gaelic Leaguers was held in Dublin 'to consider the means of bringing the principles of the Gaelic League prominently under the notice of Protestants, and inducing them to take their place prominently in the Gaelic movement'.[110] The meeting decided to send a delegation to the Dean of St Patrick's to allow a monthly Irish-language service in the cathedral, as well as to communicate with Protestant schools in Dublin about the status afforded Irish language and history. This led to the creation of the Committee of

---

[106] De Blaghd, *Trasna na Bóinne*, 94.
[107] National Museum of Ireland, EW 1290, Sinn Féin executive minutes, 3 November 1910.
[108] Military Archives, Dublin (MAD), Military Service Pensions Collection (MSPC), 34REF61665, George Irvine, Statement on IRB service (accessible online); BMH WS 265, George Irvine.
[109] See Chapter 2.
[110] *The Leader*, 11 May 1907. See also *UG*, 18 May 1907; *An Claidheamh Soluis*, 18 May 1907; *Peasant*, 11 May 1907.

Protestant Gaelic Leaguers. Deakin was chairman, and Irvine secretary. The Gaelic League gave the new body assistance.[111]

The foundation of this committee involved Rolleston in more controversy. Speaking at the opening of the Midleton Feis in May 1907, a Catholic priest, Archdeacon Hutch, welcomed the recent increase in Protestant involvement with the League. However, he warned against the creation of what he termed a specifically 'Protestant Branch of the Gaelic League'. He criticised attempts to 'ring-fence' Protestants from the rest of the organisation. In short, the archdeacon called for them to act as 'honest Protestants'.[112] Rolleston responded to Hutch's comments by stating that the Craobh na gCúig gCúigí, which the priest was alluding to, was not a Protestant-only branch, and that he would refuse to serve as an officer of any such body. He stated that Hutch had mistaken the Branch for the Committee of Protestant Gaelic Leaguers, which was not a branch of the League per se, but a committee made up of members of many different branches engaged in encouraging Protestant participation in the League, rather than ring-fencing them from it. The Craobh had simply allowed the Committee use of their rooms. Less credibly, he maintained the Craobh na gCúig gCúigí was largely Catholic in membership.[113]

The Committee sought, with mixed success, to use Young Men's Christian Association and parochial halls to hold meetings to attract laity. After one rector agreed, his parishioners were alleged to have sarcastically enquired, 'would the same facilities be given to Mr Ginnell to give a lecture on cattle-driving when he came out of gaol'?[114] They also held musical concerts; it was claimed that one, on Dublin's northside, was broken up by a group of Orangemen. The group was scarcely a success, at least in this early incarnation. With myriad other interests to attend to, O'Casey and Blythe appear to have left the organisation after a short period. The few Presbyterian and Methodist Gaelic Leaguers also drifted away. The remaining body, which was almost entirely Anglican in membership, became the Gaelic Services Committee, which sought to introduce Irish-language services to the Church of Ireland.

Although Irish-language services in Irish-speaking regions for the purpose of proselytism were a recent memory, there was much hostility towards Irish-language services in the Church of Ireland. On St Patrick's

---

[111] *UG*, 18 May 1907; *Gaelic Churchman*, November 1920.   [112] *FJ*, 27 May 1907.
[113] *FJ*, 28 May 1907. See also *An Claidheamh Soluis*, 1 June 1907; *Peasant*, 18 May 1907.
[114] *Gaelic Churchman*, December 1920. Laurence Ginnell (1852–1923), home rule politician and land agitator, led a cattle-driving campaign against farmers and graziers from 1903.

Day, 1904, the Rev. J. E. H. Murphy (three years before his spat with Hyde) preached a service in Irish in St Kevin's Church, South Circular Road, Dublin. It was originally intended that the service would be held in St Patrick's Cathedral, but the dean, John Henry Bernard, proved so uncooperative that an alternative venue was found. But it was a historic moment, and those present knew it. 'Many of [the congregation] were scanning their old Irish prayer-books, venerable yellow volumes that had not seen the light for perhaps a generation.'[115]

Eventually, on St Patrick's Day, 1906, Hannay preached a Holy Communion service in Irish in the cathedral, perhaps the first since the reign of Elizabeth. Dean Bernard wrote that he had to take precautions against the disruption of the service, as he had 'been accused of condoning a profanation of the Blessed Sacrament'.[116] The *Gazette*, although making no charge of blasphemy, was nevertheless displeased. Commenting favourably on Bernard's insistence that only those capable of understanding the service should attend, they stated, '[W]e are anxious that no love of novelty and no following of a fashionable whim, should induce our clergy to have services which the majority of the people cannot, as yet, understand'.[117]

Eager for something more substantial, the Gaelic Services Committee organised a petition asking Bernard to allow 'the tongue in which St Patrick taught [to] be heard in the cathedral called by his name'. They sought a monthly service in the language. Forty Irish speakers signed one petition pledging to attend the service, and 428 Anglicans, including the bishop of Limerick and several prominent clergy from across the country, who sympathised with the request, signed another.[118] The Dean refused permission, stating in a letter to George Irvine that there were not enough Anglican Irish-speakers in Dublin to justify it, and more significantly, 'it would be highly unbecoming to use St Patricks Cathedral for any purposes, however legitimate, other than for religious edification'.[119]

There the matter rested for six years. In April 1914 a group of Anglican Irish-language activists, many of whom had been associated with the now-moribund Gaelic Services Committee or the (still active) Craobh na gCúig gCúigí, held the first public meeting of the Irish Guild of the

---

[115] *Celtia: a Pan-Celtic monthly magazine*, March 1904.
[116] Taylor, *The life and writings of James Owen Hannay*, 58.   [117] *CIG*, 23 March 1906.
[118] *CIG*, 5 June 1908. Nelly O'Brien, who was attached to the committee, stated that the numbers did not represent all who supported the petition, due to its being advertised only through the Gaelic League, and in great haste; *CIG*, 12 June 1908. Among those who refused was an unidentified bishop who stated that the proposal 'bordered on blasphemy'; *Gaelic Churchman*, November 1920.
[119] *CIG*, 5 June 1908.

Church (Cumann Gaelach na hEaglaise).[120] Of the original IRB quartet of Blythe, O'Casey, Irvine, and Deakin, only one – Irvine – remained. The instigator of the new body was George Ruth, a civil service clerk. The Gaelic Services Committee had enjoyed little success, but the Irish Guild of the Church would prove more resilient and would demonstrate the radicalising affect cultural nationalism could have on Protestants.

The Guild sought to promote the use of Irish within the Church of Ireland, to collect from Irish sources suitable hymns and devotional literature, and to encourage use of Irish art and music in the Church.[121] The Gaelic Services Committee had faced great hostility from the Anglican establishment. Now a different mood prevailed. The Guild's senior officers included as its president Benjamin Plunket, bishop of Tuam, and as vice-presidents Bishop Orpen of Limerick, Bishop Dowse of Cork, Lord Chief Justice Richard Robert Cherry, and, in a departure from the frostiness towards the Irish language that characterized Bernard's tenure, his replacement as Dean of St Patrick's, Charles Ovenden.[122] Roger Casement welcomed the establishment of the Guild. Casement's letter to the group's secretary offers some insight into his complex relationship with the Church of Ireland:

I was brought up in the Church of Ireland, but its aloofness … from things that should be dear to all Irishmen repelled me even as a boy. What seemed to me worthy of study, examination, and often of love, I was told to regard as 'foolishness'. Where, as an Irishman I asked for bread I was offered a stone. The Church of Ireland has many things to learn, and much to unlearn – or confess – before it can claim that its attitude, as a body of Christians, is in conformity with its title.[123]

Plunket of Tuam conceded that Irish-language revivalists were still viewed with suspicion by their co-religionists. Denying that the Guild was political, he admitted there was a belief that they were

revolutionists, and that they were out against all the law and order of the Church of Ireland. They were revolutionists only in so far as they endeavoured to bring this dear old country into closer touch with its most priceless possession – the Church of Ireland.[124]

---

[120] In St Ann's Parish Room, Diocesan School, Molesworth St., Dublin: *IT*, 29 April 1914.
[121] Representitive Church Body Library, Dublin (RCBL), Irish Guild of the Church minute book, 1914–1922, 22 January 1914.
[122] RCBL, Irish Guild of the Church minute book, 29 April 1914.
[123] NLI, MS 13,664, Roger Casement to George Ruth, 25 April 1914. See also MS 13,664, F. J. Bigger to George Ruth, 27 April 1914.
[124] *IT*, 14 April 1915.

The establishment credentials of the group's senior officers ensured its respectability; within a year it reported almost 100 members, almost all from Dublin. Among the best known were Douglas Hyde, F. J. Bigger, and three TCD academics: J. E. H. Murphy, Wilbraham Fitzjohn Trench, and Edward Culverwell. The Guild enjoyed an early success when the Dean of St Patrick's granted permission for a monthly service in Irish to be held in the cathedral's Lady Chapel.[125] In mid-1915 Nelly O'Brien became a member.[126] She had initially stayed aloof from the organisation, fearing, as with several other Protestant Gaelic Leaguers, that it would introduce a sectarian element into the revival.[127] O'Brien would become the most prominent member of the Guild. The creation of the Irish Guild of the Church coincided with the final eclipse of Douglas Hyde, and his non-political vision, within the Gaelic League. At the League's ard fheis in August 1915 the group appended to its objectives the freeing of Ireland from 'foreign rule', which prompted Hyde to resign the presidency. Eoin MacNeill would later admit that the adoption of a political stance had greatly damaged the League.[128] From this point onwards, the Irish Guild of the Church would become the principal Protestant cultural revival vehicle.

These, and most of the developments in this chapter, relate to events that occurred in Dublin and the south of Ireland. In Ulster, Protestant nationalist counterculture enjoyed a largely separate development, and would have a significant impact on the development of nationalism generally. Chapter 2 will assess this tradition.

---

[125] RCBL, Irish Guild of the Church minute book, 17 June 1914; *IT*, 13 October 1914.
[126] RCBL, Irish Guild of the Church minute book, 1 July 1915.
[127] *Gaelic Churchman*, May/June 1925.
[128] Janet Egleson Dunleavy and Gareth W. Dunleavy, *Douglas Hyde: a maker of modern Ireland* (Berkeley, 1991), 327–328; *DIB* article on Douglas Hyde.

2   Dissidents, 1900–1910

Introduction

Ulster's past casts a shadow on all those who live in the province. A history of defiance, conquest, plantation, rebellion, conversion, and of loyalty and disloyalty has provided both religious communities with a rich store of historical memory with which to justify their own position, and disparage that of their rival. For Ulster unionists, the narrative was straightforward: a formerly recalcitrant, backward province was colonised by brave Protestant planters, who brought order and prosperity. Treacherous, dispossessed Catholics sought to overturn the conquest in 1641; however, in a great act of providence, they were defeated, although it was only after the Battle of the Boyne in 1690 that Protestant ascendancy in Ireland was guaranteed. Following another rebellion, in 1798, the Act of Union finally ensured the liberty and security of Irish Protestants, a liberty and security that was imperilled by home rule.

However, beginning in the early 1890s, a Protestant republican counterculture emerged in Ulster, whose adherents invoked a striking counternarrative. Ulster Protestant republicans elided over their ancestral experience as planters in the seventeenth century and as unionists in the nineteenth; instead, they sought to highlight Protestant involvement in the eighteenth-century Patriot or United Irishmen movements. So compelling was this counternarrative that even some Orangemen flirted with abandoning Orangeism's traditional unionism in favour of a radical realignment with nationalism. However, the activities of the Ulster Protestant nationalist network were anathema to unionists, and the latter's hostility would play a key role in the eventual dissolution of this group.

The Old Generation and the New

The creation of a network of mostly young activists owed much to the actions of an older generation who acted to recruit suitable young

Protestants and foster their talents. Among the most influential of these was the Episcopalian solicitor and antiquarian Francis Joseph Bigger (1863–1926). Of Scottish extraction, the Biggers were a well-established Ulster commercial family. Born in Belfast, as a sickly child he was sent to live with relatives in Mallusk, County Antrim. Seven decades after 1798, the folk memory of the rebellion remained strong in rural Ulster, and here Bigger learned about the United Irishmen and conversed with the sons and daughters of rebels.[1] Like so many Protestant nationalists, he was obsessed with 1798: he wrote a series of six biographies of United Irishmen figures, though only one, of William Orr, was ever published.[2] Bigger also developed a fascination for his grandfather, David Bigger, who had been a well-known Volunteer during the days of Grattan's parliament.[3] Another influence was his father's first cousin, Joseph Gillis Biggar (1828–1890), the Irish Party member for Cavan, a noted 'obstructionist' during the Parnell era. Also important was his mother, from whom he inherited religiously tolerant views.[4] Practising law in Belfast from 1889, Bigger threw himself into an array of Irish cultural activities. He joined the Belfast Naturalists' Field Club, becoming its secretary and later president.[5] This body was originally focussed on botany; under Bigger's influence it became more historical and archaeological. When this club's 'Celtic' class was later reorganised as the Belfast branch of the Gaelic League, Bigger was appointed to its executive.[6]

    F. J. Bigger grew to dislike English government, which, in his opinion, had been responsible for Ireland's undoing.[7] Cultural nationalism led him to political separatism. However, despite the close friendships Bigger forged with physical-force separatists, such as Bulmer Hobson and Roger Casement, he 'never breathed a word that might incite to force or violence, which in his heart he detested'.[8] His friends understood his views and took care to avoid embarrassing him: Hobson informed R. B. McDowell how just before the Great War he and Casement decided it would 'be tactful to wait until Bigger had bustled off to his city office

---

[1] J. S. Crone and F. C. Bigger (eds.), *In remembrance: articles and sketches: biographical, historical, topographical by Francis Joseph Bigger M.A., M.R.I.A., F.R.S.A.I.* (Dublin, 1927), xvi–xvii.

[2] Francis Joseph Bigger, *William Orr* (Dublin, 1906).

[3] Crone and Bigger, *In remembrance*, xvi.   [4] Crone and Bigger, *In remembrance*, viii.

[5] Roger Dixon, 'Francis Joseph Bigger: Belfast's Cultural Don Quixote', *Ulster Folklife*, Vol. 43 (1997), 40–47.

[6] *Annual Report and Proceedings of the Belfast Naturalists' Field Club for the year ending 31 March 1895*, Series II, Part II, Volume IV, 1894–1895; Crone and Bigger, *In remembrance*, 10.

[7] Crone and Bigger, *In remembrance*, x.   [8] Crone and Bigger, *In remembrance*, xi.

before they discussed certain bold projects'.[9] Although a prolific author on a great variety of Irish topics – including history, politics, archaeology, topography, and conservation, Bigger's greatest contribution to nationalism in Ulster was, as we will see, his slow cultivation of Irish ideals among the younger generation.

Another member of the older generation who sought to win converts among the young was the novelist and playwright Alice Milligan. Milligan was born in 1866, daughter of Seaton Milligan MRIA, a successful businessman, liberal unionist, and well-known antiquarian. After attending what she would later describe as a 'very high-class school in Omagh, strictly Tory and Protestant',[10] she continued her education in Methodist College, Belfast, King's College, London, and Magee College, Derry, where she trained as a teacher.

'Alice Milligan ... did not so much break away from a tradition as revert to an older one.'[11] Although this claim from the 1940s may be exaggerated, Ulster in the 1870s and 1880s was a more complex place than is sometimes understood, and there were other hereditary impulses at work. Significantly, one of Milligan's great-grandfathers and his five sons rose in 1798; they marched with the insurgents to the Battle of Antrim.[12] Even by Ulster nationalist standards she was fixated on the United Irishmen, returning constantly to this theme in her writing, and played a prominent role in organising the centenary celebrations in 1898. Born one year before the Fenian Rebellion, Milligan was raised in an environment suffused with the traditional Ulster Protestant fear of an uprising by the Catholic dispossessed: 'I was taught in my childhood that the Papists and Fenians had quite lately designed a general uprising and massacre of Protestants, and that they had gone out and assembled on the hills for that purpose'. As a child Milligan was taught that local Catholics were apportioning – in fact holding raffles – for Protestant land. 'My own ancestral farm at the time of the 1886 Home Rule Bill was reported to have reverted to a catholic country tailor man.'[13] Tales of the near-disaster of 1867 were a common theme of her childhood, as she recalled in her most famous poem:

> An army of Papists grim
> With a green flag over them,
> Red-coats and black police
>   Flying before them
> But God (Who, our nurse declared,

[9] R. B. McDowell, *Alice Stopford Green: a passionate historian* (Dublin, 1967), 80.
[10] Henry Mangan (ed.), *Poems by Alice Milligan* (Dublin, 1954), xiv.
[11] *Irish Press*, 10 July 1941.   [12] *Irish Press*, 10 July 1941.   [13] *The Leader*, 17 July 1909.

> Guards British Dominions)
> Sent down a deep fall of snow
> And scattered the Fenians.

However, even as a child Milligan had different ideas from the rest of her household:

> But one little rebel there,
> Watching all with laughter,
> Thought: 'When the Fenians come
> I'll rise and go after.'[14]

Despite an education in which 'the glories of English and foreign literature absorbed [her] attention' and in which she 'learned nothing of Ireland',[15] Milligan's interest in Irish culture was piqued by two older relatives. From a great-uncle, she gained an interest in the Irish language,[16] and from her father, she developed an interest in Irish history. 'Instinctively, since I was a child my heart went out to my own nation. In spite of all I heard, I knew that Ireland was my country and that its people were my people.'[17] On leaving Derry in 1891, she moved to Dublin, and became a supporter of the Parnellite faction of the Irish Parliamentary Party, led by John Redmond. A theme in her writing during this period was her belief that Ireland should gain self-government through public agitation rather than parliamentary negotiation. Hearing Redmond speak in 1893, she recorded: 'the spirit of independence in every line. – He convinces that he is going to rouse the country instead of waiting for Gladstonians in parliament.'[18] However, after this period she grew disenchanted with the home rule movement, and instead set up her own organisation. In November 1894 she founded the Irish Women's Association (IWA), which quickly launched branches in Belfast, Portadown, and Moneyreagh.[19] Her co-founder was Jennie Armour, wife of the home ruler and Presbyterian minister James Brown Armour, who had become deeply unpopular with Ulster unionists. The IWA sought to bring Catholic and Protestant women together in a nationalist vehicle. However, this was not a republican movement; the IWA's main stated aim, 'self-government', was far from separatist.[20]

---

[14] 'When I was a little girl', in Mangan, *Poems by Alice Milligan*, 2–4.

[15] Mangan, *Poems by Alice Milligan*, xvi.

[16] *Ulster Herald*, 18 April 1953; Mangan, *Poems by Alice Milligan*, xviii.

[17] *Irish Weekly and Ulster Examiner*, 7 September 1940.

[18] NLI, MS 47,782, Alice Milligan diary, 10 October 1893.

[19] Morris, *Alice Milligan*, 32.

[20] W. S. Armour, *Armour of Ballymoney* (London, 1934), 136; *II*, 13 January 1913; *FJ*, 3 November 1894.

In 1895 Milligan helped establish the Henry Joy McCracken Literary Society, becoming its vice-president. The society's name reflects Milligan's interest in the Protestant rebels of 1798. The new society was somewhat more advanced than the IWA, and was quite explicitly an Ulster Protestant vehicle. Milligan's column in the *Weekly Irish Independent* reminded southern readers of the existence of Protestant nationalists in the north; she wanted to 'show to you on the other side of the Boyne that it is the voice of many men in Ulster'.[21] Along with her co-editor and close friend, the Catholic Anna Johnston (pseud. Ethna Carbery), the society's paper, the *Northern Patriot*, asserted Ulster's right to equal status with the south in the nationalist movement.[22] When Milligan and Johnston were sacked from the paper – on discovery that Johnston's father, Robert, was a member of the IRB – the two founded an unequivocally separatist alternative, the *Shan Van Vocht*.[23] As with the *Northern Patriot*, it covered themes of interest to Milligan: the Protestant patriots of 1798, Thomas Davis, and the Fenian Rebellion. *Shan Van Vocht* remained the principal advanced nationalist organ until 1899, when it was replaced by Arthur Griffith's livelier *United Irishman*.

Milligan's and Bigger's activities took place within the context of a disorientated nationalist movement. Patrick Maume argues that nationalism, which was weakened by the Parnell split in 1890, enjoyed a revival in the late 1890s, due to a combination of the 1798 centenary, democracy in local government, the formation of the United Irish League, and the Boer War.[24] If the moderate nationalist movement, which reunited under John Redmond in 1900, was beginning to reorganise, the same could be said for advanced nationalists. Into this environment came Bulmer Hobson, an ambitious protégé of Milligan and Carbery.

Bulmer Hobson (1883–1969) was born into a well-established Quaker family in Belfast.[25] There was a weak tradition of nationalism in the family: his grocer father, Benjamin, was a Gladstonian home ruler.[26] His English mother, Mary Hobson, a suffragist and amateur archaeologist, was a unionist. A friend recorded: 'His father goes a little way but his mother is an English woman and shows it. He dare not discuss his plans with me in her presence. At least to avoid trouble he dare not.'[27] From the age of twelve Hobson was borrowing Standish O'Grady works from Alice Milligan. These retold Celtic myths 'opened up ... new ranges of

---

[21] *Irish Weekly Independent*, 31 August 1895.   [22] *Northern Patriot*, 15 October 1895.
[23] See Catherine Morris, 'In the enemy's camp: Alice Milligan and fin de siècle Belfast', in Nicholas Allen and Aaron Kelly (eds.), *Cities of Belfast* (Dublin, 2003), 62–73.
[24] Maume, *The long gestation*, 27.
[25] Bulmer Hobson, *Ireland yesterday and tomorrow* (Tralee, 1968), 1.
[26] Hay, *Bulmer Hobson*, 9.   [27] Hay, *Bulmer Hobson*, 14.

hitherto unimagined beauty'. Hobson was particularly affected by close proximity in Ulster to the centres of Irish mythology:

all around were the places where my heroes had lived and died. I knew Dunseverick and the Rock of Fergus. I had seen Oisin's grave and Grania's Cairn, and within a day's journey was Cuchulain's Dun and the Sea of Moyle where the children of Lir had formerly wandered.[28]

Another influence was Ethna Carbery, who used to invite Hobson to her house, where he met local Gaelic League figures, as well as Douglas Hyde, Maud Gonne, and John O'Leary.[29] While a student at Friends' School in Lisburn he subscribed to the *Shan Van Vocht*. He recalled a struggle with an Englishman teacher who held the students' purse strings. 'It caused quite a flutter in the school and definitely marked me as an eccentric. I was not perturbed and in the *Shan* I came for the first time in touch with the new forces that were beginning to stir in Ireland.'[30] One particular event that caused these forces to stir was the 1798 centenary celebrations. Hobson was still a schoolboy during these events, but they had a strong impact on him. As was the case for many others, the centenary provided impetus to learn about the – mainly Protestant – leaders of the Rising. Nor was the United Irishmen's Ulster orientation lost on the young man:

I found myself living in a city enriched by their associations. The result was that I decided to spend the succeeding years of my life in trying to complete their task. From then on I found myself integrated into the tradition of Tone. My own people completely disapproved of my views.[31]

From this period onwards, Hobson was a republican, and looked to Wolfe Tone as his exemplar. He also began to associate with the growing circle around F. J. Bigger. Confident and ambitious, Hobson was an inveterate joiner – and founder – of nationalist organisations. Between 1901 and 1903 he joined the first Antrim County Board of the GAA, and became involved in the Gaelic League in Belfast, later becoming secretary of the Belfast executive.[32] In 1900 he joined Cumann na nGaedheal, an IRB front organisation. This and other nationalist activities he fitted in while he was working long hours in a Belfast printing house.

If the period after c. 1898 saw the regeneration of the broad advanced nationalist movement, some observers expressed alarm at the small numbers of Protestants becoming involved in separatist organisations.

---

[28] Hobson, *Ireland yesterday and tomorrow*, 1.   [29] BMH WS 82, Bulmer Hobson.
[30] Hobson, *Ireland yesterday and tomorrow*, 2.
[31] *IT*, 6 May 1961. See also Hobson, *Ireland yesterday and tomorrow*, 2.
[32] Hobson, *Ireland yesterday and tomorrow*, 3–4.

One such figure was the Catholic writer Seumas MacManus (1868–1960). He used a lengthy piece in the *United Irishmen* to outline a remedy. MacManus stated:

Irish Nationality will make a great forward stride when it receives the Protestant impulse. Again and again the minds of men who wrought for Ireland were racked to find a plan for getting hold of the Protestant and making him a patriot – but racked in vain. Although many efforts to win Protestantism to our cause have failed, the stake is such an admittedly valuable one that it is worth playing for once more on a new system.

Like others, MacManus took heart from the large numbers of Protestant intellectuals who were demonstrating nationalist sympathies, through organisations such as the Gaelic League:

not since '48, if even then, have we had on the National side any band of as many and as brilliant young Protestants as you could choose today out of literary, journalistic, and propagandist circles ... With all the zeal and ability for which these young men individually are remarkable, and with all the dash and fight that is in them, if they came together as a body ... forming a Young Protestant Party, you would have a Party more remarkable, and bigger with possibilities, than any other party since the days of Young Ireland.[33]

MacManus's proposal provoked controversy. One correspondent stated that any Protestant nationalist organisation would weaken the nationalist movement, at a time when unity was required, and when unionists could muster Catholic members. The creation of a Protestant nationalist party would by definition create a Catholic nationalist party.[34] The opposite view was taken by 'An Irish Protestant'. He admitted that it was a 'paradoxical means of combatting sectarianism to form ourselves into distinctly labelled bodies' but that the plan could work. As with MacManus, he stressed the opportunities for nationalism due to the increase in Protestant interest in Irish culture:

were the Young Protestant Party founded to-morrow what is true of hundreds of young Protestants in Dublin, who are silently studying all that pertains to their country, would be true of thousands. And although the means suggested savour of sectarianism, they would be the means by which sectarianism would be, please God, stamped out.[35]

In February 1903, a Protestant National Society was founded, not in Dublin, but in Belfast. Hobson was a founding member. It aimed at 'bringing the Protestants of the North into line with the Catholics of the South on Irish National matters'.[36] In taking a leading role in this society

---

[33] *United Irishman*, 10 January 1903.   [34] *United Irishman*, 24 January 1903.
[35] *United Irishman*, 7 February 1903.   [36] *United Irishman*, 28 February 1903.

Hobson was attempting to give effect to his Wolfe Tone–inspired philosophy. McManus's suggestion would have made an especial impression on Hobson, as he was the husband of his intimate Ethna Carbery. Hobson's principal partners in the project were the playwright David Parkhill, and William McDonald, a young man Hobson had met through the Ulster Debating Club.[37] Little is known about McDonald, who died young, save Denis McCullough's memory of 'a little fella ... one of the best minds I met in all my time – he died, poor boy, of TB'.[38] Seumas MacManus gave an optimistic report on the organisation, when he visited their rooms at Donegall Street. He described a group of around twenty young men meeting in a hall decorated with portraits of Protestant heroes: Grattan, Emmet, FitzGerald, Tone, Davis, and a modern addition, Douglas Hyde. Many of those present came from the Belfast School of Art, were sons of businessmen, or, as was common for Protestant nationalists, sons of clergymen.[39] The group unanimously adopted the policy of the *United Irishman* journal as its policy.[40]

Following the successful passing of the Wyndham Land Act in 1903, the government, seeking to capitalise on a sense of general good feeling in the country, decided to organise a visit by Edward VII. Advanced nationalists, fearing that the nationalist lord mayor of Dublin, Timothy Harrington, would co-operate with a loyal address to the King, formed themselves into an opposition group called the 'National Council'. A National Council delegation, led by Maud Gonne and Edward Martyn, interrupted a United Irish League meeting in Dublin, demanding Harrington commit to not giving an address. The resulting incident, known as the 'Battle of the Rotunda', was an open riot.

In Belfast, the Protestant National Society passed a resolution congratulating the National Council on their action, and pledged it every assistance.[41] Harrington responded by attacking the Protestant National Society, suggesting to a meeting of his supporters that it was a sectarian organisation. This in turn provoked a furious counterattack from Griffith's *United Irishman*:

there is no question of misrepresentation or error – deliberately and absolutely Mr Harrington lied. 'These gentlemen', the wretched man added, 'came forward with loud praise to the President of the new Catholic Association [a Harrington slight against Edward Martyn]. The first endorsement he got was from the True

---

[37] BMH WS 82, Bulmer Hobson.
[38] University College Dublin (UCD), Denis McCullough papers (McC), P120/34 (2), transcript of interview with Denis McCullough for Ulster Television, 8 September 1964.
[39] *United Irishman*, 2 May 1903.   [40] *United Irishman*, 4 April 1903.
[41] *United Irishman*, 30 May 1903.

Blue Orangemen of Belfast – the Protestant Association.' The man who uttered this deliberate and cowardly lie occupies the highest elective position in civic life in Dublin.[42]

This proved the last controversy of the Protestant National Society's short existence. Having had, in Hobson's own words, 'little noticeable success' in spreading the gospel of Wolfe Tone, Ireland's first explicitly Protestant nationalist organisation since the IPHRA faded away.[43] Hobson changed tactics, and would never again set up a Protestant-only organisation.

Hobson's rise to prominence among Ulster radical nationalists was aided by his joining the IRB in 1904.[44] He was sworn in by Denis McCullough (1883–1968), a young Catholic activist from Belfast. McCullough was then engaged in reviving the stagnant Fenian organisation in the North, actively replacing the older generation, many of whom had become dependent on alcohol. Travelling around rural Ulster, McCullough encountered elderly Protestant Fenian relics, hangovers from the 1860s or before. Tantalised by the endurance of this tradition, he sought to revive it. However, McCullough hesitated before admitting Bulmer Hobson to the IRB. By 1904 Hobson was among the most prominent Protestant nationalist activists in Ulster.[45] Although the Belfast IRB, as with the rest of the organisation, was non-sectarian and had 'quite a good number of Protestant men in the movement at the time',[46] McCullough was fearful of admitting so well known a figure, given the North's religious tensions:

I was afraid that the RIC – G-men as we called them – would circulate, as they did circulate, that the movement would be led by Protestants, [which] would lead us into trouble deliberately ... They would work on the ... anti-Protestant and pro-Catholic idea, and we had nothing of that [i.e. sectarianism] at all ... Any stick is dirty enough to beat a dog with you know.

Hobson, in common with several other Protestant nationalists, among them Darrell Figgis, Erskine Childers, and Albinia Brodrick, gained a reputation for arrogance. McCullough remembered:

It's like most of the Protestants who came into our movement, they thought they knew all about it and they listened to no [one]. [Hobson] was a complete egoist ... if he didn't have his way he'd break up an ordinary meeting, and I had a difficult job keeping him in line.

---

[42] *United Irishman*, 6 June 1903.
[43] Bulmer Hobson, quoted in Sam Hanna Bell, *Theatre in Ulster* (Totowa, 1972), 2–3.
[44] Hay, *Bulmer Hobson*, 44; Hobson, *Ireland yesterday and tomorrow*, 35.
[45] See, for example, *United Irishman*, 30 May, 22 August 1903.
[46] UCD, McC, P120/36, transcript of BBC interview with Denis McCullough, 1964.

However, McCullough also remembered his old friend's personal charm: 'he was a very persuasive person and ... an exceedingly nice fellow'.[47]

After 1904, McCullough was able to make use of Hobson's talents to resuscitate the Ulster IRB, alongside Catholic lieutenants Sean McDermott, Pat McCartan, and Joe McGarrity, as well as Ernest Blythe. Together, this group revived the organisation.

An Orange/Nationalist Nexus?: Lindsay Crawford and Independent Orangeism

> [Most] of them were, if not actual, at least potential agnostics, and all of them anti-clericals. [O'Casey] knew few of them who might be called practising catholics, though he had had one experience how the Faith lay crystallised in the corner of their minds. He got the ... *Irish Protestant* from a friend, and in one issue was astounded to see the leading article praised the Men of '98 ... The article had been written by Lindsay Crawford, who, one way or another, had been attracted by the new Irish movement. Sean hurried down to Tom Clarke's shop with the journal.
>
> — Look, he said ... you'll find something to stir you there!
>
> As soon as Clarke's brilliant eyes saw the title of the paper, he flung it back at Sean, saying ... with no little venom, Take it away — I don't read such slanderous rubbish! Take away that anti-catholic rag!
>
> — I don't want to make a protestant of you, man! Sean said, savagely, surprised to see that the fear of the bigot lingered even in the bold heart of Tom Clarke. Here was a most intelligent man, ready to face a firing squad, afraid to face a Protestant paper ... Sean [said] ... this issue of the paper praises the Irish who died for Ireland, and says that the Protestants should be in the vanguard in Ireland's fight for freedom.
>
> Tom Clarke seized the paper, skimmed it with his gleaming eyes, turned, and said with rapture, Here, Sean, quick, get three dozen of them; go where you think they are, and get them — this is the best I've read for years![48]

Sean O'Casey's possibly apocryphal account of introducing Thomas Clarke to the *Irish Protestant* provides an accurate reflection of the joy provoked among Irish advanced nationalists at the conversion of Robert Lindsay Crawford (1868–1945) to separatism and the concomitant rupture within the Orange Order. The creation of the Independent Orange Order, and the unusual trajectory of Crawford, its chief ideologue, has

---

[47] UCD, McC, P120/36 transcript of BBC interview with Denis McCullough, 1964.

[48] Sean O'Casey, *Drums under the windows*, in *Autobiographies*, Vol. I (London, 1992 [originally published as a single volume in 1945]), 615–616.

generated a historiographical debate. Writing in 1962, J. W. Boyle argued that the Independent Order, under Crawford's influence, demonstrated nationalist sentiment analogous to the United Irishmen or Young Ireland, before his expulsion led to the organisation's reversion to sectarianism and unionist orthodoxy.[49] In 1980, Henry Patterson offered a different interpretation. Patterson stressed the sectarianism of the Independents and argued that Crawford's radicalism was essentially empty as it required alliance with a non-existent milieu of Catholic anti-clericalists.[50] More than twenty years later Peter Murray undermined Patterson's arguments, by asserting the even-handed secularism of Crawford's ideology.[51] This section will offer a new assessment of the creation of the Independent Orange Order, and the career of Lindsay Crawford, by stressing the extent to which he sought to bring together Independent Orangemen and dissident nationalists in a common anti-clericalist coalition, in the hope of undermining Protestant support for the Union.

Crawford was an Antrim-born member of the Church of Ireland, the son of a scripture reader. He initially worked in business before becoming, in 1901, the founding editor of the *Irish Protestant*, a monthly (and from October 1903, weekly) evangelical review, published in Dublin. He was a prominent Dublin Orangeman, and in the Church of Ireland synod a well-known opponent of what he deemed ritualistic liturgical practices. In its early years the *Irish Protestant* specialised in pungent anti-Catholic rhetoric. It campaigned against changes to the Royal Declaration, a solemn repudiation of Catholicism, which was required of a British monarch as part of the coronation ceremony.[52] The paper frequently charged the Church of Ireland with 'Romanising' ritualism.[53] Crawford argued that Protestants in the south and west were victims of an organised campaign of ill-treatment. He claimed, for example, that Protestant members of the Dublin Metropolitan Police suffered sectarian persecution.[54] Crawford's *bête noire* was the Catholic Association. He saw it as an open anti-Protestant conspiracy, which sought to boycott Protestant

---

[49] John W. Boyle, 'The Belfast Protestant Association and the Independent Orange Order, 1901–10', *Irish Historical Studies*, Vol. 13, No. 50 (Sep. 1962), 117–152.

[50] Henry Patterson, 'Independent Orangeism and class conflict in Edwardian Belfast: a reinterpretation', *Proceedings of the Royal Irish Academy. Section C: archaeology, Celtic studies, history, linguistics, literature*, Vol. 80C (1980), 1–27.

[51] Peter Murray, 'Radical way forward or sectarian cul-de-sac? Lindsay Crawford and Independent Orangeism reassessed', *Saothar* 27 (2002), 31–42.

[52] *Irish Protestant*, August, September, October, November 1901, April, August, 1902.

[53] *Irish Protestant*, December 1901, 2 January, 23 April, 4 June 1904.

[54] *Irish Protestant*, February, June 1902, 23 January, 23 April, 4 June 1904.

businesses and create a Catholic monopoly on public positions.[55] Crawford in some respects resembled D. P. Moran, a prominent Catholic
Association supporter. Both editors were reasonably young (Crawford
was thirty-nine when he founded the *Irish Protestant*; Moran thirty-one
when he launched *The Leader*), both were partisans for their respective
religious community, and neither observed the pieties of mainstream
unionist or nationalist politicians.[56]

Crawford's critique of the Catholic Association owed much to the
influence of Michael J. F. McCarthy (1862–1928). McCarthy was a
Catholic barrister and TCD graduate whose prolific writings – notably
Five years in Ireland (1900) and *Priests and people in Ireland* (1902) –
gained a large audience. He argued that the Catholic clergy were seeking
to dominate the country, principally through control of education.
The *Irish Protestant* supported McCarthy's abortive candidacy for
St Stephen's Green division in 1904, where he sought to run as an
independent unionist.[57] Crawford not only gained material for caustic
anti-priestly commentary from McCarthy; he also conceived that clerical
influence could be overcome through an alliance of Irish Protestants and
secular-minded Catholics.[58]

The *Irish Protestant* may seem an unlikely journal to develop nationalist
sympathies. However, Crawford had an independent spirit that was,
from the beginning, at odds with the unionist establishment. An early
edition had disavowed the 'Divine Right of Toryism' to represent Irish
Protestants. It also diverged from mainstream unionism in sympathising
with the Boers.[59] Crawford's breach with unionism was prompted by
his resistance to Conservative Party policy, particularly in education.
Between 1890 and 1905 the Conservatives embarked on a policy of
so-called constructive unionism in which ameliorative or progressive
legislation was introduced in the hope that it would impede the success
of the Irish Party and perhaps reconcile nationalists to the Union.[60] The
most controversial conciliatory measure proposed was the creation of a
Catholic university in Dublin. This was greatly desired by the Catholic
hierarchy but opposed by many Nonconformists and evangelicals. The

---

[55] *Irish Protestant*, October 1902, 2, 9, 16, 30 January, 13, 20 February, 2 July 1904. The
    United Irishman also attacked the Catholic Association as sectarian: *United Irishman*, 23
    January 1904.
[56] Siobhan Jones, 'The Irish Protestant under the editorship of Lindsay Crawford, 1901–6',
    Saothar, Vol. 30 (2005), 87.
[57] *Irish Protestant*, 19, 26 March 1904.
[58] McCarthy eventually converted to Protestantism.
[59] *Irish Protestant*, November 1901, January 1902.
[60] Cf. Andrew Gailey, *Ireland and the death of kindness: the experience of constructive unionism,
    1890–1905* (Cork, 1987).

proposal was anathema to Crawford.[61] A further turning-point was the 1902 Education Act, which enhanced clerical influence in elementary schools in England and Wales. Crawford inveighed against unionist MPs for supporting the 'iniquitous priests' Bill'.[62] Peter Murray has shown that Crawford not only criticised Catholic influence in education, but also attacked Protestant clerical control of schools and universities.[63] The *Irish Protestant* campaigned for the Divinity School to be removed from TCD and for the College to be placed under secular management.[64] (However, this latter proposal may have been informed by a belief that the Divinity School was a nest of ritualism).

Unionists sometimes argued that Catholic clergy would have such influence under home rule, that they preferred the creation of an Irish republic – which they presumed would have a continental anti-clerical character. These statements were usually flippantly made, but Crawford, quite earnestly, began to conceive a new political alliance between Protestants and anti-clerical Catholics that would ultimately lead to his espousing republicanism. An editorial in 1902 encapsulates his thinking: 'The great aim of successive Governments has been the enlistment on the side of law and order of the Church of Rome, and every effort of the present executive has been directed to that end.' Crawford maintained that continental Catholic countries, such as France, Italy, and Spain, were reducing clerical influence, while only the United Kingdom was increasing it. In an extraordinary statement, Crawford hinted at a future Protestant/anti-clericalist rebellion:

What are the signs of awakening, and on what lines will the Irish Revolution of, say, 1910 proceed? Looking at the trend of events in Continental nations, we cannot be surprised if the tide of anti-clericalism already beats on Irish shores. Mr [Frank Hugh] O'Donnell, Mr McCarthy &c., are the living indices to the Irish awakening; and Irish Protestants can do much to hasten the day which will bring Irishmen of all creeds and classes together by resolutely opposing clerical superiority in education.[65]

The editorial, mindful of alienating readers, rather weakly affirmed support for the Union. However, it is clear that by mid-1902 Crawford was moving to a nationalist position, by aligning himself with anti-clericalists, such as McCarthy and Frank Hugh O'Donnell. Frank Hugh O'Donnell (1846–1916), a maverick former Irish Party MP, had become a prominent critic of clerical-controlled education.[66] Crawford could also look to

---

[61] *Irish Protestant*, October 1901, March 1902, 9 January 1904.
[62] *Irish Protestant*, June, December 1902, 23 January 1904.
[63] Murray, 'Radical way forward or sectarian cul-de-sac?', 39.
[64] *Irish Protestant*, October 1901.   [65] *Irish Protestant*, May 1902.
[66] See Frank Hugh O'Donnell, *The ruin of education in Ireland and the Irish Fanar* (London, 1902).

Michael Davitt and Francis Sheehy-Skeffington as exemplars of anti-clericalism from a Catholic background, and, as will be seen, he perceived similar tendencies in the Gaelic League.

Ultimately, geography may have been key to Crawford's conversion to nationalism. Had he resided in Ulster he might found common cause with radicals in the unionist movement. His business interests in the south, however, ensured that his political development took on an all-Ireland, rather than Ulster character.

On 12 July 1902, a group of protestors disrupted a speech made by Colonel Edward Saunderson, leader of the Irish unionist MPs, at an Orange Order rally in Belfast. The demonstrators charged Saunderson (who was also County Grand Master of Belfast) with voting in the Commons to exempt convent-run laundries from government inspection. The protest was led by T. H. Sloan (1870–1941), a shipyard worker and Methodist lay preacher, who had some talent for public speaking. In August Sloan defeated the official unionist candidate in the Belfast South by-election, and entered parliament as an independent unionist.[67] This breach of unionist unity may have been due to the relatively quiescent political situation. In the early 1900s, the liberals were out of office and the home rule menace had receded; working-class Protestants had the luxury of critically examining their unionist representatives and questioning the merit of the Tory alliance.

Orange schism followed political rupture. A stand-off occurred when Sloan balked at giving Saunderson a written apology, leading the Grand Lodge of Ireland to revoke the warrants of three pro-Sloan lodges. On 11 July 1903 the Independent Orange Order was founded. The rebel organisation enjoyed steady growth, mainly confined to working-class Belfast and the liberal redoubt of North Antrim. By early 1904 it claimed nine lodges in Ballymoney alone, where radicalism was especially strong, largely due to the influence of the Rev. James Brown Armour.[68] The organisation peaked at forty-four lodges in 1907.[69] At the Independent Order's first rally, held outside Belfast, Sloan moved resolutions that denounced changes to the Royal Declaration, resisted proposals to create a Catholic university, and demanded mandatory inspection of convent laundries. These were familiar themes for Lindsay Crawford, who chaired the meeting.[70]

---

[67] Boyle, 'The Belfast Protestant Association', 117–124.

[68] *Irish Protestant,* 23 January 1904.

[69] Grand Orange Lodge of Ireland, Belfast (GOLI), Independent Orange Order collection, *Independent Orange Institution of Ireland, Grand Lodge report, 1907* (Belfast, 1907).

[70] *Northern Whig,* 14 July 1903, quoted in Boyle, 'The Belfast Protestant Association', 126.

By July 1904 Crawford was Imperial Grand Master in the new order. Although Sloan could provide grassroots support, he was an intellectually limited man; Crawford established himself as the organisation's ideologue. He sketched out a radical new conception of Irish nationalism partially masked by sophisticated rhetoric. Its bellicosity found favour with Independent Orange audiences, who, like Sloan, initially failed to understand its full implications. As late as January 1904 Crawford affirmed his unionism at an Independent rally.[71] Less than a month later an *Irish Protestant* editorial suggested he had converted to separatism. He lamented the death of Parnell, saying had he lived Ireland would have seen clerical influence diminish. Irish Protestants, in seeking to avoid home rule, had inadvertently strengthened Catholicism:

our Sovereign, by the advice of his Ministers, visits the Pope, makes a pilgrimage to the assembled Bishops in Maynooth, and places Ireland both by moral and administrative influence, under the suzerainty of Archbishop Walsh! ... Is Ireland to-day less under the domination of the priest than would have resulted from a parliament in College Green? Has Unionism made for national, or for Papal, progress? No right-minded Irish Protestants can continue to follow blindly in the wake of a party which, under the guise of the consolidation of the British Empire, filters Irish national ideals ... through the cesspool of Vaticanism.

The existing political parties could not be trusted:

The Unionist Party and the Home Rule Party ... are converging by parallel roads on the Highway to Rome. To neither of these parties can be entrusted the future destiny of our country. There is room at the present moment for a patriotic party, embracing all classes and creeds who ... will unite in demanding for Ireland her rightful place in the existing Constitution.[72]

Mainstream unionists argued home rule would be Rome rule; Crawford argued Ireland had Rome rule already. The 'patriotic party' Crawford had in mind would be an alliance of Independent Orangemen, southern Protestants, anti-clericalists, and perhaps the Gaelic League and Sinn Féin.

At a speech in Larne in June 1905 Crawford argued that Protestants should look to the eighteenth century for inspiration. They should 'emulate the sturdy independence of their forefathers and assume the full duties and responsibilities of their citizenship in their own country'. He had a solution to those who held that the Catholic majority would discriminate against Protestants: when Irish Protestants sought to take leadership in Ireland, the majority would follow them, and 'accord [them] that place in the government of the country which [their] patriotism and self-sacrifice had justly

---

[71] *Irish Protestant*, 23 January 1903.   [72] *Irish Protestant*, 20 February 1904.

assigned'.[73] Sloan's bland response, in which he stated that Orangemen should 'remember' they were Irishmen, suggested he did not understand the substance of Crawford's remarks.[74] The Independent brethren warmly received Crawford's speech. It is hard to imagine the majority did not understand that Crawford was proposing an Orange/nationalist nexus. The likelihood is they were thrilled by the radicalism and bellicosity of Crawford's rhetoric, believing a threat to withdraw support for the Union would effect a change in government policy.

Crawford's most famous attempt to reorient Orangeism came with the Magheramorne manifesto, which was written by him and read at an Independent Orange meeting at Magheramorne, County Antrim, on 13 July 1905. It amounted to a reiteration, rather than development, of Crawford's thinking since 1902. It made an even-handed attack on clerical involvement in education and called for the transfer of the TCD divinity school to the Church of Ireland and for the college to become non-denominational. The Independent Orange working-class base would have been pleased with a call for land purchase of town property and expediting the transfer of farmland to tenants. On the Union it was circumspect: the manifesto repudiated the Irish Reform Association's recent devolution proposals as undemocratic, which implied support for a fully elected scheme, i.e. an assembly or parliament. Sloan, who as Belfast County Grand Master signed the manifesto, gave it a cool reception, reminding members that he sat with the unionists in the Commons.[75] The unionist press reaction was unanimously negative.

One young Protestant intellectual who responded warmly to Crawford's project was Robert Lynd. Lynd's pseudonymous pamphlet, *The Orangemen and the nation*, clearly expressed the ambivalence with which Irish republicans viewed Orangemen:

The Orangeman has long been to the Irish Nationalist a source at once of eager hope and melancholy despair. He has filled us with despair because we have appealed to him so often to forget the childish quarrels of vanished ages and to take his stand at the side of Ireland, and because ... he has still allowed the honeyed words ... of some landlord whose only interest in Ireland has been to screw the last penny out of his unfortunate tenants, or of some lawyer who was willing at the first opportunity to sell his soul, with Ireland thrown in, in return for thirty pieces of Government silver. On the other hand the Orangeman inspires us with eternal hope, because he is so sincere, and so passionate, and so extreme.

---

[73] Lindsay Crawford, *Irish grievances and their remedy* (Dublin, 1905), 10.
[74] Crawford, *Irish grievances*, 10.
[75] The Magheramorne manifesto was reproduced in the *Irish Protestant*, 22 July 1905.

Lynd argued that the Magheramorne manifesto demonstrated that 'Orangemen are growing tired of a way of thinking that makes them strangers in their own country and that leads them ... to distrust their fellow-countrymen.'[76] However, Magheramorne seems to have been better received by nationalist intellectuals than it was by the Independent Orange grassroots. Ominously for Crawford, it was reported, only days after it was unveiled, that considerable numbers of Independent brethren were unhappy with the document.[77] Some resigned soon after. Sloan, fearful for his seat, disassociated himself from any sections of the manifesto held to be anti-Union.[78] There is, in fact, little evidence to suggest there were a substantial number of home rule – let alone separatist – Independent brethren. Unionists and members of the old Order charged that the Independent Order was pro-independence.[79] Some senior Independent figures were of a similar mind to Crawford: Richard Braithwaite, secretary of the organisation, voiced support for self-government in the press.[80] Braithwaite would later leave the Order, join the Gaelic League, and under the name 'Richaerd Brannigan' become secretary of the Irish Citizen Army.[81] However, only one serving Independent Orangeman, Jimmy Hope, has been identified as having joined the Dungannon Clubs. Hope was the grandson of James 'Jemmy' Hope, a 1798 rebel.[82] Independent brethren gave Crawford's early speeches a warm reception. Thrilled as they were by his fighting talk, for most members the necessity of jettisoning Unionism and allying with Catholics was a deeply dubious proposition. Ultimately, the views of figures such as Crawford, Braithwaite, and Hope were rare within the organisation.

Crawford, now isolated in the movement of which he was nominally leader, found common cause with some southern Protestants. The Rev. James Owen Hannay wrote to Crawford enthusing about the manifesto, although he doubted its principles would find wide support in the short term:

The question now is whether the rest of Ireland will respond to the call or whether the priests still have the powers to smother the national spirit. No doubt they will try & no doubt they have the control of the whole, or almost the

---

[76] Riobard Ua Fhloinn [Robert Lynd], *The Orangemen and the nation* (Belfast, 1907), n.p. For Lynd, see discussion below.

[77] *IT*, 22 July 1905.   [78] Boyle, 'The Belfast Protestant Association', 137, 140.

[79] See, for example, *UG*, 23 February, 2 March 1907.

[80] *UG*, 23 February, 16 March, 6, 20 April, 4 May 1907.   [81] See Chapter 4.

[82] BMH WS 183, Liam Gaynor.

whole, of the Irish Nationalist press. However, if the people don't respond today they will tomorrow.[83]

Another correspondent was Arthur Thomas MacMorrough Kavanagh (1888–1953), an Episcopalian, Irish speaker, and the heir to an estate in County Carlow. He stated:

You cannot understand how longingly the people look to their Protestant brothers to help them. Will you dear editor be the means of bringing them together? If our people are to be saved from Romanism Protestants must lead a little, for nothing is more hateful to our people than the rule of the foreigner. An English King planted Romanism here & it must always flourish while an English government bosses us. I have seen the results of freedom in [South] America. The people freed from Spain soon threw off the papal yoke. In Ireland it would be just the same.[84]

In May 1906 Crawford was ousted as editor of the *Irish Protestant*. The mainly unionist shareholders disliked his politics, as had readers: it had suffered a decline in circulation.[85] In November of that year he suffered a heavy defeat to William Moore in the North Armagh by-election.[86] The result illustrated the dearth of grassroots support for Crawford's views. However, in January 1907 he took over as editor of the *Ulster Guardian*, the weekly journal of the Ulster Liberal Association (ULA).[87] Crawford immediately shifted the *Ulster Guardian* to a nationalist viewpoint. He abused the Conservatives, scorned denominational education, attacked the old Order's allegiance to Britain, and supported Belfast striking workers. A series of articles on Thomas Davis invited readers to look to the Protestant past for political inspiration.[88]

An outbreak of anti-clericalism in Queen's County offered Crawford an opportunity to reaffirm his principles on a southern platform. In

---

[83] Trinity College Dublin (TCD), James Owen Hannay papers, MS 3454–6/208a, James Owen Hannay to Lindsay Crawford, 15 July 1905. Strong support came from Michael Davitt; NLI, Lindsay Crawford papers, MS 11,415, Michael Davitt to Lindsay Crawford, 22 July 1905.

[84] NLI, Crawford papers, MS 11,415, Arthur Thomas MacMorrough Kavanagh to Lindsay Crawford, 29 February [1906?].

[85] Jones, 'The *Irish Protestant* under the editorship of Lindsay Crawford', 93.

[86] Moore took 4,228 votes to Crawford's 1,433.

[87] See report, *UG*, 12 January 1907.

[88] See *UG*, 12, 26 January, 2, 9, 16 February 1907. Francis Sheehy-Skeffington wrote Crawford saying, 'I congratulate you on the immediate improvement of the *Ulster Guardian*; I hope you will have a free hand to spread the light'; NLI, Crawford papers, MS 11,415, Francis Sheehy-Skeffington to Lindsay Crawford, 13 January 1907.

August 1905 a Catholic priest cast aspersions on the morality of women who attended mixed-sex Gaelic League classes. In what was dubbed the 'Battle for Portarlington', local Gaelic Leaguers expelled the parish priest and a curate from membership.[89] In April 1907 Crawford addressed the Ruairí Ó More branch, which had been at the centre of the dispute. In his address, he congratulated members on their stand against the clergy and claimed the Gaelic League was one of the organisations that was bringing Catholics and Protestants together. He foresaw the Independent Orange Order as playing a central role in a self-governing Ireland. He said that he

looked forward to the day when the North would once again be represented in some big national council, and in the capital of Ireland, and he himself had a hope that the Independent Orangemen of Ulster would one day march through the streets of Dublin to the Nine Acres, there to proclaim once more the oneness of the Irish race, and the union of the Orange and Green.[90]

The following week Crawford followed this up with an editorial that called for a grand alliance of Sinn Féin, the Gaelic League, anti-clericalists, devolutionists, Labour, the Independent Order, and the ULA.[91]

This sort of statement was too radical for the *Ulster Guardian*'s shareholders. In 1907 the ULA was still circumspect about supporting self-government, although from December 1910 the organisation was pro–home rule.[92] For perhaps the only time in his career Crawford found himself ahead of a substantial body of Ulster Protestant opinion. However, in May 1908 he received a dual blow: he was sacked as editor of the *Ulster Guardian* and expelled from the Independent Orange Order. Sloan replaced him as Imperial Grand Master. Crawford was unable to find employment in Ireland, and in June 1910 he emigrated to Canada. Robert Lynd, writing to wish him well, argued that a dearth of like-minded Protestant nationalist intellectuals had impeded political change. 'If', he said, 'there were a hundred of us like you in Ireland, I think we'd bring about a revolution.'[93] The Independent Order went into decline under Sloan's leadership. In January 1910 Sloan lost his seat in the

---

[89] Murray, 'Radical way forward or sectarian cul-de-sac?', 38. See also Sgéal Ruaidhrí Uí Mhórdha, *Autobiography of the Ruairi O More Branch of the Gaelic League, Portarlington* (Dublin, 1906).

[90] *UG*, 6 April 1907. See also *The Republic*, 11 April 1907.   [91] *UG*, 13 April 1907.

[92] See Chapter 4.

[93] NLI, Crawford papers, MS 11,415, Robert Lynd to Lindsay Crawford, 25 May 1910.

Commons. By 1913 it had only nine active lodges in north-east Ulster.[94] Although Sloan and the Independents frequently sought to embarrass the official order by highlighting the impact the latter body's support for partition would have on the southern Protestant minority, the organisation had lost momentum and would no longer pose any threat to the unionist establishment.

Crawford's project represented a failed attempt to reorient Orangeism towards the newly buoyant advanced nationalist movement. However, another group of Ulster Protestants, looking to the Protestant past for inspiration, were at that time also seeking to inculcate nationalist sentiment among their co-religionists.

A New 'Northern Athens'?

During this period, Hobson and his associates sought to make use of the burgeoning cultural revival as a vehicle for the transformation of the political views of Ulster Protestants. In 1902 Hobson was among the founders of the Ulster Literary Theatre (ULT) and later the literary magazine *Uladh*.[95] For Hobson and his associates the creation of the ULT and *Uladh* was a political project, designed to encourage Protestant participation in political nationalism, by means of piquing their interest in Irish things through the arts. In Hobson's words he intended to 'use the Drama for propaganda purposes'.[96] Patrick McCartan was more explicit, writing to Joseph McGarrity that *Uladh*'s 'present circulation is confined to wealthy Protestants. [The] object will be to bring them along gradually to nationalism.'[97]

At first Hobson and Parkhill were the driving force behind the group, which at first described itself as the 'Ulster Branch of the Irish National Theatre'. In early 1904 they put on Belfast productions of Yeats's and Lady Gregory's *Cathleen ni Houlihan* and Æ's *Deirdre*. Both the name of the new group and the decision to perform *Cathleen ni Houlihan* without permission provoked an angry response from Yeats. Hobson and Parkhill visited Yeats in Dublin where they found the poet, who seems to have had a prejudice against Ulster, to be 'haughty and aloof', with no interest in encouraging the young men, and refusing to allow them put on the

---

[94] GOLI, Independent Orange Order collection, *Orange Independent*, January, May 1913.
[95] For a recent study of this organisation, see Eugene McNulty, *The Ulster Literary Theatre and the northern revival* (Cork, 2008).
[96] Bulmer Hobson, quoted in Margaret McHenry, 'The Ulster theatre in Ireland', PhD thesis, University of Pennsylvania, 1931, 82.
[97] NLI, Joseph McGarrity papers, MS 17,457 (2), Patrick McCartan to Joseph McGarrity, 23 December 1905.

Irish National Theatre's plays.[98] Far from being discouraged, the interview only enhanced the scope of Hobson's and Parkhill's ambition. Returning to Belfast, Hobson turned to his friend, saying, 'Damn Yeats, we'll write our own plays.'[99] Hobson and his associates changed the name of the company to the Ulster Literary Theatre, a separate body to the Irish National Theatre Society. Yeats's lack of interest had an important impact on the ULT: independent of Dublin influence, yet nationalist in ideology, it would develop its own regional character, and produced distinctively Ulster plays.[100]

A native, nationalist theatre in Belfast drew a large number of young artists and intellectuals. Hobson's wish to use cultural organisations as a means to increase Protestant engagement with nationalism paid off, at least initially. A large group of Protestants were attracted to the ULT. Perhaps the most gifted playwright was Samuel Waddell (pseud. Rutherford Mayne) (1878–1967). Born in Japan to a Presbyterian missionary, and the brother of Helen Waddell, the noted scholar, author and translator, he trained as an engineer before joining the civil service. However, he devoted much of his energies to writing and performing drama. Waddell used the theatre to undermine well-entrenched aspects of Ulster identity, such as sectarianism.[101] One of his most successful works, *The Troth*, tells of two Famine-era peasant farmers, one Protestant and one Catholic, who conspire to kill their landlord when they are threatened with eviction, with each promising to care for the other's wife if the other was caught.[102] It is a brief, yet powerful call for religious solidarity in rural Ulster.

Another figure who rose to prominence through the ULT was Harry Morrow (pseud. Gerard MacNamara) (1865–1938). Morrow came from a Belfast Presbyterian family: he was one of eight sons of Harry Morrow Sr, who ran a painter and decorator business in Belfast, almost all of whose sons made a career in the arts. An early member of the ULT, the first play he wrote for the group was *Suzanne and the Sovereigns* (1907), in collaboration with David Parkhill. This play lampooned the verities of both Catholics and Protestants, depicting the Williamite War as a bout

---

[98] Bell, *Theatre in Ulster*, 2.
[99] Flann Campbell, *The dissenting voice: Protestant democracy in Ulster from plantation to partition* (Dublin, 1991), 369.
[100] BMH WS 82, Bulmer Hobson.
[101] See Karen Vandevelde, 'An open national identity: Rutherford Mayne, Gerald MacNamara, and the plays of the Ulster Literary Theatre', *Éire-Ireland*, Spring/Summer, 2004, 36–56.
[102] See Wolfgang Zach (ed.), *Selected plays by Rutherford Mayne* (Washington, DC, 2006), 91–101.

by King William and King James for the hand of an attractive maiden, the Suzanne of the play's title.[103] The play became a great, frequently revived success. Other Morrow brothers also joined the ULT: Norman Morrow as a set designer, actor and manager, Jack Morrow as a set designer and costumer, and Fred Morrow as the group's principal producer for many years.[104]

Those drawn to the ULT included William Brown Reynolds (pseud. William Donn) (1874–1925), a Presbyterian, who worked as a composer and *Evening Telegraph* music critic. Other prominent members included the journalists Robert Lynd (Irish: Roibéard Ó Floinn) (1879–1949) and James Winder Good (pseud. Robert Harding) (1877–1930). The Belfast art scene was a fertile recruiting ground. Among the artists who joined were Paul Henry, Walter Riddall, William Robert Gordon, and John McBurney. Other members included F. J. Bigger, Marion Crimmins, and Fred Hughes. Many Catholics also joined, including Seán McEntee and Denis McCullough. Three members of the Campbell family, the poet Joseph Campbell (Irish: Seosamh MacCathmaoil) (1879–1944), the artist John Campbell (1883–1962), and their sister Josephine Campbell, were also involved.[105] Many ULT members adopted pseudonyms. To be openly involved in so avant-garde a venture was to incur the risk of parental disapproval or shunning by prospective employers. Dorothy Macardle noted, they 'worked under a *nom de guerre*; they had been gaily treading the path to perdition for several years before even their own parents knew who the players were'.[106] The requirement of secrecy by so many – particularly Protestant – members was a symptom of the political atmosphere that would see so many gifted nationalists forced to leave Ulster.

The ULT published *Uladh*, a quarterly literary journal. Influenced by Yeats's *Samhain*, it was launched in November 1904.[107] Its committee comprised Bulmer Hobson, David Parkhill, James Winder Good, John Campbell, and W. B. Reynolds. Reynolds was editor, and John Campbell manager. Although short-lived, *Uladh* is a valuable source for understanding the ideology of this group of mainly Protestant activists. The first issue's editorial struck a determinately regional note, stating,

---

[103] For MacNamara, see Kathleen Danaher, 'Introduction to the plays of Gerald MacNamara', *Journal of Irish Literature*, Vol. 17, Nos. 2–3 (May–Sept., 1988), 3–20.

[104] Campbell, *The dissenting voice*, 370; *Uladh*, November 1904, 6.

[105] In 1909 Samuel Waddell married Josephine Campbell; two years after her 1941 death he married another Campbell sister, Frances.

[106] *Irish Press*, 10 December 1931. See also Campbell, *The dissenting voice*, 469–470 n.

[107] McNulty, *The Ulster Literary Theatre*, 77–78; Hay, *Bulmer Hobson*, 34–36.

'Ulster has its own way of things.'[108] The journal was a rather sophisticated propaganda vehicle that sought to effect the slow conversion of Protestants to nationalism.[109] Over its four issues *Uladh* illustrated the extent to which Ulster cultural talent had migrated to nationalism. Bulmer Hobson, J. W. Good, Herbert Hughes, F. J. Bigger, Forrest Reid, David Parkhill, W. B. Reynolds, Robert Lynd, and Alice Milligan wrote for it, and George and Norman Morrow provided artwork. Among Catholic contributors were Joseph Campbell, P. S. O'Hegarty, and Padraig Colum. Hobson later recalled, 'It came as a surprise to most people to find how many Ulster writers there were.'[110] One highly significant figure, Roger Casement, used its pages to intervene for the first time in Irish public life. Casement (1864–1916) was born in Dublin; his family was County Antrim landed gentry. Casement joined the British colonial service in 1892, and would gain international renown for publicising the exploitation of natives in Africa and South America. Casement's *Uladh* contribution, inauspiciously, involved a recent cause célèbre, that of a farmer who was prosecuted for painting his name in Irish on his cart.[111] However, his love of the underdog and fierce sense of right and wrong would see him come to identify with the most radical strain of Irish nationalism. Good-looking, aristocratic in bearing, and prone to depression, few Irish nationalists would enjoy as romantic a career, or controversial an afterlife, as Roger Casement.

Reynolds avoided any explicit assertion of Irish separatist principles, which might scare off some readers, yet hinted at a broader agenda. *Uladh* would be 'run on broad propagandist lines' and seeks to 'roll the stone that has been only pushed at by others. Then will the heroes of the North ride forth once again: at present they only sleep within the cavern of dark prejudice and ignorance and mistrust.'[112] A later editorial developed this point further, stating that the ULT circle sought not to separate Ulster from the rest of the country but rather to use a northern revival as a means to firmly anchor the province within the Irish nation.[113] F. J. Bigger struck a similar note. His *Uladh* contributions stressed the culture and learning of pre-1800 Belfast, which led the city to be dubbed 'The Northern Athens'.[114] He extolled the virtues of the eighteenth-century city and denigrated what he saw as its modern

---

[108] *Uladh*, November 1904, 1.
[109] NLI, McGarrity papers, MS 17,457 (2), Patrick McCartan to Joseph McGarrity, 23 December 1905.
[110] McHenry, 'The Ulster theatre in Ireland,' 83. [111] *Uladh*, May 1905, 23–28.
[112] *Uladh*, November 1904, 3. [113] *Uladh*, February 1905, 1–2.
[114] See John Hewitt, '"The Northern Athens" and after', in J. C. Beckett et al., *Belfast: The making of a city* (Belfast, 1988), 71–82.

philistinism.[115] Bigger, an optimistic man, perceived the revival of this tradition in Belfast.

The polarisation of Irish public life into two separate camps was a matter of great concern to these Ulster Protestant nationalists. But it fell to a southern Protestant, Stephen Gwynn, to articulate apprehension at a separation – if only cultural – from the rest of the country. Typically, he began with reference to Ulster's history as the province that prior to the Cromwellian plantation gave greatest resistance to English rule, before recalling Ulster's historic liberalism and radicalism which spawned the Dungannon Convention and United Irishmen.[116] However, betraying a Protestant nationalist apprehension at the direction politics in the province was taking, Gwynn sought to simultaneously downgrade the city:

Taking Belfast on its merits, as a commercial centre, it might well rank ... with second rate English towns – below Newcastle, probably, but above Wigan and the like ... Belfast is encouraged to believe itself a place much in advance of Dublin. Yet, as a matter of fact, Dublin is a metropolis, and Belfast is a provincial town of little interest, except for those who wish to study almost extinct types of religious bigotry.[117]

It is clear that by 1905 the prospect of partition had come to perturb the likes of Gwynn:

if Ulster, or even Belfast, is finally divorced in spirit from Ireland, it is a pity of pities; for Ireland, wanting the hand of the North, will go maimed; but Belfast divorced from Ireland will be squalid, undignified and contemptible.[118]

One motivation for Hobson and his associates in launching *Uladh* was to create an organ that would encourage young writers to remain in Belfast, and prevent their migration elsewhere due to economic circumstance and hostility to their political beliefs. As an editorial put it, 'We have most to fear for the young men in that, if they do not find an outlet in Ulster, they will either go away, or gravitate upon the sloblands of American or English magazine work.'[119] Ironically, one significant figure given voice in *Uladh* was the journalist and essayist Robert Lynd, a man who had already migrated to those very sloblands. Lynd was born in Belfast in 1879, the son of R. J. Lynd, a liberal unionist Presbyterian minister who served as moderator of the church in 1888.[120] As with many Presbyterian intellectuals of his generation, Robert Lynd differed politically from his father. Coming from a long line of Presbyterian

---

[115] *Uladh*, November 1904, 11–12. See also *Uladh*, February 1905, 26–28.
[116] *Uladh*, February 1905, 9–12.   [117] *Uladh*, February 1905, 11.
[118] *Uladh*, February 1905, 12.   [119] *Uladh*, November 1904, 2.
[120] *Belfast News-Letter*, 19 November 1906.

ministers, he took great pride in his forbears, including one clergyman who learned Irish to preach to Ulster peasants (probably to bring about their conversion to Protestantism), and another who it was claimed hid a runaway slave in his manse.[121]

Concern for the plight of the poor caused Lynd's conversion to socialism while an undergraduate at Queen's College Belfast.[122] His conversion to nationalism came later. In 1901 he moved to England, finding work as a journalist in London:

I had come to England ... believing in my simplicity that the English spent their days and nights thinking out plans for the welfare of Ireland – for improving the land system and the education system, and for draining the regions of the Bann and the Barrow. To my surprise I found that the English were a very practical people who had enough problems of their own to solve without spending sleepless nights over the drainage of the Bann. Most of them seemed to look on the Irish as a pampered people living largely at the expense of the English taxpayer. Finding that they regarded Ireland mainly as a nuisance, I concluded ... that it would be better for the country to be governed by people who were, at least, interested in it.[123]

All but one of Lynd's six siblings became republicans too. Only Laura, the eldest of the family, remained a unionist, but, she insisted, a liberal unionist. This caused ructions in the Lynd household: when the Rev. Lynd came into the living-room, conversation, which was generally about Irish politics or culture, would cease.[124] Working as a journalist in London, Robert Lynd threw himself into Irish political and cultural associations, which would become increasingly fashionable as the decade continued. In 1901 he joined with Paul Henry, an old friend from the Royal Belfast Academical Institution, as well as Edwin, George, and Norman Morrow to form a literary club in London. He also learned Irish, and became a Gaelic League teacher. Among his pupils were fellow Protestants with Ulster roots Roger Casement and Aodh de Blacam.[125]

Writing as Roibéard Ó Floinn, Lynd was a prominent contributor to *Uladh*. His articles provide an insight into the anxieties of Ulster Protestant nationalists. One article, 'Ancestor-Worship in Ulster', was a plea for young Protestants to be unafraid of differing politically from their elders: 'To be a Unionist or a Home Ruler, or anything else, merely because one's father was this ... is to have lost caste as a human being, and to have

[121] *II*, 21 April 1979.
[122] Robert Lynd, *Galway of the races: selected essays* (Sean McMahon, ed.) (Dublin, 1990), 9–10.
[123] Robert Lynd, *I tremble to think* (London, 1936), 62.
[124] Lynd, *Galway of the races*, 11; *II*, 21 April 1979.
[125] Lynd, *Galway of the races*, 18–19; *II*, 21 April 1979.

sunk into the condition of a primitive machine.' This, Lynd argued, had seen Ulster reduced to an 'intellectual Sahara' or 'spiritual wilderness'. In reference to the employment difficulties experienced by Protestants who held unpopular political views, he spoke from experience:

Everybody who aims at getting a 'job' discovers that the easiest way to success lies in agreeing with the numerous catchwords of his father and his father's friends. If one has opinions of one's own, one finds that it pays best to keep them quiet. We fear the bigotry of our neighbours, and, with a cynical sigh, resolve to conform.[126]

As we will see in the next section, the need to get a 'job' would eventually see substantial numbers of Protestant nationalists leave the province.

By the middle of the first decade of the twentieth century, the slow process of winning converts by such figures as Bigger, Milligan, and Hobson had yielded results, and Belfast had become the centre of a vibrant circle of separatists. The mainstay of this group was that 'rubicund genial pleasant man' F. J. Bigger.[127] Ardrigh, Bigger's comfortable Belfast residence, became the focal point for informal meetings of cultural and political nationalists, both Protestant and Catholic. Unionists, even Orangemen, were welcome. Groups of thirty or forty gathered in the house for a meal followed by a céilí.[128] Among those who attended these gatherings were Bulmer Hobson, Joseph Campbell, Alice Stopford Green, Herbert Hughes, the Waddells, Roger Casement, and Denis McCullough.

Céilithe are never to everyone's taste, and several participants, despite their commitment to Bigger's cultural project, must have stifled a smile at their host's eccentricities. Casement wrote that 'those gatherings are amusing but one does not want too many of them'.[129] By 1911 he and Alice Stopford Green had developed their own code for some of Bigger's more pretentious projects:

I long to hear of your pilgrimage to Ardglass and what came of it. Are you now the woman of three (or more) cows and a Golf Links and an Irish Stronghold? Will you henceforth quarter the Red Hand – or do you propose quartering Mr Bigger? – without a Battleaxe and a Gallowglass – impossible![130]

---

[126] *Uladh*, May 1905, 9, 11.
[127] UCD, McC, P120/34 (2), transcript of interview with Denis McCullough for Ulster Television, 8 September 1964.
[128] F. X. Martin (ed.), *Leaders and men of the Easter Rising: Dublin 1916* (Dublin, 1967), 99.
[129] NLI, Roger Casement additional papers, MS 36, 204/1, Roger Casement to Alice Stopford Green, 8 September 1906.
[130] NLI, Casement additional papers, MS 36, 204/1, Roger Casement to Alice Stopford Green, 24 May 1911. Cf. Shane Leslie, *The film of memory* (London, 1938), 384–385.

Feis na nGleann ('The Glens Feis') was central to this group's endeav-
ours. This Gaelic cultural festival, first held in 1904, was held in the
Glens of Antrim, a district where the Irish language still endured. The
inaugural feis saw the participation of several women from prominent
gentry families in the locality, including Ada McNeill, Rose Young, and
Margaret Dobbs. Others who would be associated with the feis include
Roger Casement, F. J. Bigger, and Joseph Campbell.[131]

Queen's College was not immune to the impact of the nationalist
revival. The Rev. Thomas M. Johnstone, later Presbyterian moderator,
described a heady nationalism among undergraduates. He remembered
students as being 'proud to count ourselves Irish, and loved to burn
incense on the altar of patriotism'.[132] In 1906 Cumann Gaedhealach
an Cólaiste (the College Gaelic Society) was founded.[133] The creation of
such a society carried a political risk; an official college publication
stated: 'The Society is strictly non-political and non-sectarian. Any
member introducing a religious or political subject at any of its meetings
shall cease to be a member.'[134] The Gaelic Society exhibited its non-
political and non-sectarian nature through a tactful choice of patrons: the
college president the Rev. Thomas Hamilton, and Lord Castletown, a
colourful figure who combined support for home rule with leadership of
the Pan-Celticists. The group, which was largely Protestant in membership, was associated with the ULT: it put on the first productions of
Mayne's *The Turn of the Road* and Parkhill's *The Pagan*.

The most significant figure to join the Gaelic Society was Mabel
McConnell (1884–1958).[135] She was from a unionist upper-middle-class
Belfast Presbyterian family; her father, John McConnell, was managing
director of the Royal Irish Distillery, which was owned by James Craig
Sr, father of Ulster unionist politician James Craig. While a Queen's
College Belfast undergraduate, she joined the College Gaelic Society,
serving on its committee from 1906 to 1907, and took to calling herself
Meadhbh Ní Chonaill.[136] Her elder sister Lizzie – or Éilís – also became

---

[131] See Eamon Phoenix et al. (eds.), *Feis na nGleann: a century of Gaelic culture in the Antrim Glens* (Belfast, 2005).

[132] Thomas M. Johnstone, *The vintage of memory* (Belfast, 1943), 64.

[133] T. W. Moody and J. C. Beckett, *Queen's, Belfast, 1845–1949: the history of a university*, Vol. I (London, 1959), 370–371. See also *The Republic*, 16 May 1907.

[134] [Anonymous] *The book of the fete: Queen's College, Belfast: May 29, 30, 31st and June 1st 1907* (Belfast, 1907).

[135] See Conor Morrissey, '"Much the more political of the two": Mabel FitzGerald and the Irish Revolution', *Irish Studies Review*, Vol. 24, Issue 3 (2016), 291–310.

[136] [Anonymous], *The book of the fete*, 108; UCD, Desmond FitzGerald papers, MS p80/ 1477 (1), Membership booklet for the College Gaelic Society, 1905–06, belonging to

an Irish-language enthusiast.[137] The McConnell sisters may have been influenced towards nationalism by their close friendship with Robert Lynd. Two of his republican sisters, Dorothy and Lucy, were Mabel McConnell's close friends, and served with her on the College Gaelic Society's committee.[138] Éilís McConnell, though a language activist, retained her family's political unionism.[139] Mabel by contrast became a political as well as cultural radical: in Garret FitzGerald's words, 'By the time she left Queen's she seems to have become a republican, suffragette and socialist – but mainly the first.'[140] In 1908 McConnell moved to London, where, as we will see, she could continue her activism within the Irish-Ireland milieu.

Hobson and the Dungannon Clubs

Besides his project of reviving the Ulster IRB alongside McCullough and others, in 1905 Hobson founded yet another organisation, the Dungannon Clubs. Hobson was a convinced republican; he deemed Griffith's dual-monarchy concept too limited, and its emphasis on the restoration of the constitution of 1782 as arcane.[141] Furthermore, Hobson and McCullough had become dissatisfied with the levels of nationalist fervour exhibited by Cumann na nGaedheal and the National Council.[142] The new group's title recalled the Dungannon Convention of 1782, when delegates of Volunteers met in that town's Presbyterian church, and in the presence of Catholics, declared Ireland's right to legislative independence, as well as liberty of religion. The choice of name underscored one of the principal functions of the Dungannon Clubs: the recruitment of Protestants into the nationalist movement. The Club's manifesto, published in August 1905, while avoiding express reference to a republic, stated that it sought to 'regain the political independence of the country' through a programme of passive resistance. Religious solidarity was also put to the fore: 'The Ireland we seek to build is not for the Catholic or for the Protestant, but an Ireland for every Irishman,

---

Mabel McConnell; UCD, FitzGerald papers, MS 1477 (2) Membership booklet for the College Gaelic Society, 1906–07, belonging to Mabel McConnell.

[137] Correspondence with Dr Jennifer FitzGerald, in possession of the author.

[138] Jennifer FitzGerald papers, Garret FitzGerald, 'Desmond – and Mabel – FitzGerald'; [anonymous], *The book of the fete*, 108.

[139] Eilis N. Vesey [Lizzie N. McConnell], 'Letters from old Victorians', *The Victorian*, 8 (June 1923), 30–33.

[140] Jennifer FitzGerald papers, Garret FitzGerald, extract from 'Notes on the McConnell Family Tree' (1995, 1997, 2001), unpublished.

[141] Hobson, *Ireland yesterday and tomorrow*, 19–20.

[142] Hay, *Bulmer Hobson*, 46; BMH WS 82, Bulmer Hobson.

irrespective of his creed or class.'[143] In this endeavour Hobson and McCullough could call upon some influential patrons, most likely Bigger and Casement. Patrick McCartan stated: 'He has many influential Prot-estants at his back who yet remain in the dark.'[144]

The surviving minute book of the parent club, Belfast Club No. 1, indicates that it had sixty-two members, all of them men.[145] Members were young – the average age in 1905 was twenty-seven – and it included clerks, mechanics, carpenters, and art students. This was a strongly urban body: about 80 per cent of members resided in Belfast City in either 1901 or 1911. Hobson had limited success in attracting Protestants. Of the thirty-nine members whose denomination has been ascertained, fifteen, or about 40 per cent of total, were Protestants: there were three Episcopalians, three Methodists, two Presbyterians, one Quaker, one Non-subscribing Presbyterian, and five Protestants whose denomination is undetermined. Among the Protestants attracted to the club were Wallace and Herbert Jamison, the sons of the Methodist minister in Carrickfergus, County Antrim, as well as Séan Lester and Ernest Blythe.

One recruit of whom Hobson was proud was Richard Lyttle, a Non-subscribing Presbyterian minister. Hobson described him as 'a true spiritual descendent of those Protestant clergyman who worked and fought with the United Irishmen in 1798'. As with McCullough, Milligan, and others, Hobson discerned the latent spirit of rebellion among the Presbyterians of Ulster, which only required a suitable figure to harness this force. Hobson deeply regretted Lyttle's early death in 1905, seeing him as a lost leader:

In Down, as in Antrim, the memory of the United Irishmen had not died out, and many of the older generation of farmers, grandsons of men who had fought at Ballinahinch and Antrim, were deeply, if mostly secretly, in sympathy with nationalist feeling. Lyttle was the natural leader of these men. He had great charm of manner, combined with ability and energy of a high order ... With his help we could have done a great deal to bring about a Union in Ulster on the same lines as the ... United Irishmen ... Had he lived the modern history of Ireland could have been very different.[146]

It appears that Hobson's Catholic associates were almost as keen on this project as Hobson was; Joe McGarrity wrote at the time of the

---

[143] Hobson, *Ireland yesterday and tomorrow*, appendix 1, 98.

[144] NLI, McGarrity papers, MS 17,457 (2), Patrick McCartan to Joseph McGarrity, 23 December 1905.

[145] NLI, Bulmer Hobson papers, MS 12,175, minute book of the Dungannon Club.

[146] Hobson, *Ireland yesterday and tomorrow*, 24.

founding of the Clubs: 'If [Hobson] can blend the Orange and Green all will be well.'[147]

As the Clubs spread they followed a loose structure, with no over-arching leadership, but looked to Belfast Club No. 1, which had McCullough as secretary and Hobson as president, as the centre of the organisation.[148] Hobson was aided by Patrick McCartan, a medical student who founded a Dublin students' branch of the Clubs, and Sean McDermott, who became a full-time organiser, setting up branches throughout Ulster.[149] The programme of the Dungannon Clubs, with its policy of passive resistance to British rule and emphasis on developing Irish industry, resembled Griffith's Sinn Féin policy, without the dual-monarchy aspect. Marnie Hay stresses the rivalry that existed between Griffith and Hobson.[150] It is likely that to some extent the Clubs were an attempt to wrestle leadership of the advanced movement from Griffith and a Dublin set and towards Hobson and Ulster. Certainly the latter's ambition for the Clubs was enormous, with plans made to set up com-mittees that would shadow government departments: 'He expects it to do the functions of a National Government.'[151] However, nothing would come of this plan; despite the grandeur of Hobson's vision, it appears the Clubs mainly functioned as literary societies. Little, in fact, separated the Clubs from the nationalist literary and debating societies which proliferated in this era, and often operated as IRB fronts. The Clubs enjoyed modest growth. Besides McCartan's student club in Dublin, at least two more branches were formed in Belfast, as well as a Derry branch and several in Tyrone. Clubs were founded in Newcastle-upon-Tyne and Glasgow, and Robert Lynd, Paul Henry, George Gavan Duffy and P. S. O'Hegarty set one up in London.[152]

From December 1906 to May 1907 the Clubs published a newspaper, *The Republic*, initially under Hobson's editorship. The title was signifi-cant. It would be wrong to presume that unionists were considered more amenable to a 'softer' constitutional separation, i.e. home rule, than they were to a republic. There was, among IRB sympathisers, an expectation that any Irish republic would be run on secular French or American

---

[147] NLI, McGarrity papers, MS 17,458 (1), Joseph McGarrity to Patrick McCartan, 20 November 1905.
[148] Hobson, *Ireland yesterday and tomorrow*, 21.
[149] BMH WS 82, Bulmer Hobson; *The Republic*, 31 January 1907.
[150] Hay, *Bulmer Hobson*, 46. See also BMH WS 915, Denis McCullough.
[151] NLI, McGarrity papers, MS 17,457 (2), Patrick McCartan to Joseph McGarrity, 23 December 1905.
[152] Hay, *Bulmer Hobson*, 49–51; Hobson, *Ireland yesterday and tomorrow*, 21; BMH WS 82, Bulmer Hobson; *The Republic*, 13 December 1906, 10 January 1907.

lines. Protestants, even convinced unionists, frequently stated, if only hypothetically, that a separate republic would be preferable to home rule where the Catholic Church could dominate an Irish Party/Ancient Order of Hibernian–majority parliament. Separatists like Hobson were convinced that Protestants, particularly Orangemen, would be converted to republicanism or nothing at all.[153] Hobson's first editorial asserted: 'An Irish Republic is our aim. We do not ask for it as a concession from England – we take it as a right.' It was hoped that in doing so 'Catholic and Protestant would be shoulder to shoulder comrades as they were a century ago'. The Dungannon Clubs sought 'no compromise with England, no repeal of the Union, no concession of Home Rule or Devolution will satisfy the national aspirations of the Irish people'. Hobson claimed that the younger generation of Protestants were turning to nationalism, and offered an assessment of the political climate that, like the paper's title, suggested anti-clericalism: 'We are convinced that it is not love of England but fear of the Pope that stands between the men of Ulster and their duty to Ireland.'[154]

In February 1907, John Devoy invited Hobson to America to spread the advanced nationalist message.[155] En route, Hobson visited Griffith in Dublin, where he was surprised by the older man's 'hostility and coldness'. Unknown to Hobson, Griffith had already written to Devoy seeking to undertake an American speaking tour himself, and must have felt slighted that the twenty-four-year-old Ulsterman was asked in his stead. Hobson claimed he regretted inadvertently spoiling Griffith's chance of doing so.[156] One reason why Devoy chose to favour the younger man was Hobson's talents as a speaker, warm reports of which had reached America.[157] There was also another reason underpinning the invitation: Hobson's religion.

Hobson's speaking tour was a success. Beginning with addressing a meeting of 2,500 people in New York, he followed with meetings in Brooklyn, Chicago, Cleveland, St. Louis, Boston, Indianapolis, and other cities.[158] The *Gaelic American*'s report of his speech 15 February New York speech makes clear the motivation behind Hobson's invitation:

Practically every active nationalist in New York was there, and there were several who were not active nationalists but who came to listen. Among these were

---

[153] Davis, *Arthur Griffith and non-violent Sinn Fein*, 29. See also *CIG* (editorial), 28 February 1908.
[154] *The Republic*, 13 December 1906.
[155] Hay, *Bulmer Hobson*, 67; F. M. Carroll, *American opinion and the Irish question, 1910–23: a study in opinion and policy* (Dublin, 1978), 9.
[156] Hobson, *Ireland yesterday and tomorrow*, 10. [157] Hay, *Bulmer Hobson*, 66.
[158] Hobson, *Ireland yesterday and tomorrow*, 10; *Gaelic American*, 23 February 1907.

several Orangemen and other Irish Protestants who never attend such gatherings. Their reason for coming was that a young Ulster Protestant was to explain a new movement which has already made some headway among the younger generation of their co-religionists in the Northern Province. They listened attentively while Hobson was speaking and they sometimes applauded, but when it came to the singing of the 'Orange and the Green will carry the day', to the, to them, familiar air of 'The Protestant Boys', their applause was of the most vigorous kind, and there was no mistaking the pleased expression on their faces. It was for such effects as these that Bulmer Hobson was brought here and the result already has justified the invitation. There is a large Irish protestant element in the United States who are now in a receptive frame of mind, and they can be reached only by a man sprung from their own ranks.[159]

Hobson's speeches stressed his view that Catholics and Protestants were becoming politically aligned in Ireland, principally through groups such as the Gaelic League.[160] During his time in America, Clan na Gael organised meetings for Hobson with prominent Irish-American Protestant nationalists, such as Colonel Robert Temple Emmet, the great-grandson of Thomas Addis Emmet, and P. J. Kane, a former Fenian who had become a Presbyterian minister in Philadelphia.[161] The *Gaelic American* reported on the numbers of Protestant Irish-Americans, including Orangemen, who attended his meetings:

It was especially for that kind of work, *which no Catholic could do*, that Mr Hobson was invited to the United States, and it is a source of great satisfaction to know that a good beginning has been made in the work of winning Irish American Protestants to Nationality. They constitute a strong and influential section of the people of the United States, and if any large number of them could be won over ... by an intelligent propaganda, the effect on the younger generation of their co-religionists [in Ulster] would be apparent.[162]

Hobson's tour, and reactions it provoked, demonstrates that by 1907 there was a realisation there was much to be gained from winning Irish-American Protestants to the nationalist cause. This speaking tour foreshadows more organised and better-publicised attempts to win over the same demographic in the 1920s.[163]

Hobson's return to Ireland saw the advanced movement nationally in a state of consolidation, and the Belfast nationalist circle in a state of disintegration. Pressure from London-based activists and wealthy American supporters, who made amalgamation of the advanced organisations a precondition of financial aid, led to the merger of the

---

[159] *Gaelic American,* 23 February 1907.
[160] See, for example, *Gaelic American,* 2 March 1907.
[161] Hobson, *Ireland yesterday and tomorrow,* 11.
[162] *Gaelic American,* 30 March 1907. Emphasis added.   [163] See Chapter 6.

Dungannon Clubs and Cumann na nGaedheal in April 1907 to form the Sinn Féin League, which itself merged with the National Council in late August of that year to form a body known simply as Sinn Féin.[164]

If the broader advanced movement was coming together, Belfast nationalism was in decline. In May 1907 financial difficulties saw *The Republic* merged with the Dublin-based *Peasant*, thus extinguishing a voice of northern advanced nationalism.[165] Money trouble had earlier forced *Uladh* to close. With Hobson moving to Dublin in 1908 to take up a position with the *Peasant*, Ulster advanced nationalism lost its most capable leader. Sean McDermott moved south too, becoming a Sinn Féin organiser. Patrick McCartan remained in Dublin and was elected to Dublin Corporation.

In his recollections Denis McCullough stressed how young nationalists found it difficult to find work in Belfast, often due to blacklisting by the Royal Irish Constabulary (RIC). Furthermore, Ulster Protestants who held any sort of nationalist views found themselves labelled 'rotten Protestants' or 'rotten Prods' by their co-religionists, and could find themselves targets of discrimination.[166] Economic necessity also led many talented people to emigrate.[167] When James Winder Good's employers became aware of his politics, he was shunned by unionist newspapers in Belfast and forced to move to Dublin. Joseph Campbell moved to London in 1906. Samuel Waddell took a job with the Land Commission in the south. David Parkhill appears to have left Belfast in about 1907. Bulmer Hobson moved to Dublin in 1908. Both Herbert Hughes and Paul Henry lived in London. As we have seen, Mabel McConnell moved to London in 1908, Lindsay Crawford moved to Canada in 1910, and Robert Lynd had been working in England since 1901. The ULT was badly impacted by the loss of so much of the nationalist intelligentsia. Forrest Reid remembered that, without any infusion of fresh blood, 'a certain timidity, a reluctance to try experiments' crept in.[168] F. J. Bigger remained in Belfast, but many of those who enlivened evenings in Ardrigh did not. The decline of the ULT is symptomatic of the decline of Protestant nationalist activism in Belfast; the initiative would now move to Dublin and the south.

---

[164] Davis, *Arthur Griffith and non-violent Sinn Fein*, ch. 2.

[165] *The Republic*, 16 May 1916.

[166] For reference to 'Rotten Protestants', see, for example, *UG*, 10 February 1912; *FJ*, 4 April, 3 November 1917; Gwynn, *Experiences*, 277.

[167] UCD, McC, P120/34 (2), transcript of interview of Denis McCullough, for Ulster Television, 8 September 1964.

[168] London *Times*, 5 December 1922.

3   Converts, c. 1910–1916

Introduction

In the first decades of the twentieth century, Ireland was a country where the lines of demarcation between religious confession and political affiliation were closely drawn. In a time when most Protestants were unionists and most Catholics were nationalists, religious and political identity converged, and converts – or defectors – to the rival group could expect excoriation. This chapter will take a close look at the theme of conversion, both political and religious. Arthur Griffith's Sinn Féin loudly proclaimed its vision of a non-sectarian nationalist movement. But how successful was this party at recruiting Protestants? Some of those Protestants who did convert to nationalism proclaimed their new allegiance in exaggerated 'Gaelic' form; these, usually upper-class figures, nicknamed 'synthetic Gaels' will be assessed. During this period a large number of Protestant women joined the advanced nationalist movement. What was their background? And what were their formative influences? The last section will discuss religious conversion and spiritualism. How likely were Protestant nationalists to convert to Catholicism? Why did they do so? What was the attitude of those who remained Protestant to the Catholic Church? And finally, why did some Protestant nationalists adopt spiritualist, theosophist, or occultist beliefs?

Protestants and Sinn Féin, c. 1910–1916

By 1910 Sinn Féin was an electorally negligible, but intellectually vibrant organisation. Under Arthur Griffith's leadership the party continued to advocate dual monarchy, in the hope that this policy would encourage Protestants and unionists to join the movement. Ironically, many of those who were least comfortable with this policy, and advocated a republic, such as Bulmer Hobson and Alice Milligan, were themselves Protestant.[1]

---

[1] For Milligan's republicanism, see UCD, Terence MacSwiney papers, P48c/100, Diary of Terence MacSwiney, 22 April 1905.

Like John O'Leary in earlier decades, Griffith continued to cultivate Protestants, put great emphasis on the conversion of Ulster to nationalism, and surround himself with radical Protestant intellectuals. There was, indeed, a sense that Griffith's movement, in avoiding the Ancient Order of Hibernian (AOH)–inspired clericalism that was so prevalent in the Irish Party, stood a good chance of gaining substantial numbers of Protestant members. Several unsubstantiated reports from Ulster claimed that serving Orangemen had joined the organisation.[2] The dual effect of Irish Party clericalism and Sinn Féin cultivation was not lost on one observer. Rosamond Stephen wrote her mother: 'while the priests are holding out their hands to the powers that be, Sinn Féin ... are holding out theirs to the Protestants. They make up to them incessantly in countless little ways.'[3] Lindsay Crawford could even make the unlikely claim to the Young Ireland Branch of the United Irish League (UIL) that 'there was no party to which the Protestants of Ulster tended more than to the party of Sinn Féin'.[4] Sinn Féiners liked to publicly identify Protestants among their number. R. B. McDowell, writing of Harry Nicholls (1889–1975), an Episcopalian TCD graduate and party member, claims that he

was often, at a Sinn Féin meeting, the embarrassed cynosure of all eyes when an orator, dwelling on how the movement embraced men of all creeds and classes, would declaim, 'And we have on the platform a Protestant from Trinity College.'[5]

One prominent figure who believed Sinn Féin did not do enough to entice Protestants was the Rev. James Hannay. An associate and critical friend of Sinn Féin, rather than a member, as the sole Anglican clergyman to publicly identify with the movement his words carried weight. He emphasised the impact the Ne Temere papal decree had on Protestant opinion, especially in Ulster, and hoped Sinn Féin would argue against it.[6] Ne Temere, which was promulgated by Pius X in 1907, and came into effect the following year, caused outrage in Protestant Ireland. The decree invalidated religiously mixed marriages unless conducted by a Catholic priest, and led to a requirement that the children of such unions

[2] *Peasant*, 27 April 1907; *UG*, 11 May 1907.
[3] RCBL, Rosamond Stephen Papers, Rosamond Stephen to her mother, 22 June 1907. For Stephen, see Chapter 6.
[4] *Northern Whig*, 15 February 1909.
[5] R. B. McDowell, *Crisis and decline: the fate of the southern unionists* (Dublin, 1997), 208. For Nicholls and his wife, Kathleen Emerson, an Episcopalian suffragist and nationalist, see Martin Maguire, 'Harry Nicholls and Kathleen Emerson: Protestant rebels', *Studia Hibernica*, No. 35, (2008–2009), 147–166.
[6] *Sinn Féin*, 18 March 1911.

would be raised Catholic.[7] Another well-known Protestant Sinn Féiner, the Episcopalian playwright St John Ervine, stressed the importance of secular education, and argued against clerical interference in schools.[8] Griffith failed to understand these concerns. He dismissed the importance of Ne Temere, stating that it was a religious rather than civil matter, and therefore irrelevant to his party.[9] This was a mistake: the Irish Party had incurred the wrath of Protestant church leaders for failing to denounce the measure; an intervention by Sinn Féin may have demonstrated to wavering Protestants that one strand of Irish nationalism was willing to criticise edicts from Rome, and understood the concerns of the minority.

It was not only the Protestant intellectual elite who despaired of the priests. Éamonn Tomas, an Episcopalian Sinn Féin supporter from Ballina, County Mayo, complained to Desmond FitzGerald about corrupt and drunken local priests preventing inter-religious collaboration on local enterprises:

I think you know me well enough to understand that I am not moved by Protestant spite in saying this. I am far more in sympathy in every way with the Catholic than with the Protestant. But I cannot conceal from myself that the priests are too often anti-national in everything but platform oratory. And where the priests lead the people, willingly or unwillingly follow ... Who is the man of influence in Ireland today? The priest, the gombeen man, the local boss. What are their ideals? Self-interest.[10]

A more robust response from Griffith might have seen a greater number of Protestants like Tomas join Sinn Féin. Hannay felt Griffith's position was tactical. He wrote to Lindsay Crawford stating that he believed Griffith was as 'able to see the danger' of 'priestly tyranny' 'as clearly as we do' but was circumscribed by not wanting to be condemned from the altar.[11] Griffith was unwilling to denounce the priests, but he was capable of making an attack on one of their principal standard-bearers, the AOH, which had the welcome by-product of attacking the Irish Party by

[7] Eoin de Bhaldraithe, 'Mixed marriages and Irish politics: the effect of "Ne Temere"', *Studies: An Irish Quarterly Review*, Vol. 77, No. 307 (Autumn, 1988), 289.
[8] St John G. Ervine, *Sir Edward Carson and the Ulster movement* (Dublin and London, 1915), 112–115.
[9] *Sinn Féin*, 11 February 1911.
[10] UCD, FitzGerald papers, P80/1520, Éamonn Tomas to Desmond FitzGerald. Tomas is probably Edwin Thomas, who lists himself as a farmer and JP in the 1911 census, an Anglican, then resident at Newport, Co. Mayo.
[11] NLI, Crawford papers, MS 11,415, Rev. James Owen Hannay to Lindsay Crawford, 29 May 1905.

extension. He wrote that the AOH had 'given the Orangeman the only explanation for their existence. Nothing [is] more calculated to defeat Home Rule than this recrudesce of sectarianism in politics.'[12]

During this period, London, where several of its Protestant supporters were based, became a centre for Sinn Féin activity. Foremost among these was Robert Lynd, who by 1910 was employed with the London *Daily News*, but who continued to write on Irish topics. In 1909 he married the English-born poet, critic, and novelist Sylvia Dryhurst (1888–1952). Dryhurst supported Lynd's politics, and the couple became leaders of the London Irish-Ireland set. Some of the strongest exponents of these ideals had no, or only a tenuous Irish connection. Arthur Ransome recalled:

Mrs [Nannie] Dryhurst and her two daughters, Norah and Sylvia, were passionately Irish ... Mrs Dryhurst had a 'day' ... and on that day her drawing-room was full of young people who, if not Irish, at least had no objection to Home Rule. There were always more of us than there were chairs, and poets used to read their poems aloud while we sat on the floor. At about six o'clock Mr [Alfred] Dryhurst, who had never been quite forgiven for being English, used to come home ... open the drawing-room door an inch or two, enough to look in on the Irishry, and disappear again at once.[13]

London was home to much Irish-Ireland activism, centred on private homes, as well as the Irish Literary Society, the Gaelic League, and GAA. Besides T. W. Rolleston, Alice Stopford Green and W. B. Yeats, a number of younger figures were active. Mabel McConnell, who continued her nationalist activism while living in London studying and spending periods as secretary to George Moore and George Bernard Shaw, married Desmond FitzGerald, an English-born Catholic poet, in 1911. FitzGerald, although a nationalist, found McConnell's views too extreme, which was a source of friction during their courtship, as it later would be throughout their marriage.[14] (One of the children of their union was Garret FitzGerald, the future Taoiseach.) This was a period when some young Protestant women – frequently converts to nationalism – make marriages to older Catholic nationalists. For example, Nancy

---

[12] *Gaelic American*, 26 October 1912.

[13] Arthur Ransome, quoted in Lynd, *Galway of the races*, 26. Sylvia Dryhurst's mother, Nannie Dryhurst, née Robinson, was a Dublin-born suffragist and anarchist, and among the models for Ann Whitefield in George Bernard Shaw's *Man and superman*: Lynd, *Galway of the races*, 25. Alfred Robert 'Roy' Dryhurst, a Fabian, worked as an assistant keeper in the British Museum.

[14] UCD, FitzGerald papers, P80/1498 (undated, 1910), Desmond FitzGerald to Mabel McConnell.

Maude, Anglican, upper-class, and English, made an ultimately disastrous marriage to Joseph Campbell in 1911.[15]

One prominent London Sinn Féiner was Michael Collins, then employed in the Post Office. At meetings of the Irish Literary Society, Collins – always less reverential towards Protestant nationalists than many of his older associates – would invariably greet Robert Lynd with the words, 'And how is the non-conformist conscience today?' He was equally flippant with Sam Maguire (1877–1927). Maguire, a Cork-born Anglican, combined prominence in the London GAA with membership of the IRB. Collins liked to square up to Maguire, saying, 'You bloody South of Ireland Protestant', allegedly to the latter's amusement.[16]

If the Boer War had a broadly unifying effect, drawing Protestants closer to the nationalist movement, and inducing some to adopt more radical positions, the ultimate impact of the Great War was defection and disengagement. During the four years of the conflict, residual affection for the British connection materialised among a number of prominent Protestant nationalists, leading to their breach with the fiercely anti-war advanced movement. The war placed great strain on Griffith's relations with his Protestant associates. The decision of Lynd and Hannay to support the British against Germany prompted a fierce attack by Griffith, who called down fire and brimstone on Sinn Féin's two principal Protestant supporters. He thought the apostasy of Lynd

a much smaller literary man than Yeats and a less brilliant one than Hannay, was inevitable. He never realised Irish Nationality or Irish Nationalism though he believed he apprehended both. He was in essence an English philosophical radical ... [and can] ... only think in terms of England.

Griffith believed money was the cause of Hannay's attitude, stating that 'materialism and idealism struggled long for the mastery of the poor Rector of Westport, and there was a time when it seemed the nobler part of the man would conquer'.[17] Here one sees the invective hurled against T. W. Rolleston for supporting the Boer War used against two new heretics a decade and a half later.[18] Griffith used such criticism as a weapon *pour encourager les autres*, although at the cost of ensuring the reprobates' departure from the movement. Richard Davis has ascribed Lynd and Hannay's stance to 'a persistence of ancestral loyalties'.[19]

[15] See further discussion below.
[16] Margery Forester, *Michael Collins: the lost leader* (Dublin, 1971), 31. Since 1928, winners of the All-Ireland Senior Football Championship have been awarded the Sam Maguire Cup.
[17] *Nationality*, 19 January 1916.   [18] See Chapter 1.
[19] Davis, 'Ulster Protestants and the Sinn Féin press', 63.

This may have been Griffith's view too, for he wrote, not without sadness, 'It was not in them in the ultimate to become other than they have become.'[20] The loss of its two most promising Protestant supporters represented a blow to Sinn Féin. Without the propagandising and proselytising energy of these two men, the nature of the party underwent a subtle change, which eased its way towards become a largely Catholic movement after 1916.

The 'Synthetic Gael'

Writing in 1922, Warre B. Wells, a waspish and perceptive commentator, described a Dublin social stereotype. These were

comic figures to be seen in Dublin in recent years who were nicknamed by the more irreverent 'synthetic Gaels'. They were people of English extraction who insisted on being more Gaelic than the Gaels themselves. The mark of them was that they always wore a kilt and habitually murdered Gaelic with an Oxford accent.[21]

Another observer, Ernest A. Boyd, the critic and journalist, was even more caustic about these English-born nationalists:

He is unmistakeably a synthetic Gael. His kilt and Oxford accent proclaim it. Not that the mere Irishman, speaking English as usual, is permitted to judge this accent in the mutual exchange of their common tongue, for he speaks only Irish … In [his] onslaught upon the speech of the Gael one perceives something of the spirit which has made England what she is. The imported Gael is truly a boy of the bulldog breed. His not to reason why, his but to speak, or die, when he finds this new world to conquer.[22]

This section assesses 'synthetic Gaels', the usually English-born, Protestant, upper-class figures whose efforts to cast off their old identity and adopt Gaelic manners and customs led them to extremes. Although Irish-Irelanders of whatever background frequently adopted Gaelic names and national dress, an element of over-compensation can be discerned in synthetic Gaelic attempts to fit in, which was frequently highlighted by contemporaries. To some nationalist critics, figures such as Cesca Chenevix Trench, Albinia Brodrick, or Claude Chavasse were merely comic characters, whose efforts to appear more Irish than the Irish themselves engendered the opposite effect. However, as Ernest A. Boyd suggests, others viewed these figures as dangerous: the

[20] *Nationality*, 19 January 1916.
[21] Warre B. Wells, *Irish indiscretions* (London, 1923), 122.
[22] *Irish Statesman*, 20 March 1920.

Englishman still on a colonising mission, an unwanted intruder, adopting a synthetically Gaelic appearance to hide his true intent.

James Joyce may have tended towards the latter interpretation. Haines, a character in *Ulysses*, is Joyce's parody of the synthetic Gael. An unwittingly condescending English folklore student, Haines is Buck Mulligan's guest in the Martello Tower, alongside a disapproving Stephen Dedalus. Although legitimately curious about Ireland, Haines is heavy-handed and lacks any real understanding of the country. On meeting an elderly milkmaid, he addresses her in Irish; having originally mistaken his language for French, she responds, 'I don't speak the [Irish] language myself. I'm told it's a grand language by them that knows.'[23] Aaron Kelly argues that Haines is seen by Joyce as a cultural imperialist, the Irish language simply 'another of his accumulated cultural treasures while simultaneously being denied any living currency among the Irish people themselves'.[24]

Most critics accept that the Haines was modelled on Dermot (or Samuel) Chenevix Trench (1881–1909).[25] Trench, who was born in England, came from a well-known clerical and military family: his grandfather, Richard Chenevix Trench, was Church of Ireland archbishop of Dublin, and his father, Major-General Frederick Chenevix Trench, enjoyed a distinguished career in the army. Samuel Trench joined the Gaelic Society at Oxford, becoming a fluent speaker and teacher of Irish. Like many Irish-Irelanders, he changed his name to reflect his new cultural allegiance, assuming the additional name Dermot by deed poll, and became known as Diarmuid Trínseach in Gaelic League circles.[26] Dermot Trench stayed with Oliver St John Gogarty and James Joyce in the Martello Tower in September 1904. Joyce, who found Trench's manner alarmingly eccentric, and who detested his accent and attempts to convert him to the Irish-Ireland movement, avenged himself in print.[27]

Dermot Trench was responsible for bringing his cousins Frances Georgiana 'Cesca' Chenevix Trench and Margot Chenevix Trench into the Gaelic League. Cesca Chenevix Trench is a fine example of what

---

[23] James Joyce, *Ulysses*, Bodley Head ed. (1986 [1922]), 12–13.

[24] Aaron Kelly, *Twentieth-century Irish literature* (Basingstoke, 2008), 29.

[25] C. E. F. Trench, 'Dermot Chenevix Trench and Haines of *Ulysses*', *James Joyce Quarterly*, Vol. 13, No. 1 (Fall, 1975), 39–48; Richard Ellmann, *James Joyce: new and revised edition* (Oxford, 1982 [1959]), 172–173.

[26] Pyle (ed.), *Cesca's diary*, 8.

[27] Oliver St John Gogarty, 'James Joyce: a portrait of the artist', in E. H. Mikhail (ed.), *James Joyce: interviews and recollections* (Basingstoke, 1990), 30–31.

R. F. Foster has called 'those Ascendancy types whose insecurity drove them to extremes of identification'.[28] Adopting the name Sadhbh Trinseach, she joined the Gaelic League in 1908, becoming a passionate Irish-speaker, as well as a member of Sinn Féin and later Cumann na mBan. A talented artist, who studied in Paris from 1912 to 1914, she produced artwork for the nationalist movement.[29] As with so many young Gaelic Leaguers, her allegiance to the Irish-Ireland ideal was strengthened during visits to the west, the effect of which she recorded in her diary:

there was a wonderful view from that spot towards Ireland and Gobacurry, everything bright blue, mauve and green, shining, shining with the sun – Oh Ireland, love of my heart, my soul, my delight, my treasure, my darling![30]

English-born, upper-class, and an Anglican, Cesca frequently worried about her Irish credentials. Her Irish-born suitor, Diarmid Coffey, sought to reassure her, writing:

I have been thinking about what you said about not being really Irish and I am sure you only get that feeling because you have been so long in Sasanac [English] society in India and England and that the moment you land on Irish soil you will feel quite differently about it.[31]

Cesca's fears could even target other Protestant nationalists. On meeting Robert Barton in November 1914, she described him as 'rather a pleasant man ... with the manners and accent of an Englishman to a curious degree, and the appearance of one too, considering he is a nationalist. They are a funny type, these English-Irishmen.'[32]

Cesca had two rival admirers, Diarmid Coffey and Claude Chavasse. Chavasse was the archetypal synthetic Gael. The son of Albert Sydney Chavasse, professor of classical languages in Oxford, Claude Chavasse read Celtic Studies at that university. He learned Irish in the west of Ireland, took to wearing a kilt, and became an accomplished Irish teacher. Chavasse's refusal to speak English was legendary: in February 1916 he was arrested, imprisoned, and fined for insisting on speaking Irish to a policeman.[33] Contemporaries were perplexed by the extremes of his behaviour: one newspaper saw him merely as 'An Englishman ...

---

[28] R. F. Foster, *Paddy and Mr Punch: connections in Irish history and English history* (London, 1993), 14.
[29] R. F. Foster, *Vivid faces: the revolutionary generation in Ireland, 1890–1923* (London, 2014), 429–430.
[30] Pyle (ed.), *Cesca's diary*, 35.   [31] Foster, *Vivid faces*, 53.
[32] Pyle (ed.), *Cesca's diary*, 174.   [33] *Kerry News*, 16, 25 February 1916.

masquerading as an Irishman'.[34] Diarmid Coffey, by contrast, was more level-headed. A well-liked barrister and writer, from a culturally well-connected family, Coffey had been baptised Catholic but raised Protestant. He held Sinn Féin sympathies and served on the Irish Volunteer staff; however, his views were more moderate than those of Cesca. As with Mabel and Desmond FitzGerald, politics played a key role in their courtship, with Cesca frequently worrying that Coffey was not sufficiently radical.[35] Coffey eventually won Cesca's hand, and they were married in April 1918. Their happiness did not last long: Cesca died in the influenza pandemic on 30 October of that year. This was not the only tragedy to befall this set. Following unrequited love for a fellow Gaelic Leaguer (who has been identified as Mary Spring Rice), Dermot Trench shot himself in 1909.[36]

Few synthetic Gaels put on so ostentatious a display as William Gibson, 2nd Baron Ashbourne (Liam Mac Giolla Bhríde). The son of a Conservative lord chancellor of Ireland, he converted to Catholicism in Oxford, and joined the London branch of the Gaelic League, becoming a fluent and highly enthusiastic Irish speaker. His appearance attracted comment: a green kilt, green stockings, and long cloak, buckled with a large brooch. Famously, he addressed the Lords in Irish in 1918. Stories of Lord Ashbourne's eccentricity are legion. He once met Diarmid Coffey on a train, while both were in the midst of the Howth gun-running conspiracy. Coffey recalled that

the 3 o'clock train from Dublin came in. On it was ... Lord Ashbourne ... a Gaelic enthusiast and one of the few Irishmen to wear a kilt. He started a conversation on the sound of the letter 'm' in the Irish word *lámh* [hand], but soon began to make cryptic remarks about my journey which made me a bit uneasy as to how many people knew what we were up to. I found this conversation embarrassing and was glad when he left.[37]

Eccentricity ran in the Gibson family. His sister Violet Gibson, who shared his nationalist views, famously shot Benito Mussolini in Rome in April 1926, causing the Italian dictator light injuries. She was thereafter deported to Britain, where she was interned for the remainder of her life in a mental asylum.[38]

What motivated these individuals? As has been previously stated, Protestant nationalists of all varieties were often strangely unreflective.

---

[34] *Nationalist and Leinster Times*, 13 May 1916.
[35] Pyle (ed.), *Cesca's diary*, 117, 133, 137.
[36] Trench, 'Dermot Chenevix Trench and Haines of *Ulysses*', 45.
[37] Diarmid Coffey, quoted in F. X. Martin (ed.), *The Howth gun-running and the Kilcoole gun-running, 1914: recollections and documents* (Dublin, 1964), 117.
[38] See Frances Stonor Saunders, *The woman who shot Mussolini* (London, 2011).

However, the diary of Nancy Campbell (née Maude) offers insights into the political development of an English-born, upper-class woman who converted to Irish nationalism. Maude (b. 1886), was born in England, the daughter of Colonel Aubrey Maude of the Cameronian Highlanders, whose father had been Crown equerry to Queen Victoria. A branch of the Maudes were landowners in Tipperary, although she grew prouder of her distant kinship with Lord Edward FitzGerald.[39] As a sixteen-year-old Maude recorded conventionally unionist and royalist convictions. However, the following year her frustration at the narrowness of the privileged life she was leading had become apparent:

How anyone can like growing up! Think of settling down and vegetating and growing older & older and be nothing interesting all the time! Do all young people think that they can never be like the rest of the world? ... It would be worse to be contented with a cabbage-like existence than to rebel against it. And yet most people are happy with it! In ten years' time we will be able to look back and see more clearly what we are fitted for. At present there seem precipices all round & one is only safe if time would for a time stand still ... We are educated, for what? Everything we do is a preparation for life. Is life the looking after a 'linen cupboard', the entertaining of a few tiresome friends? What a black gulf the future looks if taken in this light.[40]

A year later Maude, who developed a hatred for what she viewed as the hypocrisy of upper-class Edwardian life, had determined to 'be *myself*, something far different from other people. A nice self, but an original one.'[41] She wrote poetry, entered literary competitions, and became a devotee of George Bernard Shaw. This horrified her father, who stated that young people 'should not have their convictions tampered with' and that Shaw was 'a scoffer, a puller down of sacred things'. This provoked a family row, prompting Maude to write that until recently:

I have been more or less content with the political and social views with which I was brought up. This year it seems as if a thousand new impressions have been collected. I remember how ... I was encouraged to think a pro-Boer a degraded almost devilish thing. Suddenly I see him to be quite a comprehensible one. So with Nationalists, Home Rulers, Socialists. If one does not agree entirely with their propaganda at least one can applaud their ... efforts to help the world. They at least are not selfish & unfeeling.[42]

---

[39] Norah Saunders and A. A. Kelly, *Joseph Campbell: poet and nationalist, 1879–1944* (Dublin, 1988), 48.
[40] TCD, Joseph Campbell papers, MS 10222, Diary of Nancy Campbell, August 1903.
[41] TCD, MS 10222, Diary of Nancy Campbell, 5 August 1904.
[42] TCD, MS 10222, Diary of Nancy Campbell, December 1907.

For Maude, her tenuous Irishness offered an opportunity for reinvention. By 1908 she had become a fervent Irish nationalist, remarking that Ireland had 'awakened a sleeping life', and praising dead Irish patriots, stating that Robert Emmet must have been the 'luckiest man' to be martyred.[43] In 1911 Maude married Joseph Campbell, whom she had met through Sinn Féin circles in London. Her family, who viewed her as a 'self-willed, passionate, changeable, unreasonable child', strongly disapproved of marriage to an impecunious Catholic poet, leading to an estrangement.[44] Raised Anglican, by 1912 Maude seems to have converted to Catholicism, although she appears to have later returned to Protestantism.[45] The Campbells proved temperamentally unsuited – Joseph Campbell had a notably taciturn personality – and their marriage broke up in 1924.

As we have seen, Albinia Brodrick's – or Gobnaít Ní Bhruadair's – conversion to nationalism was largely due to her aversion to Britain's actions during the Boer War.[46] However, another contributory factor was hereditary guilt over her family's history. She explained her distaste at her family's actions as harsh landlords in Cork during the penal era and Famine.[47] (Ironically, her plans to build a hospital at Ballincoona led her to evict a poor local farming family; they would never forgive her.)[48] Brodrick's endorsement of Irish nationalism prompted a breach with her family, in particular her brother St John Brodrick, later 1st earl of Midleton, who led the Irish Unionist Alliance from 1910. Both siblings were acutely embarrassed by the other's politics: she would respond to queries concerning him by saying, 'he used to be my brother'; it was suggested that his sister's activities were a factor in St John Brodrick declining the lord lieutenancy when he was offered it in 1918.[49]

One Protestant-raised and English-born nationalist whose brother did serve as lord lieutenant was Charlotte Despard (1844–1939), the suffragist, socialist, and writer. Sir John French, 1st earl of Ypres, was lord lieutenant between 1918 and 1921, during which time his sister's Sinn Féin activism proved a source of unease.[50] Such close family links with the political enemy led to the sort of esprit de corps that

---

[43] TCD, MS 10222, Diary of Nancy Campbell, 9 September 1908, 28 November 1909.

[44] TCD, MS 10222, Diary of Nancy Campbell, 25 November 1910, 8 May 1911.

[45] TCD, MS 10222, Diary of Nancy Campbell, 22 July 1912.   [46] See Chapter 1.

[47] Hubert Butler, *The sub-prefect should have held his tongue and other essays* (R. F. Foster, ed.) (London, 1990), 9; *The Kerryman*, 2 January 1965.

[48] *Sneem Parish News* (1998), 12–13.

[49] *IT*, 3 August 1968; *The Kerryman*, 7 February 1997; *Manchester Guardian*, 30 April 1918.

[50] UCD, LA18, Máire Comerford Papers, Máire Comerford unpublished memoirs.

frequently characterised relationships between Protestant nationalist women. Brodrick remarked to a friend: 'I saw Mrs Despard when I was last in Dublin, and we sympathised with each other on our respective brothers.'[51] Like Brodrick, Despard framed her decision to convert to nationalism in revulsion at her family history. Growing up in England as a member of a cadet branch of the Frenchs of Roscommon, she was appalled to hear of the Penal Laws: 'When I first heard of them as a young girl, I thought of them as a revelation of evil.'[52] For synthetic Gaels, the decision to convert to nationalism was a private act of insurrection against a system they had grown to despise.

Ordinary Irish people did not take these figures too seriously. Dublin children used to refer to Maud Gonne and Mrs Despard as 'Maud Gonne mad and Mrs Desperate'.[53] More serious, however, was a sense among some nationalists that these figures did not truly belong in the movement, or even that their involvement concealed subversive intent. Kathleen Clarke, the wife of prominent IRB man Thomas Clarke, held such views. Cesca Chenevix Trench, who worked with her in Cumann na mBan, stated that 'Mrs Clarke hates me, I think, because she thinks I'm a spy, very probably, or else because of my accent and general appearance. Anyway she doesn't approve of landlords or their relations!'[54] Cesca remained deferential in the midst of this treatment, recording on another occasion: 'It struck me very much her [Clarke] suspecting [me], she's the first I ever met who did, when so many times they might have. It's *so* reasonable, and *so* rare. But her man was 15 years in prison, a Fenian, so it's natural.'[55] Clarke was likewise ill-disposed to Roger Casement, another landed gentry nationalist, later describing him as the 'aristocratic kind and he assumed that when he went into any movement, *ipso facto*, he was one of our leaders, if not the leader'.[56] Arthur Griffith could also show great hostility to certain newcomers in the movement, among them Jack White. Captain Jack White DSO (1879–1946) was an Antrim-born Boer War veteran, the son of Field-Marshal Sir George Stuart White VC, a soldier and landowner, the 'Hero of Ladysmith'. Although raised Episcopalian, White held religiously idiosyncratic views, and came to

---

[51] NLI, Maurice Moore Papers, MS 10,556 (folder 4), Albinia Brodrick to Lady Sarah Byles, 22 May 1922.
[52] R. M. Fox, *Rebel Irishwomen* (Cork, 1935), 185.
[53] Donncha O Dúlaing, *Voices of Ireland: conversations with Donncha O Dúlaing* (Dublin, 1984), 39.
[54] Pyle (ed.), *Cesca's diary*, 145.   [55] Pyle (ed.), *Cesca's diary*, 146.
[56] Fr Louis O'Kane, interview with Kathleen Clarke, quoted in *IT*, 21 October 2015.

espouse 'Christian communism'.[57] On returning to Ireland from a
period of bohemian wandering in 1912, White, a dashing but eccentric
figure, threw himself into nationalist and socialist politics. Unsurprisingly, White was not always made welcome among nationalists. Of
Arthur Griffith, White recalled: 'I always thought [Griffith] a very
unpleasant little man. To me he seemed to emanate the suspicion of
the professional Gael towards the foreign or Protestant interloper in the
"movement".'[58] As we see throughout this book, Arthur Griffith
devoted much of his career to cultivating nationalist sentiments in
Protestants, but he was selective: his preference was for middle-class
and Ulster Protestants, rather than for more exotic English-born or
upper-class variants. Indeed, it is often impossible to deduce which
aspect of the background of nationalist 'outsiders' – Englishness, Protestantism, or gentle birth – inspired most hostility. For the Catholic
convert Maud Gonne, her Englishness was cited against her by John
MacBride during their 1904–1906 divorce proceedings. In Caoimhe
Nic Dháibhéid's words, 'her English background, English friends and
family, frequent visits to England, and worst of all, her engagement of
an English lawyer … [were] all referred to ad nauseam'.[59] In general,
the tendency for individuals such as Griffith or Clarke to view landed
gentry recruits to nationalism as dilettantes, or worse, probably
hindered their progress. And, as we will see in Chapter 7, to be a
'synthetic Gael' in time of civil war could be dangerous.[60]

Protestant Advanced Nationalist Women

From c. 1910 an unprecedentedly large number of Protestant women
became attracted to the advanced nationalist movement. A total of
ninety-one advanced nationalist women have been identified. 'Advanced
nationalist' is defined here as members or supporters of Sinn Féin,
members of Cumann na mBan, members of the ICA, members of the
Irish Guild of the Church who did not split from the group in 1918,
as well as those who propagandised for a republic through print. Protestant women's reasons for gravitating towards radical nationalist organisations were similar to those of their Catholic counterparts. The Irish

[57] See Leo Keohane, *Captain Jack White: imperialism, anarchism, and the Irish Citizen Army* (Dublin, 2014).
[58] Jack White, *Misfit: a revolutionary life* (Dublin, 2005 [1930]), 157.
[59] Caoimhe Nic Dháibhéid, '"This is a case in which Irish nationalist considerations must be taken into account": the breakdown of the MacBride-Gonne marriage, 1904–08', *Irish Historical Studies*, Vol. 37, No. 146 (November 2010), 248.
[60] See Chapter 7.

Table 3.1 *Denomination of Protestant advanced nationalist women*

Denomination	Number
Episcopalian	78
Presbyterian	6
Congregationalist	2
Methodist	2
Quaker	1
Total	**89**

Source: Nominal data for all tables in this chapter is derived from a variety of sources, including *DIB*; BMH WSs; RCBL, Irish Guild of the Church minute books (excluding those who later joined the Irish Guild of Witness); MAD, MSCP, list of ICA awards; NLI, Jacob papers, Rosamond Jacob diaries; and a survey of biographical accounts. Further biographical data is derived from Census of Ireland 1901 and 1911.

Party's hostility towards women's suffrage and discouragement of women's participation in home rule politics inclined them towards the advanced nationalist movement, which welcomed women members.[61] The sex-equality practised in the Gaelic League was also a factor, with many women who joined that organisation developing advanced nationalist sympathies. This section will discuss the denominational, geographic, and socioeconomic background of Protestant advanced nationalist women, and will discuss the formative influences of a selection of them.

The denominational background of eighty-nine of these women has been traced, as shown in Table 3.1. A strikingly high number – almost 90 per cent – of these women were Episcopalian. Although this figure is partially accounted for by members of the Irish Guild of the Church, even with these figures excluded, Episcopalians still predominate. Female members of the Church of Ireland, had, since the late nineteenth century, been heavily involved in philanthropy, education, and social activism.[62] Frequently well off, educated, and with a commitment to furthering women's rights, many Episcopalian women wished to play an influential role in society. Constitutional nationalism did not offer such women an outlet commensurate with their ambitions. Non-conformist advanced nationalist women were, by contrast, few. Even among the six

---

[61] For a fine recent study, see Senia Paseta, *Irish nationalist women, 1900–1918* (Cambridge, 2013), chs. 4 and 5.

[62] See Oonagh Walsh, *Anglican women in Dublin: philanthropy, politics and education in the early twentieth century* (Dublin, 2005).

Table 3.2 *Father's occupation of Protestant advanced nationalist women*

Occupation	Number
Clergyman	10
Solicitor	6
Civil servant	4
Landowner	4
Manager	3
Military officer	4
Peer or baronet	4
Chemist	3
Company director or banker	3
Manual trade	3
Barrister	2
Merchant	2
Rent agent	2
Other	5
Total	**55**

Presbyterians (the second largest denomination), four are accounted for by the same family, the four republican sisters of Robert Lynd.

As the majority of these women were not directly employed, father's rank or occupation offers the best determinant of their socioeconomic background. The occupation of fifty-five of these women's fathers has been identified, as shown in Table 3.2.

Clerical families, which emphasised reading and an interest in philanthropy, produced the largest number of Protestant advanced nationalist women, with ten individuals. The gentry and aristocracy were quite well represented: three of their fathers were peers of the realm, one was a baronet, and a further four were substantial landowners. The Hon. Albinia Brodrick's father, William Brodrick, 8th Viscount Midleton, owned nearly 10,000 acres split between Surrey and Cork.[63] The Hon. Mary Spring Rice's father, Thomas Spring Rice, 2nd Baron Monteagle, held 8,755 acres in counties Limerick and Kerry.[64] Sir Henry Gore-Booth, 5th Baronet, the father of Constance Markievicz, held 31,774 acres in County Sligo.[65] Nelly O'Brien's father, Edward William O'Brien, owned 4,990 acres in County Limerick.[66] The majority of the group came from the wealthy professional classes, with fathers employed as military officers, in substantial business, or the law. Working-class

[63] John Bateman, *Great landowners of Great Britain and Ireland* (London, 1876), 309.
[64] U. H. Hussey de Burgh, *The landowners of Ireland* (Dublin, 1878), 321.
[65] Bateman, *Great landowners*, 47.   [66] Hussey de Burgh, *The landowners of Ireland*, 343.

Table 3.3 *Geographic origin of Protestant advanced nationalist women*

Place of birth	Number
Dublin	25
Ulster	11
Britain	11
Connaught	7
Munster	5
British Empire	2
Leinster (excluding Dublin)	3
Total	**64**

women were scarcely represented. One consequence of the social profile of these women was an ability, or willingness, to write. Twenty-eight of the group were published authors or produced a substantial amount of journalism, including Alice Milligan, Rosamond Jacob, and Lily McManus. There were also six professional artists. These women produced a large amount of political material useful to the separatist movement. Protestant women formed, for example, a majority of regular contributors to *Bean na hÉireann*, an advanced journal.[67] Due to the education and background of these women, Irish advanced nationalism could make use of a substantial group of female propagandists.

The place of birth of sixty-four individuals has been identified, as shown in Table 3.3. Almost 40 per cent were born in Dublin. Eleven were born in Ulster, most of whom belonged to the Protestant nationalist culture forged in Belfast in the early 1900s.[68] The 18 per cent who were born in Britain largely came from landed families, who maintained residence in England. Although they had a diverse geographic origination, this was a strongly urban, Dublin-based group: almost all of those who were born in Connaught, Munster, and non-metropolitan Leinster resided as adults in Dublin. They tended to be quite young, although few were in their late teens or early twenties. The average age was thirty-two in 1910, with only five individuals aged fifty-five or over.

In summary, the Protestant women who joined the advanced nationalist movement after 1910 tended to be Episcopalian, and were usually from an upper-middle-class, often clerical background, although a substantial minority came from landed families. Most were born in Dublin, which was the centre for advanced Protestant nationalist activity, or

---

[67] Walsh, *Anglican women in Dublin*, 44.   [68] See Chapter 2.

resided there as adults, and they tended to be in their early to mid-thirties.

The following pages will briefly discuss the formative experiences of these women. For Elizabeth Bloxham, later a journalist and Cumann na mBan executive member, growing up in a County Mayo Episcopalian family, the daughter of an RIC pensioner, affection for the connection with Britain was taken for granted. 'Being Protestants, we were, as a matter of course, Unionists.'[69] She recorded a narrow school curriculum which did little to provoke political consciousness in the young:

The board of education at that time was wise in its generation in not allowing history – English or Irish – to be taught in National Schools, for if we had been taught Irish history it would have broken through the crust of our conventional unionism and even if we read English history some of us with enquiring minds might have wanted to know 'the other side of the story'.[70]

The elementary education system was noted for its 'acceptance of the prevailing social, economic and political value system', which must have alienated Bloxham.[71] Bloxham's interest in nationalist politics was piqued when she read Arthur Griffith's United Irishman as a child. Her conversion had a matter-of-fact quality to it; she later stated, 'It would, no doubt, be of interest if I could recall a struggle before accepting the outlook of such a paper. The fact is that I had no such experience ... That one's first loyalty is to one's own country seemed to me then, as it does now, to be unquestionable.'[72] By 1906 Bloxham had become a regular contributor to Griffith's Sinn Féin.

Although Bloxham's unionist family proved surprisingly sympathetic to her political beliefs, expressing admiration for her spirit, the same could not be said of other co-religionists. Bloxham was employed as a domestic economy instructress in the unionist stronghold of Newtownards, County Down, from 1911. Originally well regarded as a teacher, she found herself persona non grata when she reacted against a political sermon delivered in the local Protestant church: 'The preacher asserted that his political opponents were actuated solely by a desire to crush the Protestant religion and to take from the Protestants their way of living.' Feeling it her duty as a Protestant to protest against these remarks, she wrote a letter of protest to the Newtownards Chronicle. Reaction was swift. This letter, and other activities, including her Cumann na mBan

[69] BMH WS 632, Elizabeth Bloxham.   [70] BMH WS 632, Elizabeth Bloxham.
[71] John Coolahan, Irish education: its history and structure (Dublin, 1981), 20.
[72] BMH WS 632, Elizabeth Bloxham.

activism, led to Bloxham being shunned by many locals. Rumours that she would be physically attacked by a gang of local women caused her to be placed under police protection, much to her disgust.[73] A further example of alienation comes from Alice Milligan. Milligan was forced by financial difficulties to reside with her Ulster unionist family, who resented her activities. In a letter to Sinéad Bean de Valera she wrote: 'Since the opening of 1919 I have been more or less a prisoner, entirely secluded by circumstances amongst relatives entirely opposed to the Republican cause.'[74]

Although Maude, Brodrick, and Despard demonstrate that espousal of Irish nationalism could lead to family estrangement, at least fifteen women came from families with an existing tradition, or alleged tradition, of nationalism.[75] (Tradition is defined here as a parent, aunt or uncle, grandparent, or member of an older generation who held nationalist views.) Few could draw on such illustrious a tradition of political separatism as Nelly O'Brien. Her paternal grandfather, William Smith O'Brien (1803–1864), had been a Young Irelander before leading the disastrous Confederate rebellion in 1848. O'Brien's maternal uncle, Lord Monteagle, was a political moderate whose daughter Mary Spring Rice was a Gaelic Leaguer and ardent nationalist, who went on to take part in the Howth gun-running. O'Brien's brother, the artist Dermod O'Brien, was originally a unionist, but after 1912 aligned himself with constitutional nationalism. Another cousin was the writer and home rule MP Stephen Gwynn. Nelly O'Brien inherited her grandfather's belief that Protestants should be reconciled to nationalism, and devoted much of her adult life to the slow process of winning converts to the nationalist cause from among her co-religionists. Sarah Cecilia Harrison (1863–1941), an Episcopalian, who in 1912 became the first woman elected to Dublin Corporation, had a strong family tradition of nationalism. She was the grand-niece of United Irishmen leader Henry Joy McCracken and his sister Mary Ann McCracken, whose campaigns for the urban poor would mirror Harrison's later work in Dublin. Her brother, Henry Harrison, had served as a Parnellite MP.

---

[73] BMH WS 632, Elizabeth Bloxham. See also NLI, MS. 7981, Diary of Elsie Henry, 17 August 1914.

[74] NLI, MS 18,311, Alice Milligan to Sinéad de Valera, undated, c. 1921.

[75] Lily Duncan, Una Duncan, Maud Gonne, Rosamond Jacob, Alice Milligan, Annie and Emily Norgrove, Charlotte Grace O'Brien, Nelly O'Brien, Anna Parnell, Annie M. P. Smithson, Mary Spring Rice, Dorothy Stopford-Price, Alice Wordsworth, Elizabeth Yeats.

Rosamond Jacob came from a Quaker home rule–supporting family, and spent her youth as the sole nationalist in her Waterford Protestant girls' school.[76] She recorded a school event she attended along with her mother and brother:

All ... went to Miss Smith's breaking-up celebrations in the Protestant Hall ... It was nice enough but sickeningly loyal, God Save the King printed on the wall and portraits of ugly ecclesiastics, and bibles with crowns on them for ornaments, and a big ER on the floor, in blue chalk ... [T]here was nothing in the least Irish about the whole thing of course ... There was one horrid 'action song', all the children marching around waving union jacks and singing 'Soldiers of the King'. And they sang God Save the King twice ... everyone but Mamma, Tom and I.[77]

Jacob's parents and uncle were prominent nationalist supporters in Waterford, and took the Parnellite side in the split.[78] Her family's dislike of 'Englishers' and 'Jingoes' influenced Jacob, who disliked being questioned about her politics by the 'hotty [haughty] cross, rude English garrison misses' she hated to meet.[79] Although her family's constitutional nationalism was more moderate than that of Rosamond, who went on to join Sinn Féin and Cumann na mBan, it is likely her pre-existing family sympathies, coupled with lack of opportunities for women in the UIL and the radicalising influence of her Gaelic League involvement, played a strong role in her political formation.[80]

Growing up in an upper-middle-class unionist family in Dublin, the nurse, novelist, and trade unionist Annie M. P. Smithson had no contact with the nationalist majority: 'I had never met personally anyone with really Irish ideals, and with the snobbery of my class and times, believed that such persons belonged only to the "lower classes".'[81] Her conversion to nationalist politics was prompted by an unexpected family revelation. Her father, subsequently a unionist barrister who died when Smithson was a child, had allegedly risen in the Fenian Rebellion in 1867, while a student in TCD, making a narrow escape after the failed confrontation with the RIC at Tallaght.[82] This, coupled with her reading of Mitchel's *Jail Journal*, led to her conversion to nationalism.

---

[76] For Quaker attitudes, see Philip Ashton, 'Divided ideals: the Religious Society of Friends and the Irish home rule controversy, 1885–1886', *The Woodbrooke Journal*, No. 6 (Summer 2000), 1–27.

[77] NLI, Rosamond Jacob diaries, MS 32,582, 17 July 1903.

[78] NLI, Rosamond Jacob diaries, MS 32,582, 22 April, 6 August, 17 March 1900, 20 September 1901, 12 September 1902.

[79] NLI, Rosamond Jacob diaries, MS 32,582, 26 August 1902.

[80] For Jacob generally, see Leeane Lane, *Rosamond Jacob: third person singular* (Dublin, 2010).

[81] Annie M. P. Smithson, *Myself – and others: an autobiography* (Dublin, 1944), 94.

[82] Smithson, *Myself – and others*, 228–229.

One of the main themes of this book is the tendency for Protestant nationalists to make political converts of their family members. This propensity is evident with regard to this group. At least forty-six of these women had a close relation (defined as spouse, sibling, or cousin) who also held nationalist views. Few nationalists enjoyed so much influence over the politics of their younger family members than Alice Stopford Green (1847–1929).[83] Stopford Green, the daughter of the archdeacon of Meath, married the prominent social historian John Richard Green in 1877. Following Green's death in 1883 she established herself as a historian in her own right, as well as one of London's most prominent political hostesses. If Stopford Green's husband ensured her adoption of liberal politics, her friend the barrister John F. Taylor QC converted her to Irish nationalism.[84] She was anti-imperialist as well as nationalist: during the Boer War she visited prisoner-of-war camps on St Helena, to investigate conditions for internees. Stopford Green's historical works were a political project, which sought, by means of extolling the glories of Gaelic, pre-plantation culture, to illustrate Ireland's contemporary capacity for self-government.[85] Originally close to the Irish Party, she later came to sympathise with Sinn Féin, without ever committing herself fully to that organisation. Her philosophy was essentially a deep belief in Ireland's nationhood and the right of all nations to independence; she had nothing but hatred for 'rule of a nation by a nation', calling it 'the most tyrannous and intolerable' form of government.[86] She always claimed to be averse to political violence; however, as we will see, this did not prevent her from playing a leading role in the Howth gun-running.

Alice Stopford Green was instrumental in converting her nieces Dorothy Stopford, Edie Stopford, Alice Wordsworth (née Stopford), Elsie Henry (née Brunton), and her nephew Robert Stopford to nationalism.[87] Stopford Green's brother Edward A. Stopford was a lifelong nationalist and UIL subscriber, who was a director of the Irish Agricultural Organisation Society. His intention to seek an Irish Party seat was stymied due to ill-health.[88] There are numerous other examples of this

---

[83] See McDowell, *Alice Stopford Green*.

[84] NLI, MS 43,325, Notes on character of Alice Stopford Green by Robert J. Stopford [undated].

[85] See, for example, Alice Stopford Green, *The history of the Irish state to 1014* (London, 1925).

[86] Alice Stopford Green, *The government of Ireland* (London, 1921), 2.

[87] For a study of this family and their milieu, see Ó Broin, *Protestant nationalists*.

[88] NLI, MS 11,426, Typescript recollections of Miss [Edie] Stopford; *Irish Statesman*, 25 October 1919.

phenomenon. Parental example explains the Norgrove daughters' membership in the ICA.[89] Kathleen Lynn was a distant cousin of the Gore-Booths.[90] Gertrude Bannister, née Parry, Roger Casement's first cousin and prodigious correspondent, followed her relative into the nationalist movement, as she later would into the Catholic Church.

Few of these women actively participated in the Easter Rising, or the War of Independence, as members of Cumann na mBan. Indeed, Cumann na mBan was overwhelmingly Catholic. At time of writing, the Military Service Pension Collection lists 387 Cumann na mBan pension claimants, of which only one, Sydney Czira, can be identified as having been Protestant in adulthood.[91] However, this does not capture all Protestant members. Constance Markievicz, Mabel FitzGerald, Elizabeth Bloxham, Margaret Dobbs, Ella Young, Dorothy Stopford Price, and Cesca and Margot Chenevix Trench were among the Protestants who joined.[92] Of these, only two – Markievicz and FitzGerald – played a role in the rising. Indeed, what emerges is a preference for Protestant nationalist women to propagandise in print for a republic or to join non-military organisations such as the Irish Guild of the Church. In general, Protestant women nationalists were social, political, and cultural rebels, but were less likely to take a combat role.

Religious Conversion and Mysticism

The most conspicuous method of assimilation with a majority-Catholic movement was religious conversion. Ireland's Protestant community, mindful of their demographically precarious position, was deeply hostile to conversion to Rome. The broadcaster and writer Jack White (1920–1980) stated that Irish Protestants saw conversion to the Catholic Church as 'a social lapse, a weakening of the tribe, a desertion from the post of duty'.[93] Such action was infused with political meaning. Otto Rauchbauer argues that for an Irish Protestant in the early decades of the twentieth century, 'With all the accompanying political ramifications, a conversion was not only an act of religious conviction but one of social and political insurrection.'[94]

The largely biographical nature of the literature on Protestant nationalists has given the impression that most converted. Twenty-seven

---

[89] See Chapter 5.   [90] BMH WS 357, Kathleen Lynn.
[91] MAD, MSPC, List of Cumann na mBan pension and awards files (digital manipulation; accessed 21 January 2015).
[92] See Jones, *Rebel Prods*, ch. 7.   [93] White, *Minority report*, 6.
[94] Rauchbauer, *Shane Leslie*, 86–87.

Protestant nationalists out of the 500 that are surveyed in this book have been identified as having converted to Catholicism. This figure has been arrived at by analysis of secondary accounts, as well as by checking all names against obituaries or death notices, primarily in the *Irish Times*, *Irish Independent*, *Freeman's Journal*, and the *Irish Press*. As such, it excludes conversions of less well-known individuals, and should be treated as a minimum figure only. The tendency towards conversion was most pronounced among advanced nationalist women: 16 of the 91, or less than one-fifth, did so. Converts primarily defected from Episcopalianism: 20 individuals came from this church: two were originally Presbyterian; and two were Quaker. This section will focus on religious conversion among advanced nationalist women, as they were the most likely to convert to Rome, and the most self-reflective.

In explaining their decision, few were as frank about their motivation as Maud Gonne, who entitled the chapter of her memoirs that dealt with conversion 'The Inevitability of the Church'.[95] This work gives the impression that her decision was political in nature. Her French confessor told her: 'It is unthinkable that Maud Gonne should belong to the Church of England ... You won't recognise old Victoria politically and yet you recognise her as head of your religion.' She admitted the Anglican Church was 'the Church of the evictors, of the pious people who destroy houses and leave children to die'.[96] However, her conversion had a more prosaic rationale, which she omitted from her memoirs: her marriage a few days later to the Catholic John MacBride.[97] Marriage to a Catholic frequently prompted religious conversion. Two of Gonne's Protestant friends, Ella Young and W. B. Yeats, counselled against changing religion. Young 'came from a Presbyterian family in Antrim and ... shared her family's fears of priestly interference in nationalist affairs. She thought that, if I became a Catholic my power to work for Irish independence would be curtailed.'[98] In fact, Gonne believed conversion would increase her scope for political action: 'I have often longed to denounce the priests and could not because I was a Protestant, but now I can.'[99]

The most extraordinary series of religious conversions of this period were made by four of the six daughters of the Gifford family. Born of a prosperous Rathmines family, to a Catholic solicitor father and a

[95] Gonne, *Servant*, 261–271.   [96] Gonne, *Servant*, 263.

[97] Margaret Ward, *Maud Gonne: Ireland's Joan of Arc* (London, 1990), 79.

[98] Gonne, *Servant*, 265.

[99] Maud Gonne, quoted in W. B. Yeats to Lady Augusta Gregory, in Conrad A. Balliett, 'The lives – and lies – of Maud Gonne', *Éire-Ireland*, Fall, 1979, 33.

Protestant mother, the twelve Gifford children were raised in a 'palatine pact' compromise, whereby the boys were baptised Catholic, and the girls were raised in their mother's faith. Isabella Gifford, a strong unionist and devout Protestant, ignored her sons' Catholic baptisms and raised the entire family in the Church of Ireland. She was a domineering and often difficult force in her daughters' lives. By contrast, Fredrick Gifford was a gentle figure. Although he was conservative and unionist in his beliefs, there was some ambivalence to his politics: he admired Parnell and may have had agrarian sympathies, telling a daughter, 'it makes my blood boil to see tenants tipping their hats to agents'.[100] Gifford kinswoman Gifford Lewis has suggested that the daughters' conversion was a reaction against their domineering mother in favour of their more sympathetic father.[101] Another important influence was the family's succession of Catholic and nationalist nursemaids, whose political and religious views influenced their charges. Sydney Czira, the youngest member of the family, gave a memorable description of the children as forming 'splinter parties':

[W]e had amongst us Fabian socialists, influenced by reading Bernard Shaw; ardent Sinn Féiners, whose thought was moulded by Arthur Griffith's paper, and a few half-hearted Unionists, who remained such chiefly because they knew that all who did not conform to this political belief were ostracised in the tennis club.[102]

Far from their change of religion being a political statement signalling an intention to enter the Catholic-dominated political scene, two of the four Gifford converts did so on becoming engaged to a Catholic, and a third on the anniversary of the death of her Catholic husband. The first Gifford sister to convert was Katie, in 1909, on her marriage to Walter Harris Wilson.[103] Grace Gifford converted to Catholicism a few months after her December 1915 engagement to Joseph Plunkett. Muriel, who married another signatory of the Proclamation, Thomas MacDonagh in 1912, was received into the Catholic Church in Easter 1917, one year after the execution of her husband.[104] The two remaining daughters, Ada and Nellie, remained Anglican.[105]

Growing up in a strongly Protestant family, Annie Smithson found the presence of elderly Catholic relatives – the result of a palatine compromise – to be incongruous: 'It puzzled my childish mind ... that they ... actually went to "chapel" like the servants.'[106] Edie Stopford recorded a

[100] Czira, *The years flew by*, xi.   [101] Czira, *The years flew by*, ii.
[102] Czira, *The years flew by*, 20.   [103] *DIB* article on Nellie Gifford.
[104] Clare, *Unlikely rebels*, 200.   [105] Czira, *The years flew by*, xv–xvi.
[106] Smithson, *Myself – and others*, 25.

similar experience. On a trip to London as a child she was 'staggered to learn in the course of our drive from Euston Station that the ragged women sitting in the doorways and the ragged, barefoot children in the streets were Protestants, not Catholics; this seemed to me almost to contradict a law of nature'.[107] For Smithson, the Anglican Church failed to provide solace during a time of emotional torment. Working in Ulster as a district nurse, the failure of a love affair with a married doctor left her suffering 'desolation of the soul'. Heartbroken, she left Ulster for Britain, where she was received into the Catholic Church by the Redemptorist Fathers in 1907.[108] Although Smithson's memoirs suggest that religion played little part in her political conversion and politics was not the cause of her embracing of Catholicism, her conversion must have informed her decision to sympathise with the rebel cause after 1916.

Mabel FitzGerald did not hold particularly strong religious convictions. Raised Presbyterian, but married to a devout Catholic, she raised her four sons as Catholic and closely supervised their religious education.[109] FitzGerald did convert to Catholicism, but much later than the other women under discussion here, in 1943. According to her son Fergus FitzGerald, this was so as to prevent hurting her Presbyterian relations while they were still alive.[110]

The numbers of those who converted gave rise to fears that others may be about to jump ship as well. The religious sceptic Rosamond Jacob stated that Albinia Brodrick was 'so full of affection towards her "beloved people and their religion" that I'm in a fright now for fear she may turn Catholic herself, like Casement and Madame de Markievicz. I do dislike to have things look as if no-one could be a Sinn Féiner without being a Catholic.'[111] Such fears were ungrounded with respect to Brodrick. The Brodrick family had subscribed to evangelical Anglicanism for generations. Brodrick's earliest writings show a devotion to Anglican ritual, and she remained an ardent Protestant for the rest of her life.[112]

But these converts were a minority. The majority were securely Protestant, and showed no interest whatever in conversion. In fact, a traditional Protestant dislike of the institution of the Catholic Church, and

[107] NLI, MS 11,426, Typescript recollections of Miss [Edie] Stopford.
[108] Smithson, *Myself – and others*, 201, 214–215.
[109] Mabel FitzGerald to Desmond FitzGerald, 12 February 1916, in Desmond FitzGerald, *Desmond's rising: memoirs, 1913 to Easter 1916* (Dublin, 2006 [1968]), 208–211; Garret FitzGerald, *All in a life: an autobiography* (Dublin, 1991), 1.
[110] Correspondence with Dr Jennifer FitzGerald, in possession of the author.
[111] NLI, Sheehy-Skeffington papers, MS 22,689, Rosamond Jacob to Hannah Sheehy-Skeffington, n.d. [c. 1919].
[112] Kerry County Library and Archives, Tralee, Albinia Brodrick/Gobnait Ní Bhruadair file, Albinia Brodrick's holiday journal, 1884 [typescript].

distrust of priests, can be detected in many Protestant nationalists, just as it could in their unionist co-religionists.

Travelling around rural Ulster, seeking to revive the IRB, Denis McCullough encountered elderly Protestant Fenian relics. He recalled:

There were four brothers, they were horse dealers, and they were very strong nationalists but they wouldn't have anything to do with the Papists – they were quite right too, in my opinion [laughs]. They were quite right. They were afraid that they'd go to confession and tell the priest about it.[113]

This attitude was far from unusual. Cesca Chenevix Trench, on meeting Agnes O'Farrelly, lecturer in modern Irish in University College Dublin (UCD), and a member of Cumann na mBan, found her nationalism wanting. Cesca recorded, 'I have my doubts about her. She is a Catholic, and under the thumb of the Church, I'll never confide in her.'[114] Rosamond Jacob was fundamentally hostile to Catholicism, believing that 'the Catholic Church is one of the greatest influences for evil in the world' and that it was 'incomprehensible how any sane person of any intelligence could be a Catholic'.[115] Of a colleague, Jacob could write: 'She has wonderful sense for a Catholic, can't be a very good Catholic I think.'[116] Nellie Gifford, likewise, inherited her mother's forthright scepticism of the Catholic faith. Lady Gregory, although discreet in public, loved to sneer at 'papists' in her letters and journals.[117] Edith White, an eccentric Methodist school inspector and friend of Jacob's, believed that priests were engaged in mass hypnosis.[118] Bulmer Hobson resigned from the Society of Friends in 1914, although he showed no inclination to become a Catholic; he remained a non-denominational Protestant, and worshipped in the Church of Ireland. Catholic and Protestant nationalists occasionally engaged in light-hearted joshing about religion. When working as a dispensary doctor in West Cork in 1921, Dorothy Stopford wrote to her mother that 'I sternly refuse all efforts … to be converted & say I prefer to go to Hell. They then all exclaim that they know it's wrong but they can't believe I will go to hell. We have great sport.'[119]

Alice Milligan was a devout Protestant and a weekly attendee at Methodist or Church of Ireland services. Milligan's poems include

---

[113] UCD, McC, P120/36, transcript of BBC interview with Denis McCullough, 1964.
[114] Pyle (ed.), *Cesca's diary*, 125.   [115] Foster, *Vivid faces*, 17.
[116] NLI, Rosamond Jacob diaries, MS 32,582, 3 September 1914. See also 20 October 1914.
[117] Colm Tóibín, *Lady Gregory's toothbrush* (Dublin, 2002), 64–65.
[118] Foster, *Vivid faces*, 19.
[119] NLI, Dorothy Stopford Price papers, MS 15,341(8), Dorothy Stopford to Constance Stopford, 19 November 1921.

public criticisms of the Catholic hierarchy, something other Protestant nationalists avoided. Originally published pseudonymously, 'At Maynooth' lambasts the bishops for meeting Edward VII during his 1903 visit to the country:

> He is a King – therefore our priests may praise him
> Pure nuns yield reverence, Bishops yield before,
> Our Cardinal may bear to Rome his greeting
> From the Irish shore.[120]

Nor would Milligan have been happy in a mixed marriage with a Catholic. 'A heretic' describes leaving a Catholic lover, being unwilling to raise a child in that faith:

> Ah, then, farewell, though my heart should break,
> Faith I can feign not, even for love's sake.
> I plead not to Virgin nor Saint nor Martyr,
> And the soul of a child I shall never barter.[121]

Similarly, Susan Mitchell, who had despaired when one of her brothers had married a Catholic, was relieved when another made a more suitable choice: 'Thank God she is a Protestant ... she is not a second Ellen, thank goodness.'[122] Some of the most suggestive comments were made by Elizabeth Bloxham. She viewed her political activism as part of a wider pattern of Protestant dissent: 'I ... pointed out that I was the best Protestant of them all – for I was *protesting*.'[123] These figures may have held different political views than their co-religionists, but Protestants they remained, and the small number of converts notwithstanding, they generally retained traditional Protestant attitudes towards Catholics.

Some Catholics felt their faith under strain during the revolutionary era. Dorothy Macardle, who was raised Catholic but with an Anglican-born unionist mother, saw her faith weaken during the Civil War period, partly due to the hierarchy's condemnation of republicans. Macardle joined the Church of Ireland, and was buried in that faith.[124]

Conversion might mean estrangement from one's family. Smithson's religious conversion caused a permanent rift with her favourite aunt, the

---

[120] Originally published in *United Irishman*, 25 July 1903, under the pseudonym Iris Olkyn.
[121] 'A heretic', in Alice Milligan, *The harper of the only God: a selection of poetry by Alice Milligan* (Sheila Turner Johnston, ed.) (Omagh, 1993), 34–35.
[122] Hilary Pyle, *Red-headed rebel: Susan L. Mitchell: poet and mystic of the Irish cultural renaissance* (Dublin, 1998), 143.
[123] BMH WS 632, Elizabeth Bloxham.
[124] Nadia Clare Smith, *Dorothy Macardle: a life* (Dublin, 2007), 42; *DIB* article on Dorothy Macardle; Jennifer FitzGerald papers, Transcript of interview with George Gilmore, 27 May 1985. See also *IT*, 25 December 1958, 21 November 1995.

journalist Susan Carpenter, who refused to speak to her again and cut her from her will.[125] Maud Gonne's 1903 conversion was met, she later claimed, with tolerance. She stated that 'religious difference never cast a shadow on a friendship but politics have broken many'. This is unusual; most women related that the repercussions for religious conversion were far worse than those of renunciation of political allegiance. The key here may be the lengthy period between Gonne taking up the nationalist cause and her entering the Catholic Church. It is possible that as such a well-known nationalist activist, by 1903 she was already alienated from many of her old friends and acquaintances; those who remained were of a more tolerant breed.

Conversion to Catholicism was not the only escape route available to Protestants who found their inherited culture burdensome. A large number of Protestant nationalists became attracted to mysticism, the supernatural, and the occult. According to R. F. Foster, these were:

marginalised Irish Protestants … often living in England but regretting Ireland, stemming from families with strong clerical and professional colorations, whose occult preoccupations surely mirror a sense of displacement, a loss of social and psychological integration, and an escapism motivated by the threat of a takeover by the Catholic middle classes – a threat all the more inexorable because it is being accomplished by peaceful means and the free legal aid of the British governments.[126]

For some Protestant nationalist intellectuals – marginalised from their own community, from literate family backgrounds, and often feeling threatened by the ascent of Catholics to leadership positions – mysticism may have offered a way out of an unwanted Protestant inheritance, without converting to Catholicism.

The 1870s and 1880s saw a revival in interest in mysticism and the occult, which would come to influence some Protestant nationalists. In 1875 the Theosophical Society was founded in New York City, by, among others, Helena Petrovna Blavatsky (1831–1891), a Russian-born occultist and spirit medium. Theosophy is a system of esoteric philosophy which draws on aspects of Hinduism, Buddhism, and Gnosticism to seek direct knowledge of the presumed mysteries of being and nature, in particular the nature of divinity and the purpose and origin of the universe.[127] These ideas, which carried with them the possibility that hidden knowledge offers a path to enlightenment, proved compelling for many bohemians, intellectuals, and artists.

---

[125] Smithson, *Myself – and others*, 211–212.   [126] Foster, *Paddy and Mr Punch*, 220.
[127] See Antoine Faivre, *Theosophy, imagination, tradition: studies in western esotericism* (Christine Rhone, trans.) (New York, 2000).

Æ George Russell may have been the most influential Protestant nationalist mystic of his generation. Russell, who was a theosophist for most of his adult life, was a central figure in the promotion of esoteric philosophy in Dublin.[128] Russell's interest in the occult and mysticism can be seen in his first volume of poetry, *Homeward: songs by the way*, published in 1894. He practised clairvoyance and represented the spiritual beings he claimed to see in his painting. Among those who came to be influenced by Russell was W. B. Yeats, the Irish literary figure whose writings gave most effective expression to the esoteric philosophies which were circulating since the 1870s.

Yeats's Sligo Protestant background – where superstition and belief in ghosts were commonplace – prepared him to find aspects of mysticism and the occult congenial. While a teenager, Yeats became enchanted with supernatural beliefs. Later, he met Russell, who introduced him to mysticism. Yeats was the driving force behind the theosophical Dublin Hermetic Society, which was founded in 1885, and joined other organisations, such as the Society for Psychical Research, which sought to investigate psychic or paranormal phenomena. This marked the beginning of a lifelong preoccupation with mysticism and esoteric, frequently Eastern-influenced forms of thought, which alongside a consuming interest in Celtic mythology, ghosts, and faery-lore inform Yeats's writings.[129] Daniel Albright argues:

In the Society for Psychical Research [and similar bodies], as in Irish peasant beliefs, Yeats found corroboration ... for the existence of an anti-world, an invisible complement to the earth, keener and greater than ours, where the dead could speak with supernatural speed and sureness.[130]

Others followed suit. Susan Langstaff Mitchell (1866–1926), the poet and essayist, joined the Dublin Hermetic Society in 1902, and, under the influence of Russell, she wrote mystical verse.[131] Alice Milligan was deeply attracted to the supernatural, and claimed in 1917 that she had foreseen Roger Casement's trial and execution twenty years before in dreams, visions, and automatic writings.[132] She also believed her support for de Valera and the anti-Treaty side was decided psychically, by her brothers' automatic writing. Maud Gonne had a brief involvement with theosophy, again under the influence of Russell. Although her

---

[128] See Nicholas Allen, *George Russell (Æ) and the new Ireland, 1905–30* (Dublin, 2003), 16 and passim.
[129] See Foster, *W. B. Yeats: a life*, Vol. I, 45–52.
[130] 'Introduction', in Daniel Albright (ed.), *W. B. Yeats: the poems* (London, 1992), xxiv.
[131] Hilary Pyle, *Red-headed rebel*, 84–91.   [132] Morris, *Alice Milligan*, 51.

involvement did not last long – her biographer argues she viewed it as a diversion from nationalist politics – she did retain a lifelong interest in the supernatural.[133]

Ella Young (1867–1956), the poet and founder member of Cumann na mBan, was perhaps the most profound devotee of the supernatural among Protestant nationalist women. Young, another protégé of Russell's, gained fame for her mystical-influenced retellings of Celtic myths, notably *Celtic wonder tales* (1910). Her memoir, *Flowering dusk*, attests to her day-to-day conference with spiritual beings and travels on the astral plane.[134] In 1925 Young moved to the United States, spending ten years as lecturer in Irish myth and lore at the University of California, Berkeley. In later life, she spent time in a theosophical community in California, as well as an artists' colony in New Mexico. Her appearance was eccentric, and her views were, even by the standards of Protestant nationalist mystics, odd. One authority wrote of her:

she wore long robes of satin or velvet in brilliant colours with contrasting sleeves, and entertained occasional visitors with poetry readings in an Ulster accent. In the last year of her life, she said that she had been in communication with the occupants of a thimble-sized spaceship which came and hovered in her garden.[135]

But mysticism, like conversion to Catholicism, does not appear to have been a mainstream choice for the Protestant nationalists discussed in this book. Protestant unionists were also attracted to the arcane; according to Alice Milligan, the 'Unionist Headquarter ladies' were fascinated by psychical research.[136] The embracing of avant-garde and esoteric systems of thought was a minority response by a largely elite group to an Irish Protestant society that was viewed as stultifying. Most Protestant nationalists remained doctrinally conservative, and did not depart from their inherited beliefs.

Among the minority who did convert to Catholicism, it is clear that matrimony or sad personal circumstance partially informed their decision. However, there is no denying that for these individuals, conversion lessened the sense of incongruity that attached to them. Events between 1912 and 1916 would sharpen the religious divisions on the island, and, as we will see, would threaten to leave Protestant nationalists an unrepresentative minority in a Catholic movement.

---

[133] Ward, *Maud Gonne*, 32–33.
[134] See Ella Young, *Flowering dusk: things remembered accurately and inaccurately* (New York, 1945), passim.
[135] *DIB* article on Ella Young.   [136] Morris, *Alice Milligan*, 53.

4 Militants, 1912–1916

Introduction

Between 1912 and 1916 Ireland underwent a major constitutional crisis, which prompted an extraordinary outbreak of popular militancy. The threat of a home rule parliament in Dublin saw unionists organise and arm themselves, willing to fight to prevent self-government for Ireland. In response, nationalists formed their own force, equally willing to fight to implement the promised measure of home rule. Quite separately, Dublin workers, tired of ill-treatment by the police, formed their own armed group. By October 1914 there would be four separate, frequently mutually antagonistic private militias operating in Ireland. The popular, as opposed to elite, nature of nationalist militancy posed challenges for Protestant nationalists, who were unused to operating outside of intimate networks based on close personal allegiance. For some, the tried-and-tested method of converting individual fellow Protestants to nationalism was applied. Others took refuge in a fantasy that the Ulster Volunteers and Irish Volunteers were destined to combine and fight the British together. Although Protestant nationalists would make a substantial contribution during the Howth gun-running, it became clear during this period that the decades-long animosity that had characterised relations between the Catholic Church and advanced nationalism was coming to an end: advanced nationalism was becoming Catholic. How, then, would Protestants fit into the Irish Volunteers? What contribution did they make to the organisation? And would socialist republicanism, in the guise of the Irish Citizen Army, prove a more seductive ideology for Protestants?

The Irish Volunteers

If the dispersal of the Belfast-based Protestant nationalist set had a debilitating effect on Ulster separatism, it brought advantages to Dublin. Principal among these was Bulmer Hobson, who moved to the Dublin in

1908, and immediately set about reviving nationalism with the same fervour as he had in Belfast. In 1909 Hobson co-founded, with Constance Markievicz, Na Fianna Éireann, an explicitly advanced nationalist competitor to the Boy Scouts.[1] By 1911 Hobson was centre of the Teeling circle of the IRB and in 1912 he became chairman of the Dublin Centre's Board and subsequently Leinster representative on the Supreme Council. Hobson would find a close ally in Thomas Clarke (1858–1916). Clarke, a veteran Fenian, had returned to Ireland from exile in the United States in 1907. Initially, Clarke idolised Hobson, seeing him as a new John Mitchel. A figure of reverence because of his militant past, Clarke was co-opted to the Supreme Council where he became a father figure to the radical set. However, Clarke and Hobson took different views of political violence: Hobson wanted to strike only when victory was assured; Clarke was determined to mount a rebellion regardless.[2] The conspiracy that was planned by Clarke and his supporters would eventually lead to the Easter Rising, and result in Hobson abandoning politics.

In April 1912, H. H. Asquith, the prime minister, introduced the third home rule bill. The resultant crisis would, within two years, bring Ireland to the brink of civil war. Ulster unionists, led by Edward Carson (1854–1935), a Dublin-born barrister, and James Craig (1871–1940), a County Down–born businessman and former army officer, begin drilling and arming in opposition to the measure, with the support of influential Conservatives. By August 1912 there were more than 300 'Unionist Clubs' throughout Ulster. In January 1913, these were coordinated as the Ulster Volunteer Force (UVF), under the control of the Ulster unionist party. Mostly trained by retired British army officers, by mid-1914 it may have had as many as 110,000 members.[3] Plans were put in place for a provisional government of Ulster which would rule the province should home rule be implemented. Carson understood this was illegal:

I don't hesitate to tell you that you ought to set yourself against the constituted authority of the land ... I am told that the [Provisional] Government will be illegal. Of course, it will. Drilling is illegal. The Volunteers are illegal, and the government know they are illegal and the Government dare not interfere with what is illegal. And the reason the Government dare not interfere is because they

---

[1] See Marnie Hay, 'The foundation and development of Na Fianna Éireann, 1909–16', *Irish Historical Studies*, Vol. 36, No. 141 (May 2008), 53–71.

[2] Hay, *Bulmer Hobson*, ch. 5.

[3] Timothy Bowman, *Carson's army: the Ulster Volunteer Force, 1910–22* (Manchester, 2007), chs. 1 and 2.

know the moment they interfere with you, you would not brook their interference ... Therefore, don't be afraid of illegalities. There are illegalities that are not crimes ... They are illegalities taken to assert what is the right of every citizen – the protection of his freedom.[4]

This expression of separatist principle promptly elicited a nationalist response. In July 1913, Hobson, as chairman of the Dublin Centre's Board, proposed the creation of an Irish Volunteers. A significant intervention came from Eoin MacNeill, the professor of early and medieval Irish history in UCD, an Irish Party supporter, and a respected figure. MacNeill wrote an article proposing the creation of a home rule–supporting volunteer group. Significantly, he characterised Carson as a sort of nationalist.[5] The Irish Volunteers was founded at a huge meeting at the Rotunda Rink in Dublin in November 1913, with MacNeill as Chief of Staff. Camaraderie, the chance to handle a weapon, and the sense of embarking on a great patriotic adventure proved a popular mix: Irish Volunteer units were founded throughout the country, with numbers eventually rising to 180,000.

Hobson stated that of the original thirty-man provisional committee, twelve were members of the IRB, and thus committed to using the Volunteers as a means of instigating rebellion. The remaining eighteen were comprised of UIL representatives and unaffiliated nationalists. Of the latter group, three, Pádraig Pearse, Thomas MacDonagh, and Joseph Plunkett, later joined the IRB.[6] A fourth figure was Roger Casement, whose presence on the executive underlined his commitment to Irish politics. One prominent advanced nationalist name not on the list was James Deakin. Deakin had been elected president of the IRB Supreme Council in 1913, and he took part in preliminary discussions leading to the setting up of the Volunteers. However, he declined to join the latter organisation, pleading that his business concerns prevented his attending meetings; he may also have grown fearful at moves towards open rebellion.[7] In late 1915 he resigned from the IRB and took no further part in nationalist activities.[8]

From its inception, the Irish Volunteers strove to be regarded as non-sectarian. Its manifesto stated that its 'ranks are open to all able-bodied Irishmen, without distinction of creed, politics or social

---

[4] Edward Carson, speaking at Newry, 7 September 1913, quoted in F. X. Martin (ed.), *The Irish Volunteers, 1913–1915: recollections and documents* (Dublin, 1963), 5.
[5] *An Claidheamh Soluis*, 1 November 1913.   [6] Martin (ed.), *The Irish Volunteers*, 30–31.
[7] Piaras Béaslaí, 'Moods and memories', *II*, 11 December 1963.
[8] Martin (ed.), *The Irish Volunteers*, 25–26.

grade'.[9] (The assertion that it was 'non-political' signified that it was not – as yet – under the control of a political party.) The *Irish Times*, correlating religion with politics, stated that the Volunteers:

are supposed to be absolutely non-political and non-sectarian, but in reality they are composed almost entirely of Nationalists. In a few centres there are some Protestant young men of the shop assistant class attending the drills, and in the corps connected with the Galway College about 10% of the members are Protestant students.[10]

Although the Volunteers was open to all, there is little evidence that it attracted many Protestants into the ranks. However, a number of Protestants took leadership roles in the organisation. One of these was Ernest Blythe. Recent research has shown that Blythe's trajectory – Gaelic Leaguer, IRB man, Irish Volunteer – was less conventional than it may seem. In 1910, the twenty-one-year-old Blythe, who was working as a journalist on the unionist *North Down Herald*, joined the Newtownards District Orange Lodge. This was unknown to his colleagues in the IRB. What explains his extraordinary behaviour? David Fitzpatrick, who has uncovered this aspect of his career, suggests that Blythe sought through his dual IRB and Orange Order membership to inculcate nationalism among members of the Orange Order, and seek to convince republicans that Orangemen could play a role in nationalist politics.[11] As we have seen throughout this book, such convictions were not unusual among Protestant nationalists; what was unusual was the duplicitous and risky steps Blythe took to accomplish Orange/nationalist unity. Following his resignation from the Order in 1912, Blythe's nationalist career took on a more conventional form. In 1914 he became an organiser for the Irish Vounteers, helping to build up companies throughout the country. His activities brought him to the attention of the authorities, and he was jailed in July 1915. Following his release two months later, he resumed his activities, which led to his being arrested in March 1916 and deported to England, which prevented him from taking part in the Easter Rising.[12]

One adventurous spirit attracted to the Volunteers was the journalist and author Darrell Figgis (1882–1925). A Dublin-born tea merchant's son, Figgis, an Anglican, lived in London for much of his life, where he

[9] NLI, ILB 300 p. 7 [Item 1], 'Manifesto of the Irish Volunteers, promulgated at the Rotunda meeting, November 25th, 1913'.
[10] *IT*, 1 May 1914.
[11] David Fitzpatrick, *Ernest Blythe in Ulster: the making of a double agent?* (Cork, 2018).
[12] UCD, P24/1002, Ernest Blythe papers, Bulmer Hobson to Ernest Blythe, 9 October 1914; The National Archives, Kew (TNA), CO 904/19, Intelligence notes, 1915; TNA, CO 904/193, Intelligence file on Ernest Blythe.

worked in business and sought to build a literary reputation. In about 1912 – possibly in imitation of Synge – he moved to Achill Island, County Mayo. Figgis's obituarist wrote that in Achill he 'discovered Irish nationality; unfortunately he also discovered Irish politics'.[13] Figgis was already sympathetic to Sinn Féin ideals; news of the Rotunda meeting quickly brought him into the new movement, and he organised the Volunteers in Achill.[14] Despite Figgis's abilities – he would become one of the nationalist movement's most prolific propagandists – he had an aloof and arrogant manner which consistently antagonised colleagues and would hinder his progress.

George Irvine served as captain in B Company of the 4th Battalion Dublin Brigade, under Eamon Ceannt. Irvine's religion could make him stand out among his fellow Volunteers. Sean Corr, a Volunteer officer, recalled a training camp held in Tromague, County Tyrone, in 1915:

George Irvine, who was a Protestant, went to Church Service from the camp wearing Irish Volunteer uniform. The parson approached him and inquired what regiment he belonged to. George replied 'The Irish Volunteers'. The parson commented 'Oh, is that the way.'[15]

One early landed gentry recruit was Robert Barton. Barton, a County Wicklow landowner and member of the Church of Ireland, had held pro–home rule views since about 1908.[16] He joined the Volunteers in 1913 and worked for a period as secretary to Colonel Maurice Moore, Inspector General of the organisation.

Besides Blythe and Irvine, several other Ulster Protestants held prominent roles in the Volunteers. For Seán Lester, an Antrim-born Methodist and journalist by trade, his study of Irish history convinced him of the moral necessity of national freedom. He went on to join the Gaelic League and Dungannon Clubs while living in Belfast; in 1908 he was sworn into the IRB by Hobson in Portadown railway station.[17] As a member of the Irish Volunteers, he had, as we will see, some success in recruiting his fellow Protestants to the organisation. Robert 'Rory' Haskins, a Belfast resident and member of the Church of Ireland, was a comparatively late convert to nationalism. Having served with the British army for six years, he joined the Orange Order in 1912, and also joined the Ulster Volunteers. However, while working for the Belfast

---

[13] Andrew E. Malone, 'Darrell Figgis', *The Dublin Magazine*, April–June 1926, 18.
[14] Darrell Figgis, *Recollections of the Irish war* (New York, 1927), 10–11.
[15] BMH WS 145, Sean Corr.   [16] Boyle, *The riddle of Erskine Childers*, 144.
[17] Douglas Gageby, *The last Secretary General: Sean Lester and the League of Nations* (Dublin, 1999), 1–7; *DIB* article on Seán Lester; 'Seán Lester', by A. W. Cotton, *Focus*, July 1959, 13–14.

Gas Department, a fellow Protestant employee sparked his interest in nationalism by giving him a copy of *Irish Freedom*, the IRB journal. Haskins's progress through the republican movement was swift; he joined the Belfast Freedom Club, an IRB front, before being initiated into the IRB itself. As a Protestant with military experience, he became a prized asset among Belfast republicans. By 1914 Haskins acted as a military instructor for the Irish Volunteers in the city.[18] Archibald 'Archie' Heron (1895–1971) was an Armagh-born Presbyterian, who, under Seán Lester's influence, converted to republicanism. On moving to Belfast in 1912, he joined the IRB, and later the Irish Volunteers. Heron, who held socialist as well as republican views, helped organise the Irish Volunteers in that city, in preparation for a rebellion.[19] Another figure Seán Lester recruited to the IRB was Alfred 'Alfie' Cotton, a Derry-born Plymouth Brethren. Cotton joined the IRB in about 1910; after helping found the Belfast Freedom Club, he joined the Irish Volunteers and took part in organising the latter movement in County Kerry.[20]

These senior figures aside, there was a gulf between the interdenominational rhetoric elucidated by the official journal, the *Irish Volunteer*, and the reality of Protestant enlistment. Anti-Protestant bias seems to have been a problem in the organisation: in June 1914 the *Irish Volunteer* stated that complaints had been received of sectarianism, and warned members to respect the organisation's constitution.[21] Captain Jack White, who commanded the Derry and Inishowen Brigade, had an unhappy experience in the Volunteers: his men, whom he considered sectarian, plotted against and ousted him.[22] Little did more to highlight the Catholic nature of the organisation than the prevalence of clergy presiding over Volunteer demonstrations. In contrast to the hostility shown by the clergy to previous militant nationalist organisations, Catholic priests addressed Volunteer units in dozens of places throughout the country. One large meeting of Wexford Volunteers had twelve Catholic clergy on the platform.[23] Only one Protestant clergyman is recorded as having addressed a Volunteer meeting. In May 1914, the Rev. Dudley Fletcher, rector of Coolbanagher, Queen's County, spoke at a meeting in Mountmellick. To

---

[18] UCD, McC, P120/27, Rory Haskins to Denis McCullough, 13 September 1949; BMH WS 223, Robert 'Rory' Haskins.

[19] BMH WS 577, Archie Heron.

[20] BMH WS 184, Alfred Cotton; BMH WS 939, Ernest Blythe.

[21] *Irish Volunteer*, 6 June 1914.

[22] White, *Misfit*, 309; Andrew Boyd, *Jack White (1879–1946): first commander Irish Citizen Army* (Belfast, 2001), 29–30. See also *Irish Volunteer*, 11 July 1914.

[23] *Irish Volunteer*, 9 May 1914. For Catholic clergy and the 1916 period, see John H. Whyte, '1916 – revolution and religion', in Martin (ed.), *Leaders and men of the Easter Rising*, 215–226.

great applause, he stated that 'every man worthy of the name should be able to fight for his country when occasion arose'.[24] The defection of a Church of Ireland clergyman caused a brief sensation, and certain vestrymen sought to force his resignation. However, Fletcher, a learned and popular man, won a vote of confidence from his parishioners, and would remain the incumbent until 1929.[25] More Dudley Fletchers may have had a positive effect on Protestant recruitment; instead, by mid-1914, the religious complexion of the Volunteers was decidedly one-sided: an overwhelmingly Catholic rank and file, with a small, intimate group of Protestant republicans holding senior rank.

Differences in religious complexion notwithstanding, not all contemporaries viewed the Irish Volunteers and the Ulster Volunteers as destined to be permanently antagonistic. There had long been an aspect of nationalist thinking that, while deploring the politics of the Orange Order, admired their spirit, and sought an eventual realignment that would see unionists and nationalists combine on an anti-government programme.[26] During the home rule crisis a substantial number of nationalists, noting the anti-government rhetoric of the UVF and its leaders, convinced themselves that just such a realignment was imminent. One such figure was Arthur Griffith.

Griffith adopted an ambivalent, even mildly supportive stance on the Ulster Volunteers. He believed that the actions of the Ulstermen could see them pass a point of no return and find themselves in open revolt, with more in common with the Irish Volunteers than they had realised. He stated, 'If and when the Ulster Unionists take up arms against the United Kingdom ... Ulster will receive the sympathy and support of nationalist Ireland.' Blithely, he claimed the unionists, in creating an army and arranging for a provisional government, were putting Sinn Féin principles into practice: 'In the spirit of Sinn Féin Ulster Unionism is marching to national salvation.'[27] Similarly, the *Irish Volunteer* foresaw the Irish Volunteers and the Ulster Volunteers combining, and sought to highlight examples of good-natured rivalry between them.[28]

No one was more convinced that Irish nationalists and Ulster unionists could work together than Roger Casement. In late November 1913, Casement denied the Irish Volunteers had any intention of fighting the UVF, and claimed rather that they would come to the Ulstermen's aid in the event 'attack be made on your liberties from any quarter', i.e. Britain.[29]

---

[24] *Irish Volunteer*, 16 May 1914.   [25] *IT*, 25 May 1914.   [26] See Chapter 2.
[27] *Sinn Féin*, 24 August 1912. See also *Sinn Féin*, 7 March 1914.
[28] See, for example, *Irish Volunteer*, 6 June, 25 July, 8 August 1914.
[29] *Daily Chronicle*, 20 November 1913, quoted in Inglis, *Roger Casement*, 243.

Casement spent the next few months touring the country, recruiting for the Irish Volunteers, and making speeches in which he praised the UVF. Casement's belief may not have been entirely misguided. Comments by Carson to Redmond in the Commons raised hopes among nationalists that compromise might be possible. Carson stated:

there are only two ways to deal with Ulster ... You must ... either coerce her if you go on, or you must, in the long run, by showing that good government can come under the Home Rule Bill, try and win her over to the case of the rest of Ireland. You probably can coerce her – though I doubt it ... [Y]ou have never tried to win over Ulster. You have never tried to understand her position ... every time we came before you your only answer to us ... was to insult us, and to make little of us. I say to the leader of the Nationalist party, if you want Ulster, go and take her, or go and win her. You have never wanted her affections.[30]

An ecstatic Casement saw this statement as heralding unity between the two paramilitary groups. He wrote to an associate, stating, 'I've a good mind to write to Carson tonight, and ask him to come to Cork with me. My God! I wonder what would happen if he said, "yes".'[31] But Casement had become oversensitive to any perceived weakening of the unionist position, and saw potential converts everywhere. Casement's attitude to the UVF combined sympathy for his fellow Ulstermen, as well as a belief that a robust response from the south would neutralise northern resistance:

Until these men are convinced that they *can't* prevent Home Rule ... they will fight; and now they are really convinced that they *can* prevent it ... I think the Ulster men are the best part of Ireland in many ways – and they should be convinced by appeals to their sense of justice, affection, and at bottom, love of Ireland.[32]

The 12th of July 1913 parade prompted Casement to declare his distaste for members of the Church of Ireland and the British, and his sympathy for Ulster Presbyterians, whom he considered dupes:

Ulster Day is come and gone ... The poor duped, sincere multitude of honest boys has paraded before Carson ... [But] I *love* the Antrim Presbyterians – Antrim and Down – they are good, kind, warm-hearted souls – and to see them now, *exploited*, by that damned Church of Ireland – that Orange ascendancy gang who hate Presbyterians only less than Papishes, and to see them delirious before ... Carson (a cross between a badly raised bloodhound and an underfed hyena, sniffing for Irish blood on the track) and whooping 'Rule

---

[30] House of Commons, Vol. 58, cc. 176–178, 11 February 1914.
[31] Casement to J. J. Horgan, 16 February 1914, quoted in Inglis, *Roger Casement*, 249.
[32] Roger Casement to Alice Stopford Green, quoted in Inglis, *Roger Casement*, 233.

Britannia' through the streets is a wound to my soul. For they are Irish right through, really.[33]

He was not fearful of inter-religious war:

Everyone (here in the Glens) thinks 'Civil War' is in sight and the ladies are, most of them, terrified. Civil War, of course, means shooting papishes. In my heart I think it is the only way these outrageous people can be brought to their senses. If only the British Providence would withdraw for the island for six months and leave Ireland and 'Ulster' to settle the question man to man, we should at least see daylight in Ireland. But that can never be – and so we shall have the British Providence, in the intervals of dining, insisting on looking in on Ireland and doing the wrong thing at the usual intervals ... Civil War would be *far* better than to go on lying and pretending – if only we could be left free to fight out our battle here ourselves. I am sick of the English![34]

Casement's attempts to undermine Ulster unionism led him, along-side Jack White and Alice Stopford Green, to organise the celebrated Ballymoney Protestant home rule meeting on 24 October 1913. Ballymoney, in the 'Route' area of North Antrim, was a traditional centre of Protestant radicalism, and the home of the Rev. James Brown Armour (1841–1928), a charismatic spokesman for Ulster Protestant home rulers. Casement, White, and Stopford Green organised the event in the hope of demonstrating, in the wake of the signing of Ulster's Solemn League and Covenant by 237,368 Protestant men, that the province included a substantial dissident minority.

The Ballymoney meeting is a much-misunderstood event. Scholars are united in viewing it as a rara avis, a seemingly spontaneous manifestation of latent and hitherto undisclosed Irish nationalism among a group of Ulster Protestants, prompted by the eccentric trio of Casement, Stopford Green, and White. For unionist historians it is an aberration, the gathering of a 'little handful of cranks', which 'emphasised rather than disturbed' the great consensus.[35] For nationalists, the meeting repre-sented a final irruption of a radical nationalist tradition that had existed among Ulster Protestants since the late eighteenth century.[36] Recent research has shown that the Ballymoney meeting was, in fact, an Ulster Liberal Association meeting, given a new, denominational guise, prompted by the rhetoric inherent in the Ulster Covenant and the

[33] Roger Casement to Gertrude Bannister, quoted in Inglis, *Roger Casement*, 233–234.
[34] NLI, Casement additional papers, MS 36,204/1, Casement to Alice Stopford Green, 11 November 1913.
[35] See, for example, Ronald McNeill, *Ulster's stand for the union* (London, 1922), 158.
[36] For a recent account, see Bill O'Brien, *Alternative Ulster covenant* (Dublin, 2013).

formation of the Ulster Volunteers.[37] The Ulster Liberal Association, which had its origins in the old Ulster IPHRA, was an overwhelmingly Protestant pro–home rule organisation, which was affiliated with the Liberal Party of Great Britain, and had the broad support of about 10 per cent of Ulster Protestants. Those who attended the meeting were certainly home rulers, but they had little sympathy with the far more advanced ambitions of Casement. The meeting, which was attended by about 500 people, passed two resolutions. The first repudiated the claim of Carson to represent the Protestants of north-east Ulster, and declared the unionist 'provisional government' an 'illegal and entirely non-representative body'. The second denigrated attempts, which it claimed were being made, to separate Irishmen and women of different creeds into separate camps.[38]

Casement was not alone in describing the Ulster Protestants as the 'best part of Ireland'. Some degree of Ulster chauvinism can be detected in northern Protestant nationalists during this period. St. John Ervine, for example, wrote, 'What Ireland needs is, not Home Rule, but Ulster Rule; and when Ulster has recovered from her sulks, she will take care that Ireland gets it.'[39] These sorts of statements may have had their origin in respect for the strength of Ulster resistance, acknowledgement of the advanced northern economy, as well as a simple belief in Protestant superiority over Catholics. Nationalists, in predicting the Ulstermen's defection from unionism, while simultaneously proclaiming the emptiness of the unionist programme, were demonstrating that they simply could not imagine the country without them. However, what they failed to understand was the depth of Ulster unionist hostility to home rule, and the sincerity of their threats to fight to prevent it.

In early 1914 the threat of civil war intensified. On 20 March, in the event known as the 'Curragh incident', about sixty British cavalry officers based at the Curragh Camp in County Kildare threatened to resign rather than obey orders which they believed would lead to the disarming of the Ulster unionists.[40] The loss of government authority in the wake of this convinced many nationalists of the pointlessness of parliamentary campaigning. Then, on 24–25 April 1914 the UVF landed 25,000 rifles

---

[37] See Conor Morrissey, '"Rotten Protestants": protestant home rulers and the Ulster Liberal Association, 1906–1918', *The Historical Journal*, Vol. 61, Issue 3 (September 2018), 743–765.

[38] *UG*, 1 November 1913. For a full account of the speeches, see [various authors], *A Protestant protest: Ballymoney, Oct. 24th 1913* (Ballymoney, 1913).

[39] Ervine, *Sir Edward Carson*, 76.

[40] For a recent discussion, see Alan F. Parkinson, *Friends in high places: Ulster's resistance to Irish home rule, 1912–14* (Belfast, 2012), 233–247.

at Larne, Donaghadee, and Bangor.[41] The nationalist response, the gun-running at Howth and Kilcoole, was almost entirely organised and carried out by a network of advanced and moderate Protestant national-ists, all of whom shared a horror of events in Ulster. The key instigator was Roger Casement, alongside Darrell Figgis and Mary Spring Rice. Casement arrived in London in early May 1914, seeking support for a counter gun-running. There, he found a ready constituency of liberals alarmed by the inability of Asquith's government to face down the UVF and willing to help arm the Irish Volunteers. An ad hoc London-based committee was formed. Alice Stopford Green, who contributed gener-ously to the £1,500 raised for arms, served as chairman and treasurer. Molly Childers, the American wife of Erskine Childers, served as secre-tary. Of the seven other subscribers to the fund, five were Anglican.[42] Lady Alice Young was the Dublin-born wife of Sir George Young of Formosa Place. Mary Spring Rice was also a subscriber, along with two of her cousins, Conor O'Brien and Hugh Vere O'Brien. George Fitzhardinge Berkeley also contributed. The two Catholic subscribers were Lord Ashbourne and Josephine Mary 'Min' Ryan, the secretary of Cumann na mBan and later wife of Richard Mulcahy. Other conspirators included James Creed Meredith, a young Anglican barrister and home rule–supporter, Hervey de Montmorency, and Diarmid Coffey.

The gun-running operation was led by Erskine Childers (1870–1922). Childers was an English-born Anglican who was raised with his cousin Robert Barton in County Wicklow. A former House of Commons clerk, he had been a home ruler since 1909, and in 1911 he published a pamphlet on the topic, *The framework of home rule*.[43] Childers's central role in the gun-running reflected his growing preoccupation with Ireland. On 28 May, Figgis and Childers travelled to Hamburg, where they purchased 1,500 rifles and 49,000 rounds of ammunition. Childers captained his yacht *Asgard*, and Conor O'Brien his yacht *Kelpie*, on the expedition back to Ireland. As a well-known nationalist, O'Brien transferred his cargo off the Cornish coast to a more respectable figure, Sir Thomas Myles. Myles, an Episcopalian surgeon, was a committed home ruler who had been a prominent member of the Dublin IPHRA in the 1880s. Myles had been persuaded to join the conspiracy so as to 'show that bloody Carson that two could play his game'.[44] On 26 July the

---

[41] Martin (ed.), *The Howth gun-running*, xiii.
[42] List of subscribers given in Martin (ed.), *The Howth gun-running*, 35.
[43] Erskine Childers, *The framework of home rule* (London, 1911).
[44] Sir Thomas Myles, quoted in Eoin O'Brien and Ann Crookshank, with Sir Gordon Wolstenholme, *A portrait of Irish medicine: an illustrated history of medicine in Ireland* (Dublin, 1984), 159.

Asgard was landed at Howth, north Dublin, and its cargo distributed to waiting Volunteers and Fianna. Although the rifles – Mausers that had been previously used by the German army – were antiquated, the success of the venture was an enormous boon for the Volunteers. Cesca Chenevix Trench, who was present at Howth, described 'A great, soaring day, a glorious day. The best day I've ever had.'[45] The glorious day had a tragic coda. A group of soldiers of the King's Own Scottish Borderers, peeved at the Volunteers' success, opened fire on Bachelors Walk at a jeering crowd, killing four and wounding more than thirty.

Two days later, war broke out in Europe. For Casement, the outbreak of war prompted complete rupture with Britain. As early as 1912 he had claimed that as Britain was unwilling to grant home rule, Ireland should look to Germany for aid.[46] By the time the guns had been landed in Howth he was already in New York, seeking to raise funds for the Volunteers. In October 1914 this 'polished, Van-Dyke bearded cosmopolitan, who looked so little like the type of Irish revolutionary',[47] arrived in Germany, where he sought to convince the Imperial government to assist a rebellion in Ireland and to raise an Irish Brigade among prisoners of war. The defection of Sir Roger Casement CMG, the chronicler of the horrors of the Belgian Congo and the Amazon Basin, caused a sensation, and demonstrated that Irish advanced nationalists were willing not merely to ignore the British war effort but to forge an alliance with the enemy. In October 1915, Casement was joined in Germany by Robert Monteith, a former British soldier and Volunteer officer. Monteith, an atheist, had a Protestant family background. Casement would be sidelined in Germany, and the role he would play there marginalised him from the growing conspiracy in Ireland, and would eventually lead to his execution.

In June 1914 John Redmond issued an ultimatum to the Irish Volunteers, and took nominal control of the organisation himself, much to the disgust of the advanced nationalists around Thomas Clarke. Hobson's decision to accept Redmond's ultimatum prompted a breach with his erstwhile comrades which would have major consequences in 1916.[48] By this time, a reasonable number of country gentlemen had already taken commissions in the Irish Volunteers.[49] The *Irish Volunteer* claimed to notice a new-found admiration for the Volunteers among those who had

[45] Pyle (ed.), *Cesca's diary*, 114.

[46] Batha MacCrainn [Roger Casement], 'Ireland and the German menace', *The Irish Review*, September 1912, 343–345.

[47] Wells, *Irish indiscretions*, 60.   [48] Hay, *Bulmer Hobson*, 134ff.

[49] Fitzpatrick, *Politics and Irish life*, 62–64; Foster, *Vivid faces*, 191.

previously spurned the organisation.[50] Martial tradition, latent or recently acquired nationalist sympathies, and a sense that the Volunteers might become respectable led members of the southern gentry and aristocracy to take commissions in this period. Most of the gentry and aristocracy who joined before August 1914 had already demonstrated some pro-self-government leanings. Major Gerald Dease (d. 1934), a Catholic landowner and former member of the Irish Reform Association (a pro-devolution body), took the command of the Westmeath Volunteers in July 1914.[51] Major George Wolfe (1859–1941), an Anglican who was a well-known landowner and home ruler, led the Kildare Volunteers.[52] Sir Anthony Weldon, who reviewed the Mountmellick corps in June of that year, had also belonged to the Irish Reform Association and supported home rule.[53] Major Hervey de Montmorency, who led the Wicklow Volunteers, had been honorary treasurer of the Irish Protestant Home Rule Committee and, as we have seen, conspired in the Howth gun-running.

One significant recruit was Captain George Fitzhardinge Berkeley (1870–1955). Berkeley was an English squire, army officer, and gentleman historian. He was proud of his collateral descent from Berkeley, the bishop of Cloyne, and ascribed his liberal views to the influence of his ancestor.[54] In July 1914 he was appointed Chief Inspecting Officer for the Irish Volunteers in Belfast and counties Antrim and Down.[55] Berkeley's decision to join the Volunteers gained an ambivalent response from Richard Edmund Longfield, an Episcopalian and County Cork landowner. Longfield wrote that the 'movement you have mixed yourself up in is very dangerous', but he agreed that it is well 'for Redmond's followers to have some gentlemen leading them'.[56] Another member of that family was more hostile, saying, 'As one who has known you since you were a small boy I … must tell you how shocked I am to think you have thrown your lot in with Redmond's Volunteers.'[57]

[50] *Irish Volunteer*, 13 June 1914.   [51] *Irish Volunteer*, 18 July 1914.
[52] *Kildare Observer*, 17 October 1914.   [53] *Irish Volunteer*, 6 June 1914.
[54] BMH WS 971, George F. H. Berkeley.
[55] Cork City and County Archives (CCCA), George Fitzhardinge Berkeley papers, PR12/56, Order by Colonel Maurice Moore, Inspector General, Irish Volunteers, appointing Captain George Berkeley as Chief Inspecting Officer for the City of Belfast and counties Down and Antrim, 14 July 1914; Colonel Edmond Cotter to George Fitzhardinge Berkeley, 22 July 1914.
[56] CCCA, Berkeley papers, PR12/106, R. E. Longfield to George Fitzhardinge Berkeley, 10 September 1914.
[57] CCCA, Berkeley papers, PR12/103, Alberta Longfield to George Fitzhardinge Berkeley, 6 September 1914.

Perhaps the most unusual figure to join the Volunteers during this period was John Evans-Freke, 10th Baron Carbery (1892–1970). At the age of six, Evans-Freke inherited the title and an estate that stretched to 19,859 acres, primarily in Cork. Young, handsome, and with a daredevil streak (he was a keen amateur pilot), a family row prompted a conversion to nationalism. Lord Carbery declared: 'I am personally a supporter of the Irish Party and absolutely disassociate myself from the Unionists.'[58] In July 1914 he presided at the inaugural meeting of the Volunteers in Clonakilty, which was unanimously named the 'Lord Carbery Branch'. Eventually he would fly the tricolour over his seat at Castlefreke and discard his title, calling himself 'John Carberry' (sic). Lord Carbery's political conversion caused disquiet among Cork gentry, one of whom complained that 'young Lord Carbery [is] flying in Cork with a green flag, but [he] will not settle in Cork and has never shown any real interest in his home or people'.[59] However, as popular as Carbery's stance made him with locals, he was unsuited to a leadership role in the Volunteer movement. Emotionally unstable and arrogant, he was described as an 'unpleasant character with a cruel sadistic streak, particularly towards animals'.[60] Lord Carbery sold his Irish estate in 1919 and moved to Kenya, where he joined the infamous Happy Valley set of aristocratic hedonists. He took to beating his wife with a sjambok whip, for which she divorced him, and was gaoled for a year for currency offences, before dying in South Africa in 1970.[61]

In a speech in the Commons on 3 August, Redmond offered unconditional support for Britain in the European war.[62] He called for British troops to be withdrawn and for the Irish Volunteers and Ulster Volunteers to jointly defend Ireland, a proposal which he hoped would effect union between the two bodies and lead to a home rule settlement. Redmond's speech prompted declarations from three unionist landowners – Bryan Cooper, Lord Monteagle, and the earl of Bessborough – that they would join or support the Irish Volunteers. Cooper telegrammed Redmond: 'Your speech has united Ireland. I join National [sic] Volunteers today, and will urge every Unionist to

---

[58] Ungoed-Thomas, *Jasper Wolfe*, 135.
[59] CCCA, Berkeley papers, PR12/103, Alberta Longfield to George Fitzhardinge Berkeley, 6 September 1914.
[60] Ungoed-Thomas, *Jasper Wolfe*, 135.
[61] For Lord Carbery, see Ungoed-Thomas, *Jasper Wolfe*, 133–135; Juanita Carberry, 'Child of Happy Valley', *Ardfield/Rathbarry Journal*, No. 3, 2000–2001, 18–20; Jeremy Sandford (ed.), *Mary Carbery's West Cork Journal, 1898–1901* (Dublin, 1998), 133–154; Hussey de Burgh, *The landowners of Ireland*, 70; *IT*, 29 January 2011.
[62] House of Commons, Vol. 65, cc. 1828–1830, 3 August 1914.

do the same.'[63] This was followed by similar declarations by the marquesses of Headfort, Conyngham, and Sligo; the earls of Longford, Mayo, Meath, and Desart; Viscount Powerscourt; Lords Castletown, Langford, Trimblestown, and Fingall; Sir John Keane, and Sir Malby Crofton.[64]

Bulmer Hobson later noted with bemusement this frequently awkward aristocratic involvement. Lord Powerscourt, having declared his adhesion to the Volunteers and attended a meeting of the Bray company, tried to present them with a Union flag. However, 'As the Volunteers declined to accept the gift his connection with the movement was brief.' Hobson recalled that the Volunteer military staff

had the active assistance, for a brief period, of a large number of titled people, like the Earl of Meath, the Marquis of Conyngham and many others. For a short period the Volunteers had the more or less enthusiastic support of a very large number of titled people, and many untitled, whose respectability and steady adherence to Dublin Castle made them strange colleagues for people like us.[65]

Ordinary Volunteers recorded their dismay at being officered by those they had previously considered their enemies.[66]

The idea of the Volunteers remaining in Ireland to defend the country (and of course defend home rule if needs be) was supported by the *Irish Volunteer*.[67] However, at a speech in Woodenbridge, County Wicklow, on 20 September, John Redmond went further, stating that the Volunteers should commit not merely to defending Ireland from invasion but to fighting 'wherever the firing line extends'.[68] Redmond's speech prompted a split in the Volunteers. By late October an estimated 158,000 men formed the Redmondite National Volunteers, and about 12,300 the advanced nationalist Irish Volunteers.[69] (The radical faction retained the organisation's original name.) By this stage most of the landed recruits had become disillusioned with the organisation, when it became evident that Redmond's Volunteers would remain a nationalist vehicle and would not be subsumed into the British military: 'Some county gentlemen with military experience who joined seemingly in the hope that it would in some way become affiliated with the Forces of the Crown, appear to have either resigned or ceased to take part.'[70] Hervey de Montmorency complained to Berkeley:

[63] *Weekly Irish Times*, 8 August 1914. See also Dermot Meleady, *John Redmond: the national leader* (Dublin, 2013), 298–299.
[64] *IT*, 6–8, 10, 13 August 1914.   [65] BMH WS 50, Bulmer Hobson.
[66] See, for example, BMH WS 1423, Jeremiah Cronin.
[67] *Irish Volunteer*, 8 August 1914.   [68] Martin (ed.), *The Irish Volunteers*, 148.
[69] Meleady, *John Redmond: the national leader*, 307–308.
[70] RIC, quoted in Charles Townshend, *Easter 1916: the Irish rebellion* (London, 2005), 70.

I am sick at playing at soldiers in this awful crisis. Why don't the Volunteers Orange and Nationalist alike enlist in the K[aiser]'s army? ... I am rather fat and old to be a captain again, but it is better to be a captain in the British army than a Field Marshal in the Irish Volunteers.[71]

De Montmorency's disillusion led him to resign from the Volunteers and join the British army. His break with nationalism was complete: he returned to Ireland after the war, and became an intelligence officer for the Auxiliary Division during the War of Independence.[72]

Robert Barton took the Redmondite side in the Volunteer split, and when war broke out in 1914, he took a commission with the Royal Dublin Fusiliers. His brother, an even less likely recruit to the National Volunteers, would also join him. Erskine Barton, a DL and JP for Wexford, had scandalised nationalists in July 1914 when, at an Orange meeting in Dublin, he alleged Catholic sectarianism against Protestants in his county.[73] However, Erskine Barton underwent a change of heart and joined the National Volunteers. During the Great War he served in the British Army and was killed in 1918, during a poison gas attack.[74]

The Great War would have an enormous effect on Irish politics and society. An estimated 206,000 Irishmen fought in the war, and an estimated 27,000–35,000 died on active service.[75] The experiences of the men who fought in the 36th (Ulster) Division became a source of Ulster unionist pride and contributed to a sense of distinctiveness in the province.[76] National Volunteers, fighting in France and Belgium instead of remaining in Ireland to defend home rule, slid towards irrelevance. The initiative would pass to the advanced nationalist Irish Volunteers, and in particular, its cadre of IRB-infiltrator officers, who, unbeknownst to Eoin MacNeill, conspired to launch a rebellion.

Redmond did not gain the adherence of all Catholic clergy when the Volunteers split.[77] The RIC reported that in 1914, subsequent to the outbreak of war, some twenty-four clergymen in fourteen counties delivered anti-recruiting or pro-German addresses. By 1915 this figure

---

[71] CCCA, Berkeley papers, PR12/43, Hervey De Montmorency to George Fitzhardinge Berkeley, 13 September 1914; PR12/44a, Hervey De Montmorency to George Fitzhardinge Berkeley, 14 September 1914.

[72] Hervey De Montmorency, *Sword and stirrup: memories of an adventurous life* (London, 1936), 230–353.

[73] *The People* (Wexford), 15, 18, 25 July 1914.   [74] *II*, 11 July 1914, 27 August 1918

[75] David Fitzpatrick, 'The logic of collective sacrifice: Ireland and the British Army, 1914–1918', *The Historical Journal*, Vol. 38, No. 4 (December 1995), 1017–1018; Keith Jeffery, *Ireland and the Great War* (Cambridge, 2000), 35.

[76] See, for example, Cyril Falls, *The history of the 36th (Ulster) Division* (Belfast, 1922).

[77] See Martin (ed.), *Leaders and men of the Easter Rising*, 217–218ff.

had risen to fifty clergymen in seventeen counties.[78] The newfound affinity between advanced nationalism and Catholicism was evident on St Patrick's Day 1916, a little more than a month before the Easter Rising. At least thirty-eight Volunteer units held marches in towns and villages, which frequently culminated in attendance at Mass.[79] In Dublin, in a major show of strength, 1,500 Irish Volunteers participated in a major parade, taking control of the city centre. One Volunteer, who attended special service for the Volunteers in the Church of St. Michael and John, in Essex Quay, described the scene:

A guard of honour in full uniform had been drawn up around the altar and the chapel packed to utmost capacity with Volunteers. At the elevation the guard of honour drew their swords to the salute while the bugles rang out with a clarity that was astounding ... Patrick Pearse, The O'Rahilly, Sean McDermott and the executive who were in close attendance near the altar, appeared to look in their uniforms as if receiving a special blessing from God, and undoubtedly every man attending that Mass received such a blessing. Suddenly a rich baritone voice burst into the hymn to our Patron Saint *Hail Glorious St Patrick* and it was taken up by the whole congregation in such a fervent manner that a lump rose in my throat and I wanted to burst out crying or to do something to prove: that I was worthy of being in their company.[80]

After decades of clerical condemnation, advanced nationalism was on the verge of reconciliation with the Catholic Church.

The Labour Movement and the Irish Citizen Army

The Irish labour movement has a long-standing association with nationalist politics. In 1896 the writer and Marxist trade union leader James Connolly founded the Irish Socialist Republican Party, which sought to create a workers' republic. This tiny group, beset by infighting, was wound up in 1904.[81] The party's Belfast branch had enjoyed some success in attracting young Protestant socialists, notably Ernest Milligan, the brother of Alice Milligan.[82] Belfast, as the most Protestant city in Ireland, as well as the city with the most developed labour movement, became a minor centre for Protestant socialist activism.

---

[78] Calculation based on TNA, CO 904/19, Intelligence notes, 1915, 'Clergymen under notice'.
[79] Calculation based on TNA, CO 904/23, 'Sinn Féin Volunteer parades, 17 March 1916'.
[80] William Daly, quoted in Fearghal McGarry, *The Rising: Easter 1916* (Oxford, 2010), 93.
[81] See David Lynch, *Radical politics in modern Ireland: the Irish Socialist Republican Party, 1896–1904* (Dublin, 2005).
[82] Austen Morgan, *James Connolly: a political biography* (Manchester, 1998), 95.

In 1903, Thomas Johnson (1872–1963), among the most important trade unionists of his era, came to Belfast. Johnson was born in Liverpool, the son of a foreman in a sailmaker's yard. His childhood attendance at a Unitarian chapel, where the need for social reform was emphasised, profoundly influenced the future labour leader.[83] In 1904, Johnson became a member of the Belfast trades council, and the following year he joined its executive. Johnson took Gaelic League classes in Belfast, and he attended meetings of the Dungannon Clubs, where he gained the acquaintance of Hobson.[84]

As one of the most prominent labour leaders in the city, Johnson supported James Larkin, the Liverpool-born trade unionist, when he arrived to organise Protestant and Catholic dockworkers in 1907. The resultant Belfast dock strike, which came to involve various other workers and tradesmen, represented a departure in the politics of the city.[85] The strikers, the majority of whom were Protestant, had the support of the trade union leadership, the home rule movement (despite some misgivings), and, significantly, the Independent Orange Order.[86] The orange, green, and red complexion of the strike has, unsurprisingly, seen it mythologised in nationalist historiography.[87] However, the dispute ended with a weak settlement, and the workers drifted back into their respective religious camps, aided by a campaign against the trade union leadership in the unionist press.

In 1912, Johnson, alongside Connolly and the labour leader William O'Brien (1881–1968), established the Independent Labour Party of Ireland (ILPI).[88] The creation of this party led to a breach with the followers of William Walker (1871–1918), a prominent union leader in Belfast. Walker argued that the Belfast Independent Labour Party should remain affiliated to the Labour Party in Britain. This socialist-unionist perspective was opposed by Connolly, resulting in the creation of the ideologically nationalist ILPI, which excluded Walker and his supporters.[89] The religiously mixed leadership of the Belfast ILPI was

---

[83] J. Anthony Gaughan, *Thomas Johnson, 1872–1963: first leader of the Labour Party in Dáil Éireann* (Dublin, 1980), 15.

[84] NLI, Thomas Johnson papers, MS 17,147 (1), Biographical fragment of Thomas Johnson.

[85] See John Gray, *City in revolt: James Larkin and the Belfast dock strike of 1907* (Belfast, 1985).

[86] Gray, *City in revolt*, 89–90, 152–153, 169.

[87] For example, Campbell, *The dissenting voice*, 388–399.

[88] Gaughan, *Thomas Johnson*, 29–30.

[89] Arthur Mitchell, *Labour in Irish politics, 1890–1930: the Irish labour movement in an age of revolution* (Dublin, 1974), 31–32.

pro–home rule.[90] Johnson scorned Ulster unionist claims that they would suffer under home rule, arguing that 'so-called safeguards for loyal Ulster [should] be accompanied by some safeguards for democracy in Ireland against the political control of its capitalist and aristocratic enemies to whatever party they may have hitherto belonged'.[91]

At a meeting in St Mary's Hall, Belfast, in May 1912, a month after the introduction of the home rule bill, Johnson addressed the religious question directly, and offered a Marxist materialist response to unionist claims:

We who are Protestants give no countenance whatever to the suggestion that the Catholic majority will tyrannise over the Protestant minority. We believe that just as the working class will unite without regard to sectarian differences so the industrial capitalists and landed agriculturalists will combine to promote their respective interests without regard to religion. There may be many cross-currents, but fundamentally there will be a division of parties on economic lines rather than religious or racial.[92]

Johnson, in proclaiming that working-class Protestants were as oppressed by the wealthy elite as working-class Catholics, and could only be protected under an Irish parliament, offered an argument which might have proved enticing. This should be contrasted with the rhetoric of both home rulers and Sinn Féiners, who before and after 1916 usually took refuge in the 'Catholic, Protestant, and Dissenter' slogan, and never gave serious thought to how the large working-class Protestant population in the north-east could be incorporated into the nationalist movement.

Despite Johnson's efforts, it would appear that the ILPI in Belfast could address itself to only a small number of Protestant grassroots supporters in 1912.[93] He would later admit that he spent much of this period in largely fruitless attempts to persuade Orangemen that their fears of clerical control under home rule were unfounded, by highlighting the stance taken by Young Ireland, the Fenians, and Parnell.[94] The failure of the dock strike and near-collapse of the Independent Orange Order since about 1907 were a blow to hopes for working-class unity in the city. Worse was to follow, when the Belfast riots of 1912 saw about 500 Protestant socialists, liberals, and Independent Orangemen driven from the yards, alongside 2,000 Catholics.[95] By 1913 the main centre of labourite politics in Ireland was Dublin, rather than Belfast, and it was in

---

[90] Gaughan, *Thomas Johnson*, 29–30.   [91] Gaughan, *Thomas Johnson*, 30.
[92] NLI, Johnson papers, MS 17,203/4.   [93] Morgan, *James Connolly*, 97.
[94] NLI, Johnson papers, MS 17,231/5, Thomas Johnson to Ernest Blythe, undated [1949].
[95] Morrissey, '"Rotten Protestants"'.

that city that labour launched its most ambitious undertaking, the Irish Citizen Army.

The ICA was founded during the 1913 Dublin Lockout as a militia to protect striking workers during clashes with the Dublin Metropolitan Police.[96] The origins of the ICA are difficult to establish with certainty. There has long been a belief that it was founded in the improbable surroundings of the Rev. R. M. Gwynn's rooms in Trinity College.[97] Darrell Figgis argued as much, stating that 'there seems to have been almost a conspiracy to forget it'.[98] This story, although intriguing, is not quite true. The organisation founded in Gwynn's rooms was not in fact the ICA, and the confusion seems to have stemmed from the involvement in both enterprises of Captain Jack White. White leant his support to the workers during the Lockout. At a meeting of the Trinity College Gaelic Society in November 1913, this highly unusual socialist agitator called for the creation of a workers' volunteers to protect strikers, and for the students themselves to strike. This infuriated Provost Anthony Traill, who forbade students from attending any further meetings addressed by White; eighty students ignored his edict.[99] The students and others assembled in the rooms of R. M. Gwynn, a Larkin-sympathising Fellow and brother of Stephen Gwynn, and created a middle-class pro-strikers body called the Dublin Civic League.[100] White, in addressing this meeting, seems to have suggested the creation of some form of militia. However, White's biographer suggests that he only made a concrete appeal for the creation of what became the Citizen Army at a trade union meeting some time later.[101] Commanded by James Connolly, the Irish Citizen Army – a workers' republican militia – represented a departure in Irish history, and would contribute a socialist dimension to the Easter Rising of 1916.

How many Protestants served in the Irish Citizen Army? The Military Service Pension Collection lists a total of 210 ICA members to whom, or to the families of whom, pensions were awarded, following service in the Easter Rising. Of these, eleven, or about 5 per cent, have been identified as Protestant.[102] Although this figure is low, there was a substantial

---

[96] Townshend, *Easter 1916*, 49.

[97] See, for example, Donal Nevin, *James Connolly: 'a full life'* (Dublin, 2005), 552–553; R. B. McDowell and D. A. Webb, *Trinity College Dublin, 1592–1952: an academic history* (Dublin, 2004), 418.

[98] Figgis, *Recollections*, 9.

[99] London *Times*, 20 November 1913; White, *Misfit*, 157–159.

[100] BMH WS 1,766, William O'Brien.   [101] Keohane, *Captain Jack White*, 116–117.

[102] MAD, MSPC, List of ICA pension and awards files (digital manipulation; accessed 21 January 2015). These are: Peter Carpenter, Walter Patrick Carpenter, John Dutton Cooper, Ellett Elmes, Nellie Gifford-Donnelly, Annie Grange (née Norgrove),

involvement by Protestants in the ICA leadership until a short period before the rising. Sean O'Casey would note that four of the twenty members of the ICA committee 'were, or had been, of the Protestant way of thinking about heaven'. He was referring to himself, Jack White, Constance Markievicz, and Richard Brannigan. O'Casey left an intriguing description of Brannigan:

[He had been] a knight of the Grand Black Chapter of the Orange Order; had served time in a Northern jail for inciting a breach of the peace in the matter of a Catholic procession; had been presented with a purse packed full of sovereigns by the Orange Brethren when he came out; had joined the Gaelic League ... and had now stalked defiantly, in his Belfast way, on to the Citizen Army Committee.[103]

Richard Brannigan was the assumed name of Richard Braithwaite. Braithwaite, an Antrim-born chemist's clerk, had been an Orangeman and organising secretary of the Belfast Protestant Association, a militantly anti-Catholic body, as well as being prominent in labour politics in the city. In July 1901 he was sentenced to six months in gaol for inciting a riot at a Corpus Christi procession. Braithwaite joined the Independent Orange Order, which appears to have coincided with a change in his political views. As secretary of that organisation, his writing demonstrated nationalist sympathies.[104] By 1911 he must have broken with Orangeism, as he was recorded as having no religion on the census form of that year, in which return he also claimed to speak Irish. In April 1914 Braithwaite spoke at an ILPI demonstration against partition, which was also addressed by White and Connolly. After this, he took up residence in Dublin and became honorary treasurer of the ICA, adopting an assumed name, as he feared dismissal from his employment. There is no evidence Braithwaite took part in the rising, and his involvement in the ICA appears to have been brief.[105]

The ideology of the ICA explains the group's attractiveness for some Protestants. Like the ILPI, it was secular in nature, making it free from the Catholic ethos that some detected in other nationalist organisations.

Emily Hanratty (née Norgrove), Seamus McGowan, Alfred George Norgrove, Frederick Norgrove, and William Scott. Three further individuals had 1916 service but do not appear in MSPC files: Kathleen Lynn, Constance Markievicz, and Maria Norgrove. The MSPC has supplanted an earlier list of names assembled by R. M. Fox; see *The history of the Irish Citizen Army* (Dublin, 1943), 228–232.

[103] O'Casey, *Drums under the windows*, 608.   [104] See Chapter 2.

[105] *II*, 24 January 1963; *Irish Press*, 1, 2 October 1963, 2 May 1976; *Weekly Irish Times*, 22, 29 June, 27 July 1901; *IT*, 25 July 1901, 13 December 1905; Boyd, *Jack White*, 20–22; Gray, *City in revolt*, 213–214; Nevin, *James Connolly*, 439, 488, 756 n.; BMH WS 1,766, William O'Brien; BMH WS 585, Frank Robbins.

The ICA's 1914 constitution, which promised 'to sink all difference of birth, property and creed under the name of the common Irish people', would have recommended it to some non-Catholics.[106] The writings of James Connolly also provide a clue as to the ICA's success in securing some Protestant support. *Labour in Irish history* is a Marxist-influenced reading of the Williamite Wars period, which eschewed the traditional narrative of Catholic dispossession and injected class consciousness into the analysis. Connolly claimed the Protestant tenantry had acted against their class interest in supporting the Williamite claim to the throne, which did nothing to advance their material well-being.[107] This argument was taken up by Seamus McGowan, a Protestant ICA man, who, in the final issue of the *Worker's Republic* before it was suppressed after the Easter Rising, argued that the Catholic and Protestant working classes were equally exploited by the British, and should join forces against them.[108]

The Lockout had marked a departure in Sean O'Casey's life. Having left the IRB a few years before, he became associated with the socialist wing of advanced nationalism.[109] In 1914 he joined the ICA, drafting its constitution and becoming its secretary.[110] In his writings O'Casey, a lower-middle-class socialist, showed himself to be a particularly stern critic of his fellow Protestant nationalists. O'Casey's class animosity towards his socially superior co-religionists must hint at tensions within advanced nationalism.

Sean O'Casey and Bulmer Hobson may have seemed natural allies: both Protestant, both republican, and both outsiders with a hint of fanaticism. But O'Casey, rather than forming an alliance, cultivated a hatred of the Ulsterman. He later described Hobson as:

Protestant secretary of the IRB, editor of *Irish Freedom*, and head bottle-washer of all Nationalist activities, with his moony face, bulbous nose, long hair covered in a mutton-pie hat, a wrapped [*sic*] look on his face, moving about mysterious, surrounded by the ghostly guns of Dungannon: Ireland awoke when Hobson spoke – with fear was England shaken.[111]

Hobson's attitude to labour was key to their difference of opinion. The creation of the Irish Volunteers in November 1913 was a blow to the

[106] Irish Citizen Army Constitution, 1914, quoted in Sean O'Casey, *The story of the Irish Citizen Army* (Dublin, 1919), 14.
[107] James Connolly, *Labour in Irish history* (Dublin, 1910), 33, 39, 40, 44, 64–65. See also Conor Cruise O'Brien, *States of Ireland* (London, 1972), 90, 98–99.
[108] *Worker's Republic*, 22 April 1916.   [109] O'Casey, *Drums under the windows*, 614.
[110] Christopher Murray, *Sean O'Casey: writer at work: a biography* (Dublin, 2004), 85, 88.
[111] O'Casey, quoted in Hay, *Bulmer Hobson*, 104.

ICA; O'Casey claimed that thousands of men left for the better-led and more professionally organised group, until Jack White was left to train just one company of stalwarts.[112] Without help from the larger force, the ICA's prospects were grim. Hobson rebuffed any schemes for co-operation between the two bodies. O'Casey remembered that Hobson's 'warmest appreciation for all things pertaining to Labour was a sneer'.[113]

There was more to O'Casey's hatred than a simple clash between the advanced nationalist right and left. O'Casey resented that he had never enjoyed any material gain from his years of hard work, while Hobson, whose literary abilities he held in contempt, had become editor of *Irish Freedom*. He was also jealous of Hobson's being Thomas Clarke's 'white-haired boy'.[114] O'Casey believed Hobson exploited his religion: 'It was pathetic to see Clarke's devotion to this Protestant shit, exploiting his Protestantism in the National movement. Clarke thought him another Tone or McCracken.'[115]

By contrast, O'Casey had respect for White, who had taken on the thankless task of training the ICA: 'His efforts to understand the mysterious natures of working-men were earnest and constant, and were never fully appreciated by those amongst whom he spent his time and a good deal of his money.'[116] White sought to inject some professionalism into the ICA until political and personal differences led to his resignation in mid-1914.[117]

There was little about Constance Markievicz, with her landed background and aristocratic manner, to appeal to Sean O'Casey. O'Casey described her as a 'spluttering Catherine-wheel of irresponsibility', whose causes were 'no more to her than the hedges over which her horses jumped',[118] and doubted the sincerity of her socialist convictions. Certainly, her lack of reliance on ideology was clear to some (but not all) contemporaries. Markievicz 'has brought to the Irish Labour movement the fury of the aristocrat *déclassé* by her own choice. It is impossible to identify her with an "ism". She is that most irreconcilable of rebels – the rebel by temperament.'[119] Highly unusually, Markievicz managed to combine membership of the both the ICA and Cumann na mBan. Following Redmond's takeover of the Volunteers, O'Casey found this too much

---

[112] O'Casey, *The story of the Irish Citizen Army*, 9, 11.
[113] O'Casey, *The story of the Irish Citizen Army*, 31.
[114] O'Casey, quoted in Hay, *Bulmer Hobson*, 104.
[115] David Krause (ed.), *The letters of Sean O'Casey, Vol. II: 1942–54* (New York, 1980), Sean O'Casey to Shaemas O'Sheel, 26 May 1951, 800.
[116] O'Casey, *The story of the Irish Citizen Army*, 41.
[117] White, *Misfit*, 202; Boyd, *Jack White*, 24–28.
[118] O'Casey, *Drums under the windows*, 596.   [119] Wells, *Irish indiscretions*, 164.

and sought to force her to stand down from one organisation. In the end, however, the ICA committee decided Markievicz was a greater asset than O'Casey, and the latter resigned, thus bringing to an end his career as an Irish nationalist.[120] O'Casey was left embittered by the experience:

She wanted to be in everything and to be everywhere. She rushed into Arthur Griffith's arms, near knocking the man down; she dunced into the Republicanism of the Irish Brotherhood; she stormed into the Gaelic League, but quickly slid out again, for the learning of Irish was too much like work; she bounced into the Volunteers one night, and into the Citizen Army the next. Then she pounced on Connolly, and dazzled his eyes with her flashy enthusiasm. She found it almost impossible to reason out a question, and smothered the reasonable answer of another with a squeal. She seemed never to be able to make any golden or silver thing out of the ore of experience.[121]

Between 1914 and 1916, the ICA, having lost Jack White, Richard Braithwaite, and Sean O'Casey, became an evidently Catholic-dominated organisation. Constance Markievicz, the ICA's most prominent Protestant officer, would convert to Rome while imprisoned after the rising.[122] Although about fourteen Protestants would fight as ICA members, the loss of these senior figures would contribute to the growing perception of Catholicism as synonymous with republicanism. The true extent of the new connection between Catholicism and republicanism would become evident during, and in the aftermath of, the Easter Rising.

---

[120] O'Casey, *The story of the Irish Citizen Army*, 45–46.
[121] O'Casey, *Drums under the windows*, 596.   [122] See Chapter 5.

5   Rebels, 1916–1917

Introduction

In the aftermath of the Easter Rising, the *Catholic Bulletin* claimed that
the upsurge in popular patriotism was also giving rise to an outbreak of
popular piety:

the founts of our nationality have been stirred to their depths … there has been a
great searching of hearts and a great quickening of religious feeling. It looks as if
with the Requiem Masses for the dead, there is united as if by common consent, a
general union of prayer for Ireland amounting almost to exultation.[1]

Many have seen the rebels themselves as exhibiting similar characteristics. F. X. Martin, writing in 1967, saw the Catholic beliefs of the Easter
rebels as a 'phenomenon which is perhaps unique in the history of armed
revolts in modern European history'.[2] Few subsequent historians have
disagreed with this contention.[3] The rebel leadership saw their coming
sacrifice in Christ-like terms, and ordinary rebels showed their devotion
through frequent recitations of the rosary, even under enemy fire. The
Easter Rising, more than any other event, demonstrated the growing
Catholicisation of Irish republicanism. But what about Protestant rebels?
How did they fit into this conception of separatism? How many Protestant rebels were there? Did their experiences – particularly in captivity –
differ from those of Catholics? Were they determined to retain their
religion, or, as in the cases of Constance Markievicz and Roger Casement, was conversion inevitable?

---

[1] *Catholic Bulletin*, quoted in John Newsinger, '"I bring not peace but a sword": the
religious motif in the Irish War of Independence', *Journal of Contemporary History*,
Vol. 13, No. 3 (July 1978), 618.
[2] F. X. Martin, '1916: myth, fact, and mystery', *Studia Hibernica*, No. 7 (1967), 117.
[3] See, for example, Newsinger, 'I bring not peace but a sword'. See also an important
discussion in McGarry, *The Rising*, 160–161.

The Easter Rising

On Easter Monday, 24 April 1916, Dublin was the centre of a rebellion planned by the Military Council of the IRB, which had infiltrated the Irish Volunteers without the knowledge of its chief of staff, Eoin MacNeill. The rebellion was led by the author, schoolmaster, and Irish-language activist Pádraig Pearse and the socialist and trade unionist James Connolly. James Connolly's Irish Citizen Army also took part, along with Cumann na mBan, the women's auxiliary of the Irish Volunteers. Taking the General Post Office (GPO) as their headquarters, rebels seized key locations in Dublin and proclaimed an Irish Republic. They held out for seven days, until their surrender on April 28. The damage caused by the Easter Rising was enormous: 485 people were killed, more than half of whom were civilians.[4] Destruction of property was estimated at £2,500,000, and much of Sackville Street lay in ruins.[5]

How many Protestants rebels fought in 1916? Assembling a complete list of Protestant combatants is a challenging task. As discussed in Chapter 4, a total of fourteen ICA combatants have been identified as Protestant. A further nine Irish Volunteer and Cumann na mBan Protestants have been traced.[6] In total, twenty-three Protestant rebels, members of the Irish Volunteers, ICA, and Cumann na mBan, have been identified. This chapter will describe their experiences. However, those who took part in the fighting tell only part of the story of Protestant nationalists during the rebellion. Easter Week was characterised by a series of bewildered solo excursions into central Dublin by a wide variety of Protestant nationalists, of various political affiliations, who recorded a mixture of sympathy, ambivalence, and horror as events unfolded.

By Easter 1916 several influential Protestants had already parted from the rebels. The most famous example is Bulmer Hobson. By early 1916 Hobson had become the most prominent Eoin MacNeill supporter, favouring a defensive strategy for the Volunteers and opposing a preemptive rebellion. On Holy Thursday, 1916, Hobson learned that Pearse

---

[4] Glasnevin Trust, *1916 Necrology*, available at www.glasnevintrust.ie/__uuid/55a29fab–3b24–41dd–a1d9–12d148a78f74/Glasnevin-Trust–1916-Necrology–485.pdf, accessed 5 July 2016.

[5] Daithí Ó Corráin, '"They blew up the best portion of our city and … it is their duty to replace it": compensation and reconstruction in the aftermath of the 1916 Rising', *Irish Historical Studies*, Vol. 39, Issue 154 (November 2014), 275, 278.

[6] Irish Volunteers: Alfred Cotton, George Gilmore, Archie Heron, George Irvine, Rory Haskins, Cahal McDowell, Harry Nicholls, and Arthur Shields. Cumann na mBan: Sydney Czira. These names were identified by means of a variety of sources, especially: BMH WSs; *DIB*; MAD, MSPC, List of IRA pension and awards files (digital manipulation; accessed 26 January 2015).

and his associates were planning a rising. Although he and MacNeill confronted Pearse, the former did not take decisive action to prevent a rebellion. On Good Friday, Hobson was detained by his former comrades until the outbreak of the rebellion.[7] MacNeill issued a countermanding order, cancelling the planned rebellion for Easter Sunday, but the Military Council decided to go ahead the following day, albeit with fewer Volunteers, in a rebellion that would be mostly confined to Dublin. Few men had contributed so much to the revival of militant nationalism as Bulmer Hobson; however, his attempts to prevent a rising, which he considered to be morally and militarily disastrous, ended his nationalist career and left him a detested figure.

Others who were already alienated from the advanced men included Sean O'Casey, James Deakin, and Captain Jack White. Seán Lester, who had obeyed MacNeill's order not to fight, took no part in the rising. Roger Casement also sought to prevent a rebellion. Casement, who had been in Germany since October 1914, had become disenchanted with what he viewed as the inadequate military assistance being offered by the Imperial government, and requested to be returned to Ireland. Casement and Monteith were sent to Ireland via U-boat, with the intention of rendezvousing in Tralee Bay with the *Aud*, a German ship that carried a limited supply of arms. However, local Volunteers failed to make contact with either vessel, and eventually the German crew, having been apprehended by a British vessel, scuttled the *Aud* in Cork Harbour. On the early hours of Good Friday, Casement and Robert Monteith washed up on Banna Strand, County Kerry. Casement, exhausted and desperate to prevent a rebellion, was arrested by the RIC after 1 p.m.[8] Monteith, a resourceful character, evaded the authorities, and eventually escaped to New York. Without Casement, and without German guns, the rising would still take place.

Among the first Volunteers to be captured by the British was Captain George Irvine. Irvine served under Éamonn Ceannt in the South Dublin Union workhouse complex, south-west of Dublin city. Ceannt, Irvine, and their men arrived at the Union at about midday on Easter Monday. Irvine soon took part in what became a celebrated engagement. Acting under Ceannt's orders, Irvine, with nine men under his command, took up position in huts beside the back gate of the Union and barricaded the windows. Soon, the complex came under fire from British troops, and he and his men found themselves surrounded. The British set up a machine

---

[7] See Hay, *Bulmer Hobson*, ch. 8.
[8] Inglis, *Roger Casement*, 310–313; Ó Síocháin, *Roger Casement*, 439–440.

gun and began firing into the hut, although Irvine's men held fast and shot two soldiers who attempted to break in. Irvine later recalled:

We now occupied a back room in the hut ... but the British had closed in on us and in the evening were pouring volleys into the hut. One man just beside me, John Traynor, got a bullet through his eye. I saw we could hold out no longer and asked the men would I surrender. They agreed and I did so.[9]

Following their surrender, Irvine and his men were marched up South Circular Road under heavy escort and spent the night in Richmond Barracks, where they were interrogated. On the Saturday after the rising, Irvine and the other Volunteers were sent to Kilmainham Gaol.

Mabel FitzGerald narrowly avoided taking part in the fighting. Desmond FitzGerald had originally opposed the decision to mount a rebellion. Eventually he decided to take part, out of loyalty to the men he had trained, despite believing the project doomed without German support. On deciding to join the rebellion, he left Dublin for Bray, to say goodbye to his children, who were being looked after by a family acquaintance. At Bray station he met Mabel by chance. They rushed to see their children before catching the train to Dublin.[10] Neither Mabel nor Desmond expected to see their children again. A few hours later, seeing the flag raised on the roof of the GPO, Desmond told his wife, 'This is worth getting wiped out for.'[11] On Easter Tuesday, believing Dublin Castle to have been captured by the rebels, Pearse sent Mabel to take a flag to be hoisted above the castle. However, she later returned with the unhappy news that that the castle had not fallen, having herself narrowly escaped capture by the British garrison.[12] At this point Pearse instructed her to return home to Bray, believing that both parents of small children should not be at risk of death.[13]

The most senior female combatant was Constance Markievicz. Choosing to fight with the ICA, she served as second-in-command of their contingent on St Stephen's Green. Michael Mallin, their commander, took the highly inadvisable course of digging trenches in the Green. On Easter Tuesday, the ICA came under fire from a British machine-gun on the roof of the Shelbourne Hotel; Mallin and Markievicz were forced

---

[9] BMH WS 265, George Irvine. See also MAD, MSPC, 34REF61665, George Irvine, Evidence given before the advisory committee, 21 September 1951.

[10] UCD, FitzGerald papers, P80/1660 (1) 'Account of entering the Post Office on the first day of the Easter Rising', by Mabel FitzGerald.

[11] FitzGerald, *Desmond's rising*, 133.   [12] FitzGerald, *Desmond's rising*, 140.

[13] Jennifer FitzGerald papers, Garret FitzGerald, 'Desmond – and Mabel – FitzGerald'.

to retreat to the solidly built Royal College of Surgeons, on the north end of the Green.[14]

One ICA man who served under Mallin and Markievicz at the Green was William Scott (1872–1947). Scott, who was born near Letterbreen, County Fermanagh, was originally a member of the Church of Ireland and later joined the Plymouth Brethren. Moving to Dublin in about 1900, Scott, a bricklayer and activist in the Bricklayers' and Stonelayers' Union, joined the ICA in 1914. On Easter Tuesday, acting under orders to capture a commercial premises on the west end of the Green, Scott slipped from a roof, injuring his ankle and back, which prevented him taking part in further fighting. Scott escaped imprisonment after the rising, and would go on to serve in the 4th Battalion of the Dublin Brigade during the War of Independence, and took the anti-Treaty side during the Civil War.[15]

Further west, Dr Kathleen Lynn, the ICA chief medical officer, took part in the action to capture City Hall. Her commander was the actor and trade unionist Sean Connolly. Arriving at City Hall before midday on Easter Monday, she, Connolly, and others took up position on the building's roof. Lynn described what followed:

It was a beautiful day, the sun was hot and we were not long there when we noticed Sean Connolly coming towards us, walking upright, although we had been advised to crouch and take cover as much as possible. We suddenly saw him fall mortally wounded by a sniper's bullet from the Castle. First aid was useless. He died almost immediately.[16]

The loss of Sean Connolly had a demoralising effect on the City Hall contingent; having come under heavy fire, they surrendered that night.

Five members of one Dublin Church of Ireland family, the Norgroves, served with the ICA. George Norgrove was born in Kingstown, County Dublin, in 1876. A gas fitter and active trade unionist, Norgrove joined the ICA at its inception. Holding the rank of lieutenant, he sat as one of eight members of its governing council, and took responsibility for bomb making. During Easter Week he was initially posted to the GPO, but on Monday evening he was sent as part of a small company to reinforce City Hall. Norgrove's daughters, Emily and Annie Norgrove – aged eighteen and sixteen respectively – were already stationed at City Hall. George

---

[14] Norman, *Terrible beauty: a life of Constance Markievicz*, 141.

[15] Fermanagh 1916 Centenary Association, *Fearless but few: Fermanagh and the Easter Rising* (Castleblayney, 2015), 105–109; MAD, MSPC, 34REF1644, William Scott, Evidence given before the advisory committee, 14 February 1936.

[16] BMH WS 357, Kathleen Lynn.

Norgrove's wife, Maria, had tried to join the GPO garrison, but had been told to go home. However, she successfully joined the ICA position at the Royal College of Surgeons. George Norgrove's son Fred, aged about fifteen, worked as a messenger boy in the GPO, until Wednesday, when James Connolly ordered him to leave the garrison on account of his age.[17]

By Easter Week, Harry Nicholls was captain in A Company, 4th Battalion of the Dublin Brigade of the Irish Volunteers. On Easter Monday, upon learning that the rebellion was going ahead, he tried to cycle across town to link up with his unit. However, on reaching St Stephen's Green, he decided to fight with Mallin's ICA contingent. Nicholls led a combined Volunteer and ICA assault on the Turkish baths on Grafton Street. Nicholls's position saw only intermittent sniping with the British, and on Saturday they were evacuated to the Royal College of Surgeons, at which point Mallin surrendered. Nicholls, who in civilian life was an engineer with Dublin Corporation, was marched to Richmond Barracks, where waiting detectives were very surprised to see him among the rebels.[18]

Occasionally, evidence for the marginalisation of non-Catholics from their Catholic fellow rebels can be detected. Arthur Shields (1896–1970), an Abbey actor who came from an Anglican and socialist family, fought with the Irish Volunteers in several positions on Sackville Street. While holding a position in the Hibernian Bank, Thomas Weafer, a Volunteer officer, was shot dead. Leslie Price recalled: 'I remember, when Tom Weafer was shot, we all knelt down to say a prayer and Arthur Shields stood in a corner because he was not a Catholic.'[19] Numerous statements preserved by the Bureau of Military History describe rebels kneeling and reciting the rosary before, during, or after fighting. These devotions came naturally to Catholics, and were not intended to promote a sense of separateness from Protestants; however, they did.

The small total number of Protestant rebels has contributed to a sense that the rising was strongly connected with the Catholic faith. The decision of some Protestant rebels to convert to Rome has contributed to this perception. One Volunteer converted during the stress of

---

[17] MAD, MSPC, 34REF204, Frederick Norgrove; 34REF1764, Alfred George Norgrove; 34REF6982, Annie Grange (née Norgrove); 34REF724, Emily Hanratty (née Norgrove); Dublin *Evening Herald*, 20 August 2011.

[18] Maguire, 'Harry Nicholls and Kathleen Emerson: Protestant rebels', 147–148; MAD, MSPC, 34REF15964, Henry 'Harry' Nicholls.

[19] BMH WS 1,754, Mrs Tom Barry (née Leslie Price). For a detailed discussion of Shield's life, see Fearghal McGarry, *The Abbey rebels of 1916: a lost revolution* (Dublin, 2015), 111–115, 140, 156, 160–161, 168–173, 176–179, 264–2319ff.

heavy fighting. George Cecil 'Cahal' MacDowell was an artist and Dublin Corporation engineer who fought under Éamon de Valera at Boland's Mill. While being bombarded from Beggar's Bush, a Catholic priest began to take the men's confessions. On hearing that McDowell was not a Catholic, the priest offered to get a Protestant clergyman. But MacDowell refused, as 'he would rather not have one as they might give them away. He laid his Howth rifle beside him and the priest baptised him. A young volunteer whose name was Kavanagh was his godfather.'[20] One of Constance Markievicz's biographers describes how, on her last night in the Royal College of Surgeons, she experienced an epiphany which would prompt her conversion to Catholicism: 'she had undergone a deep mystical experience which the men and women around her had been able to express through the ritual of their Catholic prayers in a way that her own, half-believed Protestant Church upbringing had denied to her'.[21] Roger Casement was received into the Catholic Church the day before he was hanged.[22] However, these conversions, although they have received much scholarly attention, were rare. Of the twenty-four Protestant Easter rebels discussed in this book, only three have been identified as converting to Catholicism.[23]

Although Dublin city was the centre of the rebellion, isolated actions took part in other parts of the country. Three Protestant Irish Volunteers took part in the failed efforts to initiate military action in the north. During Easter Week, Belfast Volunteers were instructed to entrain for Coalisland, County Tyrone, from where it was intended they would march south and hold the line of the Shannon. Rory Haskins, who served as a drill instructor, was among them. This operation was a failure, largely due to the confusion caused by the countermanding order. Haskins was arrested in Tyrone and brought to Richmond Barracks, and latterly, Frongoch. He had few regrets, later telling Denis McCullough that 'it was great fun while it lasted'.[24] Archie Heron also joined the muster in Coalisland, but on Easter Sunday he was informed that the rising had been called off and he returned to Belfast with his men. On hearing that Dublin had risen, Heron made for Clogher, County Tyrone, where he sought to raise a force to cause an Ulster diversion. However, this plan came apart when news reached him of the surrender. Heron spent several weeks in various safe houses after

[20] BMH WS 258, Maeve Cavanagh MacDowell.
[21] Norman, *Terrible beauty: a life of Constance Markievicz*, 167.
[22] See below for further discussion.
[23] Rory Haskins, Cahal McDowell, Constance Markievicz.
[24] UCD, McC, P120/27, Rory Haskins to Denis McCullough, 13 September 1949. See also BMH WS 223, Robert 'Rory' Haskins.

the rising, and managed to evade capture.[25] Alfred Cotton had an even more peripatetic experience. Cotton, who had been expelled from Kerry under the Defence of the Realm Act in March 1916, was ordered by the Volunteer leadership to return to Belfast and attempt to return only when the rebellion broke out. On Easter Monday he made his way to Dublin and arrived at the GPO just as the building was being captured. After meeting with James Connolly and Sean McDermott, it was agreed that he would make for Kerry, and help lead the Volunteers there. He proceeded north, with the intention of linking with Volunteers in south Ulster and making his way down the Shannon. However, he halted in Drogheda, on hearing that the rest of the country had not risen. Cotton spent several frustrating days attempting to return to Dublin City, before eventually returning to Belfast. On 2 May he was arrested and, with other Belfast Volunteers, brought to Richmond.[26]

For every active Protestant rebel in 1916, there were many more Protestant nationalists with no involvement in the rebellion, who, like ordinary Dubliners, found themselves perplexed and confused partici-pants, with only an imperfect understanding of events. Their experiences demonstrate the extent to which many Protestant nationalists had become marginalised from the most radical strand of Irish nationalism. The most famous Protestant nationalist eyewitness account of the rising comes from the writer James Stephens (d. 1950). Stephens, a regular contributor to *Sinn Féin* and an associate of Arthur Griffith, published one of the earliest and most vivid eyewitness accounts of the rebellion. *Insurrection in Dublin* records the bewilderment of the crowds, the vio-lence of the Volunteers, and the brutality of the British response, in a tone of sympathy towards the rebels.[27] During Easter Week, Douglas Hyde was living in Earlsfort Place, in the south city centre. On Easter Monday morning, Hyde, who was bicycling around St Stephen's Green, was amazed to witness Mallin's men digging trenches. In the aftermath of the rebellion, some loyalists would point the finger of blame at Gaelic Leaguers for having inculcated anti-British sentiment in the country. On Thursday, Hyde received an early experience of this when he met a dentist of his acquaintance on Harcourt Street, who asked him, 'How much are you responsible for this?' and threatened to bayonet him. Hyde's reaction to events veered between thinking the Volunteers 'crim-inally careless' for putting civilians in danger, admiration at the

[25] BMH WS 577, Archie Heron; *DIB* article on Archibald 'Archie' Heron.
[26] BMH WS 184, Alfred Cotton. See also [various authors], *Kerry's fighting story, 1916–21* (Tralee, n.d., [1947]), 46–53.
[27] James Stephens, *Insurrection in Dublin* (Dublin, 1916).

organising powers of the rebels, and anger at the British government, whose handling of the Curragh incident, he believed, had led to the rebellion.[28] Another Protestant Gaelic Leaguer who witnessed the rebellion first-hand was Nelly O'Brien. O'Brien was so disconnected from advanced nationalism that for the first few days she believed the sounds of fighting came from a demonstration against conscription.[29] Within two years, she would be among the principal Protestant republican activists in Dublin. Cesca Chenevix Trench, although a member of Cumann na mBan and a more radical nationalist than her future husband Diarmid Coffey, was appalled by the rising. On Easter Monday Cesca visited Pearse in the GPO and told him she disapproved of his actions. She later told her aunt: 'This mad affair has done irreparable damage to the cause of Irish freedom which it is meant to serve, as it can only succeed by a miracle which isn't likely to occur. God help us, I think it will break all our hearts.'[30] But others were sympathetic. Nancy Campbell, who was living in County Wicklow, registered her delight that a rebellion was under way. She, her husband Joseph, and three-year-old son Gillachrist embarked on a near-suicidal excursion into Dublin city centre to see the action for themselves.[31] A similar figure was Ella Young. Young, who was living in the unionist enclave of Leinster Road, Rathmines, relished the outbreak of rebellion, but she did not take part in the fighting. However, on Easter Monday she joined the curious crowd of onlookers at Rathmines Town Hall, where she could see soldiers marching out of Portobello Barracks in the distance.[32]

Elizabeth Bloxham was working in Newtownards, County Down, when she heard news of the rising. The toleration her employers had shown of her previous political activities did not survive the new political climate, and her school committee voted her dismissal. On leaving Ulster she moved to Meath and later Wexford where she continued her Cumann na mBan activities.[33] Gertrude Bannister, who had worked in the same London school for seventeen years, was dismissed from her position a few months after the rising, due to her decision to visit her cousin Roger Casement in prison.[34] The Giffords were deeply affected

[28] TCD, MS 10343/6–7, Douglas Hyde, Diary of Easter Week.
[29] TCD, Nelly O'Brien papers, MS 10343/1, Nelly O'Brien, typescript account of Easter Week.
[30] Cesca Chenevix Trench to Francis Trench, 29 April 1916, in Pyle (ed.), *Cesca's diary*, 214.
[31] TCD, Campbell papers, MS 10238, Nancy Campbell's diary of 1916.
[32] Young, *Flowering dusk*, 123.   [33] BMH WS 632, Elizabeth Bloxham.
[34] NLI, MS 47,738, Gertrude Bannister to George Bernard Shaw, 6 August 1916.

by the rising. Nellie Gifford, the most socialist of the sisters, took part in the rising with the ICA, serving at the Royal College of Surgeons.[35] Muriel Gifford, who was married to Thomas MacDonagh, was widowed following her husband's execution after the rising, as was her sister Grace, who, in a melancholy ceremony, married Joseph Plunkett just hours before his execution.[36] The treatment of Grace Gifford was one of several factors which increased sympathy for the rebels in the months that followed. However, Grace and Muriel Gifford received little sympathy from their mother. In an interview shortly after the rising, she stated she had opposed her daughter's union with Plunkett, and that Grace was 'a very headstrong and self-willed girl, and latterly had lived a more or less independent life'. She knew who to blame for her daughters' entanglement with the rebels: 'The Countess Markievicz ... has been responsible for all along dragging them into it. They got to know her several years ago, and have been largely under her influence.'[37]

Alice Stopford Green was appalled by the rebellion. She was personally close with some British officials and supported a negotiated settlement to the Irish crisis; just prior to the rebellion she had been staying with Sir Matthew Nathan in the under-secretary's lodge in Phoenix Park, alongside her niece Dorothy Stopford.[38] Green was particularly saddened by her friend Roger Casement's arrest. This was 'a calamity brought on by an insane desire of Roger as well as the rest of the rebels to follow Wolfe Tone'.[39] Dorothy Stopford, who spent Easter Week in the under-secretary's lodge, was equally scathing, telling her brother that the rebels were 'very small and violent and heaven knows they may have wrecked Home Rule'.[40] Within two years, a combination of executions, curfews, and searches would convert Dorothy Stopford to republicanism.[41]

The rising caused a crisis in the Irish Guild of the Church. The Guild included a diverse mixture of unionists, republicans, and apolitical language activists. At first the executive committee were concerned simply to keep the organisation together, with members being informed that at

---

[35] BMH WS 256, Nellie Gifford.
[36] Clare, *Unlikely rebels*, 171–184. From Mountjoy, Kathleen Lynn recorded: 'Heard very pitiful crying, it was Miss [Nellie] Gifford, her brother told her that two brothers in law were shot, MacDonagh & Plunkett'; Royal College of Physicians of Ireland (RCPI), Diary of Kathleen Lynn, 9 May 1916. Muriel MacDonagh, née Gifford, herself died the following year, drowning while swimming alone in Skerries, Co. Dublin.
[37] *Belfast Evening Telegraph*, 8 May 1916.
[38] NLI, MS 11,426, Typescript recollections of Miss [Edie] Stopford.
[39] Alice Stopford Green, quoted in McDowell, *Alice Stopford Green*, 103.
[40] Anne MacLellan, *Dorothy Stopford Price: rebel doctor* (Dublin, 2014), 36.
[41] For Dorothy Stopford's War of Independence career, see Chapter 7.

their post-rebellion meeting, 'in the event of their alluding to the recent Rising nothing should be said likely to offend anyone'.[42] The Bishop of Tuam, seeking to impose his authority on the body of which he was president, threatened to resign unless a strong statement deploring the rebellion was passed. The resulting resolution was loyalist indeed:

> The Guild affirms its loyalty to his Majesty the King, and desires the establishment of law and order and the restoration of peace and goodwill among the people of Ireland.[43]

However, many of those who supported this resolution did so tactically. In the next two years their ranks would be joined by others, new converts to republicanism, who would entirely change the nature of the organisation.[44]

Protestant nationalists were unlucky in the religious composition of the rising. The fact that all seven signatories of the Proclamation of the Republic were Catholic, along with the conversions of Markievicz and Casement, coupled with the decision of such prominent figures as Sean O'Casey and Bulmer Hobson to part company with advanced nationalists, has given the impression of religious homogeneity among this generation of Irish nationalists. The 'poet's Rising' described by Ella Young has come to be perceived as a 'Catholic's rebellion' as well.[45] The attitudes of the rebel leaders towards religion demonstrates the extent to which Catholicism had come to influence Irish republicanism. The Catholic conception of sacrifice was central to Pearse's thought. He appropriated the death of Christ as an exemplar of the sacrifice required to redeem the Irish nation, and even viewed his own coming self-sacrifice as comparable to that of the Lord. Joseph Mary Plunkett, a devout Catholic, wrote mystical verse. Sean McDermott, a committed IRB man, had lived much of his adult life as an anti-clericalist; in the period before his execution, he was reconciled to the Catholic Church.[46] Another figure who was reconciled to his faith was James Connolly, whose last wish was that his wife, Lillie, a member of the Church of Ireland, should convert to Catholicism.[47] There were some exceptions: Thomas Clarke, the veteran Fenian, seems to have remained an anti-clericalist to the end. However, by 1916, the traditional IRB hostility to

---

[42] RCBL, Irish Guild of the Church minute book, 20 June 1916.
[43] RCBL, Irish Guild of the Church minute book, 20 June 1916, stated that this was passed only after 'considerable discussion'.
[44] See Chapter 6.   [45] Young, *Flowering dusk*, 131.
[46] David Bracken (ed.), *The end of all things earthly: faith profiles of the 1916 leaders* (Dublin, 2016), 19, 89–92, 65–67.
[47] Donal Nevin, *James Connolly*, 688.

organised Catholicism, a tradition which had proved amenable to some Protestants, was in unassailable decline.

The Aftermath

On 29 April the rebels surrendered unconditionally. Two days earlier supreme command in Ireland had been vested in General Sir John Maxwell, who was granted martial law powers. Maxwell chose to arrest 'all dangerous Sinn Féiners [sic]' including 'those who have taken an active part in the movement although not in the present rebellion'.[48] Some 3,509 people were arrested, including 79 women.[49] Of the 90 death sentences imposed by courts martial, 15 were carried out. Roger Casement, George Irvine, and Constance Markievicz were sentenced to death; Irvine and Markievicz had their sentences commuted; Casement, as we will see, was hanged after a trial. Although a large portion of those arrested were shortly released, around 1,800 were interned in Britain, principally in the Frongoch camp, north Wales, as well as various prisons. Twenty Protestants have been identified among their number.[50] The experiences of Protestant prisoners are instructive as they offer insight into the place members of these churches would hold within the nationalist movement after the rising.

After surrendering, Kathleen Lynn was imprisoned in Kilmainham Gaol.[51] Lynn's period of captivity illustrates something of the incongruity of a Protestant rebel in 1916. The Church of Ireland chaplain who came to minister Lynn and the Norgroves was the first to offer criticism: he 'thinks it a pity "Protestants should be mixed up in a revolution"'.[52] The interviews Lynn had with family members caused anguish. Lynn was close to her strongly unionist family, especially her father, the Church of Ireland rector of Cong. Throughout her period as a republican activist she would attempt – with some success – to remain on good terms with her relations despite their different politics. After her father visited her in prison she wrote: 'I am sorry sorry he came, it is hard to grieve one's father, but I could not do otherwise.'[53] She stated:

---

[48] Quoted in Townshend, *Easter 1916*, 273.   [49] Townshend, *Easter 1916*, 274.

[50] Ernest Blythe, Roger Casement (converted to Catholicism in custody), Alfie Cotton, Ellett Elmes, Darrell Figgis, Nellie Gifford, Rory Haskins, George Irvine, Kathleen Lynn, Constance Markievicz (converted to Catholicism in custody), Seamus McGowan, Herbert Moran, Harry Nicholls, Alfred Norgrove, Annie Norgrove, Emily Norgrove, Sam Ruttle, Arthur Shields, Peter Steepe, Captain Jack White.

[51] BMH WS, 357, Kathleen Lynn; RCPI, Diary of Kathleen Lynn, 2 May 1916.

[52] RCPI, Diary of Kathleen Lynn, 6 May 1916.

[53] RCPI, Diary of Kathleen Lynn, 10 May 1916.

A very black Friday. Farnie and Nan [father and sister] were here, oh, so, reproachful, they wouldn't listen to me & looked as if they would cast me off forever. How sorry I am for their sorrow! Erin needs very big sacrifices. I am glad they go home to-morrow. Why do they always misunderstand me?[54]

During these visits her family made clear their wish that she should discontinue her nationalist activities; she refused, and they banned her from the family home.[55]

While imprisoned in Mountjoy after the rising, Markievicz registered as a Catholic and sought instruction in the faith. However, she made no attempt whatever to engage with Catholic theology, preferring to enquire about her fellow rebels. The chaplain explained:

I can't understand Countess Markievicz at all. She wants to be received into the Church, but she won't attend to me when I try to explain Transubstantiation and other doctrines. She just says, 'Please don't trouble to explain. I tell you I believe all the Church teaches, Now Father, please tell me about the boys.'[56]

Markievicz formally entered the Catholic Church on her release from prison.

Roger Casement was tried for high treason in the Old Bailey in June 1916. Despite having been strongly critical of Casement's actions, Alice Stopford Green threw her energies into his defence, subscribing funds, hiring lawyers, and agitating on his conditions. Casement's fellow Ulster nationalist, Alice Milligan, travelled to lend her support, and sat beside Stopford Green during the trial. Casement's defence was undermined by British officials, who, before and during his trial, circulated sections of his diaries, which detail homosexual encounters.[57] On 29 June, Casement was found guilty and sentenced to be hanged. In his speech from the dock, Casement condemned British rule in Ireland, argued that he should have been tried before an Irish judge and jury, and claimed that the Ulster Volunteers would have combined with the Irish Volunteers, were it not for the machinations of the government.[58] Although detested as an arch-traitor by much of the British public, Casement garnered influential supporters among the British and Irish intelligentsia, including W. B. Yeats, George Bernard Shaw, Sir Arthur Conan Doyle, John Galsworthy, G. K. Chesterton, and Beatrice and

---

[54] Ó hÓgartaigh, *Kathleen Lynn*, 31.
[55] RCPI, Diary of Kathleen Lynn, 25 December 1917.
[56] Norman, *Terrible beauty: a life of Constance Markievicz*, 167.
[57] See Jeffrey Dudgeon, *Roger Casement: the Black Diaries: with a study of his background, sexuality and Irish political life* (Belfast, 2002).
[58] George H. Knott (ed.), *Trial of Sir Roger Casement* (Philadelphia, 1917), 199–205.

Sidney Webb, who agitated for a reprieve.[59] However, on 24 July the appeal failed. Casement told Father Carey, the chaplain of Pentonville Prison, of his desire to convert to Catholicism. On being informed of this, Cardinal Bourne, the archbishop of Westminster, insisted that he could only convert having first expressed sorrow 'for any scandal he might have caused by his acts, public or private'.[60] Such a statement would have meant repudiating his involvement in the rebellion, which Casement refused to do. However, in the course of discussion with the prisoner, Carey discovered that Casement had been baptised a Catholic by his mother when he was a child. This meant that Casement, rather than being baptised, merely had to be reconciled, *in articulo mortis*, to the Catholic Church. In a final apologia before his execution, Casement explained his decision to die a Catholic: 'In Protestant coldness I could not find [what I was looking for], but I saw it in the faces of the Irish. Now I know what it was I loved in them. The chivalry of Christ speaking through human eyes.'[61] The image of Roger Casement in his cell, reading *The imitation of Christ* and fingering his rosary beads, is difficult to reconcile with the Casement we saw in earlier chapters, subscribing to the Irish Guild of the Church, describing Ulster Protestants as the 'best part of Ireland', and organising home rule meetings in North Antrim. Even the *Catholic Bulletin*, in its obituary, admitted Casement had spent his entire life until his imprisonment a convinced Protestant.[62] Casement's conversion came as a result of his realisation that efforts to entice the vast bulk of Protestants towards nationalism were doomed to fail. His own people having failed him, he looked to Catholics for redemption and vindication. Casement was hanged on 3 August 1916 at Pentonville, thus bequeathing Irish republicanism a new, Catholic, martyr.

The vast majority of the men imprisoned in Britain after the rising were young, Catholic, and demonstrably religious.[63] The denominational profile of the rebel prisoners was, for some, a cause of concern. Imprisoned in Reading Gaol, with other men believed by the British to be ringleaders, Tomás MacCurtain noted that three of the twenty-seven inmates – Darrell Figgis, Ernest Blythe, and Alfie Cotton – were

---

[59] See, for example, British Library (BL), Add MS 63596, Casement Petition papers, 'A Petition to the Prime Minister on behalf of Roger Casement by Sir Arthur Conan Doyle'.
[60] Inglis, *Roger Casement*, 368.   [61] Inglis, *Roger Casement*, 370.
[62] *Catholic Bulletin*, Vol. 6, No. 9 (September 1916), 517.
[63] For the Catholic faith of the men imprisoned at Frongoch, see W. J. Brennan-Whitmore, *With the Irish in Frongoch* (Dublin, 1917), 33, 41–42, 50. For group recitations of the rosary in Richmond and Stafford prisons, see, for example, BMH WS 1,041, Thomas Doyle.

Protestant. This was, he noted, 'a good sign'.[64] The prisoners in Reading elected Figgis as captain. A largely inactive member of the Irish Volunteers, Figgis had not taken part in the rising, but was arrested at his home in Achill Island, County Mayo, in the general roundup that followed. Figgis, as we have noted, had a particularly difficult personality, and the prisoners came to regret their decision. According to Ernest Blythe, 'Very soon ... like most of the prisoners there, I came to the conclusion that Figgis was no good.' He recalled:

Ultimately it was decided to get Figgis out of office, by proposing that the office of Captain should go round and that a new election should take place every month. It was decided that I should follow Figgis lest he should allege that he was put out of office because he was a Protestant.[65]

Nor was this the sole occasion when Figgis's highly unusual public touchiness about his religion embarrassed his fellow prisoners. According to another Volunteer in Reading:

We decided also that we would have prayer ... in Irish in the small hall ... When this decision was made known ... our Protestant fellow members, including Blythe, Cotton, Seamus McGabhan [Seamus McGowan], Herbert Moran, a farmer from Co. Limerick, one of the Palatine people [Peter Steepe] ... and Darrell Figgis came along and asked [Sean] T. O'Kelly if it were true 'Yes' he said, 'but that is not stopping you from having your own prayers publicly as well.' 'Oh, we are not going to do that; all we want to know is, in what language are they being recited.' 'In Irish, of course' said Sean T. 'Well, in that case, we'll participate in it; we will show our solidarity if nothing else for the language of our country' and they did. They (the Protestant prisoners) found serious fault with Darrell Figgis on the first night those prayers were said, because Darrell knelt up on a chair instead of kneeling on the ground. They had a very heated discussion with him, saying that it was not the proper thing to do. He said he was just as good a Protestant as any other Protestants. As it was the Protestants had the discussion with him, we said nothing, for we did not mind the thing at all. They alleged that he did not have the slightest idea of what it was to be a good Protestant, and the matter ended at that, but Figgis knelt on the floor from that on.[66]

There are other examples of joint Catholic/Protestant prayer meetings. In a letter to a friend, George Irvine, while imprisoned in Lewes Gaol, described praying every morning and evening with his Catholic fellow rebels, and even requested a set of tricolour rosary beads, the better to contribute to devotions.[67]

---

[64] NLI, Florence O'Donoghue papers, MS 31,140, Typescript diary of Tomás MacCurtain, 16 July 1916.
[65] BMH WS 939, Ernest Blythe.   [66] BMH WS 1403, Eamon O'Duibhir.
[67] NLI, MS 49,909, George Irvine to Crissie M. Doyle, 21 February 1917.

The vast majority of prisoners ended up in Frongoch. Protestants formed only a tiny proportion of the 1,800 internees.[68] A total of eleven Protestant internees have been identified, including Harry Nicholls, Alfie Cotton, and Arthur Shields. There is some evidence that the ecumenical scenes described at Reading and Lewes was not as apparent in Frongoch. While in Frongoch, Protestant prisoners shared quarters with large numbers of demonstrably religious Catholic fellow rebels. Arthur Shields found this an uncomfortable experience. Adrian Frazier has shown how the stultifyingly Catholic environment disillusioned Shields and informed his decision to abandon the nationalist movement after his release. He later moved to Hollywood, where he found fame as a feature film actor, appearing in several John Ford films, including *How Green Was My Valley?* (1941) and *The Quiet Man* (1952). Years later, asked why he left Ireland, Shields said it was because he 'didn't want to pray in Gaelic'.[69] Such a comment can only hint at tensions that must have been felt by Protestant republicans after the rising.

Although numerous Protestants who held mildly nationalist sympathies were radicalised and converted to separatist principles by the events of 1916, for others, the rising served to alienate. The events of Easter Week did nothing to reverse Robert Lynd's disenchantment with the nationalist movement. Writing to Mabel FitzGerald, he stated: 'Pearse obviously died like a hero, but I have always thought his "blood-shed" gospel of Nationalism a wild delusion & a breakaway from anything for which [Thomas] Davis stood.'[70] Arthur Griffith's imprisonment, however, was the catalyst for a partial reconciliation with Lynd. As we have seen, Griffith had earlier denounced him for supporting Britain in the Great War.[71] Lynd paid a visit to Griffith in Wandsworth prison, which one eyewitness described as a 'friendly and unexpected scene'.[72] However, the visit was a personal one, not indicative of any return to an advanced-nationalist position. Likewise, for James Hannay, the rising came as an enormous shock and contributed to his leaving Ireland. Hannay's support for the Allied cause had prompted him to serve as a chaplain in France from 1915 to 1918. Although he would initially return to Ireland, taking a rectorship in Kildare from 1918 to 1922, he had

[68] For a discussion, see Sean Ó Mahony, *Frongoch: university of revolution* (Dublin, 1987), 46, 54, 123, 226.

[69] Adrian Frazier, *Hollywood Irish: John Ford, Abbey actors and the Irish revival in Hollywood* (Dublin, 2010), 107. For Shields's Irish Volunteer service, see MAD, MSPC, REF23323.

[70] UCD, FitzGerald papers, P80/1591 (1), Robert Lynd to Mabel FitzGerald, 28 May 1916.

[71] See Chapter 3.   [72] *IT*, 17 March 1951.

decisively broken from his separatist friends, and developed a revulsion for the IRA. In 1924 he accepted a living in Mells, Somerset, and would remain in England for the rest of his life.[73] Although both Lynd and Hannay would intervene in Irish politics during the War of Independence and Civil War, it would be as sympathetic outsiders, rather than as partisans of the nationalist movement.[74]

For other Protestants, the rising had a tendency to reinforce new-found beliefs and propel them towards more radical positions. One example is Albinia Brodrick. In the period after the rising, Brodrick, who had previously identified with constitutional nationalism, fell afoul of the military censors. A letter to Alice Stopford Green, which criticised the government's actions, was intercepted.[75] The censors also suppressed her poem 'Dublin – May 1916', which had been written for the *Catholic Bulletin*, in which she praised the executed rebel leaders as martyrs.[76] In fact, poetry was central to the Protestant nationalist reaction to the rising. A number responded to the rising in verse, among them Alice Milligan, Eva Gore Booth, W. B. Yeats, Æ George Russell, James Stephens, Constance Markievicz, Seumas O'Sullivan, and Augusta Gregory. The most famous poem of the rising, Yeats's 'Easter, 1916', with its refrain 'All changed, changed utterly: / A terrible beauty is born', although usually read as a paean, also carries a strong sense of ambivalence.[77]

Much like the impact of the Boer War almost two decades before, the Easter Rising had the effect of galvanising Protestant nationalist opinion, radicalising many nationalist moderates, and effecting the conversion to nationalism of some convinced unionists. Although the numbers of advanced Protestants increased in the wake of the rising, they would find the broader advanced nationalist movement a less hospitable environment than before. After the rising the initiative moved to men like Éamon de Valera, Michael Collins, and Harry Boland, who were less interested in the painstaking work of making political converts of Protestant unionists. Following the declaration of the republic, to which all Irishmen and women were expected to give allegiance, advanced nationalists showed

---

[73] Taylor, *The life and writings of James Owen Hannay*, 137–216.
[74] Davis, 'Ulster Protestants and the Sinn Féin press', 64.
[75] Bodleian Library, Oxford, Henry Duke papers, Albinia Brodrick to Alice Stopford Green, 5 August 1916.
[76] Brian P. Murphy, 'The Easter Rising in the context of censorship and propaganda with special reference to Major Ivon Price', in Gabriel Doherty and Dermot Keogh (eds.), *1916: The long revolution* (Cork, 2007), 141–168.
[77] 'Easter, 1916', in Albright (ed.), *W. B. Yeats: the poems*, 228–230. See also R. F. Foster, *W. B. Yeats: a life, Vol. II: the arch-poet, 1915–1939* (Oxford, 2003), 59–64.

less concern about promoting Protestants to prominent positions, or enticing wavering unionists to defect. There would no longer, as in the days of John O'Leary, or Arthur Griffith pre-1916, be a group of well-connected Catholics determined to win converts. Furthermore, the Conscription crisis of 1918 would soon highlight the extent to which Catholicism had become synonymous with nationalism. The post-1916 period would prove difficult for Protestant republicans.

6   Outsiders?, 1918–1921

Introduction

> The position of those who are both Protestants and nationalists has always been a difficult one. The present war has increased the strain, Easter Week was heart-breaking, the first Sunday in Lent has seen the Protestant Archbishop of Dublin utilise the pulpit of St Patrick's Cathedral to insult and vilify Nationalist Ireland. In Heaven's name when did we ask for 'Protection'? Such insults as these provoke the question. Can we not hit back? We can, indeed, and I desire to see Protestant nationalists unite.[1]

Maud Eden, who wrote these words, was an English-born Episcopalian journalist and activist in the Irish Women Workers' Union, who supported the suffrage, socialist, and republican movements.[2] She was certainly correct in stating that the outbreak of war in Europe, and then the Easter Rising, placed nationalist-supporting Protestants in a difficult position: their politics continued to alienate them from the bulk of their co-religionists, while Ulster unionist rhetoric sharpened divisions between Catholics and Protestants throughout the island. Protestant nationalists would be forced to adopt various strategies to counteract the growing impression that the republican movement was a Catholic one. These strategies included the establishment of a separate Protestant anti-conscription campaign. Another was the decision of a group of Dublin-based republicans to launch a coup within the Irish Guild of the Church and transform the organisation into a nationalist pressure group. Faced with the prospect of partition, nationalist thinkers sought to modify the Sinn Féin programme in order to appeal to the Ulster Protestant working class, a group which was believed to be especially likely to defect. Éamon de Valera, the dominant figure in advanced nationalism from this period, also made efforts to reach some accommodation with

---

[1] Maud Eden, 'Protestants, organise', *New Ireland*, 17 March 1917.
[2] *Irish Press*, 3 October 1931; *Irish Citizen*, September 1916. Eden later converted to Catholicism.

Ulster unionists. Finally, some of these developments were mirrored across the Atlantic, where a group of Protestant Irish-Americans, led by a notably eccentric clergyman, founded the Protestant Friends of Ireland, which propagandised against partition and the British government.

The Conscription Crisis

After the Easter Rising, advanced nationalism enjoyed an enormous resurgence, as the public, impressed by the bravery of the rebels and outraged at the actions of the British, abandoned the home rule movement. The republican movement forged during this period differed markedly from advanced nationalism prior to 1916: popular, mainstream, with ambitions to gain the loyalty of ordinary men and women, little effort was made to encourage individual Protestants to defect, and no grand scheme emerged to entice the Protestant working class of the north-east to defect. This tendency could be seen during the 1917 Sinn Féin convention, during which the old, dual-monarchist body was recast as a republican organisation, with Éamon de Valera as president, and Arthur Griffith accepting a demotion to vice-president. In his presidential address, de Valera devoted much of his speech to explaining that rebellion against British rule was justified under Catholic teaching, stating, 'I have never yet found the Catholic religion to be contrary to anything I hold in my conscience.'[3] There was no room in his address for any discussion of the need to persuade Protestants – particularly Ulster Protestants – to embrace Sinn Féin. The new nationalism appeared to lack the inter-religious spirit of the old one. The extent to which advanced nationalism had come to be Catholic-dominated became evident during the conscription crisis.

Early in the morning of 21 March 1918 the German army launched its greatest offensive of the war. The spring offensive saw German forces menace Paris and come close to breaking the entente's resolve.[4] The enormous British army death toll ensured that the extension of conscription to Ireland was forced on the government's agenda. Irish recruitment to the British army had originally been vigorous: an estimated 44,000 enlisted in 1914 and 45,000 in 1915, but this fell to 19,000 in 1916 and only 14,000 in 1917.[5] Britain had experienced a broadly similar decline

---

[3] TNA, CO 904/23/5, Report on the Sinn Féin convention, 1917.
[4] See Randal Gray, *Kaiserschlacht: the final German offensive of World War One* (Oxford, 1991).
[5] David Fitzpatrick, 'Militarism in Ireland, 1900–1922', in Thomas Bartlett and Keith Jeffery (eds.), *A military history of Ireland* (Cambridge, 1996), 688.

until the Military Service Act was passed in 1916, which introduced conscription in that island.[6]

Previously it had been argued that the cost of implementing the policy, in terms of potentially bloody disturbances, and the possible supplanting of the Irish Party by Sinn Féin, was too high. On 9 April, against a background of conflicting cabinet and civil service advice, Prime Minister Lloyd George introduced the Military Service Bill, which would allow for its application to Ireland by order in council.[7] The government claimed they hoped to conscript 150,000 Irishmen. Lloyd George's vague assurance that he intended to 'invite Parliament to pass a measure of self-government for Ireland' was not enough to convince the Irish Parliamentary Party to support the policy: John Dillon, Redmond's replacement as Party leader, led his supporters out of the Commons after the vote.[8] William O'Brien also led his All-for-Ireland-League MPs out of the house, declaring the measure to be a 'declaration of war against Ireland'.[9]

The announcement provoked fury among Irish nationalists, who temporarily joined forces to prevent the measure being implemented. An Irish anti-conscription committee was established, with representation by the Irish Party, Sinn Féin, the All-for-Ireland-League, and Labour and the unions. Between April and June 1918 numerous rallies were held throughout the country, where people pledged to resist the imposition of conscription. Labour held a one-day general strike in protest at the measure. The Catholic Church was strongly associated with this agitation. On 18 April, having received a deputation from the anti-conscription committee, the hierarchy pronounced the measure 'an oppressive and inhuman law which the Irish people have a right to resist by all means which are consonant with the law of God'.[10] The bishops decreed that solemn Mass of Intercession be held in every Catholic church and chapel in the country the following Sunday, 'to avert the threatened scourge of conscription from Ireland'. After Mass, a public meeting was held in every parish, where hundreds of thousands signed a pledge, modelled on the Ulster Covenant of 1912, to 'resist conscription

---

[6] Fitzpatrick, 'The logic of collective sacrifice', 1018–1021.

[7] *Military service. A bill to make further provision with respect to military service during the present war.* (16) 1918.

[8] Alan J. Ward, 'Lloyd George and the 1918 Irish conscription crisis', *The Historical Journal*, Vol. 17, No. 1 (March 1974), 109–114; Thomas Hennessey, *Dividing Ireland: World War One and partition* (London, 1998), 220–221. See also Adrian Gregory, '"You might as well recruit Germans": British public opinion and the decision to conscript the Irish in 1918', in Adrian Gregory and Senia Pašeta (eds.), *Ireland and the Great War: 'a war to unite us all'?* (Manchester, 2002), 113–133.

[9] House of Commons, Vol. 104, cc. 1362–1363, 9 April 1918.

[10] *The Irish Rosary*, Vol. 22, No. 5 (May 1918), 387.

by the most effective means at our disposal'.[11] Despite this explicit coupling of Catholicism with anti-conscription agitation, nationalist leaders claimed that the campaign was non-partisan and non-sectarian. The nationalist press highlighted Protestant participation at meetings and rallies.[12] One correspondent claimed that by late April, 'Hundreds of Protestants throughout the country have attended anti-Conscription meetings.'[13]

Attempts to emphasise the non-sectarian nature of the protest were aided by the decision of small numbers of Orangemen – probably Independent Orangemen – to join in the agitation. Kevin O'Shiel, a Sinn Féin activist, addressing a meeting in a hall near Omagh, County Tyrone, was surprised to see three Orangemen – young farmers – in attendance. They wished to join the Irish Volunteers to resist conscription. O'Shiel recalled that he 'heard of numbers of similar happenings in other parts of Ulster at the time'. He recorded that the men remained with the Volunteers for a time, before 'withdrawing into their own Orange background'.[14]

The most striking example of Orange participation in the anti-conscription campaign occurred at a large rally in Ballycastle, County Antrim. Described as 'in every sense unique', the rally was preceded by a procession headed by the Moyarget Independent Orange pipe band, with Sinn Féin and Ancient Order of Hibernian pipers following, marching alternately to such tunes as 'The Boyne water' and 'A nation once again'. The Master of Moyarget Lodge was prominent on the platform.[15] As we saw in Chapters 2 and 4, some Irish nationalists dreamed of a historic realignment that would see the mass defection of Orangemen to nationalism. Those present at Ballycastle may have believed they were witnessing just such a realignment. One Catholic nationalist who addressed the crowd stated that

it was the first time he had ever taken part in a procession, headed by an Orange Band playing 'The Boyne water', but he hoped it would not be the last ... He trusted that [this] wonderful meeting was going to be the beginning of a new era for [Orangemen] and for Ireland.[16]

---

[11] *Irish Catholic*, 27 April 1918; NLI, William O'Brien papers, LO P 114 [Item 98], Ireland's Solemn League and Covenant [Anti-conscription protest form].

[12] *FJ*, 25 April 1918 (rally in Athy, Co. Kildare); *Kildare Observer*, 27 April 1918 (rally in Stradbally, Queen's Co.); *Anglo-Celt*, 27 April 1918 (meeting in Ballymoney, Co. Antrim, attended by 'many Protestant farmers'); *FJ*, 20 April 1918 (rally in Enniskillen, Co. Fermanagh). At the latter rally 'Unionists' were also described as attending.

[13] Elizabeth Bloxham, letter to *Anglo-Celt*, 27 April 1918.

[14] BMH WS 1770, Kevin O'Shiel, 775–776.

[15] *II*, 18 April 1918. See also BMH WS 762, Liam McMullen.

[16] *Ballymoney Free Press*, 25 April 1918.

There were also reports from other parts of the province of those described as Ulster Volunteers switching sides due to opposition to conscription. One former Irish Volunteer recalled:

One very unusual feature of the conscription campaign in our part of Co. Tyrone [Dromore] was the fact that a number of young Ulster Volunteers came along to us and offered to join the Irish Volunteers in their determination to fight conscription. To my own knowledge, at least four or five came along with others to join us. The conscription menace lasted such a short time that this attitude didn't have time to develop amongst the rank and file of the Ulster Volunteers. The delight caused to us by the great rush of recruits into the Volunteers during the anti-conscription campaign turned to disappointment later on when the crisis passed, because great numbers of the men who had joined during the heat of the campaign left us.[17]

Although traces remained of the anti-government sentiment that characterised the Independent Orange Order in its early years, the anti-conscription movement seems to have gained the support of only a tiny number of Orangemen. It is likely that the short duration of the crisis ensured that those members who came to associate with nationalism slowly drifted back into the unionist movement.

The fleeting, uncoordinated participation by Orangemen and Ulster Volunteers did little to alter the perception that opposition to conscription was a largely Catholic affair. Even the most unlikely groups of Catholics declared against conscription. The Dublin Metropolitan Police Catholic Society resolved to resist the measure.[18] In an unprecedented protest, sixteen Catholic King's Counsel signed the pledge as a group, which caused outrage in the Commons.[19] One individual who grew uneasy with the religious complexion of the protest was Ernest Reginald McClintock Dix (1857–1936). Dix was an Episcopalian solicitor and Irish-language enthusiast who was prominent in Protestant nationalist circles in Dublin. In late April, he stated:

Fullest provision for signing the pledge against conscription has been made for Catholics, but ought there not to be … an opportunity for others to sign? This is a National matter, and not merely a religious one.[20]

In Dublin, a small committee, led by Nelly O'Brien, organised a Protestant counterpart, the 'Protestant protest against conscription'.[21] Analysis of the organising committee membership indicates that the

---

[17] BMH WS 721, Nicholas Smyth.
[18] NLI, LOP 114 [96], Dublin Metropolitan Police Catholic Society, anti-conscription poster.
[19] *Nationality*, 18 May 1918; *UG*, 27 April 1918; Cork *Evening Echo*, 6 May 1918.
[20] *UG*, 27 April 1918.   [21] *New Ireland*, 27 April 1918.

protest had its genesis in the Irish Guild of the Church. By 1918 many members of the Guild had become attracted to radical nationalism. A declaration in favour of conscription by the Church of Ireland arch-bishops of Armagh and Dublin seems to have spurred the members of the Guild to organise the protest.[22] One anonymous member of the Church of Ireland wrote:

The Primate and Archbishop of Dublin, in issuing their manifesto with regard to conscription, speak as though they represent the voice of the Church. Such is not the case. Sinn Féin members of the Church of Ireland, through a sense of loyalty to the Church, have for long submitted to their church being exploited for political ends. This loyalty has proved to be mistaken by our betrayal by the Primate and Archbishop, who have now placed the Church of Ireland in a position as is calculated may be used as a political weapon to separate us from our Roman Catholic fellow-countrymen, in whose national aspirations we are one.[23]

All seven members of the organising committee – O'Brien, Ernest Reginald Dix, Isabella Tuckey (a kindergarten headmistress), the Rev. Oswald Fisher, George Ruth, George Irvine, and the artist Lily Williams – were members of the Guild. At least four of these – O'Brien, Ruth, Irvine, and Williams – can be identified as Sinn Féiners, with Irvine, a 1916 Rising veteran, also serving in the Irish Volunteers. The protest adopted a pledge whose language was, again, based on the Ulster Covenant of 1912:

We, the undersigned, wish to join our Roman Catholic fellow-countrymen in protesting in the strongest possible manner against the application of Conscription to Ireland.

We believe that to force our people to act contrary to their will and conscience is a violation of the law of God, and cannot but be productive of the gravest and most disastrous moral, religious and material consequences.[24]

The campaign operated from Dublin, where, under O'Brien's direction, a large general committee was formed to publicise the protest across the country. By May, the protest was available for signature in twenty-seven counties, including several places in Dublin, the main area of activity. Organisers has some success in Ulster: the pledge could be taken in Cavan, Fermanagh, Armagh, two places in Derry, and four places in Antrim.[25] There were reports of significant degrees of success in certain

[22] *IT*, 18 April 1918.   [23] *Nationality*, 27 April 1918.
[24] NLI, LO P114 [95], Protestant protest against conscription circular.
[25] MAD, Contemporary Documents (CD) 258/8/ Protestant protest against conscription, May 1918 file, letter from organising committee to Lord Mayor of Dublin, 16 May 1918; *II*, 22 April, 6 May 1918.

areas. In Foxford, County Mayo, organisers claimed to have garnered the signatures of 'almost all' members of the Church of Ireland, including two Justices of the Peace and a synodsman.[26] In Dugort, Achill Island, County Mayo, the organiser sent O'Brien a list of signatories which included the names of ten select vestrymen and two churchwardens, one of whom was a synodsman.[27] The publicising of the protest was aided by the decision of nineteen prominent Protestants, including Douglas Hyde, Æ George Russell, and Robert Barton, to sign the pledge. All these signatories held nationalist views.[28] In the absence of more detailed lists of signatures, these can be taken as evidence of the political views of most signatories of the protest.

Æ made a noteworthy intervention in the conscription debate. Although a Theosophist, a mystic, and a dreamer, he was also a well-known political moderate, who had recently published a pamphlet calling for Ireland to be granted dominion status, similar to Australia or Canada, within the British Empire.[29] *Conscription for Ireland: a warning to England* was a furious denunciation of the government:

The people of England should realise the danger, not merely to Ireland but to the Empire, of the policy of those they maintain in power ... Our people look on this last act of British power with that dilating sense of horror a child might feel thinking of one who had committed some sin which was awful and unbelievable, as the sin against the Holy Ghost ... If [the government] insist on breaking the Irish will, there will not be a parish here where blood will not be shed.[30]

Outwardly, the Protestant protest committee maintained that the protest was proceeding satisfactorily: O'Brien informed an *Irish Citizen* representative that she was getting a 'magnificent response' to the appeal.[31] Although the nationalist press maintained that the pledge had been signed by 'thousands', the organising committee were concealing frustration at the small numbers of people taking the pledge.[32] In a letter to the Lord Mayor of Dublin, the organising committee outlined three factors that, they believed, were impeding the success of the protest: opposition of the Church of Ireland hierarchy and the heads of the other Protestant churches, opposition from employers who pressured their employees not to sign, and a boycott by the unionist press.[33]

---

[26] *Connaught Telegraph*, 4 May 1918.   [27] Cork *Evening Echo*, 3 May 1918.
[28] List of names included in MAD, CD 258/8/ Protestant protest against conscription, May 1918 file, letter from organising committee to Lord Mayor of Dublin, 16 May 1918.
[29] George Russell, *Thoughts for a convention* (Dublin, 1917), 29.
[30] George Russell, *Conscription for Ireland: a warning to England* (Dublin, 1918).
[31] *Irish Citizen*, May–June 1918.   [32] *Donegal News*, 18 May 1918.
[33] MAD, CD 258/8/ Protestant protest against conscription, May 1918 file, letter from organising committee to Lord Mayor of Dublin, 16 May 1918.

O'Brien was correct about hierarchical opposition. John Henry
Bernard, archbishop of Dublin (whose son Robert had been killed at
Gallipoli in 1915), told the *Church of Ireland Gazette* that he hoped no
Episcopalians would sign the 'mischievous and misleading manifesto'.[34]
Bernard sought to dissuade individual Church of Ireland clergymen from
taking part in the protest. He wrote to the Rev. Henry Barbor, a well-
known nationalist sympathiser, vice-president of the Irish Guild of the
Church, and rector of Castledermot, saying:

> I do not question your right to 'protest' against the introduction of compulsory
> service in Ireland, any more than I would question the right of an Orangeman to
> 'protest' against the introduction of Home Rule. But the meeting with the objects
> of which you expressed your sympathy 'declared for the Covenant to resist
> Conscription'. That is a very different matter. IF you associate yourself with
> those who resist the law, you are going beyond what is, in my judgment,
> legitimate for a Christian clergyman. You will certainly forfeit the respect and
> the confidence of your people, and you will bring dishonour on the Church of
> Ireland in this province, which has always upheld the tradition of obedience in the
> law, as a Christian duty, recommended in the New Testament.[35]

There is some evidence that the unionist press did mount a boycott.
The Dublin *Daily Express* stated in mid-May that they had been
requested to advertise the protest but they 'declined to lend our columns
to any such disloyal publication'.[36] However, both the *Church of Ireland
Gazette* and the *Irish Times* printed the Protestant anti-conscription
protest circular. Despite lack of support from the unionist press, the
organising committee maintained that the protest was supported through
the co-operation of Catholics, a friendly nationalist press (the *Irish Independent* and *Freeman's Journal* gave very favourable coverage), and the
alleged assistance of a 'not inconsiderable number of the younger clergy
of the Church of Ireland', despite episcopal disapproval.[37]

Not every nationalist newspaper was as enamoured of the Protestant
anti-conscriptionists as were the *Irish Independent* and the *Freeman's
Journal*. D. P. Moran's *The Leader* offered a denunciation not only of
O'Brien's protest but of Protestant nationalists in general:

> We think the day has gone by for people self-labelling themselves Protestant
> Home Rulers, Protestant Nationalists, Protestant Anti-Conscriptionists. What

---

[34] *CIG*, 3 May 1918. For criticism of the archbishop's stance, see *CIG*, 10 May 1918. See
also Cork *Evening Echo*, 6 May 1918.
[35] BL, John Henry Bernard Papers, Add MS52783/14, John Henry Bernard to Henry
Barbor, 23 April 1918.
[36] Dublin *Daily Express*, 15 May 1918.
[37] MAD CD 258/8/ Protestant protest against conscription, May 1918 file, letter from
organising committee to Lord Mayor of Dublin, 16 May 1918.

has their being Protestants got to do with it? There was a time when Mr [William Mills] Forsyth, the Pembroke Bumble, or Mr [Stephen] Gwynn, need only say that though he a Home Ruler was a Protestant, to evoke loud applause from a green and half-slave mob. We hope we are getting out of this sort of spirit. There is a gratuitous 'superiority' in people labelling themselves as, say, 'Protestant Home Rulers', as if it were a condescension for a Protestant to be a Home Ruler or anything else in common with an ordinary mere Irish Catholic. The plain fact that stares everyone in the place is that the non-Catholics of Ireland are apart from the Irish nation – no odd exceptions make any appreciable difference to the main fact.[38]

Moran's attack on Protestant nationalists and anti-conscriptionists, although breaching one of the nationalist movement's oldest taboos, may have reflected the submerged thinking of many 'ordinary mere Irish Catholics' in the movement.

The launch of the Protestant protest gave rise to claims that Protestant unionists were being boycotted or intimidated for refusing to sign the pledge. Major John Pretyman Newman, Conservative member for Enfield, who came from a County Cork landed family, was an active critic of the Protestant protest. In late April he enquired in the House of Commons whether the government was 'aware that threats were being used to compel the scattered loyalist population in the three [southern] provinces' to sign.[39] Newman's accusation provoked the government to investigate O'Brien's committee.[40] There may have been some truth in Newman's accusation. The *Daily Express* claimed that 'in several small country towns individuals have been threatened with all the horrors of the boycotting if they dare refuse to sign'.[41] Some members of Naas Urban District Council publicised the refusal of one member to take the Protestant pledge. Six members of Wicklow Urban Council who refused to sign an anti-conscription resolution were boycotted. Two of them were forced to leave Wicklow town; of the others, the *Irish Times* claimed that 'it is sought to drive [them] out of trade and ruin their successful business'.[42] The Rev. Bertram C. Wells, the incumbent of St Thomas's, Dugort, cast serious doubt on the claims of Episcopalian support for the Protestant protest on Achill Island. Wells alleged that his parishioners had been threatened with boycotting if they did not sign the Protestant protest, and that eight families had refused to submit to these threats. For Wells, the incident 'casts a lurid light on the sort of tolerance that would

[38] *The Leader,* 15 June 1918. William Mills Forsyth (b. 1865/6), a Methodist Belfast-born home ruler, was a member of Pembroke Urban District Council.
[39] *Ballymoney Free Press,* 2 May 1918.
[40] House of Commons, Vol. 106, cc. 200–201, 14 May 1918.
[41] Dublin *Daily Express,* 15 May 1918.   [42] *IT,* 15 June 1918.

be extended to supporters of the cause of the Allies and humanity in the event of Home Rule'.[43] Such allegations do not seem to have impressed the government. In mid-May Newman again claimed that 'Protestants are being visited and compelled to sign the pledge under threats of being immediately boycotted if they refuse', and enquired what action would be taken on the matter. Newman wondered why 'a license is being accorded to the activities of this League which was refused to a League founded with similar objects in England'. (Members of the British-based Anti-Conscription League faced arrest and imprisonment for distributing anti-conscription material.)[44] The government speaker replied that having investigated O'Brien's committee, 'I cannot find that any intimidation has been used to force persons to sign it.'[45]

On 9 June, 'Women's Day', women pledged not to replace conscripted men in the workforce. The most impressive scenes were in Dublin, where, despite heavy rain, some 40,000 took the pledge.[46] Among the women's organisations whose members took part were the Irish Women Workers' Union (which was the largest contingent, with 2,400 signing), the Irish Women's Franchise League, and the women of the Irish Citizen Army. A group of munitions workers from Rathmines organised themselves and signed as a body. Some 700 members of Cumann na mBan marshalled the event.[47] That morning a group of Protestant anti-conscription women, led by Nelly O'Brien and including Alice Stopford Green, Susan Mitchell, Sarah Cecilia Harrison and Alice Milligan, had the altercation with an official of Christ Church Cathedral described in the Introduction. In all about seventy-five signatures were appended to the Protestant women's pledge. Although this may seem tiny – 0.19 per cent – of the total estimated number of women's signatories, it must be noted that many Protestant women preferred to take the mainstream pledge. The Irish Women Workers Union group, led by Louie Bennett, an Episcopalian trade unionist, was described as including 'a large contingent of Protestant Labour women'.[48]

Although no statistics survive, it appears that hundreds of thousands of people signed the anti-conscription pledge throughout the country. Eventually, the extent of Irish resistance, alongside the immensely favourable impact of American involvement in the war, convinced Lloyd

---

[43] *IT*, 9 May 1918.
[44] See *Manchester Guardian*, 26 February 1916; *The Observer*, 27 February 1916; *The Times*, 28 February 1916.
[45] Cork *Evening Echo*, 15 May 1918.   [46] According to *II*, 10 June 1918.
[47] *II*, 8, 10 June 1918.   [48] *II*, 10 June 1918.

George to postpone the measure. Believing that party to have been the instigator of the anti-conscription agitation, on the night of 17–18 May the authorities arrested seventy-three prominent Sinn Féiners, including Éamon de Valera, on the spurious grounds of a treasonous plot between them and Germany. The 'German plot' arrests provoked a furious response from John Dillon, who believed – correctly – that further moves against advanced nationalists would destroy his own movement.[49] The Irish Party had won three by-election victories prior to the conscription crisis, which gave the impression the party had reversed the trend towards Sinn Féin.[50] However, the impact of the anti-conscription agitation, which saw the latter party greatly increase its membership and public popularity, coupled with the folly of the German plot arrests, ensured that a greatly weakened Irish Party entered the 1918 general election. In the election, which was held a month after the cessation of hostilities, the Party, which had taken seventy-four seats in the previous election, returned only six members to Sinn Féin's seventy-three. After the conscription crisis, Sinn Féin would never again have its position as the leading nationalist movement seriously threatened.

The nationalist press claimed the Protestant protest against conscription was signed by several thousand people. However, this vague figure must be treated with some scepticism: the organisers did not release figures, nor have lists survived. Perhaps the importance of the protest is in alerting us to the existence of a small but active network of Protestant nationalists, who, although generally avoiding explicit identification with Sinn Féin, worked independently to a separatist agenda, and acted collectively to undermine the appearance of Protestant political unanimity.

The Irish Guild of the Church

A year after the Easter Rising, the Irish Guild of the Church was out-wardly united. Its membership continued its project to inject the spirit of the Gaelic Revival into the Church of Ireland by means of lectures, classes, and agitation for Irish-language religious services. More ambigu-ously, it also sought, in the words of one of its most prominent activists, 'to remind her members ... that they had a place in their own land'.[51]

---

[49] Michael Laffan, *The resurrection of Ireland: the Sinn Féin party, 1916–1923* (Cambridge, 1999), 142–144; Ward, 'Lloyd George and the 1918 Irish conscription crisis', 118–120.
[50] Hennessey, *Dividing Ireland*, 230.
[51] RCBL, Rev. William Vandeleur, typescript memoirs, 23.

The position of members of the Irish Guild of the Church, or 'Gaelic Churchmen', within mainstream Anglicanism was underlined by the continued presence of Plunket of Tuam as the Guild's president. Bishop Orpen of Limerick, Bishop Berry of Killaloe, and Charles Ovenden, dean of St Patrick's Cathedral, served as vice-presidents. In April 1917 well-known republican Kathleen Lynn was blackballed.[52] However, a growing group of members, some advanced nationalists since before the Easter Rising, others more recent converts, wanted the body to adopt a position far removed from that of the Guild's senior office-holders.

The Guild's minute-books list 128 people who joined the group from 1914 to 1923. This rather unsatisfactory source provides enough detail to enable the identification of 82 members. Clergymen predominated, amounting to 44 members, four of whom were bishops. There were also seven academics, four solicitors, three teachers, three authors, and two artists. The strong attraction shown by some Anglican women towards nationalism is underlined by analysis of the membership lists. Some 49 women – 38 per cent of total – joined the Guild. Of these women, 47, or 96 per cent, were unmarried on joining. The two married women members had nationalist husbands. The tendency for Protestants to encourage their relations to join the nationalist movement is also illustrated by the Guild's membership lists: about one-fifth of members had a close relative in the Guild. The Guild had a predominantly middle-aged membership: members had an average age of forty-six in 1918. However, women members tended to be considerably younger, having an average age of thirty-five, which is comparable to the average age of advanced nationalist women discussed above.[53] This was a mostly urban, Dublin-based movement: about 70 out of 82 members resided in Dublin city or county.

Among the clergy active in the Guild were the Rev. Courtenay Moore, the Rev. John Roche Ardill, and, most prominently, the Rev. William Vandeleur. Born in County Tyrone, of a County Clare Conservative landed family, Vandeleur later claimed that his education at Marlborough College reinforced his sense of Irishness and prevented his developing what he claimed could have been an infatuation with Britain. Following his ordination, he spent two spells as a curate in the Anglican diocese of Natal, where, a liberal-minded man, he later wrote he was appalled by the mistreatment of blacks by white settlers. In 1910 he was appointed chaplain to the duke of Leinster at Kilkea. Time spent abroad had tempered Vandeleur's views, and he became critical of the Church of

---

[52] RCBL, Irish Guild of the Church minute book, 20 April 1917.   [53] See Chapter 3.

Ireland, as well as convinced that 'anti-national sprit ... has been the ruin of the Reformed Church in Ireland'.[54] In Kildare he became friends with two Anglican home rulers: Lord Walter FitzGerald, land agent to his nephew the duke of Leinster, and the Rev. Henry Barbor, rector of Castledermot. He joined the Gaelic League and attended Irish classes with Barbor. Later, when serving as curate in Malahide, he claimed to have become acquainted with Roger Casement and to have sympathised with his politics. It was while living in Malahide in April 1914 that Vandeleur attended the meeting that led to the setting up of the Irish Guild of the Church.[55] He became one of the Guild's most active clergyman members.[56]

Another inaugural member of the Guild was Margaret Cunningham (1872–1940), warden of Trinity Hall, TCD's women's hall of residence in Dartry. Cunningham was born in Buncrana, County Donegal, into a liberal, home rule–supporting Church of Ireland family. Cunningham was educated in Girton College, Cambridge, where in 1894 she took a first in the modern and medieval languages tripos. A pioneer in women's education, she lectured in French and German in Victoria College, Belfast, from 1896 to 1900, and served as senior lecturer in German in the Royal Holloway College of London University from 1900 to 1906. In 1908 Cunningham came to Dublin as first warden of Trinity Hall. She sought to emulate the intellectual and progressive atmosphere of Girton for her charges, and proved a popular figure among her students. She was never, however, invited to lecture by university authorities.[57]

At the Guild's annual meeting in 1918, George Irvine moved a reso-lution which rescinded the post–Easter Rising declaration of loyalty and replaced it with a declaration that 'the [Guild] expresses no opinion whatever in regard to the relations at present existing between the two nations of Ireland and England'.[58] The apolitical nature of this motion was undermined by his proud display of a republican badge while addressing the meeting.[59] The bishop of Killaloe, who chaired the

---

[54] RCBL, Rev. William Vandeleur, typescript memoirs, 32.
[55] RCBL, Rev. William Vandeleur, typescript memoirs, 20 (c).
[56] See, for example, RCBL, Irish Guild of the Church minute book, 29 April 1914.
[57] For Cunningham, see *IT*, 4 July 1940, 24 April 1936, 4 March 1911; Ó Broin, *Protestant nationalists*, 38; RCBL Irish Guild of the Church minute book, 22 January 1914; BMH WS 391, Helena Molony; BMH WS 687, M. J. Curran; McDowell and Webb, *Trinity College Dublin*, 351; Rosa Pilcher, *Trinity Hall, 1908–2008: Trinity College Dublin residence* (Dublin, 2013), 25–37; Susan M. Parkes (ed.), *A danger to the men? a history of women in Trinity College Dublin 1904–2004* (Dublin, 2004), 75–78, 104–105.
[58] RCBL, Irish Guild of the Church minute book, 14 May 1918.
[59] Dublin *Daily Express*, 15 May 1918.

gathering, reminded members of their Christian obligation of loyalty to civil power. Responding to this, the Rev. Oswald Fisher (1889–1920) drew a contemporary parallel, asking, 'Were the clergy of Belgium disloyal to their Church because they did not recognise the Kaiser?'[60] The resolution was passed after a stormy session, and as a result the bishops, as well as many other office-holders and members, resigned.[61] Susan Mitchell, who had recently joined the organisation, was moved to the chair.[62] The ultra-unionist Dublin *Daily Express* was scandalised that so many Protestants were willing to be 'exploited' by Sinn Féin.[63] One observer described the scene:

The ultra-loyal element present at the meeting were absolutely dumb-founded at the course which events had taken. It would be impossible to give an adequate idea of the appearance of the Bishop [of Killaloe], but the poor man seemed to think he had strayed into a Sinn Féin club.[64]

By mid-1918 the original, purely language-activist Guild had become an organisation of about ninety mainly Dublin-based Episcopalians, who supported independence.

As a result, a breakaway body, the Irish Guild of Witness (Comhluadar Gaodhalach na Fiadhnuise), was formed.[65] The new group incorporated Rosamond Stephen's Guild of Witness organisation, which had sought to promote unity among Christian denominations.[66] Although they claimed to be non-political, its profession of loyalty to the Book of Common Prayer, with its prayers for the royal family and lord lieutenant, amounted in effect to a political test.[67] The Rev. William Vandeleur, who joined the Irish Guild of Witness after resigning from the Irish Guild of the Church believed that both bodies' 'ideals were much the same except

---

[60] *Young Ireland*, 25 May 1918.
[61] *IT*, 15 May 1918; RCBL, Irish Guild of the Church minute book, 14 May 1918.
[62] Pyle, *Red-headed rebel*, 177.   [63] Dublin *Daily Express*, 15 May 1918.
[64] *Donegal News*, 26 October 1918. For a reaction to Irvine's resolution from one of the dumbfounded, see Miss S. E. E. West, letter to the editor, in *CIG*, 31 May 1918.
[65] RCBL, Irish Guild of Witness minute book, Final Report 1918; Irish Guild of the Church minute book, 20 November 1918; *IT*, 19 May 1919.
[66] For the amalgamation, see RCBL, Irish Guild of Witness minute book, Final Report 1918; Irish Guild of Witness minute book, Rev. Paul Quigley to Rosamond Stephen, undated [c. October 1918]. For Rosamond Stephen (1868–1951), who founded the Guild of Witness in 1901 and sought to promote reconciliation between Belfast Protestants and Catholics, see Oonagh Walsh (ed.), *An Englishwoman in Belfast: Rosamond Stephen's record of the Great War* (Cork, 2000).
[67] For the Irish Guild of Witness's profession of loyalty to the *Book of Common Prayer*, see RCBL, Irish Guild of Witness minute book, Rev. Paul Quigley to Rosamond Stephen, undated [c. April 1919]; Irish Guild of Witness minute book, Constitution of Irish Guild of Witness. See also RCBL, Irish Guild of Witness, Early general records book, *Law and Order*, pamphlet published by Irish Guild of Witness, November 1920.

that those who belonged to the former were content to be regarded as loyal to the British connection, while the latter tended to a more radical political position'.[68] The bishops deserted the Guild of the Church for the new group. Bishop Berry of Killaloe became president, and Bishop Plunket of Tuam and Bishop Gregg of Ossory were among its vice presidents. Other prominent members included Rev. Canon John Godfrey Fitzmaurice Day (who in 1920 replaced Gregg as bishop of Ossory), Rev. Walter Gahan of Gorey, and Rosamond Stephen, who served as honorary treasurer.[69]

Of the 83 members elected from 1918 to 1920, a total of 20, or about 24 per cent, had been members of the Irish Guild of the Church. The Irish Guild of Witness was even more clergy-dominated than the older group. Some 31 of its members, about 40 per cent of total, were clergymen. As with the Guild of the Church, a substantial number of women joined the new association: 43 women were admitted as members, 52 per cent of the total. Married women were more likely to join the Irish Guild of Witness: 18 did so, of whom four were married to a co-member. The majority of women members – 58 per cent – were unmarried. The new organisation also set up a Belfast branch, with fourteen members.[70] Over 80 per cent of members resided in either Belfast or Dublin. Guild of Witness members had the same average age – forty-five – as members of the Irish Guild of the Church, although its female members showed no tendency to be younger, with an average age of forty-four.

These two Church of Ireland reform associations, one whose members were generally sympathetic to separatism, and the other whose members professed loyalty to the Crown, may have seemed antithetical, especially in the context of the 1918 general election and War of Independence, but there is evidence of cooperation between the two groups, not least in petitioning the hierarchy for Irish-language services.[71]

The split marked the Irish Guild of the Church as clearly within the advanced nationalist pale. This was underlined by the immediate election of high-profile republicans Albinia Brodrick and Kathleen Lynn to the Guild, with the latter being elected to the group's executive.[72]

---

[68] RCBL, Rev. William Vandeleur, typescript memoirs, 32–33.
[69] See RCBL, Irish Guild of Witness minute book, Irish Guild of Witness Pamphlet [1919], for list of officers and committee members.
[70] See RCBL, Irish Guild of Witness minute book, membership list, 1920; RCBL, Irish Guild of Witness, Early general records book, Annual report May 1920, Annual report November 1922, Annual report November 1923; *IT*, 21 May 1920. See also *CIG*, 30 January 1920.
[71] See, for example, RCBL, Irish Guild of the Church minute book, 16 October 1919.
[72] RCBL, Irish Guild of the Church minute book, 20 November, 30 May, 18 June 1918.

Lynn, being Dublin-based, became an active member.[73] The most prominent member of the Cumann was Nelly O'Brien, who along with honorary secretary George Ruth provided much impetus to the group. After Plunket's defection to the Irish Guild of Witness, the Rev. Canon William Ireton Willis replaced him as president of the Irish Guild of the Church. However, O'Brien, as vice-president, was the leading activist. From March 1919 the Guild published, under O'Brien's editorship, its own journal, the *Gaelic Churchman*. The *Churchman* is a useful source not just for the Irish Guild of the Church but for Protestant advanced nationalists generally.

The split damaged the cause nearest the hearts of Gaelic Churchmen: Irish-language services. There was some progress in this area: there had been an annual 17 March service in St Patrick's Cathedral since 1906; and in April 1918, at the Guild's urging, the Dean of St Patrick's granted permission for a regular weekly service in the cathedral.[74] However, Dean Ovenden rescinded permission for any Irish-language services after George Irvine's resolution was passed.[75] With St Patrick's closed to the Irish language, the Guild made representations to the Dean of Christ Church, who was equally unreceptive. This provoked an angry response from O'Brien, who railed against 'clerical snob[s]'. She said clergymen should 'remember that he is a minister of God, and not an agent of the British Empire', and linked decline in church attendance to clerical preference for unionist politics and the company of the upper classes.[76] The Irish-language services issue was partially resolved in December 1919 when permission was granted for a monthly service in St Andrew's parish church, under the aegis of the Irish Guild of Witness.[77] These services were a lesser prize than a weekly service in one of the city's two cathedrals, and agitation continued.

Many members were unhappy with the Irish language Prayer Book then in use, and sought to replace it with something closer in spirit to the antiquarian perspective of members. A *Gaelic Churchman* leader called for the General Synod to appoint a committee to produce a book based on the 'ancient Catholic liturgical forms of the [pre-Reformation] Irish Church'. It stated that 'the English Prayer Book, being the product of the Teutonic mind in England and the Continent, is quite unsuited for Irish use'.[78] By 1921 Nelly O'Brien's ambitions were greater than this. Stating

[73] See, for example, RCPI, Diary of Kathleen Lynn, 18 October 1918, 1, 31 January 1919; 14 December 1920, 4 September, 30 October 1921.
[74] *CIG*, 23 July 1920; RCBL, Irish Guild of the Church minute book, 12 April 1918.
[75] *IT*, 16 May 1918.   [76] *Gaelic Churchman*, June 1919.
[77] *Gaelic Churchman*, February, June 1920; *IT*, 21 May 1920.
[78] *Gaelic Churchman*, June 1919.

that 'there will be no true national unity until religion is included', she made a call for the amalgamation of the Church of Ireland and the Catholic Church into a single Irish-speaking national church, based on her understanding of the pre-Reformation 'Celtic Church'.[79] This proposal was strongly criticised by members of the Guild. Typical was a letter from one pro–Sinn Féin Anglican who claimed such a proposal was unworkable due to the doctrinal differences between the churches. The most that could be hoped for was the reform of the Church of Ireland to make it less hostile to nationalism.[80] Although some Anglican nationalists such as Kathleen Lynn and Dorothy Stopford Price did attend Catholic services in addition to their own, there is little evidence of widespread ecumenist views among this group, let alone for O'Brien's proposal. It is possible that in this regard, O'Brien was in a minority of one.

By now the Irish Guild of the Church was fully outside the Church of Ireland mainstream, as distrusted by laity as they were by clergy. One correspondent stated that they were 'a sect everywhere spoken against'.[81] George Irvine believed the attitude of the hierarchy to nationalism was a danger to the survival of the Church of Ireland itself. He criticised the Primate and others who had publicly linked loyalty to the Crown to membership of the Church. 'What about an Irish Republican?' Irvine asked. 'Are we outside the pale?' He condemned what he viewed as the complacent laity, who clung to unionist politics while the rest of the country sought independence:

A God-sent move of Freedom is sweeping over the earth, and is surely approaching our own shores. How is the Church of Ireland preparing to receive it? There is no use shrugging one's shoulders and saying 'England will never allow it' or in prating smugly – and falsely – of 'the Church that has served Ireland faithfully for centuries' or in hoping that peace will some day be restored to our 'dear' country.

In every way it is proclaimed that those who are loyal to Ireland cannot be loyal members of the Church of Ireland. IRELAND IS GOING TO BE FREE. Don't stick your heads on the sand, but face the question, 'What will happen to the Church of Ireland then?'[82]

By late 1919, Gaelic Churchmen were actively campaigning for the hierarchy to abandon their policy of support for British rule and hostility to Irish nationalism. Although initially reluctant to do so, O'Brien eventually wrote on the Guild's behalf to the bench asking they 'disassociate

---

[79] *Gaelic Churchman*, April 1921.
[80] *Gaelic Churchman*, July 1921. See also *Gaelic Churchman*, August 1921.
[81] *Gaelic Churchman*, May 1919.   [82] *Gaelic Churchman*, January 1920.

themselves from those who see no remedy for our national troubles but coercion and more coercion'.[83] In late 1920 the Guild sent a delegation to the Archbishop of Dublin seeking his intervention to get a reprieve for the condemned young Volunteer Kevin Barry (1902–1920).[84]

The radical nationalist spirit of the Guild was evident in a resolution unanimously passed by the Guild at their 1919 annual general meeting. A disapproving *Irish Times* called it a 'remarkable resolution':

That we, members of the Irish Guild of the Church, while affirming our entire loyalty to the Church, desire to express our great regret and dissatisfaction that she is so constantly identified with the reactionary forces in this country by our Bishops, clergy and representative laymen. We consider it illogical and disastrous that the Church, which claims to be the National Church, should be so completely out of sympathy with the ideals of the great majority of the Nation which she professes to serve. We cannot help noticing it as inconsistent that the Church expresses her abhorrence of deeds of violence on the one side, while she refrains from condemning the actions of those in power ... In this we are voicing not only our own opinions, but those of a growing body of clergy and laity.[85]

The Guild may have been exaggerating the extent to which they had the support of fellow Anglicans. The movement was never strong enough to force the bishops to move towards a nationalist position. The creation of the Irish Guild of Witness had much reduced the Guild of the Church's membership; although it recovered somewhat over the coming years, and several members of the former organisation returned, it reported only 85 members in 1922.[86]

As a religious body, the Irish Guild of the Church had avoided explicitly endorsing Sinn Féin: however, its publicly expressed concerns about hunger strikers, mistreatment of Catholics in the North,[87] the fate of Kevin Barry, or criticisms of the 'reactionary' instincts of the clergy revealed its sympathies. By late 1921 the Guild's leadership had decided that, with negotiations with London taking place, they could 'justifiably take the line of cordial recognition of de Valera and his colleagues as the accredited delegates for the working out of peace'.[88]

In November 1921, the Irish Guild of the Church hosted Éamon de Valera at a reception in his honour.[89] The purpose was to 'provide the opportunity for members of the Church of Ireland to show their

---

[83] Nelly O'Brien to Archbishop of Dublin, 16 December 1919, in *Gaelic Churchman*, January 1920.

[84] See RCBL, Irish Guild of the Church minute book, 29 October 1920.

[85] *IT*, 27 January 1920; *Gaelic Churchman*, February 1920. See RCBL, Irish Guild of the Church minute book, 11 December 1919, for the origins of the resolution.

[86] *Gaelic Churchman*, March 1922.   [87] See Chapter 7.

[88] *Gaelic Churchman*, October 1921.   [89] *IT*, 11 November 1921.

sympathy with him in this difficult task'.[90] The reception afforded Protestants who had previously avoided public association with the Sinn Féin leadership an opportunity to do so. A total of 118 people, 55 of them women, were listed as having attended or having sent regrets.[91] Although held under the aegis of the Irish Guild of the Church, only a minority of its members – 24 – were listed as attending. Three members of the Irish Guild of Witness attended, and three others – Bishop Plunket, now translated to Meath, Bishop Berry of Killaloe, and Bishop Day of Ossory – sent regrets. Among those who attended were Douglas Hyde, Jack and Cottie Yeats, Kathleen Lynn, Lily Williams, Alice Stopford Green, Louie Bennett, Joseph Johnston, Ernest Blythe, Mia Cranwill, and James Douglas.

The decision of one clergyman to attend aroused fury among his largely unionist congregation. The Rev. Ernest Henry Lewis-Crosby, rector of Rathmines, held views that were at odds with the vast bulk of his congregation. Although Lewis-Crosby took an active part in aiding the Great War effort, he also 'sympathised with the sincerity' of the Anglicans who joined the republican movement, which included several members of his own congregation. He proved a friend to Church of Ireland Sinn Féiners, and appealed to the British government on their behalf.[92] Lewis Crosby's activities scandalised the best part of his flock, but he refused to curtail his dealings with his nationalist parishioners.[93]

De Valera offered little evidence that Sinn Féin intended to take dramatic steps to encourage Protestants to subscribe to its programme. His speech was characterised by complacency on the issue of politics and religion. 'The fact that the lines of political division ran to a certain degree parallel to the lines of religious division – a circumstance which they knew was accidental – gave an unfortunate foothold for all those who wished to misrepresent the position.'[94] Nor did he take advantage of this opportunity to make overtures to working-class Protestants, either in Dublin or in the north-east. De Valera, unlike Arthur Griffith (at least before 1916), showed little or no interest in outlining a conception of Irish nationalism that would tempt the industrialised Protestant populations towards nationalism. Not even here in Dublin, before an elite body of Protestant nationalists, could the Sinn Féin leader offer any

[90] *Gaelic Churchman*, December 1921.
[91] For an account of the reception, see *Gaelic Churchman*, December 1921.
[92] E. C. Hodges, *A valiant life, 1864–1961* (Dublin, 1963), 24. This memoir of Lewis-Crosby was prefaced by a letter from Éamon de Valera which stated that the late Dean of Christ Church had 'proved to be a staunch champion of some dear friends of mine': de Valera to E. C. Hodges, 4 September 1962, in Hodges, *A valiant life*, 10.
[93] Hodges, *A valiant life*, 24.   [94] *Gaelic Churchman*, December 1921.

imaginative programme. This was unfortunate: de Valera's reluctance to advance a conception of Irish nationality that surmounted the 'Catholic, Protestant and dissenter' cliché helped ensure that the ideology ascribed to by Gaelic Churchmen remained a minority one.

The Ulster Problem

During the post-1916 period, some nationalists, having previously largely ignored Ulster, began to consider new strategies to win over enough northern Protestants to avert partition. As we will see, these efforts were unsuccessful for several reasons, among them a tendency for nationalists to continue to equate Catholicism with Irishness. Protestant-born converts to Catholicism could cause especial embarrassment to the nationalist leadership. Aodh de Blacam (1891–1951) was an English-born journalist from a Protestant evangelical background who, having become an Irish republican – due in part, he claimed, to discovering his Ulster-born father had been a home ruler – converted to Catholicism in 1913.[95] A prominent Sinn Féin publicist, de Blacam outlined his vision of an independent Ireland in *Towards the republic* (1919) and *What Sinn Féin stands for* (1921). Heavily influenced by Catholic social teaching and his understanding of pre-Norman Ireland, he envisaged the implementation of what he called 'Gaelic social ideals', signifying a rural-based polity, organised co-operatively.[96] De Blacam saw Catholicism as being intrinsically bound with Irish nationhood. He could be tactless, stating:

It is the worst mistake possible to suppose that Ulster can be converted by preaching Sinn Féin under a disguise. No one is quicker than an Ulsterman is to detect disguises or resent them. The Ulsterman's bark is worse than his bite and the fact is he would come to terms with St Ignatius Loyola sooner than with a camouflage Nationalist. He could be, and maybe, some day will be reconciled to the Pope sooner than he would give way to a mongrel nationalism. He has got to live with Papists and it is useless to pretend to him that we are not Papists.[97]

In his journals, Griffith would discourage this sort of plain speaking, which although probably an expression of what a large section of nation-alists actually thought, threatened to damage Sinn Féin's attempts to gain ground among Ulster Protestants, and to demonstrate to the British and American public that the movement had cross-religious appeal.[98]

---

[95] Patrick Maume, 'Anti-Machiavel: three Ulster nationalists of the age of de Valera', *Irish Political Studies*, 14 (1999), 55.
[96] Aodh De Blacam, *What Sinn Féin stands for* (Dublin, 1921), 149–176.
[97] *Old Ireland*, 24 July 1920.   [98] Davis, 'Ulster Protestants and the Sinn Féin Press', 71.

A contrasting attitude was taken by William Forbes Patterson, another Sinn Féin journalist and publicist. A Presbyterian schoolmaster's son who was born in Derry, Patterson worked for a time as a bank clerk before the Great War. His family was unionist: both his father William and brother James Ross Patterson signed the Ulster Covenant. Patterson claimed to have lost his position as a bank clerk 'because I expressed indignation at the flagrant injustice of the British Government and sympathy with the just cause of my fellow-countrymen'.[99] At the outbreak of the war he enlisted as a private soldier in the 30th Battalion of the Canadian Infantry. On being demobilised he found himself alienated by what he perceived as a lack of concern for his interests shown by the unionists of Ulster and instead turned to 'the only real friendship I have found in Ireland': Sinn Féin. Patterson brought a labour-oriented perspective to Ulster republicanism. In his journalism, and when addressing public meetings – his religion found favour with organisers – he maintained that the Ulster Protestant working class had been duped into supporting the 'commercial magnates and Ascendancy party' only after Devlin had assumed the presidency of the Board of Erin faction of the AOH.[100] Patterson proved a perceptive critic of the treatment of his co-religionists by Sinn Féin members. Stating that suspicions of Protestants had increased in the aftermath of the Rising, he claimed that:

[If] a Unionist dared to enquire into Sinn Féin ideals he was treated with suspicion. One Sinn Féiner complained to me that So-and-so, a Protestant, had been trying to 'draw him', and he had no satisfactory answer to my retort, 'Why not be drawn?'. Those who did join the movement were distrusted: the pilgrim Protestant finds himself in a perfectly awful atmosphere of suspicion. The sinister word 'Spy' meets him, expressed and implied.[101]

One nationalist who agreed that the labour movement offered the best vehicle for indoctrinating Ulster Protestants was the Tyrone-born Catholic barrister and activist Kevin O'Shiel (1891–1970). Despite his recent conversion from the home rule movement to Sinn Féin, he had

---

[99] *II*, 6 February 1919.
[100] *II*, 6 February 1919; Public Record Office of Northern Ireland (PRONI), Ulster Covenant, signature sheet 1834/10 (William Patterson), signature sheet 1879/4 (James Ross Patterson) (accessible online); Canadian Great War Project, Canadian Expeditionary Force Soldier Detail, entry for Private William Forbes Patterson, at http://canadiangreatwarproject.com/searches/soldierDetail.asp?ID=105276, accessed on 2 June 2012; *Derry People*, 4 October 1919; *FJ*, 29 January 1920. In 1948 Patterson married Florence Fulton Hobson (1881–1978), the pioneer woman architect and sister of Bulmer Hobson.
[101] *Old Ireland*, 7 February 1920.

little faith that the latter party could elicit much Protestant working-class support. Instead, he argued, an alliance with the Irish Labour party, which could call on some Belfast Protestant trade unionist members, would provide the most effective means of propagating nationalist views among Ulster Protestants.[102] Although O'Shiel was himself free of prejudice and was more concerned than most about the need to encourage Protestants to join Sinn Féin, he was associated with a sorry episode that undermined the movement's claims to represent people of every faith.

Under the terms of the 1918 election pact, a plebiscite was held to determine which of the two nationalist parties should contest North Fermanagh.[103] North Fermanagh was a mixed constituency, with a unionist member, but it was believed in nationalist circles that the introduction of manhood suffrage and the granting of votes to women over thirty could lead to the return of a nationalist.[104] Such a victory could even ensure that the county was included in a southern Irish state in the event of partition. Sinn Féin won the local plebiscite.[105]

The Fermanagh Sinn Féin executive had already endorsed George Irvine to contest the seat.[106] He was a well-qualified candidate. A Fermanagh-born Protestant, Easter Rising veteran, and lately Irish Guild of the Church bête noire of the hierarchy, he was also widely liked in Sinn Féin, and his unassuming manner was admired. He was also a senior officer in the Dublin Brigade of the IRA. Irvine, who was well connected in his native county, believed he could rely on enough Protestant votes to overturn the small unionist majority. However, an unexpected complication emerged when the local AOH refused to accept the result of the plebiscite. They first complained that the vote was rigged or that electors had been placed under duress. Eventually it was admitted that they would not vote for Irvine, whose parents, they alleged, had been proselytisers.[107] The Hibernians might have been persuaded to lend their votes to a Catholic Sinn Féiner, but not a Protestant one, particularly one with Irvine's family background. The succeeding campaign to force Irvine to revoke his candidature was orchestrated by Patrick Keown (d. 1946), Catholic parish priest of Enniskillen and a well-known clergyman. Even youthful indiscretion was unearthed and used against

---

[102] *New Ireland*, 16 June 1917. For O'Shiel, see Eda Sagarra, *Kevin O'Shiel: Tyrone nationalist and Irish state-builder* (Dublin, 2013), 71–86.
[103] NLI, n. 3651, p. 3269, Sinn Féin standing committee minute book, 16 October 1918.
[104] Sagarra, *Kevin O'Shiel*, 118.
[105] *FJ*, 3 December 1918; *II*, 3 December 1918. The result was Sinn Féin, 3,737; Irish Parliamentary Party, 2,026.
[106] *Ulster Herald*, 17 October 1959.
[107] BMH WS 1770, Kevin O'Shiel, 813–814; *Ulster Herald*, 17 October 1959.

Irvine: it was alleged that as a Portora schoolboy he had broken a convent window with a stone.[108]

Fiercely disappointed, Irvine renounced his candidature. Kevin O'Shiel, despite, he later claimed, serious misgivings, replaced him on the ticket.[109] Irvine remained in the constituency to campaign with him.[110] Irvine believed his exclusion had more far-reaching implications than his own thwarted ambition:

> I had been promised the support of a large Protestant contingent, but these shrewd Northerners, when I approached them to transfer their votes to Mr O'Shiel told me that, though they would gladly have voted for myself, they had determined to abstain altogether since the religious question had been introduced. If the promise given by the UIL before the plebiscite had been kept, I believe the votes of this Protestant contingent would have turned the scale and that we would have won the seat by a narrow majority. If that had taken place it is practically certain that Fermanagh would have been included in the Free State; but to my mind, a more deplorable result was that these Protestants were made to feel that their help was not wanted and that their hope of all sections coming together was disappointed.[111]

O'Shiel narrowly lost the North Fermanagh election by 6,236 votes to his unionist rival's 6,768.

The Sinn Féin standing committee, outraged at events in Fermanagh, suspended the North Fermanagh Comhairle Ceanntair in retaliation for their acquiescing to Irvine's decision to stand down.[112] However, their indignation should be placed within the context of a derisory return of Protestants after the general election. The Sinn Féin victory saw only two Protestants elected out of seventh-three MPs. In West Wicklow, Robert Barton overturned The O'Mahony, then a Bulgarian Orthodox, although an Anglican communicant, by 12,232 votes to 1,247. Ernest Blythe's successful campaign in North Monaghan made great play of his religious background, with voters reminded that he would be a 'worthy follower in [the] footsteps' of the Protestant patriots of 1798 and 1848.[113]

The return of nineteen unionists for Ulster constituencies in 1918, alongside three Labour unionists, forced some in Sinn Féin to acknowledge that their attempts to convert Ulster Protestants to nationalism were not working. There was some evidence of innovative thinking on the platform of the Sinn Féin ard fheis, where the issue of working-class Ulster Protestant antipathy to nationalism was prominent. One speaker,

---

[108] *Ulster Herald,* 17 October 1959.   [109] BMH WS 1770, Kevin O'Shiel, 814–815.
[110] *Impartial Reporter,* 12 December 1918.   [111] *Irish Press,* 4 November 1935.
[112] BMH WS 1770, Kevin O'Shiel, 836; *Ulster Herald,* 17 October 1959.
[113] UCD, Blythe papers, P24/1017, 'The career of Ernest Blythe: candidate for North Monaghan'.

John McSparran, a Catholic priest from Lurgan, praised the Irish Transport and General Workers' Union's success in organising the Belfast workers. They were, he said, 'doing a great deal to smash up the capitalistic opposition to nationality'.[114] Forbes Patterson went further and suggested Sinn Féin should form a close alliance with the Irish Labour Party. 'They must approach these men [the Ulster Protestant working class] through Labour only. They must approach them, if possible, from Liberty Hall, and not from 6 Harcourt Street, and give them a pure Labour ticket.'[115]

At that same ard fheis, Ernest Blythe, Sinn Féin's most prominent Protestant Ulsterman, stated that propaganda work was needed among his co-religionists in the north. If this was done, he said, 'great numbers could be brought over'.[116] This sentiment gained the support of Father McSparran, who told the convention that a propaganda campaign aimed at Ulster Protestants could be successful only if conducted by Protestant republicans. Joseph Devlin was excoriated for his involvement with the AOH, which it was claimed gave Carson the opportunity to win the support of the Protestant workers. Advanced nationalist journal the *Irishman* heartily endorsed Blythe and McSparran's proposals:

By Protestants, therefore, should the Sinn Féin propaganda be carried into the Protestant North now. Sinn Féin has a splendid band of Protestant thinkers, writers, speakers and workers who, with Belfast as their centre, could not undertake better work for the Republic than in such a campaign amongst their co-religionists in Ulster.[117]

One of this 'splendid band', William Forbes Patterson, took this advice. Between October and December 1920 he published *Red Hand Magazine*, a periodical aimed at an Ulster Protestant readership. Its labour-influenced tone suggested that some in Sinn Féin had modified its message in an attempt to win Protestant working-class support. In the 1918 general election the Irish Labour party agreed to stand aside in Sinn Féin's favour, to allow the election be decided on the relationship between Britain and Ireland alone.[118] This decision, which probably contributed to the marginalisation of Labour in Irish politics, has proved controversial. Furthermore, it had the effect of losing to nationalist politics a constituency of Protestant socialists in the north-east, a fact which some Sinn Féiners belatedly came to recognise. Captain Jack White claimed he received a friendly response to the programme of 'the

---

[114] *The Irishman*, 26 April 1919.   [115] *IT*, 12 April 1919.   [116] *IT*, 12 April 1919.
[117] *The Irishman*, 26 April 1919. See also *Old Ireland*, 5 June 1920.
[118] Gaughan, *Thomas Johnson*, 120.

most uncompromising Labour Sinn Féinism' he outlined at a meeting in Antrim. Sinn Féin, White maintained, was gaining Protestant adherents due to increased co-operation with the unions.[119] The magazine offered little further evidence of fresh thinking among the movement's band of propagandists. Contributors adopted a threatening tone towards Ulster unionists. Even while the Government of Ireland Bill was being debated in the Commons, Edmund B. FitzGerald, a Glasgow-based nationalist, was writing that Ulster unionists must be 'shown by every coercive means that the authority of the Mother is stronger naturally and actually, than the instinct for rebellion in any untoward offspring'.[120] Patterson, too, threatened war: nationalists would 'fight forever' rather than accept partition.[121] Such sentiments offered little inducement for wavering Protestants to defect.

The following year another propaganda journal emerged, which unlike *Red Hand Magazine* gave the impression of wishing to speak to a readership beyond a small band of enthusiasts. Rumly entitled *The Unionist*, it was the work of James Winder Good, Seán MacEntee, Seán Lester, and – unpromisingly – Aodh de Blacam. It adopted a more conciliatory approach than previous Sinn Féin propaganda, in suggesting a nine-county Ulster could enjoy a large degree of independence in a united Ireland: 'The old Unionism is dead. Long live the new Unionism! A united Ulster in a united Ireland. That is the gospel *The Unionist* has been founded to preach.'[122] *The Unionist* was a de Valera mouthpiece, and it was reflecting a significant change in his thinking in relation to Ulster. John Bowman has shown how before 1921 de Valera adopted an assimilationist approach to the province. He viewed unionist opposition as largely a consequence of British scheming: once their forces were withdrawn 'we'll put a South of Ireland Catholic on a platform in Ulster and an Ulsterman on a platform in the South, and in ten words they will have dispelled the bogy illusion of religious differences'. Furthermore, de Valera maintained that 'racially' Ulster 'remains Irish', and that after 'more than 300 years of intermarriage' there were 'few native born Ulstermen or Ulsterwomen today in whom Gaelic blood does not predominate'.[123] Bowman argues that in 1921 his position shifted towards seeking an accommodation with Ulster unionists, on the basis of

[119] *Red Hand Magazine*, September 1920. For White's attempts to inculcate socialist sentiment in Sinn Féin, see Keohane, *Captain Jack White*, 197–205ff.
[120] *Red Hand Magazine*, October 1920.   [121] *Red Hand Magazine*, December 1920.
[122] *The Unionist*, 7 May 1921.
[123] Éamon de Valera, quoted in John Bowman, *De Valera and the Ulster question, 1917–1973* (Oxford, 1982), 41, 42.

decentralisation of authority from a Dublin parliament to Belfast.[124] In early May 1921, in a statement outlining his party's policy as part of elections being held under the aegis of the Government of Ireland Act, de Valera stated that an independent Ireland, while 'undivided and a unit with regard to other nations', would allow a degree of devolution to Ulster ample for 'the satisfaction and contentment of all sections of the people'.[125] *The Unionist* enthusiastically endorsed this proposal, stating that a partitioned six-county state would be unable to sustain itself economically.[126] The editors scorned James Craig for seeking safeguards from de Valera for southern Protestants. Only in union with the rest of Ireland could the interests of southern Protestants be safeguarded, they maintained.[127] The timing of this policy was poor: the Government of Ireland Act, which introduced partition, had passed, and in the south the War of Independence was about to end in truce. Moreover, de Valera, the man behind the policy of accommodation, was singularly unsuited to effecting détente with Ulster: he knew little of the place and showed no real interest in understanding Protestant concerns. The last issue of *The Unionist* was published on 24 May 1921, the same day as the first elections to the Northern Irish parliament.

Protestant Friends of Ireland

On 1 June 1919, de Valera left Ireland for the United States. The objectives of the president of Dáil Éireann were to gain recognition of the Irish Republic and to secure a substantial loan from the American public.[128] His expedition was a success, and the itinerary highly exacting: the *Gaelic American* estimated that during his first major tour, in October to December 1919, he made 130 speeches and about half as many brief talks. De Valera's tour illustrates the extent to which Irish controversies over the correlation between religious denomination and political affiliation had transferred across the Atlantic.

Irish-American Protestants proved a generally less obtrusive group than their Catholic compatriots. However, recent work on Irish political culture in New York has highlighted a culture of freemasonry and Orange brotherhood in that city.[129] Protestant Irish America included an Irish nationalist element, exemplified by John Mitchel after 1854, and

---

[124] Bowman, *De Valera and the Ulster question*, 44–47.   [125] *II*, 4 May 1921.
[126] *The Unionist*, 14 May 1921.   [127] *The Unionist*, 21 May 1921.
[128] Carroll, *American opinion*, 150.
[129] Mary C. Kelly, *The shamrock and the lily: the New York Irish and the creation of a transatlantic identity, 1845–1921* (New York 2005), ch. 3.

by Dr Thomas Addis Emmett, leader of the Irish National Federation of America from the 1890s. Irish-American Protestant nationalists gravitated towards the Friendly Sons of Saint Patrick, a secular social organisation. In 1919 an explicitly Protestant Irish-American nationalist organisation was formed: the Protestant Friends of Ireland (PFOI).[130] Its leader was the Rev. James Grattan Mythen (d. 1925), a former Episcopalian clergyman. Described by an obituarist as 'a stormy petrel in religion as well as politics', Mythen was an American-born son of a Protestant father and a Catholic mother who supported Irish republicanism. Mythen had – or claimed – a tradition of nationalism or patriotism in his family: collateral descent from Henry Grattan. Holding strongly advanced nationalist sympathies, during the Great War he did not conceal his support for Germany and distrust of Great Britain. However, he served in the United States navy for part of the conflict, volunteering as an ordinary recruit. Mythen's Irish nationalist activism brought him into conflict with the Episcopalian hierarchy: this may have been a factor in his ordination into the Liberal Catholic priesthood in August 1917. (Separate from the Catholic Church, the Liberal Catholic Church allowed its members a wide degree of intellectual independence, with many holding Theosophist views). In 1920 he converted again, this time to Orthodoxy, taking the name Patrick in religion. Mythen immediately became an influential figure in American Orthodoxy, advancing to archimandrite and bishop of Alaska. The leader of a group of convert priests, he was instrumental in founding the first convert parish church in America, the Church of the Transfiguration in New York. In 1925, just before his violent death (see later discussion), Mythen made an approach to Rome: while remaining a priest of the Eastern Church, he declared himself to be under the jurisdiction of the pope.[131]

It would be a mistake to exaggerate the extent of the PFOI's activities. Although it claimed membership in the hundreds and maintained a close association with Clan na Gael (the separatist sister of the IRB) and the Friends of Irish Freedom, the body was weakened by internal division. The relationship between Mythen and the PFOI's secretary, Dr Norman Thomas, a former Presbyterian minister and prominent socialist, was

---

[130] *The Sun* (New York), 13 December 1919; *Kentucky Irish American*, 20 December 1919.
[131] *Butte Independent*, 16 May 1925; Kelly, *The shamrock and the lily*, 103; David Fitzpatrick, *Harry Boland's Irish revolution* (Cork, 2003), 142; Alexei Krindatch (ed.), *Atlas of American Orthodox Christian Churches* (Brookline, MA, 2011), 25–26; *Gaelic American*, 3 January 1920; 'A short history of the liberal Catholic Church and St. Raphael's Parish', available at http://srlcc.tripod.com/lcchist.htm, accessed 30 July 2013; T. J. Tobin, 'President de Valera at Notre Dame', *Notre Dame Scholastic*, Vol. 53, No. 4 (1919), 58.

badly strained.[132] Thomas was a critic of Mythen's role in the organisation and accused him of misuse of PFOI finances. Mythen retaliated
by stating that Thomas was not of Irish blood.[133] Nor was the group
fully independent: it was dominated by the Friends of Irish Freedom.
Minuscule, weakened by disagreement, and led by a man – Mythen – of
dubious judgement, the PFOI nevertheless played a role in rebutting
potentially damaging criticisms of the effect of Sinn Féin policy on
religious freedom in Ireland.

In November 1919 a seven-man 'Ulster delegation' visited the United
States, seeking to elicit American Protestant sympathy for the unionist
cause. Buoyed by a sympathetic Protestant church press, the delegation
visited twenty-four cities in three months. They were enthusiastically
received in Protestant churches, where they informed bulging congre-
gations of the threat Sinn Féin posed to Irish Protestant liberties.[134] The
Irish World suggested that the peculiar denominational make-up of the
delegation – three Methodist clergyman, three Presbyterian clergymen,
and an Episcopalian clergyman – represented an attempt to influence
American Methodist opinion.[135] Although Methodists amounted to just
1.54 per cent of the total Irish population (and 5.48 per cent of the
Protestant population) in 1911, American Methodism had seen sharp
growth, embracing almost 6 per cent of the total US population in 1920.
The presence of the Ulster delegation and its associated publicity vexed
de Valera and his lieutenant Harry Boland. Boland's allies resorted to
disrupting the delegation's meetings in several cities.[136] Several Protestant nationalists resident in North America were inspired to launch a
response to charges of Sinn Féin intolerance.

Some of the staunchest criticism of the Ulster delegation came
from Robert Lindsay Crawford, then resident in Canada. Following his
forced resignation from the editorship of the Ulster Guardian in 1908 and
expulsion from the Independent Orange Order, he had emigrated to
Canada.[137] Crawford joined the editorial staff of the Toronto Globe
(1910–1918), until his political views saw him removed, again, from his
position. In July 1918 he became founding editor of a new liberal journal,
the Statesman. His politics had by now undergone further revision:
formerly a proponent of Irish self-government, he now favoured a

---

[132] For Thomas, see Fitzpatrick, Harry Boland, 142, 372 n.
[133] Kelly, The shamrock and the lily, 103.
[134] Fitzpatrick, Harry Boland, 141; Edward Cuddy, 'The Irish question and the revival of
Anti-Catholicism in the 1920's', Catholic Historical Review, Vol. 67, No. 2 (April
1981), 242.
[135] Irish World, 22 November 1919.   [136] Fitzpatrick, Harry Boland, 142.
[137] See Chapter 2.

republic. By 1920 he had become closely associated with the PFOI.[138] Crawford's writing offers insight into his political trajectory, from champion of proletarian Protestantism to Lake Ontario–based propagandist of the Irish Republic. He claimed that 'Carsonism is the rump of the old Protestant Ascendancy, the residuary legatee of the special privileges claimed by the Protestant settlers.' Since disestablishment, he alleged, Presbyterian industrialists had aped the worst elements of the landed class.[139] As for the 'sectarian crusaders', or Ulster delegation, he drew a parallel between their campaign and an earlier anti-revolutionary intervention in North America: they called to his mind 'the mercenary Hessian troops of George III [who] overran the Thirteen Colonies in an effort to stem the tide of American revolt'.[140]

In 1920 de Valera was introduced to the Rev. James Alexander H. Irwin, a republican-sympathising Presbyterian minister from Killead, County Antrim, who was visiting America to recuperate from illness. Irwin agreed to accompany de Valera on a leg of his tour, where he addressed numerous meetings.[141] Irwin's presence at the side of the Sinn Féin president (or, as some Americans called him, the 'President of the Irish Republic') offered some rebuttal to unionist claims that Ulster Protestants were unanimously anti-republican. This was certainly how the Irish republican press viewed Irwin's association with the de Valera tour.[142]

The Ulster delegation's presence influenced de Valera's rhetoric. His speeches were replete with references to the Protestant patriots of the eighteenth century, the substantial amount of Protestant support of Irish independence, and the conversion of Ulster Protestants to republicanism, which he promised his audiences was imminent.[143] The extent of the political choreography employed to counter the Ulster delegation's claims was impressive. A front organisation, the 'Inter-Church League for Irish Independence', was set up, which sought to counter the 'slander' against Protestants that they were instinctively imperialist.[144] Organisers of de Valera's public meetings strove for the appearance of ecumenical harmony: they ensured a presence of both Protestant and

---

[138] See John W. Boyle, 'A Fenian Protestant in Canada: Robert Lindsay Crawford, 1910–22', *Canadian Historical Review*, Vol. 52, No. 2 (June 1971), 165–176.

[139] Lindsay Crawford, *The Problem of Ulster* (New York, 1920[?]), 4, 5, 9.

[140] Crawford, *The Problem of Ulster*, 13, 10.

[141] BMH WS 394, James Alexander H. Irwin.   [142] *Old Ireland*, 17 April, 5 June 1920.

[143] *Gaelic American*, 10 January, 12 July, 23 August 1919.

[144] *Irish World*, 22 November, 20 December 1919.

Catholic clergymen on platforms.[145] At ten of his rallies de Valera claimed Ulster Protestant support for Irish separatism.[146]

The ecumenical theme reached its zenith at a rally held in April 1920 in Carnegie Hall, New York, under the auspices of the PFOI. In his address to the meeting, Grattan Mythen offered an apology for the existence of the PFOI. The organisation was, he said, only necessary to counter the 'bitterness', 'vindictiveness', and 'bigotry' of groups such as the Ulster delegation, whose claims of uniform Protestant support for imperialism they needed to counter. Mythen was followed by Irwin, whose presence on the platform the *Gaelic American* deemed to be 'an assurance that the spirit of 1782 and 1798 still lives in Ulster'. De Valera highlighted the significance of Irwin's appearance on the platform: he claimed that the presence of the Presbyterian clergyman illustrated the success of Sinn Féin ideals in penetrating Ulster.[147]

The Ulster delegation declared themselves satisfied with their American tour. They secured numerous resolutions from Church bodies demanding the United States cease interference in Irish politics.[148] Supporters of the PFOI, too, had reason to be satisfied. Although it is unlikely their propagandising won many new supporters to their cause, their assertion of non-sectarian principles offered, at least briefly and in the wrong continent, some concrete evidence of the veracity of the 'Catholic, Protestant and Dissenter' slogan.

On Irwin's return to Ulster he became victim of a campaign of harassment by members of his church, seeking to have him removed from his position. He was briefly jailed during the War of Independence when a revolver, gun, thirty-five rounds of ammunition, and an Irish Volunteer badge were found in his house.[149] In 1926 he left Killead to take a post in Edinburgh, before being appointed minister in Lucan, County Dublin, in 1935. He died in his manse in Lucan in 1954.

James Grattan Mythen's life had a more tragic coda. In 1925, Mythen was brutally murdered in 'mysterious circumstances', after a 'terrible struggle'. His obituarist, while drawing attention to his kindness and sense of humour, also reported on his physical and mental ill-health: he was 'a tortured mind in a tortured body'. Mythen's death, it was stated,

---

[145] See, for example, *Gaelic American*, 2 April 1920.
[146] John Bowman, 'De Valera on Ulster, 1919–1920: What he told America', *Irish Studies in International Affairs*, Vol. 1, No. 1 (1979), 9.
[147] *Gaelic American*, 17 April 1920.
[148] Cuddy, 'The Irish question and the revival of Anti-Catholicism', 242.
[149] BMH WS 394, James Alexander H. Irwin; *Old Ireland*, 5 June 1920; *The Witness*, 18 March 1921.

'deprives the Irish movement of a most picturesque figure'.[150] It was a sad end to an unusual career.

De Valera's mission to the United States happened in the context of the ongoing Irish War of Independence. Chapter 7 will assess this conflict and seek to identify the extent of Protestant involvement as active combatants in the Irish Republican Army.

[150] *Butte Independent,* 16 May 1925.

7   Revolutionaries, 1919–1923

Introduction

The Irish War of Independence is traditionally described as beginning with the 21 January 1919 ambush and killing of two policemen in Soloheadbeg, County Tipperary, by a detachment of Volunteers led by Seán Treacy.[1] Coincidently, Dáil Éireann first met that day, comprised of Sinn Féin members elected in the 1918 election. The Dáil elected a cabinet, which created independent ministries, in an effort to supersede the British administration. Dáil courts were set up, which sought to undermine the established system of justice. A guerrilla war slowly developed, with the Irish Volunteers, which gradually became known as the IRA, on one side, and the RIC and the military on the other.[2] In 1920 the British government, seeking to reinforce the RIC, created two new forces, the 'Black and Tans' and the Auxiliary Division, which became responsible for highly publicised acts of brutality against the IRA and the public. The conflict led to the deaths of 405 members of the police, 150 British soldiers, and around 750 Volunteers and civilians.

The outbreak of war saw many socially elite, mild nationalists, who had previously advocated home rule or had confined themselves to the cultural sphere, declaring their allegiance to a republic. During this period Dorothy Stopford would write that 'all sorts of upper-class respectable people' were supporting Sinn Féin.[3] Dublin's literary salons would gain additional frisson by the introduction of guerrilla fighters, men with mysterious pasts and prices on their heads. Michael Collins, for example, would become a regular visitor at Alice Stopford Green's house at 90 St Stephen's Green. Even TCD got a poorly disguised Sinn Féin club during this period, the 'Thomas Davis Society'. This group

---

[1] Michael Hopkinson, *The Irish War of Independence* (Dublin, 2002), 25.
[2] The term 'Irish Volunteer' remained in use during this period: for a discussion of the partial adoption of the term 'Irish Republican Army', see Charles Townshend, *The Republic: the fight for Irish independence, 1918–1923* (London, 2013), 89.
[3] MacLellan, *Dorothy Stopford Price*, 50.

represented the first attempt by Trinity students to form a nationalist society on campus since Provost Mahaffy had suppressed the Gaelic Society in 1914.[4] George O'Brien, a patrician Catholic and later a leading economist, described the atmosphere in Dublin about 1919:

I had become quite a romantic young rebel. The Arts Club, the Abbey Theatre, the Irish Bookshop, the Crock of Gold and the Sod of Turf were all full of rebels – rebels with genteel outlooks and upper-class accents. The real rebels were far away in the background.[5]

Who were the 'real' Protestant rebels?

The War of Independence, 1919–1921

A small number of Protestants fought in the IRA during the War of Independence and in the anti-Treaty republican forces during the subsequent Civil War. The Irish revolutionary period is especially well documented, which has allowed scholars to trace the social and economic profile of IRA men.[6] However, the scarce number of Protestants in the IRA, their wide geographical dispersal, and the lack of autobiographical accounts they generated impedes detailed prosopographical analysis.[7] Although it is estimated that more than 100,000 men were in the Volunteers at some point during the revolutionary period, there were only about 5,000 active, committed guerrilla fighters.[8] Only a tiny number of the latter group were Protestant. For example, during the Civil War, analysis of the unusually complete records of the National Army Cork Command shows there were 235 Catholic prisoners, one atheist, and no Protestants.[9] Locating the thin scattering of Protestant rebels throughout the country is a challenging task. Using a wide variety of sources, this author has uncovered a total of thirty-seven Protestants who were active

---

[4] *Gaelic Churchman*, May 1920. For the suppression of the TCD Gaelic Society, see Tomás Irish, *Trinity in war and revolution, 1912–1923* (Dublin, 2015), 167–169.

[5] James Meenan, *George O'Brien: a biographical memoir* (Dublin, 1980), 76.

[6] Fitzpatrick, *Politics and Irish life*, 168–170; Peter Hart, *The IRA at war, 1916–1923* (Oxford, 2003), 110–138.

[7] For references to Protestant republican fellow-prisoners during the Civil War, see, for example, Ó Fiaich Library and Archive, Armagh, O'Kane collection, LOK IV B.05, interview with Patrick Hennessey.

[8] Hart, *The IRA at war*, 112–113.

[9] MAD, CW/P/13/02, Ledger of political prisoners, Cork Command, August 1922; CW/P/13/08, Ledger of political prisoners, Cork Command, October 1922. Likewise, Peter Hart conducted a survey of 917 prisoners convicted under the Defence of the Realm Act from 1917 to 1919, and found one agnostic and no Protestants: Hart, *The IRA at war*, 123.

in the IRA or anti-Treaty republican forces at some point from 1919 to 1923.[10] Protestants, likewise, formed only a very small proportion of grassroots Sinn Féiners. For example, analysis of Sinn Féin members in Mullinabreena, County Sligo, in 1918, found that of the 126 individuals that could be traced to the census, only one was Protestant.[11]

Protestant hesitancy about joining the IRA in substantial numbers is partially explained by the organisation's strongly Catholic ethos. The IRA was officially a secular organisation, which kept religion and politics strictly separate, and this spirit was valued by many IRA men.[12] However, the overwhelmingly Catholic nature of the organisation was reflected in habits such as companies parading on Sundays outside Mass, as well as frequent recitations of the rosary, neither of which was likely to encourage Protestant recruiting. It is likely that the small number of Protestant volunteers found that their religion marked them as outsiders. Certainly, the sole National Army Protestant to write about his experiences did not encounter antagonism, but was struck by the demonstrative Catholicism of his fellow-soldiers.[13] Ernie O'Malley recalled in his autobiography a 'pitying commiseration' for Protestants and atheists.[14] For Todd Andrews, the revolution was imbued with religion: he spoke of the 'profound Catholic faith' of the Volunteers.[15] Frank Busteed (1898–1974), of Cork No. 1 Brigade, was a rare atheist among Volunteers. Born in Doughcloyne, County Cork, he was the son of an Episcopalian father and Catholic mother. Busteed believed that his Protestant surname – rather than his atheism – hindered his progress in the IRA.[16]

However, some republican tradition of anti-clericalism did endure. Certain republicans, alienated by the Catholic hierarchy's support for the pro-Treatyites, moved away from the church. Dorothy Macardle, as we have seen, joined the Church of Ireland. The Rev. William Vandeleur recalled one curious incident that happened in County Wexford:

[10] Robert Basil Anderson, Robert Barton, William Beaumont, Robert Bradshaw, Peter Carpenter, Walter Patrick Carpenter, Geoffrey Coulter, Ellett Elmes, Charlie Gilmore, George Gilmore, Harry Gilmore, Rory Graham, James Hawe, Jim Heuston, Frank Hoffman, George Imbush, George Irvine, James Johnston (né Nethercott), Bertie King, Alfred George Norgrove, Frederick Norgrove, Seamus McGowan, Liam McMullen, Ian Graeme Baun 'Scottie' MacKenzie Kennedy, Charles MacWhinney, Walter Mitchell, Séan Nethercott, George Nugent, George and James Plant, Thomas Pollington, David Lubbock Robinson, William Scott, Peter Steepe, Francis Stuart,, Alfred Ward, Percy Ward.
[11] Laffan, *The resurrection of Ireland*, 184.   [12] Hart, *The IRA at war*, 123.
[13] See Chapter 8.   [14] Ernie O'Malley, *On another man's wound* (London, 1936), 24.
[15] C. S. Andrews, *Dublin made me: an autobiography* (Dublin, 1979), 99.
[16] Townshend, *The Republic*, 57.

the Roman Catholic Church ... threw its weight on the side of the Cosgrave Party. There were among its members those who favoured a Republic and some of these men were quite definitely anti-clerical and resented what was to them the leaning of the bishops. This feeling took a strange form sometimes. Once, when a group of Republicans called on a country rector in the town of Ferns, they enquired on what terms they could be admitted to the Church of Ireland![17]

The motivating influences of Protestant Easter rebels is relatively easy to discern: Irish Volunteers were generally radicalised through intimate personal networks forged first in the Gaelic League classroom, then occasionally Sinn Féin, and then the IRB; ICA members were usually urban workers, attracted by the promise of a socialist republic. The motivation of Protestants who fought in the War of Independence or in the republican side in the Civil War is more obscure. Certainly, seven were long-term republicans and had fought in the Easter Rising with the ICA or Irish Volunteers.[18] Others give the impression of simply joining in with their Catholic neighbours, acting on a personal slight against the British, or wishing to take part in a grand adventure. George Imbush, who fought in Limerick, recalled that as a youth, local Volunteers on parade had made a great impression on him.[19] In 1916, George and James Plant, aged twelve and thirteen, respectively, were beaten in custody by RIC seeking information about two local republicans. As a result, the Plants, who came from a Church of Ireland farming family in Fethard, County Tipperary, developed a hatred of the law. Two years later they joined the Moyglass unit of the 7th Battalion of the 3rd Tipperary Brigade.[20] Similarly, William Beaumont, who had served with the Dublin Fusiliers during the Great War, was taking a tram home to Dawson Street one evening, when it was searched by Auxiliaries, and found it difficult to persuade them he was not a member of the IRA. According to his brother, Sean Beaumont,

He came home furious with indignation about the way that he and the other passengers, particularly the women, had been treated and the first thing he said to me when he came in was that, if I got him a gun, he would shoot some of the Auxiliaries.[21]

Rather than shooting any Auxiliaries, under his brother's influence, William Beaumont befriended them, and collected information which was passed to Michael Collins. By contrast, little is known about what

---

[17] RCBL, Rev. William Vandeleur, typescript memoirs, 31.
[18] Ellett Elmes, George Gilmore, George Irvine, Seamus McGowan, Alfred George Norgrove, Frederick Norgrove, William Scott.
[19] UCD, Ernie O'Malley papers, P176/130, interview with George Embush [sic].
[20] DIB article on George Plant.   [21] BMH WS 709, J. N. (Sean) Beaumont.

motivated a group of Galway Protestants, including James Hawe and George Nugent, who were active in Aughrim; brothers Alfred and Percy Ward, from Roundstone; Bertie King, from Carna; or Thomas Pollington, from East Connemara, to join the Volunteers.[22] The Galway Protestant community was tiny, and it is likely that these men saw a better future fighting side-by-side with their neighbours, rather than continuing to uphold loyalism. Rory Graham, from Cregagh, Belfast, was one of a small number of Protestants to serve with the IRA in Ulster. He was arrested by B-Specials (the Ulster Special Constabulary) in Labby, near Magherafelt, County Derry. Fr Louis O'Kane recalled:

[Graham] said that being a Protestant he was a sort of a white-blackbird as far as the Catholic Irish Volunteers were concerned. He remained in Belfast until it got too dangerous, and the IRA Intelligence decided that if Rory were captured by the Specials, being a Protestant in the IRA, he would be very brutally killed … When he was asked his name (upon his arrest in Labby) he said he was Lawrence Roderick McGlone, and that he was a student for the priesthood of the Diocese of Baltimore, USA … To keep up the disguise which had been arranged weeks before, Mary Toner from Labby came and innocently asked the guard at the gate to see prisoner McGlone, that he had left his rosary beads behind him when he was arrested.[23]

Likewise, James Johnston (né Nethercott), a Fermanagh-born Anglican and commandant in the East Down Battalion, IRA, thought it prudent to serve under his mother's maiden name.[24]

The highest-ranking Protestant Irish Volunteer of the War of Independence was George Irvine. In 1918 he was appointed vice-commandant of the 1st Battalion Dublin Brigade, under the command of Thomas F. Byrne.[25] Irvine was charged with visiting the thirteen battalion companies, and inspected its first aid, machine-gunning, and other classes.[26] His men affectionately called him 'The Grey Ghost'.[27] Irvine, who had led a republican putsch in the Irish Guild of the Church against unionist clergy and laity, was less assertive in Catholic company:

[22] Cormac Ó Comhraí, *Sa bhearna bhaoil: Gaillimh 1913–1923* (Gaillimh, 2015), 326.

[23] Fr Louis O'Kane, interview with Rory Graham, quoted in *Irish News*, 9 November 2015.

[24] *Irish Press*, 22 August 1955. For Johnston's brother, Séan Nethercott, an IRA intelligence officer who converted to Catholicism at some unspecified point prior to 1922, see PRONI, HA 5/1644, Intelligence file on Séan Nethercott.

[25] MAD, MSPC, 34REF61665, George Irvine, Application for a service certificate; and testimony of Oscar Traynor on Irvine's military service, 22 November 1950.

[26] MAD, MSPC, 34REF61665, George Irvine, Evidence given before the Advisory Committee, 21 September 1951.

[27] *II*, 1 July 1954.

None of his old comrades ever knew much about George Irvine's family associations in County Fermanagh ... His accent betrayed his Northern origin, though he was not a man who spoke much at any time, even among [his] small circle of friends.[28]

Irvine adopted something of a dual character during this period: to his mainly Catholic colleagues in the IRA, he was a distant, unassuming character, whose Protestant background was rarely visible; but to his co-religionists, he was an iconoclast, who sought rupture with the past.[29]

The most colourful Protestant Volunteer of the War of Independence era was Ian Graeme Baun 'Scottie' MacKenzie Kennedy (1899–1922). MacKenzie Kennedy was born in Inverness-shire in the Scottish Highlands to a Church of Scotland family. There was a military tradition in Kennedy's family: his father was a major and his uncle had been a major general in the British army. The death of his brother fighting in France prompted his mother to move to Ireland with Kennedy in 1916, where she believed he would be far from violence. Initially MacKenzie Kennedy and his mother lived with Albinia Brodrick in Kerry. Here, MacKenzie Kennedy, a Scots Gaelic speaker and bagpiper, with a deep interest in his clan heritage, immersed himself in the Irish language. He joined the D Company of the 8th Battalion, Cork No. 1 Brigade, based in Ballingeary, and took part in a gun-running expedition to England in 1921. At some point during his time in Kerry he and his mother converted to Catholicism. Having taken the republican side in the Civil War, MacKenzie Kennedy was aged twenty-three when he was killed by National Army forces in Rochestown, County Cork, in August 1922.[30]

Albinia Brodrick was able to put her training to use to help the Volunteers. At her hospital in Caherdaniel, County Kerry, she offered nursing care and a safe-house for men on the run. One Volunteer recalled:

It was during the trouble in the mountains. I was in the Column. There was twenty-five of us altogether ... she was helping us and looking after us and bringing us clothes ... she had posters and that to join the IRA ... and she'd be there at the head of the table and telling everything.[31]

As a well-known republican, Brodrick's hospital was a frequent target of Black and Tan raids. After one such incident, General Sir Nevil

---

[28] *Donegal News*, 10 July 1954.   [29] See Chapter 6.
[30] Stephen Coyle, 'Ian Graeme Baun MacKenzie Kennedy – "Scottie" 1899–1922: a Scottish Gael who died for the Irish Republic', at www.rsfcork.com/ianmackenziekennedy.htm, accessed 10 June 2014; *Southern Star*, 25 June 2011; *Sunday Independent*, 8 October 1922.
[31] Morrissey, 'Albinia Brodrick', 100.

Macready, the commander of British forces in Ireland, wrote to Lord Midleton: 'I was sorry the other day that we had a slight altercation with Miss Brodrick, but I am afraid her sympathies are not altogether on our side.'[32]

After she completed her final examinations in medicine from TCD in 1921, Dorothy Stopford moved to West Cork where she became medical officer to the IRA in the region, as well as lecturing on first aid to local members of Cumann na mBan. This was the culmination of an accelerated ideological trajectory that took her from unionist and close friend of Sir Matthew Nathan prior to the rising, beyond her aunt's support for nationhood within a commonwealth, towards republicanism.[33] Máire Comerford remembered:

Dorothy Stopford disappeared from our circle and it was only very rarely, when I saw her, that I knew she was on to something good, about which she never spoke. The truth was that she had gone to be medical officer in charge of a secret IRA cottage hospital, somewhere near Kilbrittan, in Tom Barry's country.[34]

The reason for her discretion was that having passed her finals, she did not wish her activities to come to the attention of college authorities until she had been awarded her degree.[35] In a series of lively letters to her mother, Stopford described an exciting, full life in the midst of war. Her republicanism did not prevent her from befriending local Protestants, which could lead to weird contrasts: 'I went to a work party at the Rectory the other day & sewed an apron & we had prayers & sang hymns. I was much amused … Next minute I am out fishing or ferretting with the IRA. You can guess which I prefer.'[36]

Differences of opinion about the War of Independence caused disagreement between Kathleen Lynn and her family. Banished from her family home for the four years since the rising, in Christmas 1920 she was finally readmitted. A St Stephen's Day sermon preached by her father angered her: 'Evening sermon annoyed me much, hate my father to be unfair. He should say nothing if he can only think of the police.'[37] The next day she had a disagreement with her family: 'We had an

[32] TNA, Lord Midleton papers, PRO30/67/44, General Sir Nevil Macready to Lord Midleton, 19 February 1921.
[33] See MacLellan, *Dorothy Stopford Price*.
[34] UCD, LA18, Máire Comerford unpublished memoirs.
[35] Ó Broin, *Protestant nationalists*, 169–170.
[36] NLI, Stopford Price papers, MS 15,341(8), Dorothy Stopford to Constance Stopford, 19 November 1921. See also MS 15,341(8), Dorothy Stopford to Constance Stopford, 4 July 1921.
[37] RCPI, Diary of Kathleen Lynn, 26 December 1920.

argument re. Murders etc. before I left. I hope they will take it as it was meant, for they only see one side.'[38]

By early 1921, Lloyd George understood that the IRA was not going to be defeated militarily; any end to violence would require a negotiated agreement. In seeking to resolve the conflict Lloyd George would have to rely on the support of Albinia Brodrick's estranged brother St John Brodrick, now earl of Midleton. By 1921 Midleton had become concerned at the spate of Big House burnings and other violence and was eager to salvage something for the beleaguered southern Protestant minority in any settlement. Along with his cousin James Francis Bernard, the 4th earl of Bandon, a prominent Cork landowner, he began agitating to introduce 'Dominion Home Rule' status for Ireland.[39]

At around 6:30 in the morning of 21 June 1921, Castle Bernard, the seat of Lord Bandon, was burnt to the ground by an IRA company led by Commandant Sean Hales (1881–1922).[40] Lord Bandon, who was kidnapped during the attack, was targeted due to his involvement with Midleton in the Dominion scheme, and as a hostage against the execution of prisoners held by the British in Cork City Jail and Mountjoy Prison.[41]

Recovering from her ordeal, Lady Bandon retired to the gardener's cottage. Guarded by an officer and platoon from Bandon garrison, she was visited by her niece, Mary Gaussen. On the Sunday after the attack Gaussen and Lady Bandon were shocked to receive a visitor: Albinia Brodrick. Brodrick's politics were well known, making her persona non grata among her relatives. At first Lady Bandon refused to see her cousin-in-law, though such was the latter's insistence that Gaussen records the Countess 'finally consented and that terrible woman came in'. The IRA had sent Brodrick as an emissary to give Lady Bandon terms for Lord Bandon's release. Brodrick stated that she had no information on him, having not seen 'our leaders', but advised Lady Bandon to put pressure on the Government to release the prisoners.[42] A British officer recorded:

A well-known lady [Brodrick], who had become an ardent Sinn Féiner, came down to Castle Bernard and said to Lady Bandon, 'I have been sent down to Castle Bernard to warn you that, unless the government conclude a Truce, Lord

[38] RCPI, Diary of Kathleen Lynn, 27 December 1920.
[39] *New York Times*, 22 June 1921; *Cork Constitution*, 23 August 1920.
[40] *Cork Examiner*, 22 June 1921.
[41] The earl of Midleton, *Records and reactions: 1856–1939* (London, 1939), 261.
[42] Diary of Mary Gaussen, quoted in Bence-Jones, *Twilight of the ascendancy*, 211.

Bandon will be killed.' The reply was 'If that is all you have to say, you had better go home.'[43]

However, Gaussen declined to have her detained, explaining, 'We had no officer up here at the moment and I'm afraid it wouldn't have done if I had asked the Corporal to arrest her.'[44]

Although appearing cruel to her relatives, Brodrick exerted pressure on the republican leadership to treat her cousin well, or even to release him. A few days after the kidnapping, Anna Hurley-O'Mahony, a Cumann na mBan officer in Bandon, was surprised to find Brodrick at her door:

I brought the little lady in ... and she explained that she had walked the whole way out from Bandon to ask me to put her in touch with the Column as she wished to intercede for the safety of her cousin. She had been directed to me by the Cumann na mBan in the town and that was good enough for me, so while the Hon. Albina [sic] was having her tea I arranged for a pony and trap and driver to bring her on her way to Coomhola where the Column was at the time. She set off and eventually, travelling by relays of traps, she got to her destination away beyond Bantry and there interviewed the Brigade staff.[45]

Brodrick's mission was unknown to her family.

Pressure for the release of Lord Bandon was also applied by Midleton; he made it a pre-condition of any talks with de Valera. At his speech at the opening of the new Northern Irish parliament on 22 June, George V made an appeal for peace in Ireland. This was followed by an invitation from Lloyd George to de Valera to come to London for talks. Before doing so de Valera and Arthur Griffith met Midleton in the Mansion House in Dublin, where they agreed to various safeguards for the Protestant community. They also agreed, as a pre-truce token of good faith, to release Lord Bandon, who had been well treated by his captors.

Albinia Brodrick had no faith in British honesty; she sought a meeting with Michael Collins, the Dáil minister for finance and IRA director of intelligence, to warn him of what she saw as their duplicity. She stated: 'I know what I am talking about, for I lived with British diplomats and worked in the War Office itself.' This belief extended to her own brother, whom she believed to be a 'dangerous enemy':[46] she warned the Sinn Féin leadership that he ought not to be trusted. This was unfair – Midleton served as an honest broker in the

[43] Major Arthur Percival, quoted in Meda Ryan, *Tom Barry: IRA freedom fighter* (Dublin, 2003), 140–141.
[44] Diary of Mary Gaussen, quoted in Bence-Jones, *Twilight of the ascendancy*, 213.
[45] BMH WS 540, Anna Hurley-O'Mahony.
[46] UCD, LA18, Máire Comerford unpublished memoirs.

negotiations leading to the Truce of 11 July 1921, despite scepticism about the process.

Collins declined to listen to Brodrick's warnings: on 6 December 1921 he and Arthur Griffith led a delegation which signed the Anglo-Irish Treaty, bringing an end to the War of Independence. It provided for the establishment of the Irish Free State, a self-governing dominion, with authority over the twenty-six southern counties. The six north-eastern counties would remain within the United Kingdom: the exact border between Northern Ireland and the Free State was left undetermined; a boundary commission would deal with the issue at a later date. To the outrage of republicans, members of the Free State parliament would be compelled to take an Oath of Allegiance to the Crown. Such an agreement may have been acceptable to pragmatists such as Collins and Griffith, but a republican group, looking to de Valera as leader, sought to overturn it.

Anti-Treatyites and the Irish Civil War, 1922–1923

This controversy split Sinn Féin into two rival factions, destroying the fragile advanced nationalist unity that had existed since 1917. Although the Treaty enjoyed widespread public support, as well as the support of the Catholic hierarchy, the majority of the IRA were opposed. The large degree of autonomy enjoyed by local commanders during the War of Independence created an environment where units could ignore both national military and political leadership. If Collins and Griffith were to defend the settlement, they would need to use force.[47] Ella Young, on hearing rumours of an agreement with Britain, sought out Kathleen Lynn. 'I hurried to Doctor Kathleen Lynn. She ... had ... no explanation: nothing but perplexity, ignorance, and foreboding.'[48] Women, including Protestant women, were among the most significant anti-Treaty activists. Indeed, the diverse group of republicans, which would include cousins Erskine Childers and Robert Barton, came to be nicknamed the 'Women and Childers Party'.[49] Few, in fact, were as conspicuously anti-Treaty as Protestant women. (Though not all: Chapter 8 will assess Protestant nationalist pro-Treatyites.) Throughout this period, figures such as Maud Gonne, Kathleen Lynn, Albinia

---

[47] For the politics of this period generally, see Bill Kissane, *The politics of the Irish Civil War* (Oxford, 2005).
[48] Young, *Flowering dusk*, 171.
[49] Norman, *Terrible beauty: a life of Constance Markievicz*, 234.

Brodrick, and Rosamond Jacob gave the impression of unyielding refusal to compromise. Why was this the case?

'Like most converts to the cause, I was zealous to the point of fanaticism.'[50] Thus Dorothy Macardle explained her opposition to the Treaty. That some reacted with the 'zeal of the convert' is undeniable. This author has conducted a survey of twenty-four Protestant women who declared themselves against the Treaty.[51] The majority came from a unionist background: eighteen of the twenty-four can be identified as having at least one unionist parent.[52] Religion may be a further factor: at least eight had converted to Catholicism.[53] For most, the decision to join the nationalist movement, and in many cases to convert to Rome, led to separation from their family or social milieu. The failure to achieve a republic after such sacrifice was unthinkable.

Protestant nationalist women's backgrounds could be highlighted during the notoriously-acrimonious Treaty debates. On one occasion, Kerry pro-Treaty TD (member of parliament) Fionán Lynch, on stating that 'I can speak for the people of South Kerry', received an unexpected reply from the public gallery:

'No!'

The House was thunderstruck. The dissenting voice was that of a sombre lady sitting in the body of the hall. All eyes were turned upon her, and Fionán Lynch, with biting emphasis, completed his sentence –

'With one exception – an Englishwoman.'

The interrupter was asked to leave the Chamber. Quietly closing her notebook, and still smiling, the Honourable Albinia Broderick [sic], Republican sister of a Southern Unionist Peer, left the hall.[54]

Constance Markievicz used her speech to argue against the addition of an upper house of parliament, which would include numerous representatives of the landed gentry class, whom she felt had betrayed the people. Despite this, pro-Treaty deputies highlighted Markievicz's

---

[50] BMH WS 457, Dorothy Macardle.
[51] Dulcibella Barton, Elizabeth Bloxham, Albinia Brodrick, Nancy Campbell, Sidney Czir; Charlotte Despard, Kathleen Emerson, Mabel FitzGerald, Nellie Gifford, Maud Gonne, Mary Louisa Gwynn, Mary Irvine, Rosamond Jacob, Luba Kaftanikoff, Kathleen Lynn, Dorothy Macardle, Dora Maguire, Mary Maguire, Constance Markievicz, Lily McManus, Alice Milligan, Annie M. P. Smithson, Dorothy Stopford-Price, Ella Young.
[52] Barton, Bloxham, Brodrick, Campbell, Czira, Despard, Emerson, FitzGerald, Nellie Gifford, Gwynn, Lynn, Macardle, Dora and Mary Maguire, Markievicz, Milligan, McManus, Smithson.
[53] Campbell, Despard, FitzGerald, Gonne, Gwynn, Dora Maguire, Markievicz, Smithson.
[54] Padraig De Burca and John F. Boyle, *Free State or republic?* (Dublin, 2003 [1922]), 17.

own landed family background during the debates.[55] Eventually the Dáil approved the Treaty by a vote of 64 to 57, with all six female deputies, including Constance Markievicz, the sole woman from a Protestant background, opposing. De Valera resigned as president of Dáil Éireann on 9 January and was replaced by Arthur Griffith.

Less than a month after de Valera led his followers from the Dáil, Cumann na mBan held a convention in the Mansion House, Dublin. The Treaty was overwhelmingly rejected, by 419 to 63, thus aligning Cumann na mBan with the anti-Treatyites.[56] This led to the resignation of several members, among them Jenny Wyse Power, Annie Blythe, and Mabel Fitzgerald.[57] Pro-Treaty women created their own alternative to Cumann na mBan, known as Cumann na Saoirse.[58]

Mabel FitzGerald had always been a more uncompromising nationalist than her husband. After his release from prison in 1921 Desmond was reappointed Minister for Publicity, and attended the Treaty negotiations in London.[59] The resulting settlement was entirely unsatisfactory for Mabel FitzGerald. She was, in the words of a contemporary observer, 'an out-and-out Republican, and contemplated nothing short of the Republic'. In 1921, foreshadowing the Treaty split, she warned that even if the War of Independence did not lead to complete independence, the fight would continue: 'If we do not get a Republic at the end of this, there will always be a Republican party, and I shall belong to it. We will never give up the Republic.'[60] Married to a government minister who helped negotiate the agreement, with whom she had a young family, the period between the signing of the Treaty and the end of the Civil War caused a personal crisis, in which she contemplated leaving her husband. Given FitzGerald's well-known republican sympathies there may have been surprise when she resigned from Cumann na mBan. She did not, however, join Cumann na Saoirse.[61] Desmond FitzGerald's support for the agreement during and after the Treaty debates strained their marriage. Máire Comerford later recorded: 'Some [of the women pro-Treatyites] were married to Free Staters. Mabel FitzGerald crossed the bridge very reluctantly; we continued to

---

[55] Norman, *Terrible beauty: a life of Constance Markievicz*, 234–235.
[56] *II*, 6 February 1922; *FJ*, 6 February 1922.
[57] Margaret Ward, *Unmanageable revolutionaries: women and Irish nationalism* (London, 1995), 172.
[58] See Chapter 8.
[59] Jennifer FitzGerald papers, Garret FitzGerald, 'Desmond – and Mabel – FitzGerald'; *DIB* article on Desmond FitzGerald.
[60] Joyce M. Nankivell and Sydney Loch, *Ireland in travail* (London, 1922), 178.
[61] *IT*, 18 March 1922, 12 February 1923; *DIB* article on Desmond FitzGerald.

meet over cups of coffee in Bewley's.'[62] In fact, to what an extent she 'crossed the bridge' is open to question. Only family considerations prevented her from separating from her husband.

FitzGerald did not keep her sympathies from her boys, who took their mother's side in the dispute. At family meals Pierce FitzGerald remembered addressing their father thus: 'Pass the salt, traitor.'[63] FitzGerald was in a position to offer more concrete support to the anti-Treaty side. She used her position as wife of a Free State minister to seek improvements in conditions for anti-Treaty prisoners in Mountjoy.[64] It has also been claimed that FitzGerald passed information on government activities to the anti-Treatyites through her letters to Ernie O'Malley, then a republican prisoner.[65] She certainly occasionally used the underground post to contact him, which would suggest that the content of the letters was frowned upon by the authorities.[66] FitzGerald's activities during the Civil War period illustrate the difficulty anti-Treaty women faced when married to men who held contrary views. Faced with a crisis of conscience over whether to remain living with a man who supported the settlement, she agreed for the sake of her children to forsake public political activism entirely. However, those who knew her had no doubts about where her true allegiance lay; nor did she balk at offering support to prisoners on the republican side.

Between June 1922 and May 1923 the Irish Civil War was fought between those in the republican movement who accepted the compromise of the Anglo-Irish Treaty and those who rejected the agreement. George Irvine was among those who had condemned the Treaty; he addressed a republican demonstration in Harold's Cross in March 1922, alongside Constance Markievicz and Erskine Childers.[67] The following month, anti-Treatyites, led by Rory O'Connor, occupied the Four Courts and several other buildings in central Dublin. Fighting began on 28 June, when the Provisional Government's new National

---

[62] Ward, *Unmanageable revolutionaries*, 172.

[63] Correspondence with Dr Jennifer FitzGerald, in possession of the author.

[64] Ernie O'Malley to Mabel FitzGerald, 24 November 1923, in Cormac K. H. O'Malley and Anne Dolan (eds.), *'No surrender here!': the Civil War papers of Ernie O'Malley, 1922–1924* (Dublin, 2007), 410.

[65] Jennifer FitzGerald papers, Garret FitzGerald, 'Desmond – and Mabel – FitzGerald'.

[66] Ernie O'Malley to Mabel FitzGerald, 24 November 1923, 410; Ernie O'Malley to Mabel FitzGerald, 1 December 1923, 449; Ernie O'Malley to Mabel FitzGerald, 10 December 1923, 465, in O'Malley and Dolan (eds.), *'No surrender here!'*.

[67] *IT*, 18 March 1922.

Army bombarded the Four Courts and attacked anti-Treaty positions in the city centre.[68] Irvine had a very brief war. Arrested by National Army men in a position on Bolton Street on 30 June, he could see the Four Courts burning in the distance. He was interned in Mountjoy until his release on 12 December 1922, having signed the form of undertaking to keep the peace.[69]

The ICA had been largely quiet during the War of Independence, but during the Civil War a substantial section of the organisation chose to support the anti-Treatyites.[70] One such figure was Ellett Elmes (1886–1958). Elmes, a Dubliner, was an Episcopalian trade unionist who had fought in the Easter Rising and was imprisoned in Frongoch. When the Civil War broke out he took part in the fighting in Dublin until his arrest in August 1922, and was interned until the following November.[71] Other Protestant ICA Easter Rising veterans who joined with the anti-Treatyites included Seamus McGowan, Frederick Norgrove, and Alfred Norgrove.

One Protestant family that came to some prominence during the Civil War was the Gilmores. George, Harry, and Charlie Gimore were the Dublin-born sons of Philip Gilmore, a well-to-do accountant and evangelical preacher. Despite their background, the Gilmore sons developed a strongly socialist and anti-sectarian form of republicanism. George Gilmore had been liminally involved in the Easter Rising, before becoming active in the South County Dublin Battalion of the IRA. George, along with his brothers, took the anti-Treaty side during the Civil War, for which he was imprisoned.[72] At least twelve of the Protestant anti-Treatyites identified were imprisoned by the Free State authorities.[73] In contrast to the post–Easter Rising period, little is known about Protestant anti-Treaty prisoners as a group.[74] However, reports emerged in late 1922 that Church of Ireland prisoners were being denied facilities for worship, seemingly due to the unwillingness of chaplains to minister them.[75]

---

[68] Townshend, *The Republic*, 406–412.   [69] MAD, Civil War ledgers (prisoners).
[70] Brian Hanley, 'The Irish Citizen Army after 1916', *Saothar*, Vol. 28 (2003), 40–41.
[71] MAD, MSPC, REF866, Ellett Elmes.
[72] UCD, O'Malley papers, P176/b/106, interview with George Gilmore; *IT*, 25 May 1976, 24 June 1985, 17 January 1987.
[73] Robert Barton, Robert Bradshaw, Walter Patrick Carpenter, Geoffrey Coulter, Charlie Gilmore, George Gilmore, Harry Gilmore, George Irvine, Walter Mitchell, Frederick Norgrove, David Lubbock Robinson, Francis Stuart: names checked against MAD, Civil War ledgers (prisoners).
[74] See Chapter 5.   [75] *Gaelic Churchman*, December 1922.

During the civil war, nationalists who had previously merely poked fun at 'synthetic Gaels' began to view these figures as potentially dangerous interlopers. After 1919, the advance of several of these, such as John Chartres and Erskine Childers, to prominent positions in the movement inspired comment and suspicion. P. S. O'Hegarty, the writer and nationalist, later recalled:

> I met [John] Chartres, of course, but I don't know how he 'came in'. He was one of those queer birds like [Erskine] Childers and Darrell Figgis who sort of wandered in by some personal reason that must have been obscure to themselves.[76]

Figgis was the least queer of these three individuals, as he had been born in Dublin and had joined the Irish Volunteers in 1913. Having been gaoled after the German plot arrests, he was released in 1919 and appointed secretary of a Dáil commission into the resources and industries of Ireland from 1919 to 1922. A man who easily provoked hatred and contempt in others, Figgis's rebarbative personality impeded his career in politics, although he enjoyed the patronage of Griffith, with whom he shared a mistrust of the militant wing of the republican movement. In June 1922 he was elected an independent pro-Treaty TD for County Dublin. His high margin of victory was partially accounted for by the sympathy he engendered having been recently assaulted by a group of republicans. The group, which included Robert Briscoe, a Jewish IRA man, forced their way into Figgis's house, and shaved off half his beard, which he had believed gave him a resemblance to Parnell. In the Dáil, his unlikeable personality and questions over his financial affairs left him isolated. Figgis's career ended in tragedy: following the suicide of his wife Millie in 1924, and the death following an abortion of his mistress, he gassed himself in his rented rooms in London in October 1925. One obituarist wrote of him that he was 'fated to provide material for the scoffer and the maker of caricatures'.[77]

Another incongruous figure was John Chartres (1862–1927). Chartres was an English-born Episcopalian, the son of a British army staff surgeon, whose Huguenot family had been established in Ireland since the mid-seventeenth century. After working as a barrister and journalist, he joined the intelligence branch of the ministry of munitions in 1915. From 1917, he became involved in Irish politics, first contributing articles to the Griffith press, and latterly as a gun-runner for Michael Collins. In

---

[76] NLI, Michael J. Lennon papers, MS 22,288 (iii), P. S. O'Hegarty to Michael J. Lennon, undated [1953/1954].
[77] Malone, 'Darrell Figgis', 15.

1918 he acted as a republican informant in the British civil service. He resigned from the civil service in 1921, by which time his activities had led to suspicion from the authorities. In October 1921 he was appointed a secretary to the Irish Treaty delegation, and played a prominent role in drafting the document. Chartres, due to loyalty to Griffith and Collins, supported the Treaty, and later served in the statistical committee of the Department of Industry and Commerce. Chartres's English birth, upper-class bearing, and intelligence background aroused republican suspicion: allegations have frequently been made that he was a British spy, although no substantiating evidence has ever been presented.[78]

Synthetic Gaels who opposed the Treaty became major objects of hate on the opposing side. The Free State Local Government Department inspector, in a letter to Minister Austin Stack in February 1922, criticised Albinia Brodrick, who was proving a particularly troublesome member of Kerry County Council. Brodrick had, he said, 'Irished her name' as Gobnait Ní Bhruadair, which meant she still 'ruled the roost' in Kerry local democracy, much, he claimed, as she had under British rule. In reference to Brodrick's landed origin he hoped that 'Kerry people will soon prefer to regard her rather as a member of the Midleton family than a poor Kerry woman striving for the betterment of her people.'[79] Such sentiments were typical of the views of senior Free State officials about anti-Treatyites with upper-class and English backgrounds. During the Civil War Brodrick continued her nursing activities at Ballincoona, this time for republican forces. Shortly after fighting began she was arrested by Free State troops and held in custody in the Lansdowne Arms Hotel in Kenmare. Finding escape impossible, she demonstrated her displeasure by smashing every object in the room and throwing them out the window, including the mattress, which she had torn open. The soldiers, exasperated by her actions, pronounced her an 'impossible woman', and simply released her.[80] In April 1923, she was involved in a more serious incident. A column of republicans, whom Brodrick had been aiding, were holding out in the Sneem area of County Kerry. Free State troops, on receiving this intelligence, decided to attack them from the rear. A convoy of two or three Crossley Tenders set out from Waterville to engage them. Brodrick, on hearing of this, set off from her hospital to warn 'her boys'. She rode her bicycle into Sneem, where the Free State

---

[78] See Brian P. Murphy, *John Chartres: mystery man of the treaty* (Dublin, 1995).

[79] NAI, 12/16, Dáil Éireann Local Government file on Kerry County Council, Eamon Coogan to Austin Stack, February 1922.

[80] T. E. Stoakley, *Sneem: the knot of the ring* (Sneem, 1986), 119; *The Kerryman*, 26 December 1964.

troops caught up with her. She refused repeated orders to halt, and continued,

keeping to the middle of the road and refusing to give way, so that she could not be passed without being run down. This strange procession went on until the stretch of road through Moneyflugh townland was reached, when Albinia, who was then just about sixty, was dead beat and turned into a boreen. Then, in the words of the narrator, 'Some silly b——— took a shot at her and drilled her clean through the buttocks.'[81]

Brodrick, who survived the incident, did not resent being injured; the sound of the gun, she later claimed, gave the republicans the chance to flee.

For Erskine Childers, the failure of the Irish Convention of 1917–1918, outrage at the policy of reprisals by British forces, as well as the imprisonment of his cousin Robert Barton effected an accelerated trajectory from constitutional nationalist ideologue to doctrinaire republican. In May 1921 he was elected TD for Kildare-Wicklow and, as he was a gifted publicist, he was appointed that same year as Dáil Éireann director of propaganda. Childers's close relationship with de Valera led to his appointment as a secretary to the Treaty delegation. He fiercely opposed the settlement and sought unsuccessfully to dissuade Robert Barton from signing it. As with Chartres, Childers's intelligence background aroused suspicions that he was a British agent, an accusation that Arthur Griffith made in the Dáil.[82] Griffith was famously hostile towards Childers, calling him a 'damned Englishman'.[83] During the Civil War, Childers made for a pitiable sight: the IRA men in Cork, where he had fled, distrusted him as an outsider and allowed him no military role. Frank O'Connor, who left a fine pen-portrait of Childers in his final weeks, remembered:

Apart from his accent, which would have identified him anywhere, there was something peculiarly English about him; something that nowadays reminds me of some old parson or public-school teacher ... conscientious to a fault and overburdened with minor cares.[84]

In late October 1922, alongside his friend David Lubbock Robinson, Childers made a clandestine journey to County Wicklow. Robinson (1882–1943) was an Episcopalian clergyman's son who had served as a captain in the tank corps on the western front, where he lost an eye, and

[81] Stoakley, *Sneem*, 118. Brodrick was aged sixty-two at the time of the incident.
[82] Boyle, *The riddle of Erskine Childers*, 308.
[83] Dáil Éireann, Vol. T, No. 17, cc. 416–417, 10 January 1922.
[84] Frank O'Connor, *An only child* (London, 1972 [1961]), 168.

received the DSO, before converting to republicanism. On 10 November they were arrested at Barton's residence, Glendalough House. Two weeks later, Childers, who had become the principal hate-figure of the pro-Treatyites, was executed by a National Army firing squad. In O'Connor's words, 'in a family row it is always the outsider who gets the blame'.[85] O'Connor was right: 'outsiders' such as Brodrick, Childers, or Maud Gonne were frequent targets of allegations during this period. However, most of those who were impugned in such a manner were upper class, and English-born; for an Irish Protestant to be treated in such a manner was rare. Although upper-class republicans had admirers in the nationalist movement both during their lifetimes and beyond, a considerable number found their interventions unwelcome, a fresh English assault on Irish liberty, cloaked in ill-fitting republican garb.

By December 1922 the National Army, which had received arms from the British government and had been transported by the Royal Navy, were in effective control of the country. However, it was only with the death of the irreconcilable Liam Lynch, the anti-Treaty IRA Chief of Staff, in April 1923 that an end to hostilities became possible. On 30 April 1923 Lynch's successor, Frank Aiken, declared a ceasefire. The Civil War was over. Victory came a cost to the pro-Treatyites: Arthur Griffith, worn out by the worries of office, died of a cerebral haemorrhage in August 1922; ten days later Michael Collins was killed during an anti-Treaty ambush near his birthplace in County Cork. The bitterness occasioned by the Civil War was extraordinary: Kathleen Lynn, on hearing of the death of Collins, could merely say, 'He was beloved of a certain set.'[86]

The Spectre of Sectarianism

In late 1919 Wilbraham Fitzjohn Trench, professor of English literature in TCD, published a pamphlet, *The way to fellowship in Irish life*, which must have unnerved Protestants in the south and west. Trench warned of the 'self-destruction' caused by his co-religionists in refusing to adopt a nationalist stance, without which, 'Protestantism in Ireland is doomed.'[87] Events of 1920–1922 would give Trench's community reason to be fearful. The outbreak of the Irish War of Independence would precipitate an outbreak of violence in the north-east from 1920 to 1922. Ulster loyalists, reacting to the breakdown of law and order in the south, launched a campaign of riots, sectarian attacks, and expulsions of

---

[85] O'Connor, *An only child*, 182.   [86] RCPI, Diary of Kathleen Lynn, 23 August 1923.
[87] Wilbraham Fitzjohn Trench, *The way to fellowship in Irish life* (London, 1919), 24, 13.

Catholics from the shipyards. In 1920 alone, an estimated 11,000 Catholics were forced to leave their jobs.[88] This placed the Protestants of the south and west in a precarious position: many feared they would suffer reprisals due to the actions of their northern co-religionists.

In Belfast, a group representing Catholic businessmen, clergy, and Sinn Féiners presented a petition to the Dáil calling for a commercial boycott of north-east Ulster.[89] The petition stated: 'It should be strictly enjoined that Protestants in other parts of Ireland are not to be molested in any way on account of the actions of their co-religionists in Belfast.'[90] Although Ernest Blythe, the sole Protestant Ulsterman in the Dáil, spoke against the boycott, the action was sanctioned, and an embargo was placed on the purchase of goods from the north-east. The economic boycott quickly affected Protestant businesses in the south. During August to September 1920, a period that coincided with some of the worst violence in the north, Protestant commercial interests throughout the rest of the country also suffered.

As in every fight for independence, the detection and neutralisation of spies and traitors was paramount: southern Irish Protestants, the vast majority of whom were loyalists, became the focus of unwanted attention by the IRA. Between 1911 and 1926 the Protestant population of what became the Free State fell by almost a third. Although recent research finds no evidence of an organised sectarian campaign against southern Irish Protestants, few dispute that the strong IRA presence in the country proved uncongenial enough to persuade a minority to leave Ireland.[91]

The killing of thirteen Protestant men in the Dunmanway area of West Cork in late April 1922 stunned the British and Irish public.[92] The Dunmanway killings, coming within the context of continual attacks on Belfast Catholics, were at the time generally assumed as being sectarian in nature.[93] It was alleged that more than a hundred Protestant families

---

[88] Michael Farrell, *Northern Ireland: the Orange state* (London, 1976), 29.

[89] Alan F. Parkinson, *Belfast's unholy war: the troubles of the 1920s* (Dublin, 2004), 73.

[90] Dáil Éireann, Vol. F, No. 16, cc. 192–193, 6 August 1920.

[91] Andy Bielenberg, 'Exodus: the emigration of southern Irish Protestants during the Irish War of Independence and the Civil War', *Past & Present*, Vol. 218, No. 1 (2013), 199–233; David Fitzpatrick, 'Protestant depopulation and the Irish Revolution', *Irish Historical Studies*, Vol. 38, No. 152 (November 2013), 643–663. Cf. Hart, 'The Protestant experience of revolution in Southern Ireland', in Richard English and Graham Walker (eds.), *Unionism in modern Ireland* (Dublin, 1996), 81.

[92] See, for example, *IT*, 28, 29 April 1922; London *Times*, 28, 29 April 1922.

[93] For the Dunmanway killings, see Andy Bielenberg, John Borgonovo and James S. Donnelly Jr. '"Something of the Nature of a Massacre": The Bandon Valley Killings Revisited', *Éire-Ireland* 49, no. 3 (2014), 7–59; Peter Hart, *The IRA and its enemies: violence and community in Cork, 1916–1923* (Oxford, 1998), chapter 12.

fled West Cork, fearing more attacks.[94] Speaking in the Dáil on behalf of the provisional government, Arthur Griffith denounced the killings:

the terrible murders at Dunmanway ... require the exercise of the utmost strength and authority of Dáil Éireann. Dáil Éireann ... will uphold, to the fullest extent, the protection of life and property of all classes and sections of the community. It does not know and cannot know, as a National Government, any distinction of class or creed. In its name, I express the horror of the Irish nation at the Dunmanway murders.[95]

A few weeks later *Young Ireland* struck a less remorseful tone. Only the 'mentally deformed', it wrote, could believe the killings showed Protestant liberties were under threat. 'They are outrages which all recognise as sullying the fair name of the nation and putting a strain on the hitherto unblemished record in the South for tolerance and goodwill by the majority' towards the Protestant minority.[96]

Southern Protestants reacted with horror to what they perceived as a sectarian attack on members of the isolated west Cork community.[97] A fortnight later, Michael Collins, as chairman of the provisional government, received a delegation from the Church of Ireland Synod, who asked 'whether the Government desired to retain them in Ireland, or wanted them to go'. Collins gave the delegation assurances that the Free State would guarantee religious liberty, and denounced the 'outrages' against the Protestant community in the south.[98]

Southern Protestant anxiety found its fullest expression in the Protestant Convention, which met in Dublin on the same day that the Synod delegation met Collins.[99] Seventeen of the twenty-nine members of the preliminary organising committee of the convention represented large commercial enterprises in the south and west, which suggests that the main motive of the organisers was to protect Protestant firms from damage and boycotting, rather than to offer political solidarity with the provisional government.[100] The convention, which was held in a packed hall in the Mansion House, passed an apolitical set of resolutions, which condemned the murders and expressed hope that Protestants could live

---

[94] Niall C. Harrington, *Kerry landing: August 1922, an episode of the Civil War* (Dublin, 1992), 8. The *CIG* stated that 'considerable people have fled from West Cork in terror of their lives': 23 June 1922. For the fear engendered among west Cork Protestants, see Willie Kingston, 'From Victorian boyhood to the troubles: a Skibbereen memoir', *Skibbereen and District Historical Society Journal*, Vol. 1 (2005), 34.

[95] Dáil Éireann, Vol. S2, No. 6, cc. 332–333, 28 April 1922.

[96] *Young Ireland*, 13 May 1922.

[97] *CIG*, 5 May 1922 (statement by Archbishop Gregg on killings).

[98] Dublin *Evening Telegraph*, 12 May 1922; *Dublin Evening Mail*, 12 May 1922.

[99] For accounts of this assembly, see *IT*, 12 May 1922; *FJ*, 12 May 1922; *Dublin Evening Mail*, 12 May 1922; *Gaelic Churchman*, June 1922.

[100] List of members of the preliminary organising committee given in *IT*, 3 May 1922.

in peace with their neighbours.[101] The only dissenting voice at the convention was that of Æ George Russell, who declined to attend. His letter of explanation was read to delegates:

he could not, without deep feelings of shame and pain, take part, for he would be expected to repudiate fears he did not feel, and deny persecution which he had never experienced, and all lest a group of fanatics in Belfast, calling themselves co-religionists, should seem to implicate the Protestants who live in Southern Ireland in their action and sentiments.[102]

Indeed, the organisers may have overestimated the level of fear that had been engendered among their co-religionists. Dunmanway proved an isolated incident, and assurances by Free State leaders that Protestants and their property would be respected seems to have convinced a good many to remain.

Events in Dunmanway, as they were then understood, did however pose difficulties for IRA-sympathising Protestants, whose views resembled Æ's. Protestant nationalists almost never conceded that sectarian persecution took place, but instead argued that it was the loyalist politics of most southern Protestants, rather than their faith, which placed them in danger. These comments, by the Rev. William Vandeleur, were typical:

Those who were supposed to be in any sense agents of the British Government … had a dangerous time. One [suspected agent] was murdered and there was always the risk of ill-treatment. There was no *religious* persecution. Houses might be raided and there was always the risk of undisciplined youths letting off guns, but no persecution existed on religious grounds.[103]

Nelly O'Brien's *Gaelic Churchman* avoided any full discussion of the Dunmanway killings. In its otherwise approving report of the Protestant Convention, it regretted that:

One or two speakers dwelt rather much on the recent murders in Cork, but Mr [James] Douglas had quite plainly the sympathy of the meeting with him when he said that denunciation of such outrages should be left to the Roman Catholic community, as they had condemned them, and that our duty was to condemn the intolerance and outrages of the North.[104]

Protestant republicans were very uncomfortable criticising their Catholic fellow-nationalists; they were unwilling to risk jeopardising efforts to build a cross-religious movement by highlighting supposed sectarian incidents, such as the killings in Dunmanway. The typical attitude was

[101] Resolutions circulated in *IT*, 3 May 1922.   [102] *Dublin Evening Mail*, 12 May 1922.
[103] RCBL, Rev. William Vandeleur, typescript memoirs, 28.
[104] *Gaelic Churchman*, June 1922.

that Catholic nationalists should react to attacks on Protestants, and Protestant nationalists ought to decry attacks on Catholics. In Rathmines, Kathleen Lynn chose to disbelieve the news reports, recording in her diary, 'Six Protestants murdered in Co. Cork. Surely agent provocateurs.'[105] These events clearly played on her mind, for she returned to the theme four days later, probably having sought reassurance on the matter: 'No doubt at all Cork murders = agent provocateurs.'[106]

The Irish Guild of the Church's complacent attitude towards the killings of their co-religionists in the south needs to be contrasted with their views on the attacks on Belfast Catholics, about which it was extremely exercised. The Guild developed something of an obsession with the violence in the north. Their journal frequently denounced the attacks and set up a fund for workers expelled from the shipyards.[107] Kathleen Lynn's response mirrored that of the Guild. She recorded: 'Slaughter in B.fast goes daily on, how long! It is horrible.'[108] Speaking of the attacks as 'extermination',[109] she accused Britain of organising it, as she would the Dunmanway killings: 'State of affairs seems almost hopeless for R.Cs & it is all engineered by England.'[110] The view that England was responsible for fostering sectarianism as part of a divide et impera policy was a common one. Casement, for example, had held it. The *Gaelic Churchman* wrote that 'sectarianism has been sedulously fostered by British rule and British influence which has always aimed at keeping Ireland weak and divided in order to dominate her more easily'.[111]

Many nationalists from a Protestant background adopted a strangely ambivalent attitude to the violence, which by 1926 would greatly decrease the size of the southern Protestant community. Meeting Sydney Czira, Kathleen Lynn recorded her stating that: 'Unionists all want to leave. Many wld. be no loss.'[112] Although there were numerous Catholic unionists in Ireland during this era – particularly in the South Dublin suburbs – the 'Unionists' who Czira and Lynn were referring to would have come overwhelmingly from their own religious background. Others preferred to deny accusations of attacks altogether. Albinia Brodrick

---

[105] RCPI, Diary of Kathleen Lynn, 28 April 1922.
[106] RCPI, Diary of Kathleen Lynn, 4 May 1922.
[107] *Gaelic Churchman,* October 1920, February, October 1921. The *Gazette* also denounced events in Belfast; see, for example, *CIG,* 23 June 1922.
[108] RCPI, Diary of Kathleen Lynn, 11 March 1922.
[109] RCPI, Diary of Kathleen Lynn, 23 May 1922.
[110] RCPI, Diary of Kathleen Lynn, 7 April 1922.
[111] *Gaelic Churchman,* February 1921.
[112] RCPI, Diary of Kathleen Lynn, 7 October 1921.

sought to enlist her co-religionists in a letter-writing campaign, in response to the stream of accounts appearing in the British press claiming IRA violence against Protestants. Rosamond Jacob received a 'hot letter ... blasting southern Protestants in general because they don't speak up and say they are not persecuted'.[113] The question of whether southern Protestants faced persecution qua Protestants or qua unionists was deeply contentious in the early 1920s, as it is to this day. Protestant nationalists, who had already detached themselves from the vast majority of their co-religionists, were not particularly qualified to assess the nature of ill-treatment of minorities by republicans. They were, and had been for many decades, a sub-group, a counterculture, which shared a religious faith, but not a political outlook or social sphere, with their fellow Protestants.

---

[113] NLI, Sheehy-Skeffington papers, MS 22,689, Rosamond Jacob to Hannah Sheehy-Skeffington, n.d. [c. 1919].

Introduction

The signing of the Anglo-Irish Treaty, the Treaty split, and resultant Irish Civil War are among the most significant occurrences in the country's recent history. The civil war destroyed the delicate unity of Sinn Féin, eased the way towards partition, and left Irish politics with a peculiar structure that has endured to this day. Nationalists, as we have seen in Chapter 7, in choosing whether to support the compromise with Britain, were making a decision that would have profound personal and political compromises. This chapter will assess two distinct groups: Protestant nationalists who chose to support the Treaty and the Irish Free State, and, second, a new group, Protestant servicemen in the pro-Treaty National Army. Why did some Protestant nationalists support the Treaty? And who were the Protestant National Army soldiers? Where did this second group come from? And what motivated them?

Treatyites

Throughout 1921, as war took its toll on the country, the Church of Ireland hierarchy and the *Church of Ireland Gazette* made frequent, vaguely formulated calls for the end to violence and for a peaceful, agreed settlement.[1] Even some representatives of the Presbyterian Church, whose members were the most hesitant among Protestants in engaging with southern politics, expressed similar sentiments.[2] It was unsurprising, then, that southern unionists greeted the signing of the Anglo-Irish Treaty in December 1921 with relief. Their leader, however, did not. Lord Midleton saw the agreement as containing little to safeguard the

---

[1] See, for example, accounts of St Patrick's Day services in Dublin churches in *IT*, 18 March 1921.
[2] See remarks by the Rev. J. Denham Osborne, *IT*, 18 March 1921.

southern unionist and landed interest. Although he was offered a seat in the Free State Senate, he declined, and played no further part in Irish affairs.

The Church of Ireland hierarchy sought to ensure their flock would support the new state. John Allen Gregg, archbishop of Dublin, preaching after the signing of the Treaty, argued that, although the Union was the wisest form of government, Anglicans ought to offer the new state 'our loyalty and our good-will'.[3] A fellow bishop and member of the Irish Guild of Witness, Godfrey Day of Ossory, went further. In a St Patrick's Day sermon he stated:

> the Provisional Government of this country has been ... lawfully established by the authority of our King and his Ministers, has been accepted by the representatives of the people, our representatives ... It is our duty as Christian men and women ... to support the Government ungrudgingly, loyally, and wholeheartedly, with the same willing obedience and service with which we supported the old; to hold it in every means in our power to discharge its functions for the happiness of the people and for the peace and prosperity of our beloved land.[4]

Comments such as these may have spurred Church of Ireland recruitment into the Free State Army. The southern unionist – or perhaps former unionist – press strongly supported the provisional government which was set up in the wake of the Treaty.[5] Even Arthur Griffith, who they had for decades denounced as a dangerous radical, was praised for exhibiting a previously undetected conservatism.

Speaking in the Dáil, during the Treaty debate, Constance Markievicz launched an attack on southern unionists, whom she described as 'traitors and oppressors' and the 'English garrison against Ireland'.[6] The *Gazette* was impressed by Griffith's staunch defence of the minority:

> We are glad ... to record that ... Griffith, the new leader of Nationalist Ireland, has declared his policy in regard to the people whom we represent, and that it is entirely satisfactory. The loyalists of Ireland want no place of privilege in the Irish Free State. But they do want a square deal, and ... Griffith is prepared to give it to them. They are no traitors to Ireland, they love their country at least as dearly as the most eloquent member of the Sinn Féin party, but they do not usually proclaim their virtues from the house tops.[7]

---

[3] *IT*, 12 December 1921.
[4] Godfrey Day, quoted in [no author], *The voice of the Protestant Church in Ireland* (n.p., n.d. [c. 1922]), 1.
[5] See, for example, *Dublin Evening Mail*, 11 May, 20 June 1922; *CIG*, 10, 17 February, 7 April 1922.
[6] Dáil Éireann, Vol. T, No. 10, cc. 181–183, 3 January 1922.   [7] *CIG*, 13 January 1922.

If Protestant unionists throughout the south were desperate for an end to violence, and relieved that a treaty had been agreed, what then of their nationalist co-religionists? The largely biographical nature of the literature on Protestant nationalists may give a misleading impression that these figures were irreconcilably radical, solely committed to achieving an all-Ireland republic. In fact, numerous Protestant nationalists supported the Treaty and gave their allegiance to the Irish Free State.

The most prominent Protestant pro-Treatyite was Ernest Blythe. As his remarks during the boycott indicate, by the early 1920s Blythe had become eager to conciliate Ulster Protestant opinion. In a memorandum circulated to his cabinet colleagues, he stated that the provisional government should seek good relations with Ulster until unity would 'come to be regarded as a wise and economical thing, by the majority in the Six Counties'. Blythe warned his colleagues that

The unity of Ireland is of sufficient importance for us to take a chance in the hope of gaining it. The first move lies with us. There is no urgent desire for unity in the North-East and it would be stupid obstinacy for us to wait till the Belfast attitude improved.[8]

The Treaty came as a great relief to W. B. Yeats. Horrified by the British policy of reprisals, yet unimpressed by what he perceived as republican fanaticism, he had long sought a dominion settlement without the coercion of Ulster. With the signing of the agreement, he too perceived the transformation of Griffith into a conservative hero. He told Æ:

I am by constitution a pessimist & never thought they would get as much out of Lloydd George & am so pleased, nor am I distressed to see Madam Markiewicz and other emotional ladies among the Non-jourors. I expect to see Griffith, now that he is the universal target, grow almost mellow, and become the fanatic of broad mindedness and accuracy of statement. Hitherto he has fired at the cocanuts but now that he is a cocoa nut himself he may become milky.[9]

Alice Stopford Green supported the Treaty out of fear that renewed conflict would lead to Boer War–type oppression.[10] The decision of Stopford Green and most of her large family to so publicly support the Treaty – she and her brother Edward distributed pro-Treaty pamphlets

---

[8] Ernest Blythe, Memorandum with regard to policy on north-east Ulster, 9 August 1922, quoted in Daithí Ó Corráin, '"Ireland in his heart north and south": The contribution of Ernest Blythe to the partition question', *Irish Historical Studies*, Vol. 35, No. 137 (May 2006), 64.

[9] W. B. Yeats to Æ George Russell, quoted in Foster, *W. B. Yeats: a life*, Vol. II, 206. Yeats had distrusted Griffith since the *Playboy* riots of 1907.

[10] UCD, LA18, Máire Comerford unpublished memoirs.

in the streets of Dublin – was noted by several observers at the time.[11] Indeed, Robert Barton was moved to write to the one anti-Treaty family member, Dorothy Stopford, to congratulate her 'on having remained a republican with so many of your relations gone wrong'.[12] Douglas Hyde, like Yeats, saw the Treaty as offering peace, and a chance to rebuild. He told a friend:

> We seem to have really hammered out a measure of real freedom ... So far as I can see, we have got almost everything we want ... I think we got the very most we could ... without war, and war is too awful to contemplate again.[13]

F. J. Bigger, who always detested violence, also welcomed the Treaty, believing that the 'tide of Anglicisation had been successfully rolled back', and hoped for a speedy reconciliation between the north and south.[14] The most significant Protestant nationalist endorsement came from the Irish Guild of the Church's official organ, the *Gaelic Churchman*. Despite the presence of hard-line republicans, such as Geoffrey Coulter and Albinia Brodrick in the organisation, the *Churchman* argued that there was a Christian obligation to support the new state, as it was approved of by the majority of the public.[15]

Cumann na Saoirse, the 'Society of Freedom', the women's pro-Treaty organisation, also included Protestant nationalists among its senior members. Alice Stopford Green was prominent on the platform at its first, well-attended, meeting in the Mansion House, Dublin, on 13 March 1922.[16] Cumann na Saoirse was a more sedate and less effective version of Cumann na mBan: it worked for the return of pro-Treaty candidates in the 1922 election, helped distribute government propaganda, and provided material assistance to Free State troops. It had no military function. However, perhaps its most important role was to counter the claim that Irish women were mainly anti-Treaty. Annie Blythe, the Catholic wife of Ernest Blythe, stated that the organisation sought 'to demonstrate that there was no justification, in fact, for the claim made that the great bulk of the women of Ireland were opposed to the acceptance of the Treaty'.[17] We lack detailed data on the member-ship of Cumann na Saoirse, which makes it difficult to establish the

---

[11] McDowell, *Alice Stopford Green*, 109.
[12] Quoted in Ó Broin, *Protestant nationalists*, 191. This strained relations between Dorothy and her pro-Treaty family: NLI, MS 11,426, Typescript recollections of Miss [Edie] Stopford.
[13] Hyde, quoted in Dunleavy and Dunleavy, *Douglas Hyde*, 351.
[14] Crone and Bigger, *In remembrance*, xi.
[15] *Gaelic Churchman*, June, October, November 1922.
[16] *FJ*, 14 March 1922; *II*, 14 March 1922.   [17] *IT*, 12 February 1923.

extent of Protestant participation in the organisation. However, three of the eighteen members of its executive, Alice Stopford Green, Alice Spring Rice and Alice Wordsworth, were Protestant, and a fourth, Edith Costello, was an Anglican convert to Rome.

Other Protestant nationalist pro-Treatyites included Darrell Figgis, who, as we have seen, was elected an independent pro-Treaty TD in 1922, Susan Mitchell, and Æ George Russell. What all these figures had in common was a desire to accept a compromise they thought was fair, a wish for nationalists to put aside constitutional abstraction, and a hope that elected representatives would concentrate on building a new self-governing state. For many Protestant nationalist pro-Treatyites, the year 1922 represented the first time in decades that they had shared the same political views as the bulk of their co-religionists. However, the War of Independence had caused previously unwavering positions to harden, and soon hundreds of southern Protestants would join the Free State colours. Their presence would help demonstrate that support for independence was no longer confined to Catholics or nationalists, but could now be seen in every aspect of southern society.

The National Army

Under the terms of the Anglo-Irish Treaty, a provisional government was set up, to which Britain transferred administrative power over the southern twenty-six counties. Michael Collins assumed the chairmanship of the provisional government. During the Civil War he would combine this role with the title of commander-in-chief of a new force, the 'National Army', which sought to defend the newly created Irish Free State.[18] Patriotism, economic necessity, as well as a sense that the coming order would restore political stability saw an enthusiastic response to Collins's call for recruits to the army. Recruitment proceeded at a rate of 1,000 per day, peaking at 60,000 men. With most of the IRA opposing the Treaty, the provisional government augmented the National Army with ex-British servicemen, as well as new, frequently young, Irish recruits. Nicknamed 'Trucileers', these men's supposed callowness and affected patriotism was derided by some anti-Treatyites.[19]

Although better armed and more professionally led than the IRA could ever have been, there were important commonalities between the

---

[18] Michael Hopkinson, *Green against green: the Irish Civil War* (Dublin, 1988), 34–46, 52–69.

[19] Hopkinson, *Green against green*, 16. For an example of anti-Treaty antipathy to 'These footlight-hungry warriors', see BMH WS 1,741 Part I, Michael V. O'Donoghue.

National Army and the pre-1922 organisation. The largely Catholic ethos remained and was institutionalised: Catholic chaplains were appointed; soldiers paraded outside church on Sundays; days were punctuated with the intonation of the rosary. Little wonder that in 1923, Daniel Cohalan, the Catholic bishop of Cork, declared that 'the Irish National Army was the Army of the most Catholic nation in the world'.[20] However, the new army was not exclusively Catholic. According to the Free State Army census of the night of 12–13 November 1922, 251 Protestants were serving in the National Army. This amounts to 0.76 per cent of total army strength of 33,210 on that night. The army census provides the basis for much the following discussion.[21] The existence of these Protestant soldiers represents an unresearched and entirely forgotten aspect of Civil War history. The following section will discuss their experiences.

The British government, keen to see the Free State established and its authority asserted throughout the twenty-six counties, provided support in creating the new army. The National Army recruited a substantial number of mostly Irish ex-British servicemen, with the British Ex-Servicemen's Federation providing assistance in procuring suitable soldiers, as well as advisors and drill instructors to augment numbers.[22] Thirty-one Protestant soldiers provided British addresses for their home address and for their next of kin. These soldiers, who were likely British recruits, rather than Irish Protestants, are outside the scope of this book and will not be discussed. Table 8.1 shows the denominational breakdown of the remaining 220 Irish Protestant recruits, alongside a comparison with numbers of Protestants in the Free State.

Episcopalians, who comprised about three-quarters of southern Protestants, produced 86 per cent of National Army soldiers. Methodists were the second-largest category, significantly ahead of Presbyterians, whose members were always the most reluctant to identify with any pro-self-government organisation. There was one Jewish serviceman.[23]

---

[20] *IT*, 4 June 1923.

[21] Findings derived from MAD, Free State Army census returns, November 1922 (10 Vols.). This task was conducted prior to the recent digitisation of these records. Although the census is a valuable source, its limitations must be noted: it provides information for only one night, and at a time when the army was still recruiting heavily.

[22] MAD, A/3696 (recruiting), Richard Mulcahy to P. Walker, 24 October 1922.

[23] Louis Goldfoot, aged twenty in 1922, served in the infantry corps. Born in Dublin city, he was the son of Russian-born Hyman Goldfoot, listed in 1911 as working as a jeweller, and resident in the Wood Quay district of the city.

Table 8.1 *Denomination of Irish Protestants in the National Army*

Denomination	#	%
Episcopalian	190	86.36
Presbyterian	12	5.46
Methodist	9	4.09
'Protestant'	6	2.74
Christian Brethren	1	0.45
Plymouth Brethren	1	0.45
United Free Church of Scotland	1	0.45
Total	**220**	**100.00**

Source: Nominal data for this and other tables in this chapter is derived from MAD, Free State Army census returns, November 1922 (10 Vols.). Further biographical data is derived from Census of Ireland 1901 and 1911.

Table 8.2 *Denominational comparison between Protestants in the National Army and Protestants in the Irish Free State, 1926*

Denomination	Free State Army (%)	All Protestants (%)
Episcopalian	86.36	75.66
Presbyterian	5.45	14.94
Methodist	4.09	4.91
Other*	4.1	4.49
Total	**100.00**	**100.00**

Source: Data for Irish Free State Protestant population is compiled from *Census of population, 1926*, Vol. III (religions and birthplaces) (Dublin, 1926).
* The 1926 Census report analysed religion under the headings Roman Catholic, Episcopalian, Presbyterian, Methodist, Jewish, Baptist, and other. The 'other' category thus includes statistically insignificant numbers of atheists, agnostics, and others.

The 1901 and 1911 census returns offer insight into the economic profile of these soldiers, ninety-one of whose fathers' occupations can be traced.

The vast majority of Protestant Free State Army men came from a working-class or lower middle-class background. Examples include Henry Bovenizer, an Anglican private soldier from Dublin, whose father was a general labourer; Isaac Bradley, an Anglican volunteer from Kilkenny, whose father was a harness-maker; and David Marshall, a member of the United Free Church of Scotland, whose father was a coppersmith. Only five of the ninety-one of these men's fathers belonged to the educated or professional classes. These included John Bowers, a

Table 8.3 *Father's occupation of Protestants in the National Army*

Occupation	Amount
Manual tradesman	20
Farmer	14
Labourer	13
Clerk	8
Policeman	6
Porter	4
Coachman/driver	3
Domestic servant	3
Civil service official	2
Merchant	2
Other	16
Total	**91**

Table 8.4 *Military rank of Protestants in the National Army*

Rank	Number	Percentage
Private	118	53.63
Volunteer	61	27.72
Sergeant	16	7.27
Lieutenant	12	5.45
Corporal	9	4.10
Captain	4	1.83
Total	**220**	**100.00**

nineteen-year-old Anglican private soldier from Kilkenny, whose father was a JP and farmer; Antony Tatlow, a nineteen-year-old Anglican volunteer from Dublin, whose father Alfred Piers Tatlow was a solicitor; and William John Thornton, an eighteen-year-old Anglican private, whose father William Henry Thornton was a substantial general merchant in the Curragh Camp.

In October 1923, in reply to an enquiry by James Douglas, Mulcahy's office stated that there were at most eighteen Protestant officers in the National Army.[24] According to the army census, there were, eleven months earlier, two fewer than that. Of the Protestants who served in the army, the vast majority, or almost 82 per cent, held the lowly ranks of volunteer or private. This might suggest that they were mostly recent

---

[24] MAD, A/10307, Return of Protestants serving in the National Army.

recruits, who had played no role in the War of Independence. Certainly, almost no connection can be drawn between the Protestant republican counterculture described in previous chapters and membership of the National Army. Only one among the 220 can be identified as having been an active guerrilla during 1919–1921. Peter Steepe, a member of the Limerick Palatine community, was a farmer's son, a member of the Church of Ireland, and an Easter Rising veteran. Imprisoned after 1916, he went on to serve in the East Limerick Flying Column during the War of Independence.[25] In 1922 Steepe served with the 18th Infantry Battalion, held the rank of sergeant, and was posted to Knocklong, County Limerick.[26] Among the Protestant officers was Thomas Aston, a Dublin-born member of a prominent Methodist pro–home rule family. Aston, who had served in the Royal Flying Corps during the Great War, was appointed captain by General Eoin O'Duffy in July 1922. He was appointed as Command Transport Officer in Kerry in September 1922, and was demobilised in October 1923.[27] Another officer with Great War service was Barry Duke. Duke served for four and a half years in the 2nd Battalion, Royal Munster Fusiliers, where he held the rank of corporal. A member of the National Army Cork Reserves until January 1923, he then joined the staff of the General Officer Commanding in Collins Barracks, Cork, before being appointed adjutant of the 15th Infantry Battalion from April 1923 until his demobilisation in December of that year.[28] James Gardiner, a Kilkenny-born Episcopalian and labourer's son, served as an intelligence officer in the 2nd Southern Division. A second lieutenant, he died as a result of a gunshot wound to the head on 10 December 1922, and was buried in his native county two days later.[29]

About two-thirds of Protestant Free State Army men came from Leinster. This province, which included Dublin, was the most populous in the Free State and had the largest concentration of Protestants outside Ulster. Hesitancy about volunteering among the Protestants of Muster and Connaught is unsurprising: these small, mostly farming communities were highly conservative and included few who met the socio-economic profile of Protestant National Army soldiers.

---

[25] *Limerick Leader*, 11 November 1989. For Steepe's War of Independence career, see Thomas Toomey, *The war of independence in Limerick 1912–1921: also covering actions in the border areas of Tipperary, Cork, Kerry and Clare* (Limerick, 2010), 331, 334, 472.

[26] MAD, Abstract of service, Peter Steepe.

[27] MAD, Abstract of service, Thomas Aston.

[28] MAD, Abstract of service, (Richard) Barry Duke.

[29] MAD, Abstract of service, James Gardiner.

Table 8.5 *Geographic origin of Protestants in the National Army*

Place	Number	Percentage
Dublin	91	41.36
Rest of Leinster	54	24.54
Munster	45	20.45
Ulster	12	5.45
Connaught	7	3.19
Britain	8	3.64
Unknown	3	1.37
Total	**220**	**100.00**

One of the principal themes of this study is the tendency for Protestant nationalists to be closely related by blood: for example, 20 per cent of members of the Irish Guild of the Church had a close relation in the organisation. The figure for Protestants in the National Army is lower. Census records suggests that sixteen men, or about 7 per cent of the cohort, were closely related. As has been discussed in earlier chapters, Protestant nationalists invested great energy in cultivating separatist instincts in their friends and relations. The lower number of members of this cohort with a relative also serving might be a further indication that most of these men joined the army for primarily economic reasons, rather than the patriotic zeal which characterised Protestants who served in the pre-1922 Irish Volunteers, the anti-Treaty IRA, or similar bodies.

Accounts of the experiences of these Protestant soldiers are few. However, one article in *An t-Óglach*, then the official journal of the National Army, is illuminating. The anonymous writer maintained that on stating his religion to the recruiting officer, he, knowing the army to be predominantly Catholic, 'felt an involuntary thrill of apprehension', and that he anticipated his religion would prove a problem. In fact, writing nine months after his enlistment, he recorded a generally positive experience. He was excused Church parade, and facilities were offered for him to worship in the Church of Ireland. He claimed that the first rector he met while on service 'tendered me a hearty welcome and we had a good long talk'. Indeed, such was his experience of the clergy in every village where he had been stationed. He maintained that his fellow soldiers showed no antagonism:

Of course, one has occasionally met a sincere Catholic, who has endeavoured to reason to one as to the 'wrong' belief held, but such talks have always been conducted with due reverence to the subject, and no antagonism has arisen.

Elements of Catholic ritual did cause some unease:

> The only time that actual embarrassment occurs is at meal times, the sounding of
> the Angelus, and on retiring or rising. Then, certain devotions are paid by my
> comrades in which I do not join. But no remark passes on my failing to do so.

Finally, the writer maintained that his religion was no bar to advance-
ment in the National Army: he had been promoted from volunteer to
lieutenant.[30]

The death of Lieut. H. A. L. Pierson, a young Limerick Protestant who
was killed fighting in Kerry in April 1923, gave the National Army the
opportunity to demonstrate its acceptance of Protestant servicemen, and
the Protestant community to show its allegiance to the new state. Pierson's coffin, which was covered by the tricolour, was accompanied
through the streets of Limerick by a full military guard of honour. Many
businesses, including the Protestant Young Men's Christian Association,
which had previously been closely associated with unionism, closed out
of respect. Crowds lined the streets of the city, and heads were reverently
uncovered as the cortège processed.[31]

The influx of a sizeable number of Protestants into the army did not
escape the attention of the minister for defence. In November 1922 Richard Mulcahy wrote to the Church of Ireland archbishop of Dublin
seeking to create chaplaincy arrangements to minister the spiritual needs
of Anglican soldiers.[32] Plans were made to approach the other Protestant
denominations as well. This, however, did not come soon enough for the
rector of Rathmines, the Rev. Ernest Lewis-Crosby. In a trenchant letter
to Mulcahy, Lewis-Crosby claimed that he had frequently applied to the
commander-in-chief at Portobello Barracks, which lay within his parish,
for the right to visit the sixteen members of his church who were stationed there, but that he had been refused admittance. The rector
demanded that he be appointed acting chaplain to the barracks with right
of access to the soldiers and any Church of Ireland prisoners as well.
He threatened to take the matter up with one his parishioners, Professor
William Thrift, the Dáil Éireann TD for the University of Dublin, but

[30] 'As others see us: Protestant recruit's experience in the army', *An t-Óglach*, 24
March 1923.
[31] *Cork Examiner*, 23 April 1923.
[32] MAD, A/7091 box 6 (Chaplains other than Catholic), 9 November 1922, Mulcahy to
Archbishop Gregg; A/7091 box 6 (Chaplains other than Catholic), 'Memorandum re.
Chaplains – Protestant, etc.', 21 November 1922.

did not 'want to trouble him unless it is necessary'.[33] The rector received a hasty reply from Mulcahy, who apologised for the situation and stated – correctly – that he had already been in contact with Dr Gregg about appointing Church of Ireland chaplains to the army. Lewis-Crosby was appointed officiating clergyman to Portobello Barracks, a role he retained until he moved parish two years later.[34]

Lewis-Crosby was not the sole Church of Ireland clergyman who sought appointment as a chaplain. Defence Order No. 3 created the position of residential chaplains – one would be appointed for the Curragh Camp – and for local officiating clergymen.[35] There was something of a tussle for these positions: numerous representations were made seeking the appointments, which carried a reasonable stipend.[36] Following the withdrawal of the British army from the Curragh Camp in 1922, the Methodist chapel and its clergy house were handed over to the Church of Ireland, the old wooden-structure Anglican church being deemed too large. This Methodist chapel became the new Church of Ireland. In September 1923 the Rev. R. C. Madden was appointed the first resident Church of Ireland chaplain to the army.[37] Archbishop Gregg visited the Garrison Church to celebrate confirmation in 1924 and 1925, at which latter occasion the Church of Ireland contingent at the Curragh was estimated at 120 men.[38]

Although they fought, and in some cases died, for an independent Irish state, Protestant National Army soldiers cannot quite be described as nationalists. The evidence suggests that they were probably mostly former unionists, who joined the army for economic reasons, as well as from a desire to defeat republicans and to make the new state work. Nor did they make any attempt to lobby or organise themselves as a unit. This should not surprise us: after the signing of the Treaty, hostility towards the idea of an independent Ireland gave way to unobtrusive engagement with the new state, and joining the National Army is just one example of

[33] MAD, A/7091 box 6 (Chaplains other than Catholic), 22 November 1922, Lewis-Crosby to Mulcahy.
[34] MAD, A/7091 box 6 (Chaplains other than Catholic), 23 November 1922, Mulcahy to Lewis-Crosby; A/7091 box 6 (Chaplains other than Catholic); 10 December 1924, minister for defence (Peter Hughes) to Lewis-Crosby.
[35] MAD, A/7091 box 6 (Chaplains other than Catholic), Defence Order No. 3, 9 November 1922.
[36] See, for example, MAD, A/7091 box 6 (Chaplains other than Catholic), Commander-in-chief to White, bishop of Limerick, 28 October 1922; Major M. Moran to Commander-in-chief, 22 December 1922; Chaplaincy application A6881, 22 September 1922 (re. the Curragh chaplaincy).
[37] RCBL, Curragh Camp Church, Parish of Ballysax, 1923–1934, Preacher's book, 2 September 1923.
[38] IT, 23 April 1924, 8 June 1925.

this. During the 1920s, Cumann na nGaedheal, the pro-Treaty party, moved steadily to the right, largely under the influence of Kevin O'Higgins, its dominant minister. This stance was amenable to many southern Protestants.[39] Protestants also found a home in the Farmers' Party and later the National Centre Party during the 1920s and 1930s. Southern Protestants would never achieve the same level of political, social, and economic dominance that they had enjoyed before independence, but life in independent Ireland was probably better than many had expected. But what about Protestant nationalists? How did they experience the decades after independence?

---

[39] John M. Regan, *The Irish counter revolution, 1921–1936: Treatyite politics and settlement in independent Ireland* (Dublin, 1999), 245–271.

Conclusion

In the years prior to independence, nationalist representatives frequently assured their audiences that the attainment of national freedom would prompt the economic, social, and cultural reconstruction of the country. Farming would be modernised, new industries would be established, and the Irish language would be revived. If prompted, the same politicians would give assurances that the rights of the Protestant community would be fully respected by an independent state. And at least initially, the Irish Free State government did make good on their promises to respect the rights of Protestants. The unionist spectres of expropriation, forced assimilation, or even exile never came to pass. The government reached out to the minority and sought to encourage their participation in public life.

Seeking to promote a spirit of inclusivity, the new government appointed a significant proportion of southern unionists to the upper house of parliament. W. B. Yeats and Alice Stopford Green added a Protestant nationalist dimension, sitting beside such moderates as Horace Plunkett and Edward MacLysaght. However, the creation of a culturally diverse senate did not inaugurate a new period of Protestant assertiveness: the minority community generally avoided active engagement in politics and largely stayed within their own social, commercial, and educational networks.[1] But what about Protestant nationalists? What was their experience of the first decades of independence?

If partition was distressing for most nationalists, it was deeply traumatic for those of a Protestant background. The creation of a Northern Ireland state, with its seemingly impregnable unionist majority, Orange ethos, and anti-Catholic discrimination marked the final defeat of the Protestant nationalist dream of a secular, independent Irish state. There is a sense, from the 1920s, of the Protestant nationalist counterculture in decline, as activists grew older, became disenchanted, or died.

---

[1] See, for example, Terence Brown, *Ireland: a social and cultural history, 1922–79* (London, 1981), 106–137.

Regeneration, the great strength of this tradition, whereby individuals cultivated nationalist convictions in their co-religionists, largely came to an end. Although there remained Protestant nationalist activists, many of them prominent, their activities are harder to place within a discernible network, and their actions were largely without the sense of optimism that characterised the early part of the century.

Æ George Russell was central to the frequently bitter controversies that characterised the early years of independence. His journal, the *Irish Statesman*, criticised conservative Catholic influence, which led to censorship of books and films and the prohibition of divorce. These policies, which were largely introduced at the behest of groups such as the Catholic Truth Society, appalled Russell. The last five years of his life were bleak. The *Statesman*, although providing a fine forum for political and cultural debate, went out of business. Revolted at growing intolerance in the country, he took to complaining about 'squalid Catholic materialism' and 'smug Catholic self satisfaction'.[2] In 1933 he left Ireland, dying two years later.

W. B. Yeats's defiance was more theatrical. Yeats's senate speech on divorce, in June 1925, argued that prohibition was an attack on civil liberties and would 'crystallise' partition. The coda, a robust defence of Irish Protestants, has become famous.

We against whom you have done this thing are no petty people. We are one of the great stocks of Europe. We are the people of Burke; we are the people of Grattan; we are the people of Swift, the people of Emmet, the people of Parnell. We have created the most of the modern literature of this country. We have created the best of its political intelligence.[3]

Terence Brown has argued that the poet was 'deliberately fomenting conflict in identifying his own stock, the Protestant people of Ireland, with an elitist libertarianism that the country could ill afford to lose'.[4] It was the culmination of more than two decades of anxiety about the intolerant nature of Catholicism.

With the coming of independence, the Irish Guild of the Church, which, as we have seen, had supported the Treaty, returned to its roots, becoming largely middle-class and respectable. It held (and to this day still holds) regular services in Irish, without encountering ecclesiastical hostility. With the death of Nelly O'Brien in 1925, the organisation lost

---

[2] Æ George Russell, quoted in Francis Flanagan, *Remembering the revolution: dissent, culture and nationalism in the Irish Free State* (Oxford, 2015), 155.
[3] Donald R. Pearce (ed.), *The senate speeches of W. B. Yeats* (London, 1960), 99.
[4] Terence Brown, *The life of W. B. Yeats: a critical biography* (Dublin, 2001), 300.

its leading figure, and three years later the *Gaelic Churchman* folded, extinguishing a distinctive voice of Protestant nationalism.

Only one Protestant nationalist of the revolutionary era held cabinet rank in the Free State. Ernest Blythe served as minister for finance between 1923 and 1932. His conservative tenure, characterised by cuts in public expenditure (including, notoriously, the old-age pension) and support for laissez-faire free trade, proved highly damaging for the Cumann na nGaedheal government, and allowed the opposition Fianna Fáil to position itself as defenders of the poor. Blythe became personally unpopular during this period, and his religion was used against him: a Fianna Fáil rival during the September 1927 election stated that Monaghan was a Catholic county and should be represented by Catholics.[5] In opposition during the 1930s he was an enthusiastic supporter of the far-right Blueshirt movement, although he would eventually play a key role in removing Eoin O'Duffy, the group's unpredictable leader. Blythe returned to his roots in cultural and language activism, becoming, from 1935 to 1967, a controversial and authoritarian director of the Abbey Theatre.[6]

Others remained unreconcilable, and would have nothing to do with the new state. Living alone in Ballincoona, Albinia Brodrick became increasingly isolated. Originally a supporter of de Valera, she broke with him in 1926 when he founded Fianna Fáil, and she remained in the now much-diminished Sinn Féin. She was involved in another split in 1933, at the Cumann na mBan convention. Feeling the organisation had become too concerned with social reform to the detriment of the 'National Question', she resigned in protest, alongside Mary MacSwiney, Eileen Tubbert, Noneen Brugha, and others. They formed a splinter group, Mná na Poblachta (Women of the Republic), devoted to campaigning 'for the glory of God and the Glory of Ireland'. Fearing that the government would convert her hospital to a military base after her death, in the late 1930s she had it dismantled. It remains a ruin to this day. Brodrick remained in Sneem, nursing the local community and operating a small shop until 1945. She died in poverty, aged ninety-three, in 1955.[7]

Few attempted the difficult task of winning Northern Irish Protestants over to nationalism. One famous exception was George Gilmore, who would devote much of his life to securing Protestant/Catholic unity as the basis for a revived republicanism. Gilmore was expelled from the IRA in 1934, and then helped set up the left-wing Republican Congress. In that

---

[5] *DIB* article on Ernest Blythe.   [6] See Welch, *The Abbey Theatre*, 132, 141ff.
[7] UCD, LA18, Máire Comerford unpublished memoirs; *Sneem Parish News*, (2000), 24.

year he succeeded in bringing several busloads of Belfast Protestants, including a bus from the Shankill, to the Wolfe Tone commemoration in Bodenstown. However, this excursion ended in violence when the Congress group were set upon by the IRA. Gilmore would later say, 'It will be a long time before "Come on the Shankill" will be heard at Bodenstown again.'[8] Gilmore (d. 1985), along with his brothers Harry (d. 1976) and Charlie (d. 1987), was active in a variety of socialist and republican organisations for the rest of his life.[9]

With the election of de Valera's Fianna Fáil in 1932, social and public policy became steadily more influenced by the Catholic hierarchy, and in particular by John Charles McQuaid (1895–1973), later archbishop of Dublin. This change in tone, which vindicated at least some unionist fears about life in independent Ireland, disillusioned some. Dorothy Macardle, who had worked closely with de Valera when writing her enormous account, *The Irish republic* (1937), the semi-official anti-Treaty history, grew increasingly worried throughout the 1930s. The 1937 Constitution, which stated that women's place was within the home, and which granted a 'special position' to the Catholic Church, led to a bitter quarrel between Macardle and de Valera.[10] Another victim of the stultifyingly Catholic atmosphere was Dr Kathleen Lynn. Lynn, who had co-founded St Ultan's Hospital for Infants on Charlemont Street, Dublin, in 1919, found that her work to reduce infant mortality was impeded by McQuaid, who objected to Protestant involvement in Catholic hospitals and worked to prevent a proposed merger between St Ultan's and Harcourt Street Children's Hospital. De Valera offered no support: by 1937 Lynn recorded she had 'nothing but contempt for him and his party'.[11]

The most extraordinary reversal was that of Mabel FitzGerald. Confiding in George Bernard Shaw, she admitted that not only was she now opposed to an Irish republic, but that she was against universal adult suffrage:

the state of Europe [has] convinced me that it was folly to try to stand alone as a separate Republic. And now the last folly of complete isolation may be committed

---

[8] *IT*, 24 June 1985.
[9] For a discussion of George Gilmore's career in the decade and a half after independence, see Richard English, *Radicals and the republic: socialist republicanism in the Irish Free State, 1925–1937* (Oxford, 1994), passim.
[10] Jennifer FitzGerald papers, Transcript of interview with George Gilmore, 27 May 1985. See also *IT*, 21 November 1995.
[11] Eugenio Biagini and Daniel Mulhall (eds.), *The shaping of modern Ireland: a centenary assessment* (Sallins, 2016), 150.

if what is really a [de Valera] dictatorship is consolidated. A dictatorship supported by the most ignorant and unthinking whose views it voices.

I have changed my own views greatly since youth. About adult suffrage, for instance. I find the masses always wrong, they seem to stand for the worst in man ... Also I am convinced that education is necessary to the forming of views that are worth while at all, and I don't believe that the majority of people can take education. If poverty and dirt and disease could be abolished, and I hope they may be, the multitude would want more dog racing, more drink, more pictures, more tabloid views from the cheap press supplied, the only demand for more education would be for the sort of education that would get better jobs for their families, not the education that would make them think better.[12]

Almost forty years after the republican, socialist, and suffragist Meadhbh Ní Chonaill had left Belfast, Mabel FitzGerald exhibited the reactionary views of her father John McConnell.

Others found their niche in independent Ireland. David Lubbock Robinson, who took the anti-Treaty side in the Civil War and participated in a forty-one-day hunger strike, was elected to the senate in 1931 and served as that body's vice-chairman in the three months before it was abolished in May 1936. De Valera appointed him to the reconstituted senate in 1938. While serving in the senate, Robinson often represented the state at Protestant functions.[13] Some supported the new state from further afield. As we have seen, Lindsay Crawford enjoyed perhaps the most unusual trajectory of all those covered in this book: from prominent Dublin Orangeman to editor of the Low Church *Irish Protestant*, grand master of the Independent Orange Order, convert to home rule, and Canada-based propagandist for an Irish republic. There would be one further permutation: Crawford ended his career as Irish Free State trade representative in New York.

In 1938 de Valera supported the nomination of Douglas Hyde as first president of Ireland. This was deeply symbolic and politically astute: it underlined the state's commitment to Irish, represented a gesture towards Protestants on either side of the border, and quieted those critics who believed de Valera wished to expand the office into a dictatorship.[14] Although suffering a stroke in April 1940 and confined to a wheelchair thereafter, Hyde carried out his duties with dignity and established a precedent for scrupulous impartiality in office. When Hyde retired in 1945, Seán Lester, who had enjoyed a successful diplomatic career as high commissioner of Free State of Danzig and last secretary-general of

[12] UCD, FitzGerald papers, P80/1664, Mabel FitzGerald to George Bernard Shaw, 26 May 1944.
[13] *DIB* article on David Lubbock Robinson.
[14] Dunleavy and Dunleavy, *Douglas Hyde*, 368–372ff.

the League of Nations, was rumoured as a candidate to replace him, but in the end the post went to Seán T. O'Kelly, a member of cabinet.[15]

As we have noted, Protestant nationalists were generally reticent about discussing their religion in public and went to lengths to avoid the appearance of criticising Catholics. George Irvine was discreet about his religion around Catholics, but an advocate for radical change among his fellow Anglicans. Following his release from prison in 1922, he avoided conventional politics, and instead became prominent in a wide variety of progressive causes, including animal welfare, the republican cause in the Spanish Civil War, and the plight of political prisoners. The increasingly Catholic ethos of the state must have angered him, as became apparent in 1949.

Throughout June of that year, the *Dublin Evening Mail* published a bad-tempered correspondence in relation to the state subsidy to Trinity College, in which some letter-writers denigrated the patriotism of Trinity, and of Irish Protestants generally.[16] This elicited an angry, and highly revealing, response from Irvine.

The persecution of Roman Catholics was not the work of the Church of Ireland, or any other Protestant denomination, but of the British government of the time ... Ireland owes a lot to Protestants, and the spirit of Protestantism, even the absolute independence of the twenty-six counties. The struggle for Irish independence is generally represented as extending over many centuries, but in reality the demand for a sovereign independent republic arose with the Protestant Wolfe Tone. The Irish princes and chieftains were fighting for their own supremacy, but acknowledged allegiance to England's King or Queen. Granuaile, whose name in ballads has become a synonym for Ireland, was a friend of Queen Elizabeth ... Patrick Sarsfield fought to restore James II. Wolfe Tone alone demanded the sovereign independence which has been gained for part of Ireland, and Protestants played their part in this struggle – the Hopes, Joys, and McCrackens in the North, Lord Edward FitzGerald, Robert Emmet, the brothers Sheares in the South ...

How many rifles outside the British Army were there in Southern Ireland when the rifles were landed in Larne Lough? Very few ... But the rifles of Larne Lough were followed by those of Howth, and they came in fast enough after that. We Protestants, both directly and indirectly, have paid our footing in the Irish Republic – and here we mean to stay.[17]

Irvine's argument, that Irish republicanism was largely the inspiration of Protestants, and that Catholic leaders were historically loyal to the Crown, probably reflected the submerged thinking of many from his background. However, this statement is notable as he eschewed the usual

---

[15] *DIB* article on Seán Lester.   [16] See *Dublin Evening Mail,* 7–11, 15, 20 June 1949.
[17] *Dublin Evening Mail,* 22 June 1949.

'Catholic, Protestant and Dissenter' slogan in favour of an explicit and insulting reference to the old Catholic tradition of loyalty. This was an unusual statement in 1949, and would have been exceptionally rare (in public anyway) before 1923. However, with a republic declared, partition entrenched, and the Catholic hierarchy dominant, he did not wish to pretend anymore.

Like most – or all – revolutionaries, Protestant nationalists did not achieve their aims. However, like most revolutionary groups, they reward our scrutiny and prompt us to reconsider the era from which they came. What can we learn from Protestant nationalists? First, study of Protestant nationalist activists demonstrates the continued centrality of religious denomination during the early decades of the twentieth century. Although nationalist leaders in early 1900s (and today) could hide behind the words 'Catholic, Protestant and Dissenter', this study shows that members of this group formed identifiable religion-based networks, either informal, such as that around F. J. Bigger that was described in Chapter 2, or explicit, by means of associations such as the Irish Guild of the Church. Throughout this book, the capturing of members of one's own tribe was fundamental: activists spent vast amounts of time seeking to inculcate nationalist sentiment in their fellow Protestants. But it was not individual conversions they were seeking; rather, they wished to see the realignment of their entire religious group and, indeed, for that group to take a leading role in the Irish nation. Furthermore, there is little evidence for a link between the holding of nationalist views and the adoption of 'progressive' attitudes on religion. As we have seen in Chapter 3, many Protestant nationalists were dismissive of, or hostile to, the Catholic Church. And as we saw in Chapter 2, even Orangemen could be nationalists.

Second, this study shows the importance of associational culture as a category of historical research. These activists rarely, if ever, worked alone; they forged their own culture, which allowed them to collectively counter those aspects of majority Protestant opinion they found undesirable. This book is not the only recent study with such an emphasis. R. F. Foster's *Vivid faces* is an exploration of the lives and ideology of the revolutionary generation in Ireland from 1890 until 1923. Professor Foster tracks the formative influences, as well as familial and personal relationships, of a large, primarily Catholic, body of activists, to illuminating effect.[18] Individual historical actors, no matter how

---

[18] Foster, *Vivid faces*, passim.

significant, can often be best understood in relation to the formal and informal networks they inhabited.

Finally, this book draws our attention to the diversity of Protestant society during this era. Irish Protestants, clearly, were not unanimously in favour of the Union, but the extent to which a significant nationalist counterculture emerged, which traversed social and denominational diversions, and could develop largely independently, in separate population centres, can be seen here. For Irish Protestants, dissent could mean more than one thing.

The often-melancholy experiences of Protestant nationalists outlined earlier should not surprise us. Partition, in creating the conditions for a Protestant-dominated state in the north and a Catholic-dominated state in the south, would always be inimical to the sort of ethos that the subjects of this book wished to cultivate. The success of the Protestant nationalist perspective depended on the creation of the sort of pan-confessional secular front that had been the desire of many republicans since Wolfe Tone, but which was ultimately unattainable. The vast majority of Irish Protestants were probably beyond conversion to nationalism: their affection for the Crown and the Union was too heartfelt, their mistrust of Catholicism too strong, and their conservatism too fundamental.

Throughout the period 1900–1923, Catholic nationalists faced a major, insurmountable problem: the lack of a numerically significant Protestant nationalist movement that shared their aims and worked to promote their agenda, and thus undermine the argument for the Union or for partition. The Protestant nationalist counterculture was never significant enough to allow for this. In later years this generation of Catholic nationalists came to understand this, and their recollections are sometimes marked by nostalgia for Protestant nationalist activity, which, they believed, had carried the tantalising prospect of a more widespread realignment. In 1964 Denis McCullough was interviewed by Ernest Strathdee for Ulster Television. Strathdee asked the now-elderly former revolutionary for his finest memory. McCullough did not choose to recall his reorganisation of the IRB in Ulster, his presidency of the Supreme Council of that organisation, or even his successful peacetime career in business. Instead, an emotional McCullough turned his mind to 1903 and to an obscure body of which he had not even been a member:

There was a Protestant National Society founded by Bulmer Hobson and a little fella, young fellow called Willie McDonald ... one of the best minds I met in all my time – he died, poor boy, of TB. Willie McDonald, David Parkhill, who founded the Ulster Literary Theatre, the Morrows, and all the men who went with them, all these men, liberal-minded men, who looked on Ireland as their Ireland and not as an outside country. I wish that was back again.[19]

The Protestant nationalist counterculture was vibrant and many of its protagonists were profoundly talented; however, its ambitions were too great, and its adherents too few, to achieve its ultimate aims.

---

[19] UCD, Denis McC, P120/34 (2), transcript of interview with Denis McCullough, by Ernest Strathdee, for Ulster Television, 8 September 1964.

Bibliography

Primary Bibliography

Manuscript Collections

Bodleian Library, Oxford
 Henry Duke papers

British Library, London
 John Henry Bernard papers
 Casement Petition papers

Cork City and County Archives, Cork City
 George Fitzhardinge Berkeley papers

Grand Orange Lodge of Ireland, Belfast
 Independent Orange Order collection

Kerry County Library and Archives, Tralee, County Kerry
 Albinia Brodrick/Gobnait Ní Bhruadair File

Military Archives, Dublin
 Abstracts of service
 Chaplains other than Catholic records
 Civil War files (recruiting)
 Civil War ledgers (prisoners)
 Contemporary Documents collection
 Free State Army census returns, November 1922 (10 Vols.)
 Ledger of political prisoners, Cork Command, August 1922
 Ledger of political prisoners, Cork Command, October 1922
 Military Service Pensions Collection
 Return of Protestants serving in the National Army

National Archives, Kew
 Intelligence file on Ernest Blythe
 Intelligence notes, 1915
 Lord Midleton papers
 Report on Sinn Féin Volunteer parades, 17 March 1916
 Report on the Sinn Féin convention, 1917

National Archives of Ireland, Dublin
    Bureau of Military History, Witness Statements
    Census of Ireland, 1901
    Census of Ireland, 1911
    Crime Branch Special Records
    Dáil Éireann Local Government file on Kerry County Council

National Library of Ireland, Dublin
    Roger Casement additional papers
    Lindsay Crawford papers
    Dublin Metropolitan Police Catholic Society, anti-conscription poster
    Elsie Henry diary
    Bulmer Hobson papers
    Rosamond Jacob papers
    Thomas Johnson papers
    Letter from Gertrude Bannister to George Bernard Shaw, 1916
    Letter from George Irvine to Crissie M. Doyle, 1917
    Letter from Alice Milligan to Sinéad de Valera, undated, c. 1921
    Letters of Roger Casement and F. J. Bigger to George Ruth, 1914
    Michael J. Lennon papers
    Manifesto of the Irish Volunteers
    Joseph McGarrity papers
    Alice Milligan diary
    Minute book of Dublin branch of the Irish Protestant Home Rule
        Association
    Maurice Moore papers
    Notes on character of Alice Stopford Green by Robert J. Stopford
        [undated]
    William O'Brien papers
    Florence O'Donoghue papers
    Protestant protest against conscription circular
    Sheehy–Skeffington papers
    Sinn Féin standing committee minute book
    Dorothy Stopford Price papers
    Typescript recollections of Miss [Edie] Stopford, undated.

National Museum of Ireland, Dublin
    Sinn Féin executive minutes

Ó Fiaich Library and Archive, Armagh
    O'Kane collection

Private Collection
    Jennifer FitzGerald papers, Cardiff-by-the-Sea, Encinitas,
        California

Public Record Office of Northern Ireland, Belfast
    Intelligence file on Séan Nethercott
    Ulster Covenant signature sheets

Representative Church Body Library, Dublin
       Curragh Camp Church, Preacher's book, 1923–1934
       Irish Guild of Witness, Early general records book
       Leslie, Canon J. R., *Biographical Index of the Clergy of the Church of Ireland*, 4 Vols.
       Minute books of the Irish Guild of the Church
       Minute books of the Irish Guild of Witness
       Rosamond Stephen papers
       Rev. William Vandeleur, typescript memoirs

Royal College of Physicians of Ireland, Dublin
       Kathleen Lynn, diary

Trinity College Dublin, Library
       Joseph Campbell papers
       Erskine Childers papers
       James Owen Hannay papers
       Douglas Hyde, Diary of Easter Week
       Nelly O'Brien papers

University College Dublin, Archive
       Ernest Blythe papers
       Máire Comerford papers
       Desmond FitzGerald papers
       Terence MacSwiney papers
       Denis McCullough papers
       Ernie O'Malley papers

Newspapers and Periodicals

All Ireland Review
An Claidheamh Soluis
Anglo-Celt
Ballymoney Free Press
Belfast Evening Telegraph
Belfast News-Letter
British Journal of Nursing
Butte Independent
Catholic Bulletin
Celtia: a Pan-Celtic monthly magazine
Church of Ireland Gazette
Connaught Telegraph
Cork Constitution
Cork *Evening Echo*
Cork Examiner
Derry People
Donegal News
Dublin *Daily Express*

Dublin *Evening Herald*
Dublin Evening Mail
Dublin *Evening Telegraph*
Freeman's Journal
Gaelic American
Gaelic Churchman
Impartial Reporter
Irish Catholic
Irish Citizen
Irish Daily Independent
Irish Independent
Irish News
Irish Press
Irish Protestant
Irish Rosary
Irish Statesman
Irish Times
Irish Volunteer
Irish Weekly Independent
Irish Weekly and Ulster Examiner
Irish World
The Irishman
Kentucky Irish American
Kerry News
The Kerryman
Kildare Observer
The Leader
Limerick Leader
London *Times*
Manchester Guardian
Nationalist and Leinster Times
Nationality
Nenagh Guardian
New Ireland
New York Times
North and South
Northern Patriot
Northern Whig
The Observer
Old Ireland
Orange Independent
Peasant
The People (Wexford)
Red Hand Magazine
The Republic
Sinn Féin
Sneem Parish News

Southern Star
The Sun (New York)
Sunday Independent
The Times
Uladh
Ulster Guardian
Ulster Herald
The Unionist
United Irishman
The Victorian
Weekly Irish Times
The Witness
Worker's Republic
Young Ireland

Official Publications

Census of population, 1926, Vol. III (religions and birthplaces) (Dublin, 1926).
Dáil Éireann debates
House of Commons debates
Military service. A bill to make further provision with respect to military service during the present war. (16) 1918.

Printed Organisation Minutes and Reports

Annual Report and Proceedings of the Belfast Naturalists' Field Club for the year ending 31 March 1895, Series II, Part II, Volume IV, 1894–1895.
Annual Report and Proceedings of the Belfast Naturalists' Field Club for the year ending 31 March 1896, Series II, Part III, Volume IV, 1895–1896.
Report of the Gaelic League for the year ended 30th September 1894 (Dublin, 1895).

Memoirs, Published Diaries, Collected Speeches, and Letters

Andrews, C. S., *Dublin made me: an autobiography* (Dublin, 1979).
Brennan-Whitmore, W. J., *With the Irish in Frongoch* (Dublin, 1917).
Carberry, Juanita, 'Child of Happy Valley', *Ardfield/Rathbarry Journal,* No. 3 (2000–2001), 18–20.
Colles, Ramsay, *In castle and court house: being reminiscences of thirty years in Ireland* (London, 1911).
Czira, Sidney Gifford, *The years flew by* (John Hayes, ed.) (Galway, 2000 [1974]).
De Blaghd, Earnán [Ernest Blythe], *Trasna na Bóinne* (Dublin, 1957).
De Montmorency, Hervey, *Sword and stirrup: memories of an adventurous life* (London, 1936).
Figgis, Darrell, *Recollections of the Irish war* (New York, 1927).

FitzGerald, Desmond, *Desmond's rising: memoirs, 1913 to Easter 1916* (Dublin, 2006 [1968]).

FitzGerald, Garret, *All in a life: an autobiography* (Dublin, 1991).

Gonne MacBride, Maud, *A servant of the Queen: reminiscences* (London, 1938).

Gwynn, Stephen, *Experiences of a literary man* (London, 1926).

Hobson, Bulmer, *Ireland yesterday and tomorrow* (Tralee, 1968).

Johnstone, Thomas M., *The vintage of memory* (Belfast, 1943).

Krause, David (ed.), *The letters of Sean O'Casey, Vol. II: 1942–54* (New York, 1980).

Leslie, Shane, *The film of memory* (London, 1938).

MacBride White, Anna, and Norman, Jeffares A. (eds.), *The Gonne–Yeats letters, 1893–1938: always your friend* (London, 1992).

Midleton, the earl of, *Records and reactions: 1856–1939* (London, 1939).

O'Casey, Sean, *Drums under the windows*, in *Autobiographies*, Vol. I (London, 1992 [originally published as a single volume in 1945]).

O'Connor, Frank, *An only child* (London, 1972 [1961]).

O'Donnell, William H., and Archibald, Douglas N. (eds.), *The collected works of W. B. Yeats, Vol. III: Autobiographies* (New York, 1999).

O'Leary, John, *Recollections of Fenians and Fenianism*, Vol. II (London, 1896).

O'Malley, Cormac K. H., and Dolan, Anne (eds.), *'No surrender here!': the Civil War papers of Ernie O'Malley, 1922–1924* (Dublin, 2007).

O'Malley, Ernie, *On another man's wound* (London, 1936).

Pearce, Donald R. (ed.), *The senate speeches of W. B. Yeats* (London, 1960).

Pyle, Hilary (ed.), *Cesca's diary, 1913–1916: where art and nationalism meet* (Dublin, 2005).

Sandford, Jeremy (ed.), *Mary Carbery's West Cork Journal, 1898–1901* (Dublin, 1998).

Smithson, Annie M. P., *Myself – and others: an autobiography* (Dublin, 1944).

Walsh, Oonagh (ed.), *An Englishwoman in Belfast: Rosamond Stephen's record of the Great War* (Cork, 2000).

Wells, Warre B., *Irish indiscretions* (London, 1923).

White, Jack, *Misfit: a revolutionary life* (Dublin, 2005 [1930]).

Young, Ella, *Flowering dusk: things remembered accurately and inaccurately* (New York, 1945).

Works of Fiction

[Various authors], *Poems and ballads of Young Ireland* (Dublin, 1888).

Albright, Daniel (ed.), *W. B. Yeats: the poems* (London, 1992).

Birmingham, George A., *The seething pot* (London, 1905).

Brodrick, Albinia, *Verses of adversity* (London, 1904).

Clark, David R., and Clark, Rosalind E. (eds.), *The collected works of W. B. Yeats, Vol. II: the plays* (New York, 2001).

Joyce, James, *Ulysses*, Bodley Head ed. (1986 [1922]).

Mangan, Henry (ed.), *Poems by Alice Milligan* (Dublin, 1954).

Milligan, Alice, *The harper of the only God: a selection of poetry by Alice Milligan* (Sheila Turner Johnston, ed.) (Omagh, 1993).

Zach, Wolfgang (ed.), *Selected plays by Rutherford Mayne* (Washington, DC, 2006).

Contemporary Accounts

[Anonymous] *The book of the fete: Queen's College, Belfast: May 29, 30, 31st and June 1st 1907* (Belfast, 1907).
The voice of the Protestant Church in Ireland (n.p., n.d. [c. 1922]).
'As others see us: Protestant recruit's experience in the army', *An t-Óglach*, 24 March 1923, 7.
[Various authors], *A Protestant protest: Ballymoney, Oct. 24th 1913* (Ballymoney, 1913).
Béaslaí, Piaras, 'Moods and memories', *Irish Independent*, 11 December 1963.
Bigger, Francis Joseph, *William Orr* (Dublin, 1906).
Childers, Erskine, *The framework of home rule* (London, 1911).
Clery, Arthur E., 'The Gaelic League, 1893–1919', *Studies*, Vol. 8, No. 31 (September 1919), 398–408.
Connolly, James, *Labour in Irish History* (Dublin, 1910).
Cotton, A. W., 'Seán Lester', *Focus*, July 1959, 13–14.
Crawford, Lindsay, *Irish grievances and their remedy* (Dublin, 1905).
The Problem of Ulster (New York, 1920[?]).
Crone, J. S., and Bigger, F. C. (eds.), *In remembrance: articles and sketches: biographical, historical, topographical by Francis Joseph Bigger M.A., M.R.I.A., F.R.S.A.I.* (Dublin, 1927).
De Blacam, Aodh, *What Sinn Féin stands for* (Dublin, 1921).
De Burca, Padraig, and Boyle, John F., *Free State or republic?* (Dublin, 2003 [1922]).
Dinneen, Patrick, 'The Gaelic League and non-sectarianism', *Irish Rosary*, Vol. 11, No. 1 (January 1907), 5–13.
Eden, Maud, 'Protestants, organise', *New Ireland*, 17 March 1917.
Ervine, St. John G., *Sir Edward Carson and the Ulster movement* (Dublin, 1915).
Falls, Cyril, *The history of the 36th (Ulster) Division* (Belfast, 1922).
Forde, Patrick, *The Irish language movement: its philosophy*, Gaelic League pamphlet No. 21 (London, n.d. [1901]), 27–28.
Griffith, Arthur, *The resurrection of Hungary: a parallel for Ireland* (Dublin, 2003 [1904]).
Hannay, James Owen, *Is the Gaelic League political?: lecture delivered under the auspices of the Branch of the Five Provinces on January 23rd, 1906* (n.p., n.d.).
Johnston, Joseph, *Civil war in Ulster: its objects and probable results* (Dublin, 1913).
Knott, George H. (ed.), *Trial of Sir Roger Casement* (Philadelphia, 1917).
MacCrainn, Batha [Roger Casement], 'Ireland and the German menace', *The Irish Review*, Vol. 2, No. 19 (September 1912), 343–345.
Malone, Andrew E., 'Darrell Figgis', *The Dublin Magazine*, April–June 1926, 15–26.
McNeill, Ronald, *Ulster's stand for the union* (London, 1922).
Moran, D. P., *The philosophy of Irish Ireland* (Dublin, 1905).
Nankivell, Joyce M., and Loch, Sydney, *Ireland in travail* (London, 1922).

Nicholls, Harry, 'Memories of the Contemporary Club', parts I and II, *Irish Times*, 20, 21 December 1965.

O'Casey, Sean, *The story of the Irish Citizen Army* (Dublin, 1919).

O'Donnell, Frank Hugh, *The ruin of education in Ireland and the Irish Fanar* (London, 1902).

O'Hegarty, P. S., *The victory of Sinn Féin* (Dublin, 1998 [1924]).

O'Leary, John, *Young Ireland: the old and the new* (Dublin, 1885).

Rolleston, T. W. (ed.), *Prose writings of Thomas Davis* (London, 1890).

Rolleston, T. W., *Ireland, the Empire, and the War* (Dublin, 1900).

Russell, George, *Thoughts for a convention* (Dublin, 1917).

Conscription for Ireland: a warning to England (Dublin, 1918).

Sgéal Ruaidhrí Uí Mhórdha, *Autobiography of the Ruairi O More Branch of the Gaelic League, Portarlington* (Dublin, 1906).

Stephens, James, *Insurrection in Dublin* (Dublin, 1916).

Stopford Green, Alice, *The government of Ireland* (London, 1921).

The history of the Irish state to 1014 (London, 1925).

Tobin, T. J., 'President de Valera at Notre Dame', *Notre Dame Scholastic*, Vol. 53, No. 4 (1919), 58.

Trench, Wilbraham Fitzjohn, *The way to fellowship in Irish life* (London, 1919).

Ua Fhloinn, Riobard [Robert Lynd], *The Orangemen and the nation* (Belfast, 1907).

Secondary

Note: With the exception of certain seminal works, only those studies listed in the footnotes are included in the bibliography.

Unpublished Theses

McCann, Oliver, 'The Protestant home rule movement, 1886–1895', MA thesis, University College Dublin, 1972.

McConnel, James Richard Redmond, 'The view from the backbench: Irish nationalist MPs and their work, 1910–1914', PhD thesis, University of Durham, 2002.

McHenry, Margaret, 'The Ulster theatre in Ireland', PhD thesis, University of Pennsylvania, 1931.

References and Directories

Bateman, John, *Great landowners of Great Britain and Ireland* (London, 1876).

Burke, Bernard (ed.), *A genealogical and heraldic history of the landed gentry of Ireland* (London, 1904).

Burke, Bernard, *Burke's genealogical and heraldic history of the landed gentry of Ireland*, 4th ed. (L. G. Pine, ed.) (London, 1958).

Burke's Peerage and Baronetage, 105th ed. (London, 1970).

Castree, Noel, Kitchin, Rob, and Rogers, Alisdair, *A dictionary of human geography* (Oxford, 2013).

A catalogue of graduates of the University of Dublin, Vol. II (Dublin, 1896).

A catalogue of graduates of the University of Dublin, Vol. IV (Dublin, 1917).

A catalogue of graduates of the University of Dublin, Vol. V (Dublin, 1931).

Curtis, Edmund and McDowell, R. B. (eds.), *Irish historical documents, 1172–1922* (New York, 1968).

De Burgh, U. H. Hussey, *The Landowners of Ireland* (Dublin, 1878).

Matthew, Colin, Harrison, Brian, and Goldman, Lawrence (eds.), *Oxford Dictionary of National Biography* (Oxford, 2004).

McGuire, James and Quinn, James (eds.), *Dictionary of Irish biography* (Cambridge, 2009).

Snoddy, Theo, *Dictionary of Irish artists: 20th century* (Dublin, 2002).

Vaughan, W. E., and Fitzpatrick, A. J., *Irish historical statistics: population, 1821–1971* (Dublin, 1978).

Walford's County Families of the United Kingdom, or Royal Manual of the Titled and Untitled Aristocracy of England, Wales, Scotland, and Ireland (London, 1918).

Walker, Brian M. (ed.), *Parliamentary Election Results in Ireland, 1801–1922* (Dublin, 1978).

Who Was Who, Vol. I: 1897–1915 (London, 1988).

Who Was Who, Vol. II: 1916–1928 (London, 1962).

Who Was Who, Vol. III: 1929–1940 (London, 1967).

Books and Pamphlets

[Various authors], *Kerry's fighting story, 1916–21* (Tralee, n.d. [1947]).

Akenson, Donald Harman, *Small differences: Irish Catholics and Irish Protestants 1815–1922: an international perspective* (Kingston, 1988).

Allen, Nicholas, *George Russell (Æ) and the new Ireland, 1905–30* (Dublin, 2003).

Anderson, Benedict, *Imagined communities: reflections on the origin and spread of nationalism* (London, 1983).

Arrington, Lauren, *Revolutionary lives: Constance and Casimir Markievicz* (Princeton, 2016).

Armour, W. S., *Armour of Ballymoney* (London, 1934).

Bartlett, Thomas, *The fall and rise of the Irish nation: the Catholic question, 1690–1830* (Dublin, 1992).

Beckett, J. C., *The Anglo-Irish tradition* (London, 1976).

Bell, Sam Hanna, *Theatre in Ulster* (Totowa, 1972).

Bence-Jones, Mark, *Twilight of the ascendancy* (London, 1987).

Beneš, Jakub S., *Workers and nationalism: Czech and German social democracy in Habsburg Austria, 1890–1918* (Oxford, 2016).

Berresford Ellis, Peter, *The Celtic dawn: a history of Pan Celticism* (London, 1993).

Bew, Paul, *C. S. Parnell* (Dublin, 1980).

Enigma: a new life of Charles Stewart Parnell (Dublin, 2011).

Biagini, Eugenio, and Mulhall, Daniel (eds.), *The shaping of modern Ireland: a centenary assessment* (Sallins, 2016).

Bjork, James E., *Neither German nor Pole: Catholicism and national indifference in a Central European borderland* (Ann Arbor, MI, 2008).

Blaney, Roger, *Presbyterians and the Irish language* (Belfast, 1996).

Bourke, Marcus, *John O'Leary: a study in Irish separatism* (Tralee, 1967).

Bowman, John, *De Valera and the Ulster question, 1917–1973* (Oxford, 1982).

Bowman, Timothy, *Carson's Army: the Ulster Volunteer Force, 1910–22* (Manchester, 2007).

Boyce, D. George, *Nationalism in Ireland* (London, 1995).

Boyd, Andrew, *Jack White (1879–1946): first commander Irish Citizen Army* (Belfast, 2001).

Boyle, Andrew, *The riddle of Erskine Childers* (London, 1977).

Bracken, David (ed.), *The end of all things earthly: faith profiles of the 1916 leaders* (Dublin, 2016).

Brooke, Peter, *Ulster Presbyterianism: the historical perspective 1610–1970* (Dublin, 1987).

Brown, Terence, *Ireland: a social and cultural history, 1922–79* (London, 1981).
  The life of W. B. Yeats: a critical biography (Dublin, 1999).

Bryant, Chad, *Prague in black: Nazi rule and Czech nationalism* (Cambridge, MA, 2007).

Butler, Hubert, *The sub-prefect should have held his tongue and other essays* (R. F. Foster, ed.) (London, 1990).

Campbell, Fergus, *The Irish establishment: 1879–1914* (Oxford, 2009).

Campbell, Flann, *The dissenting voice: Protestant democracy in Ulster from plantation to partition* (Dublin, 1991).

Canny, Nicholas, *Making Ireland British, 1580–1650* (Oxford, 2001).

Carroll, F. M., *American opinion and the Irish question, 1910–23: a study in opinion and policy* (Dublin, 1978).

Clare, Anne, *Unlikely rebels: the Gifford girls and the fight for Irish freedom* (Cork, 2011).

Clark, Gemma, *Everyday violence in the Irish Civil War* (Cambridge, 2014).

Coffey, Diarmid, *Douglas Hyde: president of Ireland* (Dublin, 1938).

Comerford, R. V., *Ireland* (London, 2003).

Connolly, S. J., *Religion, law and power: the making of Protestant Ireland, 1660–1760* (Oxford, 1992).

Coolahan, John, *Irish education: its history and structure* (Dublin, 1981).

Cullen Owens, Rosemary, *Louie Bennett* (Cork, 2001).

Daly, D. P., *The young Douglas Hyde: the dawn of the Irish revolution and renaissance* (Dublin, 1974).

Davis, Richard, *Arthur Griffith and non-violent Sinn Fein* (Dublin, 1974).

Dudgeon, Jeffrey, *Roger Casement: the Black Diaries: with a study of his background, sexuality and Irish political life* (Belfast, 2002).

Dunleavy, Janet Egleson, and Dunleavy, Gareth W., *Douglas Hyde: a maker of modern Ireland* (Berkeley, 1991).

Dwan, David, *The great community: culture and nationalism in Ireland* (Dublin, 2008).

Elliott, Marianne, *Wolfe Tone: prophet of Irish independence* (New Haven, 1989).

When God took sides: religion and identity in Ireland – unfinished identity (Oxford, 2009).

Ellmann, Richard, *James Joyce: new and revised edition* (Oxford, 1982 [1959]).

Emerson, Caryl, *The Cambridge introduction to Russian literature* (Cambridge, 2008).

English, Richard, *Radicals and the republic: socialist republicanism in the Irish Free State, 1925–1937* (Oxford, 1994).

Irish freedom: the history of nationalism in Ireland (London, 2006).

Faivre, Antoine, *Theosophy, imagination, tradition: studies in western esotericism* (Christine Rhone, trans.) (New York, 2000).

Farrell, Michael, *Northern Ireland: the Orange state* (London, 1976).

Fermanagh 1916 Centenary Association, *Fearless but few: Fermanagh and the Easter Rising* (Castleblayney, 2015).

Fitzpatrick, David, *Politics and Irish life, 1913–1921: provincial experience of war and revolution*, rev. ed. (Cork, 1998 [1977]).

The two Irelands, 1912–1939 (Oxford, 1998).

Harry Boland's Irish revolution (Cork, 2003).

Descendancy: Irish Protestant histories since 1795 (Cambridge, 2014).

Ernest Blythe in Ulster: the making of a double agent? (Cork, 2018).

Flanagan, Francis, *Remembering the revolution: dissent, culture and nationalism in the Irish Free State* (Oxford, 2015).

Forester, Margery, *Michael Collins: the lost leader* (Dublin, 1971).

Foster, R. F., *Modern Ireland, 1600–1972* (London, 1988).

Paddy and Mr Punch: connections in Irish history and English history (London, 1993).

W. B. Yeats: a life, Vol. I: the apprentice mage (Oxford, 1997).

W. B. Yeats: a life, Vol. II: the arch-poet, 1915–1939 (Oxford, 2003).

Words alone: Yeats and his inheritances (Oxford, 2011).

Vivid faces: the revolutionary generation in Ireland, 1890–1923 (London, 2014).

Fox, R. M., *Rebel Irishwomen* (Cork, 1935).

The history of the Irish Citizen Army (Dublin, 1943).

Frazier, Adrian, *Hollywood Irish: John Ford, Abbey actors and the Irish revival in Hollywood* (Dublin, 2010).

The adulterous muse: Maud Gonne, Lucien Millevoye and W. B. Yeats (Dublin, 2016).

Gageby, Douglas, *The last secretary general: Sean Lester and the League of Nations* (Dublin, 1999).

Gailey, Andrew, *Ireland and the death of kindness: the experience of constructive unionism, 1890–1905* (Cork, 1987).

Garvin, Tom, *The evolution of Irish nationalist politics* (Dublin, 1981).

Nationalist revolutionaries in Ireland, 1858–1928 (Oxford, 1987).

1922: The birth of Irish democracy (Dublin, 2005).

Gaughan, J. Anthony, *Thomas Johnson, 1872–1963: first leader of the Labour Party in Dáil Éireann* (Dublin, 1980).

Gellner, Ernest, *Thought and change* (London, 1964).

Nations and nationalism (Oxford, 1983).

Gray, John, *City in revolt: James Larkin and the Belfast dock strike of 1907* (Belfast, 1985).

Gray, Randal, *Kaiserschlacht: the final German offensive of World War One* (Oxford, 1991).

Grosby, Steven, *Nationalism: a very short introduction* (New York, 2005).

Groves, Patricia, *Petticoat rebellion: the Anna Parnell story* (Cork, 2009).

Harrington, Niall C., *Kerry landing: August 1922, An episode of the Civil War* (Dublin, 1992).

Hart, Peter, *The IRA and its enemies: violence and community in Cork, 1916–1923* (Oxford, 1998).

The IRA at war, 1916–1923 (Oxford, 2003).

Hastings, Adrian, *The construction of nationhood: ethnicity, religion and nationalism* (Cambridge, 1997).

Haverty, Anne, *Constance Markievicz: an independent life* (London, 1988).

Hay, Marnie, *Bulmer Hobson and the nationalist movement in twentieth-century Ireland* (Manchester, 2009).

Hebdige, Dick, *Subculture* (London, 1979).

Hennessey, Thomas, *Dividing Ireland: World War One and partition* (London, 1998).

Hill, Jacqueline, *From Patriots to unionists: Dublin civic politics and Irish Protestant patriotism, 1660–1840* (Oxford, 1997).

Hill, Judith, *Lady Gregory: an Irish life* (Stroud, 2005).

Hobsbawm, Eric, *Nations and nationalism since 1780: programme, myth, reality* (Cambridge, 1990).

Hodges, E. C., *A valiant life, 1864–1961* (Dublin, 1963).

Holroyd, Michael, *Bernard Shaw: the one-volume definitive edition* (London, 1998).

Hopkinson, Michael, *Green against green: the Irish Civil War* (Dublin, 1988).

The Irish War of Independence (Dublin, 2002).

Hurley, Michael (ed.), *Irish Anglicanism, 1869–1969: essays on the role of Anglicanism in Irish life, presented to the Church of Ireland on the occasion of the centenary of its disestablishment, by a group of Methodist, Presbyterian, Quaker, and Roman Catholic scholars* (Dublin, 1970).

Hutchinson, John, *The dynamics of cultural nationalism: the Gaelic Revival and the creation of the Irish nation state* (London, 1987).

Inglis, Brian, *Roger Casement* (London, 1973).

Irish, Tomás, *Trinity in war and revolution, 1912–1923* (Dublin, 2015).

Jackson, Alvin, *The Ulster Party: Irish unionists in the House of Commons, 1884–1911* (Oxford, 1989).

Ireland, 1798–1998: war, peace, and beyond, 2nd ed. (West Sussex, 2010).

Jeffery, Keith, *Ireland and the Great War* (Cambridge, 2000).

Jones, Valerie, *Rebel Prods: the forgotten story of Protestant radical nationalists and the 1916 Rising* (Dublin, 2016).

Keats-Rohan, K. S. B. (ed.), *Prosopography approaches and applications: a handbook* (Oxford, 2007).

Kedourie, Elie, *Nationalism* (London, 1960).

Kelly, Aaron, *Twentieth-century Irish literature* (Basingstoke, 2008).

Kelly, M. J., *The Fenian ideal and Irish nationalism, 1882–1916* (Woodbridge, 2006).

Kelly, Mary C., *The shamrock and the lily: the New York Irish and the creation of a transatlantic identity, 1845–1921* (New York, 2005).

Keohane, Leo, *Captain Jack White: imperialism, anarchism, and the Irish Citizen Army* (Dublin, 2014).

Kiely, Kevin, *Francis Stuart: artist and outcast* (Dublin, 2007).

Kissane, Bill, *The politics of the Irish Civil War* (Oxford, 2005).

Krindatch, Alexei (ed.), *Atlas of American Orthodox Christian Churches* (Brookline, MA, 2011).

Laffan, Michael, *The resurrection of Ireland: the Sinn Féin party, 1916–1923* (Cambridge, 1999).

Lane, Leeane, *Rosamond Jacob: third person singular* (Dublin, 2010).

Lynch, David, *Radical politics in modern Ireland: the Irish Socialist Republican Party, 1896–1904* (Dublin, 2005).

Lynd, Robert, *I tremble to think* (London, 1936).

Galway of the races: selected essays (Sean McMahon, ed.) (Dublin, 1990).

Lyons, F. S. L., *Charles Stewart Parnell* (London, 1977).

Culture and anarchy in Ireland, 1890–1939 (Oxford, 1979).

MacDonagh, Oliver, *States of mind: a study of Anglo-Irish conflict, 1780–1980* (London, 1985).

MacLellan, Anne, *Dorothy Stopford Price: rebel doctor* (Dublin, 2014).

Mansergh, Nicholas, *The Irish question, 1840–1921* (London, 1965).

Martin, F. X. (ed.), *The Irish Volunteers, 1913–1915: recollections and documents* (Dublin, 1963).

Martin F. X. (ed.), *The Howth gun-running and the Kilcoole gun-running, 1914: recollections and documents* (Dublin, 1964).

(ed.), *Leaders and men of the Easter Rising: Dublin 1916* (Dublin, 1967).

Mathews, P. J., *Revival: the Abbey Theatre, Sinn Féin, the Gaelic League and the Co-operative movement* (Cork, 2003).

Maume, Patrick, *D. P. Moran* (Dundalk, 1995).

The long gestation: Irish nationalist life 1891–1918 (Dublin, 1999).

Maye, Brian, *Arthur Griffith* (Dublin, 1997).

McBride, Ian, *Eighteenth-century Ireland: the isle of slaves* (Dublin, 2009).

McConnel, James, *The Irish Parliamentary Party and the third home rule crisis* (Dublin, 2013).

McCormack, W. J., *Fool of the family: a life of J. M. Synge* (London, 2000).

McCracken, Donal P., *The Irish pro-Boers* (Johannesburg, 1989).

McDowell, R. B., *Alice Stopford Green: a passionate historian* (Dublin, 1967).

The Church of Ireland, 1869–1969 (London, 1975).

Crisis and decline: the fate of the southern unionists (Dublin, 1997).

McDowell, R. B., and Webb, D. A., *Trinity College Dublin, 1592–1952: an academic history* (Dublin, 2004).

McGarry, Fearghal, *The Rising: Easter 1916* (Oxford, 2010).

The Abbey rebels of 1916: a lost revolution (Dublin, 2015).

McInerney, Michael, *The riddle of Erskine Childers* (Dublin, 1971).

McNulty, Eugene, *The Ulster Literary Theatre and the northern revival* (Cork, 2008).

Meenan, James, *George O'Brien: a biographical memoir* (Dublin, 1980).

Meleady, Dermot, *John Redmond: the national leader* (Dublin, 2013).

Mitchell, Arthur, *Labour in Irish politics, 1890–1930: the Irish labour movement in an age of revolution* (Dublin, 1974).

Moody, T. W., and Beckett, J. C., *Queen's, Belfast, 1845–1949: The history of a university*, Vol. I (London, 1959).

Morgan, Austen, *James Connolly: a political biography* (Manchester, 1998).

Morris, Catherine, *Alice Milligan and the Irish cultural revival* (Dublin, 2012).

Mulholland, Marie, *The politics and relationships of Kathleen Lynn* (Dublin, 2002).

Murphy, Brian P., *John Chartres: mystery man of the treaty* (Dublin, 1995).

Murphy, Rose, *Ella Young: Irish mystic and rebel: from literary Dublin to the American West* (Dublin, 2008).

Murray, Christopher, *Sean O'Casey: writer at work: a biography* (Dublin, 2004).

Nevin, Donal, *James Connolly: 'a full life'* (Dublin, 2005).

Norman, Diana, *Terrible beauty: a life of Constance Markievicz* (Dublin, 1988).

O'Brien, Bill, *Alternative Ulster covenant* (Dublin, 2013).

O'Brien, Conor Cruise, *States of Ireland* (London, 1972).

O'Brien, Eoin, and Crookshank, Ann, with Wolstenholme, Sir Gordon, *A portrait of Irish medicine: an illustrated history of medicine in Ireland* (Dublin, 1984).

Ó Broin, Leon, *Protestant nationalists in revolutionary Ireland: the Stopford connection* (Dublin, 1985).

Ó Comhraí, Cormac, *Sa bhearna bhaoil: Gaillimh 1913–1923* (Gaillimh, 2015).

O'Connor, Ulick, *Oliver St. John Gogarty* (London, 1981 [1963]).

O Dúlaing, Donncha, *Voices of Ireland: conversations with Donncha O Dúlaing* (Dublin, 1984).

O'Faoláin, Seán, *Constance Markievicz: or, the average revolutionary; a biography* (London, 1934).

O'Halpin, Eunan, *The decline of the union: British government in Ireland, 1892–1920* (Dublin, 1987).

O'Hegarty, P. S., *A history of Ireland under the Union* (London, 1952).

Ó hÓgartaigh, Margaret, *Kathleen Lynn: Irishwoman, patriot, doctor* (Dublin, 2006).

Ó Loingsigh, Pádraig, *Gobnait Ní Bhruadair: the hon. Albinia Lucy Brodrick* (Baile Átha Cliath, 1997).

Ó Mahony, Sean, *Frongoch: university of revolution* (Dublin, 1987).

O'Neill, Marie, *Grace Gifford Plunkett and Irish freedom: tragic bride of 1916* (Dublin, 2000).

Ó Síocháin, Séamas, *Roger Casement: imperialist, rebel, revolutionary* (Dublin, 2008).

Ó Snodaigh, Pádraig, *Hidden Ulster: Protestants and the Irish language* (Belfast, 1995).

Ó Tuama, Seán (ed.), *The Gaelic League idea* (Cork, 1972).

Parkes, Susan M. (ed.), *A danger to the men? a history of women in Trinity College Dublin 1904–2004* (Dublin, 2004).

Parkinson, Alan F., *Belfast's unholy war: the troubles of the 1920s* (Dublin, 2004).

Friends in high places: Ulster's resistance to Irish home rule, 1912–14 (Belfast, 2012).

Paseta, Senia, *Irish nationalist women, 1900–1918* (Cambridge, 2013).

Phoenix, Eamon, et al. (eds.), *Feis na nGleann: a century of Gaelic culture in the Antrim Glens* (Belfast, 2005).

Pilcher, Rosa, *Trinity Hall, 1908–2008: Trinity College Dublin residence* (Dublin, 2013).

Power, T. P., and Whelan, Kevin (eds.), *Endurance and emergence: Catholics in Ireland in the eighteenth century* (Dublin, 1990).

Pyle, Hilary, *Red-headed rebel: Susan L. Mitchell: poet and mystic of the Irish cultural renaissance* (Dublin, 1998).

Rauchbauer, Otto, *Shane Leslie: sublime failure* (Dublin, 2009).

Regan, John M., *The Irish counter revolution, 1921–1936: Treatyite politics and settlement in independent Ireland* (Dublin, 1999).

Regan-Lefebvre, Jennifer, *Cosmopolitan nationalism in the Victorian Empire: Ireland, India and the politics of Alfred Webb* (Basingstoke, 2009).

Reid, B. L., *The lives of Roger Casement* (New Haven, 1976).

Reid, Colin, *The lost Ireland of Stephen Gwynn: Irish constitutional nationalism and cultural politics, 1864–1950* (Manchester, 2011).

Ryan, Meda, *Tom Barry: IRA freedom fighter* (Dublin, 2003).

Sagarra, Eda, *Kevin O'Shiel: Tyrone nationalist and Irish state-builder* (Dublin, 2013).

Saunders, Frances Stonor, *The woman who shot Mussolini* (London, 2011).

Saunders, Norah, and Kelly, A. A., *Joseph Campbell: poet and nationalist, 1879–1944* (Dublin, 1988).

Smith, Anthony D., *Nationalism and modernism: a critical survey of recent theories of nations and nationalism* (London, 1998).

Smith, Nadia Clare, *Dorothy Macardle: a life* (Dublin, 2007).

Stanford, W. B., and McDowell, R. B., *Mahaffy: a biography of an Anglo-Irishman* (London, 1971).

Stewart, A. T. Q., *The narrow ground: aspects of Ulster 1609–1969* (Belfast, 1997 [1977]).

Stoakley, T. E., *Sneem: the knot of the ring* (Sneem, 1986).

Taylor, Brian, *The life and writings of James Owen Hannay (George A. Birmingham), 1865–1950* (New York, 1995).

Tiernan, Sonja, *Eva Gore-Booth: an image of such politics* (Manchester, 2012).

Tóibín, Colm, *Lady Gregory's toothbrush* (Dublin, 2002).

Toomey, Thomas, *The war of independence in Limerick 1912–1921: also covering actions in the border areas of Tipperary, Cork, Kerry and Clare* (Limerick, 2010).

Townshend, Charles, *Easter 1916: the Irish rebellion* (London, 2005).

The Republic: the fight for Irish independence, 1918–1923 (London, 2013).

Ungoed-Thomas, Jasper, *Jasper Wolfe of Skibbereen* (Cork, 2008).

Walsh, Margaret, *Sam Maguire: the enigmatic man behind Ireland's most prestigious trophy* (Midleton, 2003).

Walsh, Oonagh, *Anglican women in Dublin: philanthropy, politics and education in the early twentieth century* (Dublin, 2005).

Ward, Margaret, *Maud Gonne: Ireland's Joan of Arc* (London, 1990).

Unmanageable revolutionaries: women and Irish nationalism (London, 1995).

Welch, Robert, *The Abbey Theatre, 1899–1999* (Oxford, 1999).

White, Jack, *Minority report: the Protestant community in the Irish Republic* (Dublin, 1975).

Wilkinson, Burke, *The zeal of the convert* (Gerrards Cross, 1978).

Wilson, T. K., *Frontiers of violence: conflict and identity in Ulster and Upper Silesia 1918–1922* (Oxford, 2010).

Articles and Book Chapters

Ashton, Philip, 'Divided ideals: the Religious Society of Friends and the Irish home rule controversy, 1885–1886', *The Woodbrooke Journal*, No. 6 (Summer 2000), 1–27.

Balliett, Conrad A., 'The lives – and lies – of Maud Gonne', *Éire-Ireland*, Fall, 1979, 17–44.

Bielenberg, Andy, 'Exodus: the emigration of southern Irish Protestants during the Irish War of Independence and the Civil War', *Past & Present*, Vol. 218, No. 1 (2013), 199–233.

Bielenberg, Andy, Borgonovo, John and Donnelly, James S. Jr. '"Something of the Nature of a Massacre": The Bandon Valley Killings Revisited', *Éire-Ireland 49*, no. 3, (2014), 7–59.

Blanke, Richard, '"Polish-speaking Germans?": language and national identity among the Masurians', *Nationalities Papers*, Vol. 27, No. 3 (1999), 429–453.

Bowman, John, 'De Valera on Ulster, 1919-1920: what he told America', *Irish Studies in International Affairs*, Vol. 1, No. 1 (1979), 3–18.

Boyle, John W., 'The Belfast Protestant Association and the Independent Orange Order, 1901–10', *Irish Historical Studies*, Vol. 13, No. 50 (September 1962), 117–152.

'A Fenian Protestant in Canada: Robert Lindsay Crawford, 1910–22', *Canadian Historical Review*, Vol. 52, No. 2 (June 1971), 165–176.

Cuddy, Edward, 'The Irish question and the revival of Anti-Catholicism in the 1920's', *Catholic Historical Review*, Vol. 67, No. 2 (April 1981), 236–255.

Danaher, Kathleen, 'Introduction to the plays of Gerald MacNamara', *Journal of Irish Literature*, Vol. 17, Nos. 2–3 (May–September 1988), 3–20.

Davis, Richard, 'Ulster Protestants and the Sinn Féin press, 1914–22', *Éire-Ireland*, Winter 1980, 60–85.

De Bhaldraithe, Eoin, 'Mixed marriages and Irish politics: the effect of "Ne Temere"', *Studies: An Irish Quarterly Review*, Vol. 77, No. 307 (Autumn, 1988), 284–299.

Dixon, Roger, 'Francis Joseph Bigger: Belfast's cultural Don Quixote', *Ulster Folklife*, Vol. 43, 1997, 40–47.

Fitzpatrick, David, 'The logic of collective sacrifice: Ireland and the British Army, 1914–1918', *The Historical Journal*, Vol. 38, No. 4 (December 1995), 1017–1030.

'Militarism in Ireland, 1900–1922', in Thomas Bartlett and Keith Jeffery (eds.), *A military history of Ireland* (Cambridge, 1996), 379–406.

'Protestant depopulation and the Irish Revolution', *Irish Historical Studies 38*, no. 152 (November 2013), 643–663.

Garvin, Tom, 'National identity in Ireland', *Studies: An Irish Quarterly Review*, Vol. 95, No. 379 (Autumn, 2006), 241–250.

Gogarty, Oliver St John, 'James Joyce: a portrait of the artist', in E. H. Mikhail (ed.), *James Joyce: interviews and recollections* (Basingstoke, 1990), 21–32.

Gregory, Adrian, '"You might as well recruit Germans": British public opinion and the decision to conscript the Irish in 1918', in Adrian Gregory and Senia Pašeta (eds.), *Ireland and the Great War: 'a war to unite us all'?* (Manchester, 2002), 113–133.

Hanley, Brian, 'The Irish Citizen Army after 1916', *Saothar*, Vol. 28 (2003), 37–47.

Hart, Peter, 'The Protestant experience of revolution in Southern Ireland', in Richard English and Graham Walker (eds.), *Unionism in modern Ireland* (Dublin, 1996), 81–98.

'The social structure of the Irish Republican Army, 1916–1923', *The Historical Journal*, Vol. 42, No. 1 (March 1999), 207–231.

Hay, Marnie, 'The foundation and development of Na Fianna Éireann, 1909–16' *Irish Historical Studies*, Vol. 36, No. 141 (May 2008), 53–71.

Hayton, David, 'Anglo-Irish attitudes: changing perceptions of national identity among the Protestant ascendancy in Ireland, ca. 1690–1740', *Studies in Eighteenth-Century Culture*, Vol. 17 (1987), 151–152.

Hewitt, John, '"The northern Athens" and after', in J. C. Beckett et al., *Belfast: the making of a city* (Belfast, 1988), 71–82.

Jones, Siobhan, 'The Irish Protestant under the editorship of Lindsay Crawford, 1901–6', *Saothar*, Vol. 30 (2005), 85–96.

Kingston, Willie, 'From Victorian boyhood to the troubles: a Skibbereen memoir', *Skibbereen and District Historical Society Journal*, Vol. 1 (2005), 4–36.

Levitas, Ben, 'A temper of misgiving: W. B. Yeats and the Ireland of Synge's time', in Senia Paseta (ed.), *Uncertain futures: essays about the Irish past for Roy Foster* (Oxford, 2016), 110–122.

Loughlin, James, 'The Irish Protestant Home Rule Association and nationalist politics, 1886–93', *Irish Historical Studies*, Vol. 24, No. 95 (May 1985), 341–360.

Maguire, Martin, 'A socio-economic analysis of the Dublin Protestant working class, 1870–1926', *Irish Economic and Social History*, Vol. 20 (1993), 3–61.

'Harry Nicholls and Kathleen Emerson: Protestant rebels', *Studia Hibernica*, No. 35 (2008–2009), 147–166.

Martin, F. X., '1916: myth, fact, and mystery', *Studia Hibernica*, No. 7 (1967), 7–126.

Maume, Patrick, 'Anti-Machiavel: three Ulster nationalists of the age of de Valera', *Irish Political Studies*, Vol. 14 (1999), 43–63.

McGee, Owen, 'Fred Allan (1861–1937): Republican, Methodist and Dubliner', *Dublin Historical Record*, Vol. 56, No. 2 (Autumn, 2003), 205–216.

McMahon, Timothy G., '"All creeds and all classes"? just who made up the Gaelic League?', *Éire-Ireland*, Vol. 37, Nos. 3–4 (Fall–Winter, 2002), 118–168.

Morris, Catherine, 'In the enemy's camp: Alice Milligan and fin de siècle Belfast', in Nicholas Allen and Aaron Kelly (eds.), *Cities of Belfast* (Dublin, 2003), 62–73.

Morrissey, Conor, 'Albinia Brodrick: Munster's Anglo-Irish Republican', *Journal of the Cork Archaeological and Historical Society*, Vol. 116 (2011), 94–108.

'"Much the more political of the two": Mabel FitzGerald and the Irish Revolution', *Irish Studies Review*, Vol. 24, No. 3 (2016), 291–310.

'"Rotten Protestants": Protestant home rulers and the Ulster Liberal Association, 1906–1918', *The Historical Journal*, Vol. 61, No. 3 (September 2018), 743–765.

Murphy, Brian P., 'The Easter Rising in the context of censorship and propaganda with special reference to Major Ivon Price', in Gabriel Doherty and Dermot Keogh (eds.), *1916: The long revolution* (Cork, 2007), 141–168.

Murray, Peter, 'Radical way forward or sectarian cul-de-sac? Lindsay Crawford and Independent Orangeism reassessed', *Saothar*, Vol. 27 (2002), 31–42.

Newsinger, John, '"I bring not peace but a word": the religious motif in the Irish War of Independence', *Journal of Contemporary History*, Vol. 13, No. 3 (July 1978), 609–662.

Nic Dháibhéid, Caoimhe, '"This is a case in which Irish nationalist consider- ations must be taken into account": the breakdown of the MacBride–Gonne marriage, 1904–08', *Irish Historical Studies*, Vol. 37, No. 146 (November 2010), 241–264.

O'Brien, Maria, 'Thomas William Rolleston: the forgotten man', in Betsey Taylor FitzSimon and James H. Murphy (eds.), *The Irish revival reappraised* (Dublin, 2003), 154–166.

Ó Conaire, Breandáin, 'Na Protastúnaigh, an Ghaeilge agus Dubhghlas de hÍde', *Seanchas Ardmhaca: Journal of the Armagh Diocesan Historical Society*, Vol. 15, No. 2 (1993), 130–150.

Ó Corráin, Daithí, '"Ireland in his heart north and south": the contribution of Ernest Blythe to the partition question', *Irish Historical Studies*, Vol. 35, No. 137 (May 2006), 61–80.

'"They blew up the best portion of our city and … it is their duty to replace it": compensation and reconstruction in the aftermath of the 1916 Rising', *Irish Historical Studies*, Vol. 39, No. 154 (November 2014), 272–295.

O'Halpin, Eunan, 'H. E. Duke and the Irish administration, 1916–18', *Irish Historical Studies*, Vol. 22, No. 88 (September 1981), 362–376.

Paseta, Senia, '1798 in 1898: the politics of commemoration', *The Irish Review*, No. 22 (Summer, 1998), 46–53.

Patterson, Henry, 'Independent Orangeism and class conflict in Edwardian Belfast: a reinterpretation', *Proceedings of the Royal Irish Academy. Section C: Archaeology, Celtic Studies, History, Linguistics, Literature*, Vol. 80C (1980), 1–27.

Stone, Lawrence, 'Prosopography', *Daedalus*, Vol. 100, No. 1 (Winter, 1971), 46–79.

Trench, C. E. F., 'Dermot Chenevix Trench and Haines of *Ulysses*', *James Joyce Quarterly*, Vol. 13, No. 1 (Fall, 1975), 39–48.

Trench, R. B. D., 'J. O. Hannay and the Gaelic League', *Hermathena*, Vol. 102 (Spring, 1966), 26–52.

Vandevelde, Karen, 'An open national identity: Rutherford Mayne, Gerald MacNamara, and the plays of the Ulster Literary Theatre', *Éire-Ireland*, Spring–Summer, 2004, 36–56.

Ward, Alan J., 'Lloyd George and the 1918 Irish conscription crisis', *The Historical Journal*, Vol. 17, No. 1 (March 1974), 256–275.

Whyte, John H., '1916 – revolution and religion', in F. X. Martin (ed.), *Leaders and men of the Easter Rising: Dublin 1916* (Dublin, 1967), 215–226.

Zahra, Tara, 'Imagined noncommunities: national indifference as a category of analysis', *Slavic Review*, Vol. 69, No. 1 (Spring, 2010), 93–119.

Web Pages

Coyle, Stephen, 'Ian Graeme Baun MacKenzie Kennedy – "Scottie" 1899–1922: a Scottish Gael who died for the Irish Republic', www.rsfcork.com/ianmackenziekennedy.htm.

'*1916 Necrology*', by Glasnevin Trust, www.glasnevintrust.ie/__uuid/55a29fab-3b24-41dd-a1d9-12d148a78f74/Glasnevin-Trust-1916-Necrology-485.pdf.

'Private William Forbes Patterson', http://canadiangreatwarproject.com/searches/soldierDetail.asp?ID=105276.

'A Short History of the Liberal Catholic Church and St. Raphael's Parish', http://srlcc.tripod.com/lcchist.htm.

Index